Ina Sander

Critical Datafication Literacy

Digitality and Education | Volume 2

Editorial

In a world where digital transformation is a central social issue, education is proving to be the key response to the complex challenges people face in the context of digitality, persistent crises and social inequalities. But how does education position itself in the face of these complex issues? What solutions does it offer beyond formal education strategies and policies? Which practices are closely linked to digitality and manifest themselves as forms of education? What implications does this have for educational research in relation to digital transformation?
These questions are at the heart of the 2023 series on **Digitality and education**.
Since we believe that the topics covered in the series should be accessible to all interested parties, all publications are open access.
The series is edited by Mandy Schiefner-Rohs, Sandra Hofhues, Nina Grünberger and Jane Müller.

Ina Sander (Dr.), is a postdoctoral research fellow at Helmut-Schmidt-University Hamburg. Before this, she conducted her doctoral research at the Data Justice Lab, Cardiff University, Wales, and undertook a research fellowship at the Center for Advanced Internet Studies, Bochum, Germany. Her research focusses on how data systems transform our societies and on ways to empower and critically educate citizens about data technologies.

Ina Sander

Critical Datafication Literacy

A Framework and Practical Approaches

[transcript]

This research and the open access publication of the findings were supported by the Economic and Social Research Council Wales as part of the "Collaborative Doctoral Training Partnership" pathway [grant number ES/P00069X/1].

Bibliographic information published by the Deutsche Nationalbibliothek
The Deutsche Nationalbibliothek lists this publication in the Deutsche Nationalbibliografie; detailed bibliographic data are available in the Internet at https://dnb.dnb.de/

First published in 2024 by transcript Verlag, Bielefeld

Cover layout: Maria Arndt, Bielefeld
Cover illustration: go2/photocase.de (modified); background of the cover: svetlanais/Adobe Stock
Printed by: Majuskel Medienproduktion GmbH, Wetzlar
https://doi.org/10.14361/9783839473788
Print-ISBN: 978-3-8376-7378-4
PDF-ISBN: 978-3-8394-7378-8
ISSN of series:
eISSN of series:

Printed on permanent acid-free text paper.

Contents

Appendix

Acknowledgements

This PhD would not have been possible without the support of a number of people. First, I would like to thank my supervisor Joanna Redden for her enthusiasm about my research and her unwavering support – from the initial project idea through the chaotic pandemic times and even after changing institutions. I would also like to thank my supervisor Arne Hintz for accepting the challenge of joining this project halfway through, and for his invaluable feedback and guidance. I am further grateful to my second supervisor Francesca Sobande for her enriching supervisory support and her encouragement. Likewise, thanks to the whole Data Justice Lab for their important research and a stimulating research environment.

I would also like to thank the project collaborator, the NGO Privacy International, for a fruitful collaboration with a great outcome. In particular, thank you, Gus Hosein, for your time, your insights, your enthusiasm for my research, and for all of your work in raising awareness and educating about data technologies.

I am further grateful to all participants of my study. Thank you for sharing your time and very valuable insights, thoughts and experiences on critically educating about datafication. I have learned so much.

I also want to thank my colleagues at the Helmut-Schmidt-University Hamburg for countless fruitful discussions and their collegiality. Special thanks to Sigrid Hartong for her ongoing support and understanding, and the invaluable insights from many inspiring conversations in the last years.

Last, but not least, I want to express my deepest gratitude to those closest to me. I would like thank my partner Ashley for her immeasurable support every step of the way throughout these PhD, pandemic and remote working years. I would also like to thank my family for always having my back and for their endless belief in me; and my friends for cheering me up, encouraging, or – if needed – distracting me. Finally, thanks to my proofreaders, specifically to Angela for going above and beyond in being an extremely supportive friend and proofreader.

This PhD and the open access publication of the findings were supported by the Economic and Social Research Council Wales as part of the "Collaborative Doctoral Training Partnership" pathway [grant number ES/P00069X/1].

List of Figures

List of Tables

1. Introduction

1.1 Why Critical Data Education is Urgently Needed

How Digital and Data Technologies Affect Our Lives

Data-based technologies are a part of all our lives. In the United Kingdom, almost all (94%) adults are connected to the internet, and, on average, they spend nearly four hours online each day (Ofcom 2022). Both during this active use of the internet – using search engines, social media or online shopping sites – and during the time that people spend doing other activities – such as walking down the street, driving, working, shopping, exercising or using their smart home appliances – they encounter and disclose data to countless data-based systems. Most digital technologies today function by collecting, processing, analysing and outputting data with the help of algorithms. These data-based technologies increasingly exert influence over our lives and our societies, for example when data that is collected about individuals feed numerous predictive and automated decision-making systems, which are used to guide decisions such as who is considered for a new job position, who is likely to commit a felony, or whose children are at risk of being neglected (see e.g., O'Neil 2016; Kitchin 2021; Dencik et al. 2022).

In light of these ubiquitous influences of data technologies, scholars speak of the "datafication" of our societies. This neologism describes a "profound transformation in how society is ordered, decisions are made, and citizens are monitored through 'big data'" (Hintz et al. 2019, p. 2f). Key aspects of the datafication of our societies include the massive production of data which track human activity and behaviour; rapid technological advances in how data is being processed; and the social, economic, cultural and political consequences of these data technologies (Pangrazio and Selwyn 2020, p. 4). Besides hopes for financial savings, more efficiency and less subjective decision-making, many risks and controversial or even harmful impacts of these systems have been identified. As data and algorithms can never be truly neutral or "raw" (Dalton and Thatcher 2014, no page number) their use can lead to biased decisions and increased discrimination (O'Neil 2016; Redden 2018b). Moreover, these systems can come with risks for citizens' privacy; potentially increased surveillance; a 'chilling effect' on free speech; new opacities due to data technologies' 'black box nature'; new power imbalances; and risks for democratic societies (e.g., Kennedy and Moss 2015; Zuboff 2015; O'Neil 2016; Hintz and Milan 2018; Redden 2018b).

The Knowledge Gap

In addition to these risks, research on citizens' knowledge of how digital and data technologies function and how they affect our lives and our societies has repeatedly shown a "major understanding gap" (Doteveryone 2018, p. 5). Studies have demonstrated that the large majority of British people (83%) are not aware that information shared about them by others is collected or that free apps make money from data (70%) (Miller et al. 2018, pp. 17; 21). Two years after this initial study, the British citizens' understanding "remains shallow", especially with regards to technology companies' business models and the way they use data (Miller et al. 2020, p. 15). Even in 2022, the majority of respondents from a large international study did not know why Google and Facebook are free of charge to use or that they earn money from advertisers (Akman 2022, p. 22). However, studies also repeatedly show that people are concerned about the use of their data, and that the claim that most people do not mind disclosing their data because they feel like they have 'nothing to hide' does not hold true. Research from recent years has highlighted that the public is highly concerned about certain data uses and that they want more knowledge about the way their data is used; more control over how much data they share; the ability to enact their data rights; and better control and regulation of these systems along with more ethical and responsible data technologies (Grzymek and Puntschuh 2019; Miller et al. 2020; Kennedy et al. 2021b; Ada Lovelace Institute 2022).

Responses to Challenges around Datafication

In light of the risks related to data technologies, citizens' understanding gap and the clear concerns of the public, many scholars argue that *change is needed*. Several solutions have been suggested, including regulatory, tactical and educational responses. However, regulatory approaches come with many hurdles and the difficult balance of protecting citizens while ensuring the freedom to connect and share with others online (Pangrazio and Sefton-Green 2020, p. 212). Tactical responses, on the other hand, such as blocking or anonymisation tools, compromise users' internet experiences, require sophisticated technical skills and ongoing maintenance, and shift the responsibility of data protection to the individual (ibid.). Therefore, educational responses to datafication have been posited as "the *most plausible and successful strategy to combat the challenges of datafication*" (ibid., emphasis added). While better regulation of data technologies is still urgently required, critical education can be seen as a key component or even *prerequisite of legal and tactical responses* to datafication (ibid., p. 218). Moreover, education is generally often regarded as a preparation for future members of society (Wringe 2012, p. 2). In line with this, my study argues that an understanding of how data systems affect our lives and societies and the ability to make enlightened choices about one's technology use are essential prerequisites for participating in today's societies in an informed and empowered manner and are further necessary for establishing regulatory solutions that correspond with citizens' attitudes to these systems.

As a response to the urgent need for more education about data, many new educational approaches have emerged in recent years. Besides new definitions for *media literacy*, *digital literacy* and *data literacy*, a variety of further literacies has been suggested. These include information literacy, statistical literacy, coding literacy, data visualisation literacy, internet literacy, new media literacy, big data literacy or data infrastructure literacy (Philip et al. 2013; Frank et al. 2016; Gray et al. 2018; Hug 2019). In light of this wave of new literacies, some scholars even speak of the "literacification of everything" (Hug 2019, p. 146). Particularly the term *data literacy* has rapidly gained attention and popularity in recent years, both in academia and in mainstream debates and policy interventions. Today, data literacy is considered a key "future skill" (Schüller et al. 2019) that is fostered by numerous large European Union funded research projects,[1] various new projects and start-ups,[2] educational initiatives and foundations,[3] countless online courses[4] as well as by new curricula and university courses.[5] Despite this increasing interest in data literacy, there is a tremendous imbalance in the data literacy field. The overwhelming majority of data literacy projects and initiatives takes a practical, skills-based perspective on data literacy, usually aiming to foster people's ability to read, work with, analyse and argue with data (e.g., QlikTech International AB 2018; Schüller et al. 2021). More research on ways to increase critical understanding of datafication is urgently needed.

Why Technical Skills Are Not Enough

While learning how to use data can be important for today's and future citizens, such skills-based approaches often neglect to foster *understanding* of how the data technologies around us function, including their limitations, and *reflection* on how they affect our lives and societies. Although a small number of practical data literacy approaches include such questions (see chapter 2.2.2), the vast majority focusses

---

1 E.g., DigComp (EU Science Hub – European Commission [no date]), DATALIT (Taibi [no date]), the Data Literate Project (Urbšienė et al. [no date]), or DaLi (Wasson [no date]).

2 E.g., Data Literacy – Learn the Language of Data (Data Literacy, LLC [no date]), The Data Literacy Project (QlikTech International AB [no date]).

3 E.g., Data Literacy Education by the German Stifterverband ([no date]), "Data Literacy" by the Valhalla Foundation ([no date]).

4 E.g., The Data Literacy Course (Maugain 2022), Data Literacy Foundations (Rochester Institute of Technology [no date]), Data Literacy for All (Tableau Software LLC [no date]).

5 E.g., Data Literacy Certificate (Derntl [no date]), Strengthening Data Literacy across the Curriculum (Louie [no date]).

on *using* data for one's individual purposes. However, data usage skills alone cannot solve the risks and challenges of datafication outlined above. Moreover, recent research even suggests that teaching skills alone can in fact be *harmful*, particularly for children and young people. A 2021 evidence review examined 34 studies with 12- to 17-year-olds and found that "greater digital skills are linked, directly or indirectly, to more exposure to online risks" (Livingstone et al. 2021a, p. 21). Thus, the authors conclude that "teaching or promoting technical skills alone emerges as a problematic strategy" (ibid.). This is a worrying, yet crucial finding in light of the strong emphasis on technical skills in IT education and digital and data literacy approaches. A recent evidence review by the Ada Lovelace Institute adds to this picture, arguing that public concerns around data should be taken seriously, and that "simply raising awareness about the benefits of data will not increase public trust" (Ada Lovelace Institute 2022, p. 3).

Thus, my study argues that what is needed are not merely better skills or more awareness, but *critical education about datafication*. Citizens need to understand how the data-driven technologies that they encounter on a daily basis function, how these technologies collect and use their data, which implications these systems entail, and how citizens can enact their rights and better protect their data. Such critical literacy is essential for "democratic participation and social inclusion in the digital age" (Polizzi 2020b, p. 2). However, critical reflection of digital technologies is not something that people can learn on their own. Rather, research shows that in order to be critical of the digital, people need support, and to be prompted to critically reflect (Pangrazio and Selwyn 2020, p. 16).

In academic research, this perspective is examined by a small but fast-growing research field on *critical data literacy*, which has suggested educational approaches such as Big Data Literacy (D'Ignazio and Bhargava 2015), data infrastructure literacy (Gray et al. 2018), personal data literacies (Pangrazio and Selwyn 2019), data citizenship (Carmi et al. 2020), or my own previous suggestion of critical big data literacy (Sander 2020a; Sander 2020c). As argued by Pangrazio and Sefton-Green and demonstrated in chapter 2.2 of this study, however, a more complete theorisation of critical data literacy is required (2020, p. 208). Only few studies thoroughly review and analyse existing conceptual suggestions, and even fewer connect critical data literacy approaches to traditional educational concepts that this new and emerging field could learn from. Moreover, implementing the abstract objectives of an academic literacy concept into practice is challenging and there is a lack of practical models for educators (ibid., p. 211; 215). Thus, both an in-depth theoretical framework for critical education about datafication and research on ways to foster such education in practice are urgently needed. This study aims to contribute to both of these gaps in research.

1.2 Goals and Purpose of This Study

Background of the Study

It is not only these gaps in academic research that shaped this study, but also my previous experience in the field. In the years before starting this study, I investigated how online data literacy resources affect university students' privacy attitudes and their actions, and how they perceive these resources (research conducted in 2018/19: Sander 2020a); organised an international working group on critical data literacy together with the German education scholar Dr Harald Gapski in 2019; and, based on this working group, co-founded the "Critical Big Data and Algorithmic Literacy Network" – an international and interdisciplinary network for scholars and practitioners that Harald Gapski and I continue to co-coordinate. In the following years, I was involved in developing a database for critical data literacy resources and organising several events on critical data literacy, such as workshops and a debate series, both in the context of this network and other critical data literacy initiatives that I am involved in. These experiences equally demonstrated how much research and practice in terms of critical education about data already takes place, but also how many gaps remain and how under-researched some highly relevant literacy practices still are. In particular, the experiences of practitioners of critical data education and the connections of critical data literacy to traditional education scholarship urgently need more research.

The Study's Novel Approach to Researching Critical Data Literacy

My study's approach to addressing the gaps in research outlined above is novel in two regards: First, it takes a *holistic perspective* to developing a new, theoretically grounded framework for *critical datafication literacy* by combining an extensive theoretical analysis with empirical research and insights from practice. Already the frameworks' terminology highlights that this literacy takes a particular perspective to education about data: it aims for critical, systemic understanding of datafication and its implications, empowering learners to become active and enlightened citizens in datafied societies (see chapters 3.4; 7).[6] To develop such a novel and well-grounded literacy framework, not only existing digital and data literacy concepts were reviewed and analysed, but the study further examined what can be learnt from more traditional approaches in education research and from practitioners of critical data education. Three relevant educational approaches were analysed in detail and the unique characteristics of each of these well-established approaches were

6 In this study, the term "critical data literacy" is used as a generalising descriptor of different academic and practical approaches to critical education about data technologies. The term "critical datafication literacy" is used when referring to the specific literacy framework that is developed throughout the study.

identified and analysed in terms of what insights they offer for a more grounded theoretical framework for critical datafication literacy. This theoretical analysis not only considered educational approaches from English-speaking parts of the world, but my bilingualism also allowed me to analyse core theoretical concepts from the German academic discourse. Education research is a strong research field with a long history in Germany, which has produced a number of influential and internationally renowned theoretical concepts, for example "Bildung" (e.g., von Humboldt 1986). These concepts offer numerous points of connection to critical data literacy concepts that have hardly been explored so far.

The holistic nature of my study's theoretical framework is not limited to making new theoretical connections, but the study also aims to learn from practitioners of critical data education. This highlights the second regard in which my study takes a novel approach: it *closely interconnects theory and practice*. It does this in a number of ways. To begin, the study included a collaboration with the non-governmental organisation (NGO) Privacy International.[7] With over 30 years of experience in raising awareness and educating the public about risks surrounding digital technologies, Privacy International (PI) constituted an ideal collaboration partner to complement my own academic knowledge. Knowledge exchange with the NGO took place in several stages of the research, with the NGO acting as an advisor and providing important feedback on different methodological decisions.

Moreover, the theoretical and empirical research of the study are closely interconnected. The study empirically examined ways in which critical education about data already takes place, including the goals and strategies that practitioners follow. These findings offered valuable insights for the development of an in-depth framework for critical datafication literacy, as they reflected practitioners' year-long experiences in fostering critical understanding of data technologies. Furthermore, these findings on literacy practices could in turn help implement the critical datafication literacy framework developed in my study into practice. As Pangrazio and Sefton-Green highlight, the translation of abstract objectives of an academic literacy concept into "a practical model that can be operationalised by educators" is challenging (2020, p. 215). Learning about the strategies and approaches that are already used to educate about data provides a meaningful starting point for developing such practical models. To further support educators and interconnect theory and practice, the final stage of my study consisted of a knowledge mobilisation project conducted in

---

7 This study was funded by the Economic and Social Research Council Wales as part of the "Collaborative Doctoral Training Partnership" pathway. This pathway supports collaborative research projects between doctoral candidates and non-academic organisations, in this case the non-governmental organisation Privacy International. This collaboration was thus embedded in the project from the start, but how the collaboration was realised could be determined by the project partners.

close cooperation with Privacy International. In this project, the theoretical and conceptual findings on what critical datafication literacy should entail as well as the empirical findings on resources and strategies to foster critical education about datafication were mobilised for educators. Thus, my study takes the interconnection of theory and practice seriously by not only calling for more literacy education, but also providing educators with the information and the resources they need to foster critical datafication literacy.

Goals of the Study

Critical education about datafication can be fostered in a number of contexts, including in the classroom or in textbooks, but also for example in youth social work, in museums and exhibitions or through documentary movies. Pangrazio and Sefton-Green differentiate between formal data literacy pedagogies, personal pedagogies of data and "folk pedagogies of data" (2020, p. 217). The latter describe "a range of open, public programmes" that raise awareness and critical understandings of data "through creativity, visualisation and/or interactivity" (ibid.).

One format that fits into this category and that also constitutes one of the longest-standing and most established approaches to critical data education is what I would term *online critical data literacy resources*. This term describes web-based resources of various formats, such as websites, short videos, interactive tools, online courses and many others, that aim to raise awareness and critically educate about datafication. Online resources were used to educate about data as early as 2006,[8] and have developed into a popular approach with countless examples since then. They provide innovative, creative, diverse and often entertaining approaches to raising critical understanding of data. Nevertheless, these critical data literacy efforts have been examined in very few studies so far (e.g., Milioni and Papa 2019; Sander 2020c; Alegre 2021), and a comprehensive overview of such resources and research into their goals, educational strategies, and their creators' considerations are lacking. Thus, we know little about the perspective of their creators – one of the most important communities who currently implement critical education about datafication into practice – nor about the contexts in which these resources are used and how they are perceived.

8 For example the interactive website "Panopti.com" from 2006, which used animated short videos and texts to highlight surveillance in a citizen's daily life and informed about risks and ways to protect one's data. Unfortunately, the website is not available anymore.

My study attempts to address these gaps in empirical and theoretical research and aims to:

1) *Develop an in-depth theoretical framework for critical datafication literacy*, which not only takes existing critical data literacy concepts into consideration, but also learns from established education scholarship and from practitioners of critical data education;
2) *Investigate critical data literacy practices* – examining online educational resources about datafication and how they are created and used by educators as one way to teach about data;
3) *Mobilise the new knowledge for practitioners* of critical data literacy together with the NGO Privacy International.

The Purpose of the Research

The broader purpose of my study is to contribute to ongoing debates on what critical data education should entail and what such literacy education could look like in practice. The development of a framework for critical datafication literacy, which constitutes the core of my study, aims to provide a more complete theorisation of such literacy by taking theoretical insights and practical experiences into consideration, and to make a stronger call for *critical and reflexive* approaches to data literacy, which are often overlooked by large data literacy projects, agendas, policy initiatives or curricula such as the ones referred to above. Moreover, the study provides findings on strategies, approaches, formats and design options to implement this literacy into practice. The findings mostly relate to online critical educational resources as these are the key research objects of the study. However, it is likely that the identified strategies and approaches can be adapted to different contexts of critical data literacy education. These practical suggestions contribute to the highlighted gaps in data literacy approaches and practical models for educators. Through the knowledge mobilisation project that took place after the research and analysis were completed, Privacy International and I further aimed to directly support educators in teaching about topics around data by providing information on datafication, advice on how to find the right educational resource for a specific group of learners, and suggestions on how to create their own learning material.

1.3 Methodological Approach and Research Questions

In its first, theoretical stage, my study examined the research question "How can an extended critical datafication literacy be conceptualised?". Here, research on datafication and its implications for society was reviewed along with existing (critical) data literacy conceptualisations (chapter two). This was complemented by an in-depth analysis of a small number of relevant theoretical approaches from traditional education scholarship (chapter three). Three educational approaches were selected as most suitable: education about (digital) media, including media literacy and digital literacy concepts; the German approach of "Bildung", including "politische Bildung"; and the Freirean "critical pedagogy". Key texts for each approach were selected, analysed in detail and key insights transferred to the conceptualisation of critical datafication literacy. Chapter 3.4 then presents a preliminary framework for this literacy based on the study's theoretical findings.

The second stage of this study comprised of different empirical approaches that aimed to investigate online critical data literacy resources from several angles. After discussing the applied methodological approaches in chapter four, chapter five addresses three research questions:

1) What is the range, shape and focus of *online critical data literacy resources*?
2) What are the goals, strategies, and experiences of *creators* of online critical data literacy resources?
3) What are *educators'* experiences with the topic of datafication and what do they need and wish for from a critical data literacy resource?

A quantitative content analysis of 75 resources was conducted in order to address the first research question and to provide an overview and initial analysis of existing online critical data literacy resources (chapter 5.1). After this, ten resources were selected out of those examined in the content analysis, and expert interviews with the creators of these resources were conducted to learn about their goals and strategies in critically educating about data (chapter 5.2). Finally, a qualitative survey with the second key community of critical data literacy practitioners – educators who are interested in teaching about digital and data technologies – was conducted (chapter 5.3). The goal here was to better understand the 57 participants' experiences and approaches in teaching about digital and data technologies, including whether or not they already use the priorly examined online resources; and to ascertain what educators' needs and wishes for critical data literacy resources are. Chapter six then interweaves the findings of all three empirical approaches and discusses them in relation to the academic literature. Finally, chapter seven presents the new critical datafication literacy framework that is developed throughout the study, reflects on the study's limitations and offers concluding remarks.

After the study's theoretical and empirical analyses were completed, the knowledge mobilisation project took place. Together with the NGO Privacy International, the knowledge developed in my study and insights from PI's practical experience were mobilised to support educators in their teaching about data. As a result, a learning resource was created that aims to provide educators with everything they need – understanding, critical perspectives and educational material – to foster critical education about datafication. While this book highlights research findings that have influenced the creation process of this learning resource, the development of the resource itself was not part of the research and is thus not included in the following chapters. A report on the creation process and the outcome of the knowledge mobilisation project can instead be found in appendix IX.

2. Literature Review

2.1 Why Do We Need Education about Datafication?

2.1.1 Introduction into Critical Data Studies

The Datafication of Our Societies

In recent years, our societies have become increasingly governed by data. With the growing collection of data and use of data analytics, today's governments and corporations have a staggering amount and range of data available – more than any other institution in history before them (Ruppert et al. 2017, p. 1). Even more disruptive, however, are the uses of these data masses. In enabling and powering a large variety of algorithmic systems, data not only pose risks around "privacy, surveillance, social discrimination, personalisation and control" (Kennedy and Moss 2015, p. 5), they also lead to new forms of capitalism (Zuboff 2019) and "a power shift" (Hintz 2022, p. 86), creating "new forms of power relations and politics" (Ruppert et al. 2017, p. 2), and altering the "nature of citizenship" (Graham et al. 2019, para.4). In our "data-driven world" (Kitchin 2021, p. 219), citizens are increasingly "profiled, categorized, scored and assessed" (Dencik et al. 2022, p. 8), but they "lack agency over how their data is used" (Ada Lovelace Institute 2020, p. 7). Considering these wide-reaching implications of data systems on how we make sense of our world, how we govern our societies and organisations, and how democracy is understood (Kitchin 2021; Dencik et al. 2022), many scholars speak of the *datafication* of our societies.

The term datafication was coined by Mayer-Schönberger and Cukier, who explained that datafying a phenomenon means to "put it in a quantified format so it can be tabulated and analysed" (2013, p. 78). They argue that this datafication is happening to our entire societal systems, as more and more information about human behaviour and people's attitudes and sentiments is turned into data points that can be analysed and used for making decisions and predicting future behaviour (ibid.). Mayer-Schönberger and Cukier see datafication not only as the "back bone of many of the Web's social media companies", but also describe it as a "great infrastructure project" that our societies are undertaking (2013, p. 91; 96). Taking a more critical perspective, van Dijck highlights that this datafication of our lives is not an objective process, but rather "staked in ideological assumptions, which are, in turn, rooted in prevailing social norms", and thus requires critical interrogation (2014, p. 200). In a more recent publication, Hepp, Jarke and Kramp further outline "the double character of datafication's processuality" (2022, p. 5). They argue that datafication describes both the individual translations of social processes into data, which are not as neutral and objective as they are often portrayed, and the overall transformation of society: "how society changes when 'online quantified data' become increasingly widespread" (ibid., p. 6).

In order to understand this datafication in more detail and to outline why more education about datafication is needed, several additional key terms need to be clarified. At their core, data systems consist of *data* and *algorithms*. Neither of these are neutral or benign measures. Data are representations of the world that are "never raw", but always shaped by decisions made in the collection, handling and analysis of the data (Kitchin 2021, p. 5). Algorithms are broadly understood as "a series of steps undertaken in order to solve a particular problem or accomplish a defined outcome" (Diakopoulos 2015, p. 400). This can, for example, be mathematic formulae in the form of equations, or computer programmes that consist of many algorithms that together "form large, often complex, recursive decision trees" (Kitchin 2017, p. 17). In the context of datafication, algorithms usually describe software systems that process data in order to – autonomously or with human involvement – take decisions or apply measures that have impacts on the individual or collective level (Directorate-General for Communications Networks, Content and Technology 2018, p.ii).

In the past decade, new, more complex and extensive "*big data*" systems emerged, that are often defined by their huge volume, high velocity and diverse variety (3V definition, Laney 2001) as well as their exhaustiveness, their fine-grained resolution and their relational and flexible nature (Kitchin 2014). Yet, other scholars have argued that big data is "less about data that is big than it is about a capacity to search, aggregate, and cross-reference large data sets" (boyd and Crawford 2012, p. 663), and have highlighted big data's sociotechnical nature (e.g., Ruppert et al. 2015; Zuboff 2015). Such critical approaches emphasise that big data is not a technology or a technology effect, but that it "originates in the social, and it is there that we must find it and know it" (Zuboff 2015, p. 75). Academic research further speaks of the "sociotechnical assemblage" that makes up (big) data (Kitchin 2014, p. 24). The notion of *data assemblage* describes the combination of "technological, political, social and economic apparatuses and elements that constitutes and frames the generation, circulation and deployment of data" (Kitchin and Lauriault 2014, p. 1).

All these terminologies aim to describe how today's data systems differ from earlier digital technologies, and how they affect our lives and societies. One type of data systems distinctly illustrates these changes: *automated decision-making systems* (ADMs). These systems consist of a "decision-making model, an algorithm that translates this model into computable code, the data this code uses as an input [...] and the entire political and economic environment surrounding its use" (Algorithm Watch 2019, p. 9). In other words, ADMs use data and algorithms to make decisions that can affect many aspects of our lives and societies, such as who is deemed creditworthy, what social services a person is eligible for and how likely it is that they will commit a crime (e.g., Directorate-General for Communications Networks, Content and Technology 2018, p. 10f; Algorithm Watch 2019).

Critical Data Studies – Research on Risks around Datafication

While many data systems are developed and implemented with good intentions (such as increased efficiency, less subjective decision-making or saving resources), the outcome often does not align with these original intentions (Redden et al. 2022). As the following section will highlight, the datafication of our societies comes with considerable risk and can lead to substantial individual and collective harm. The underlying cause for many of these problematic issues is the misleadingly assumed objectivity and accuracy of data that was already outlined above. Numerous scholars have highlighted that big data is "never a neutral tool" (Dalton and Thatcher 2014), that numbers do not speak for themselves (boyd and Crawford 2012, p. 670), and that claims of big data's extraordinary accuracy need to be treated with caution as "all datasets are necessarily limited representations of the world" (Dalton and Thatcher 2014).

Research from the field of *Critical Data Studies* has played an important role in exploring and developing such arguments. The original call for the field was made by Dalton and Thatcher, asking "what does a critical data studies look like, and why do we care?" (2014). The term "critical data studies" was taken up by Kitchin and Lauriault in the same year (2014) and has since developed into a growing, transdisciplinary research field. Critical Data Studies can be seen as "a response to the increasing spread of digital data and data infrastructures for decision- and meaning-making" (Hepp et al. 2022, p. 6), as the field examines the "unique cultural, ethical, and critical challenges" of data systems (Iliadis and Russo 2016, p. 1) and reflects on how "corporations, institutions and individuals collect and use 'big' data – and what alternatives to existing approaches could look like" (Richterich 2018, p. 8). In its essence, the field is "concerned with the significance (and power) of digital data in contemporary society and how it relates to societal transformation" (Hepp et al. 2022, p. 6).

Residing at the "intersection of science and technology studies, social science, policy and legal fields, and the humanities" (Neff et al. 2017, p. 86), Critical Data Studies is inherently inclusive and "open to self-critique and dialog" (Iliadis and Russo 2016, p. 2). In its transdisciplinary nature, Critical Data Studies further has many overlaps with related research fields, such as *Science and Technology Studies*, which has already existed for several decades, and aims for "understanding and critiquing the role of technology in our lives" (Moats and Seaver 2019, p. 2). Another closely related field is *Critical Algorithm Studies*, which argues for a need for more insight into algorithms (Gran et al. 2021, p. 1779), and challenges and critiques the many claims of data technologies' "objectivity and legitimacy", instead emphasising that "data science is politics by other means" (Moats and Seaver 2019, p. 2). Many overlaps exist in particular between Critical Algorithm Studies and Critical Data Studies, and the terms are sometimes used interchangeably (e.g., Yeung 2018).

In the past years, critical scholars have highlighted many ways in which datafication impacts our lives, our politics, economics and societies as a whole. Key concerns can be summarised as: "less privacy, more surveillance and social discrimination, and a new means of controlling how publics come to be represented and so understood" (Kennedy and Moss 2015, p. 2). Privacy – considered a key human right in many countries (e.g., Germany, see Deutscher Bundestag 1949) – is endangered through the ubiquitous collection and analysis of citizens' data, which increasingly leads to a "surveillance culture" (Lyon 2017), or "dataveillance – the monitoring of citizens on the basis of their online data" (Van Dijck 2014, p. 205). Datafication transforms and increases surveillance, allowing for "user-generated surveillance" (Lyon 2018, p. 5) through social media platforms and even leading to a "new economic order", as Zuboff argues (2019, no page nr.). This new *surveillance capitalism*, according to Zuboff, "claims human experience as free raw material for hidden commercial practices of extraction, prediction and sales" and constitutes a "profoundly antidemocratic social force" (ibid., p. 513).

Dencik, Hintz, Redden and Treré speak of datafication as a "political-economic regime" and highlight how datafication changes power relations, with citizens being increasingly monitored and profiled, while those who govern have access to new datafied management and governance techniques that citizens have "no knowledge about" (Dencik et al. 2022, p. 7; Hintz 2022, p. 81). Because of this "asymmetric relationship between those who collect, store, and mine large quantities of data, and those whom data collection targets" (Andrejevic 2014, p. 1673), it has been argued that datafication poses "severe challenges for democracy" (Hintz et al. 2022, p. 81) and limits citizens' agency (Baack 2015; Milioni and Papa 2019; Dencik et al. 2022). Data-based surveillance has even been called an "authoritarian and illiberal practice in the digital realm" (Hintz and Milan 2018, p. 3939).

Another implication of the increased surveillance through datafication is the "chilling effect" (e.g., Zuboff 2015, p. 82; Hintz and Milan 2018, p. 3949), which describes "people's sense of being subject to digital dataveillance" that causes them to "restrict their digital communication behavior", for example in the form of self-censorship (Büchi et al. 2022, p. 1). Equally, microtargeting – targeting small groups of online users with specific content – and "hypernudging" constitute datafied processes that can have problematic impacts. By showing each internet user the message that could persuade this individual to make a certain decision, hypernudging aims to "shape individual decision-making to serve the interests of commercial Big Data barons" (Yeung 2017, p. 119). Such attempts at "behaviour modification" (Zuboff 2019, p. 19) are becoming increasingly common in commercial as well as political advertising, as can be illustrated by the 2018 Cambridge Analytica scandal (see e.g., Cadwalladr and Graham-Harrison 2018), and pose significant risks for democratic processes.

A big part of the problem lies in the *opacity* of data practices. As the algorithmic models behind these systems are usually proprietary, their workings are frequently black-boxed and only rarely "open to public scrutiny and supervision" (Kennedy and Moss 2015, p. 2; Kitchin 2017; Redden 2018b). Thus, most of the time we cannot be certain how these data systems make their decisions or what data they base them on. This is particularly problematic when it comes to flawed and biased data systems. Not only can algorithms "make mistakes and operate with biases" (Diakopoulos 2015, p. 398), but also data that is "drawn from a world that is unequal will reflect that inequality" (Redden 2018b). Moreover, datafication reinforces existing discriminations, for example through search engines that produce racist results (Noble 2018), in consumer finance, where "risky groups" are denied credit, or in social policy, where "specific communities associated with particular behaviours can be targeted for increased surveillance" (Ruppert et al. 2015, p. 2). Scholars have argued that this algorithmic discrimination is the result of the "epistemological foundation" of big data systems: "data fundamentalism, post-explanatory anticipatory pragmatics, and anti-political solutionism" (Prietl 2019, p. 2); and that it tends to disproportionally affect communities that are already disadvantaged (Eubanks 2018), and places where "people, laws, and human rights are the most fragile", such as in the global South (Milan and Treré 2019, p. 319). In light of these social justice concerns that arise through datafication, scholars have called for improved "data justice" (Dencik et al. 2016; Dencik et al. 2022).

However, datafication is not only associated with risks that *may* negatively affect people, but people "are *already* being negatively affected by algorithmic systems" (Redden 2022, p. 60, emphasis in original). Redden has collected such harms and has developed a taxonomy of the negative influences that data systems have on people's lives (ibid., p. 60ff). She found that people have been targeted and exploited based on "inferred vulnerabilities"; that discriminatory social sorting practices have disproportionately disadvantaged people based on their "ethnicity, gender, sexuality and income"; that the "manipulation of information and targeting of voters" has undermined democratic processes and sowed social division; that the automation of government systems has prevented people "from accessing the necessities of life"; and that work surveillance and data breaches have led to physical and mental harms (ibid., p. 71f).

2.1.2 Citizens' Lacking Knowledge and Resignation

Informed Consent?

Another significant problem with the datafication of our societies is people's lack of knowledge and understanding of data collection and algorithmic practices as well as many people's dissatisfaction with these practices when learning about them. Although data collectors like to argue that their users "consent" to these practices, research increasingly shows that this is often not the case. Studies have found that up to 69% of British users accept terms and conditions without reading them (Ofcom 2019, p. 8; see also Meier et al. 2020; Larsson et al. 2021), and that 51% do not understand them when they try to read them (Doteveryone 2018, p. 17). This is not surprising given that most terms and conditions and privacy policies are written in legal jargon and, already in 2008, it would have taken a user around 25 days a year if they read every privacy policy they encountered online (McDonald and Cranor 2008). In fact, Draper and Turow argue that privacy policies deliberately use rhetorical practices of obfuscation to provide a misleading sense of the data that is collected (2019, pp. 7; 9; see below). While the General Data Protection Regulation (GDPR) that came into effect in May 2018 may have led to more transparency on the web, it has not been very effective in fostering users' consent (Degeling et al. 2019). Rather, scholars argue that it may have induced "a false sense of privacy and security for users" as few websites offer their users an actual choice regarding cookie-based tracking (ibid., p. 14), and users tend to assume that the mere existence of a policy protects their privacy (Turow et al. 2018). Overall, the notion of "*meaningful* consent" (Johnson et al. 2017, p. 37, emphasis in original), that is explicit, informed and freely given has been seriously questioned due to internet users' lacking knowledge; their acceptance of cookies because they "feel they have no choice" (Larsson et al. 2021, p. 117); and due to the "dark patterns" of internet services that nudge users toward the "least privacy friendly options" (Forbrukerrådet 2018, p. 4) and implement new "features that cannot be turned off, or settings that are invisible to the user" (Shade and Chan 2020, p. 332).

Lacking Knowledge

Moreover, recent research has increasingly found internet users' knowledge and understanding of data practices to be fragmentary at most. These findings span country borders and various aspects of data collections and analysis: For example, although 94% of British adults have internet access at home and they spend an average of nearly four hours daily online (Ofcom 2022), 24% do not know how technology companies make money, with more than two-thirds (70%) unaware of how free-to-use apps, social media (62%) and search engines (57%) make money from data (Miller et al. 2018, pp. 6; 21). Similarly, less than half of Europe's population knows what an algorithm is or is aware that algorithms are already being used in many areas of life

(Grzymek and Puntschuh 2019, p. 10), and Americans are found to not have "the basic knowledge to make informed cost-benefit choices" about how their data is used by marketers and often base their choices on incorrect information (Turow et al. 2015, p. 16f). Similarly, people's understanding of social media platforms appears to be limited, with 84% of Facebook users not knowing that Facebook categorises their interests (Hitlin and Rainie 2019, p. 8), and many being unaware that an algorithm curates their News Feed (Eslami et al. 2015, p. 153).

These numbers have not increased much over time, with newer studies identifying some increases in people's awareness of data collection and the use of their data between 2018 and 2020, but no significant increase in their understanding of technology companies' business models (Miller et al. 2020). Thus, also in 2020, the British people's understanding "remains shallow" and their ability to shape their online experiences based on their knowledge is poor (ibid., p. 15). Further, a German study found that while people's knowledge has increased in some areas between 2018 and 2022, the number of people who understand the influence of algorithms and artificial intelligence on their lives remains very small (merely increased from 27% to 29%) (Overdiek and Petersen 2022, p. 9). Similarly, Yates et al. described British citizens' knowledge as "patchy", and they found a "very limited understanding" of how technologies work and the "economics and technical ecosystems" that underpin these platforms (2021, pp.xiii, xii). The underlying narrative of these findings seems to be that while people may be aware that their data is being collected online, their understanding of the business models of the internet platforms they use daily remains limited (see also Johnson et al. 2017). This correlates with findings of a recent large-scale international study that found that the majority of internet users do not know how Google or Facebook are free of charge to use (Akman 2022, p. 22). Moreover, the study demonstrated that only a third of respondents knew how a search engine ranks its results and nearly a quarter had "no idea" how this takes place (ibid., p. 26).

Some scholars even speculate that this lacking knowledge and understanding, or "the inability to anticipate the potential uses of such data", may not be "an artifact of laziness or ignorance" but could rather be intentional, constituting a "defining attribute of data-mining processes" (Andrejevic 2014, pp. 1673; 1685). Similarly, Draper and Turow argue that "capitalist systems benefit from the cultivation of resignation as a strategy to neutralize critical or political action" and therefore engage in "obfuscatory communication practices" to hamper people's understanding of data mining processes (2019, pp. 5f; 7; see also below). However, despite the opacity of online platforms, people experience, make sense of and try to imagine how algorithms function, which has been described as people's "algorithmic imaginary" (Bucher 2017, p. 40). These feelings towards data practices have often been found to be negative and uneasy ones, as will be outlined in the next section.

Internet Users Feel Uncomfortable

Contrary to the common argument that users feel like they have 'nothing to hide', research from recent years has repeatedly found that people are concerned about their data, how it is used and how they can protect it (Miller et al. 2018; Selwyn and Pangrazio 2018; Miller et al. 2020; Müller-Peters 2020; Kennedy et al. 2021b). This concern is not dependent on people's knowledge about data practices: studies have found that people's concerns "correlate with both high and low levels of understanding" (Ada Lovelace Institute 2022, p. 20), and even without a good understanding of data practices, people still have strong emotional responses that they are able to articulate clearly (Kennedy et al. 2021a). In fact, many people feel uncomfortable with current data practices, articulating that targeted advertising and state surveillance make them feel "uncomfortable" and "uneasy" (Bucher 2017, p. 39; Dencik and Cable 2017, p. 771), that they find it "intrusive or creepy" (Akman 2022, p. 25), think it is "unacceptable" after learning more about it (Worledge and Bamford 2019, p. 5), and that they (nearly half of participants) feel negatively about receiving it (Miller et al. 2018, p. 15). Looking at Facebook in particular, studies found that people reacted with "surprise and anger" when becoming aware of the curation of their News Feeds through an algorithm (Eslami et al. 2015, p. 153), and that they feel "not very or not at all comfortable" with the way Facebook analyses their interests and traits (Hitlin and Rainie 2019, p. 8).

Moreover, people are unhappy about not being able to better protect their own data online (Miller et al. 2018, p. 16) and they want clearer information about data practices, better regulations and more ethical and responsible technologies (Ada Lovelace Institute 2022). Several studies have identified the creative tactics users apply to resist data collection and profiling, to mislead algorithms and thus to enact small forms of agency (Bucher 2017; Gangneux 2020; Kennedy et al. 2020; Larsson et al. 2021). Besides these clear findings on people's wishes for more understanding and control of their data, studies have also identified the complex and often conflicted and contradictory feelings that people have about how their data is used. People often show "mixed feelings" towards algorithms and data practices, appreciating benefits such as time savings, quality of services, convenience or personalisation, but at the same time voicing their concern, mistrust, anxiety and fears of a "risk of manipulation" (Grzymek and Puntschuh 2019, p. 10; Doteveryone 2018; Ofcom 2019; Overdiek and Petersen 2022; Shade and Shepherd 2013). These mixed feelings may be explained by the different contexts of data practices, as the context of data collection and use, the actors behind these practices and many other factors maintain or undermine trust in data practices (Kennedy et al. 2020). However, in some studies, respondents have both articulated that they have "nothing to hide", but also their "strong concerns about their privacy" (Demertzis et al. 2021, p. 131), or that they dislike being targeted with advertisement, but still would not be willing to pay for the online services they use in exchange for their data (Akman 2022).

Resignation towards Data Practices

This complex picture of people's attitudes towards data practices is further complicated when taking into consideration that many people seem to feel resigned towards data collection. Various studies have found evidence for such a "resignation" (Turow et al. 2015); "digital resignation" (Draper and Turow 2019); "surveillance realism" (Dencik and Cable 2017); "online apathy" (Hargittai and Marwick 2016) or "privacy cynicism" (Hoffmann et al. 2016). Despite some differences in their foci, samples and methods; in their core, these studies examine the same phenomenon. Digital resignation describes a situation where users believe that any efforts to protect their data are futile because data collection – and therefore the possibility of surveillance – is inevitable, and they assume that they can never gain control over their data. Importantly, these users do not consent to datafication, nor are they indifferent about it (see e.g., Kennedy et al. 2020, pp. 24; 48) or see data collection as a "tradeoff for benefits they receive" (Turow et al. 2015, p. 3), but they rather feel *powerless*. Because resigned users can show privacy behaviours that are similar to those who feel indifferent about big data practices, "resignation can obscure signals that people care deeply about privacy" (Draper and Turow 2019, p. 11). Instead, data collection is seen as negative and undesirable *because* people still value their privacy and are concerned about surveillance. These findings correspond with other studies on privacy and data collection that emphasise people's concerns around privacy and a "lack of control" (see above; European Commission et al. 2015, p. 115).

Internet users' resignation toward the collection of their data has further been identified in a number of empirical studies. For example, Worledge and Bamford found that a key reason why nearly nine in ten participants did not click on advert preference messages was that they felt not "able to do anything about it" (2019, p. 12). Other studies have found that people "accept cookies even though they do not want to" because they feel that they "have no choice" (Larsson et al. 2021, p. 117), and that people feel "resigned but also 'uneasy'" about data tracking (Yates et al. 2021, p.xii). Resignation might even increase over time, with Doteveryone's 2018 report finding that 25% of British internet users felt like "there's no point" in changing their privacy settings as "companies will get round them anyway" (Miller et al. 2018, p. 17), and their 2020 report identifying "a strong feeling of resignation" in the British public, with two-thirds feeling that they "don't have any say in what technology companies do" (Miller et al. 2020, p. 24). Digital resignation scholars argue that internet users' resignation derives from a perceived necessity of using the internet and social media (Hargittai and Marwick 2016, p. 3751) and fear of "significant social and economic penalties" in case of opting out (Turow et al. 2015, p. 9) in combination with uncertainty of how data systems work (Dencik and Cable 2017, p. 770), concerns about privacy violations (Hargittai and Marwick 2016, p. 3749), and lacking control over their data (Turow et al. 2015, p. 20).

Resignation as a Reasonable Response?

Many scholars argue that this reasoning is in fact "not paradoxical", but "a pragmatic response to the contemporary networked social environment" (Hargittai and Marwick 2016, p. 3752f). Thus, resigned or cynical attitudes are seen as a "coping mechanism" that is developed in order "to avoid cognitive dissonance" (Hoffmann et al. 2016, p. 2), and that constitutes a "rational response to a seemingly inevitable outcome" – consumer surveillance (Draper and Turow 2019, p. 5). Another explanatory model explains resignation with the power of imagination, arguing that the "sheer ubiquity of surveillance infrastructures" makes it difficult to think they can be challenged, and that our "hampered imagination" lets datafication and surveillance be seen as inevitable (Dencik 2018, p. 37f). In short, resignation scholars seem to agree that this attitude constitutes a reasonable and pragmatic response to the apparent inevitability of intrusive data practices.

Some authors even go further and argue that resignation not only constitutes a rational response to data practices, but that companies actively foster resignation among internet users through their obfuscatory practices (Draper and Turow 2019, p. 7). Examples of this "placation, diversion, jargon, and misnaming" are incomprehensible privacy policies and incomplete transparency initiatives (ibid., p. 9). This reiterates Andrejevic's argument that internet users' lacking knowledge constitutes a defining attribute of data mining processes and supports the notion that it might be in the digital platforms' interests to keep users' knowledge of data practices limited (2014; see above). However, the last years have seen a shift in technology companies' approach to privacy and some big technology firms now use data privacy as a "strategic competitive advantage", as examined in a recent Master's Thesis (Trindade 2020). Moreover, it is uncertain whether resignation leads to more data disclosure based on the belief of its inevitability and perhaps a perceived lack of technical ability (as suggested by, among others, Hoffmann et al. 2016; Dencik and Cable 2017), or rather to active resistance against data collection by engaging in privacy-protecting behaviour, avoiding certain internet services, and applying "a variety of imperfect, but creative, social strategies" to maintain at least a certain degree of control over one's data (Hargittai and Marwick 2016, p. 3753; see also Draper and Turow 2019; Yates et al. 2021).

2.1.3 Working towards a More Informed Citizenry

Calls for More Literacy and Public Involvement

In light of these problematic findings on internet users' resignation as well as the "major understanding gap around technologies" (Doteveryone 2018, p. 5) that was outlined throughout this chapter, many calls for more *education* about data and more *societal and public involvement* have been made (e.g., Zuboff 2015; O'Neil 2016; Marwick and Hargittai 2018; Miller et al. 2018; Müller-Peters 2020). On the one hand, scholars have argued that our democratic institutions need to respond to datafication by "developing a means to make black-boxed processes and the implications of changing systems open to wider debate and intervention" (Redden 2018a, p. 10). On the other hand, the need for a "greater public awareness" that might "open up discussion of policy solutions to regulate such [data] practices" has been emphasised (Marwick and Hargittai 2018, p. 14). One way to work toward such greater awareness is *data activism*.

Data Activism's Role in Challenging Datafication and Raising Awareness

The term data activism is used to describe "new forms of civic engagement and political action" that take a critical approach towards datafication (Milan and van der Velden 2016, p. 58). Data activism constitutes a "theoretical construct grounded in empirical observations" (Milan and Gutiérrez 2015, p. 121). Scholars have highlighted that data activists play an important role not only in working toward more socially just datafication processes, but also in acting as "mediators" between data and ordinary citizens, as "literacy promotion" is seen as one of the key tasks of data activists (Beraldo and Milan 2019, p. 5). Examples for data activism practices include the use of open data to foster citizens' understandings and their agency (e.g., Baack 2015; Meng and DiSalvo 2018); engaging citizens in political matters related to data (e.g., Baack 2018); and projects that raise awareness about data practices (e.g., Milioni and Papa 2019), also through unusual approaches such as using "theatre and performance as instruments of critical data studies" (Windeyer 2019, p. 316).

These examples already hint at an important distinction in data activism projects: data activism that *applies data practices* and activism *about big data* (which does not necessarily take place digitally, see Windeyer 2019). The first type, "proactive" data activism, uses data and data technologies from a bottom-up perspective to "provoke social change", to offer alternative narratives and empower citizens (Milan and van der Velden 2016, pp. 66; 67). The second type, "re-active" data activism, perceives massive data collection by state and industry as a threat to our "values, freedoms and activities" and encourages practices of resistance, such as "self-defence, civil disobedience and disruption" as well as using "technical means like encryption or anonymity networks" to prevent monitoring from state or corporation (Milan and van der Velden 2016, p. 67).

Despite their different approaches, both types of data activism conflate to various degrees and constitute "two facets of the same phenomenon, which has data and information at its core" (Milan and Gutiérrez 2015, p. 123). Moreover, both contain an explicit *pedagogical dimension* and often aim to foster citizens' agency (Baack 2018, p. 51f), critical reflection and "critical imagination" of alternative data narratives (Milan 2017). This emphasises data activism's relevance for my study. Moreover, one of the most similar empirical studies to my study comes from the field of data activism: Milioni and Papa's analysis of eight online data activism case studies combines data activism with affordance theory (2019). The authors highlight how these online resources provide "hidden affordances", "new affordances", "meta-affordances", and "anti-affordances" that aim to empower users and foster their critical understanding (ibid., pp. 7–10). Several of the analysed tools also fall into my study's definition of critical data literacy resources. Moreover, Milioni and Papa warn against shifting "responsibility from data industries and regulatory agencies to the 'enlightened' user" (ibid., p. 11f) – a highly relevant point that will be further discussed in the next chapter.

Calls for More Literacy about Datafication

A second key approach of working towards greater public awareness of data practices and more societal and public involvement is to *promote education about datafication*. The hope behind this is that more "reflexive, active and knowing publics" (Kennedy and Moss 2015, p. 1) might not only empower citizens, but also lead to a much-needed broader public discussion about "the transparency, accountability and oversight of data systems required for protecting citizens' rights" (Redden 2018b). When outlining ways to better educate the public about data practices, scholars have suggested a number of ideas and concepts, which will be analysed in detail in the next chapter. Many highlight the need to support "digital education" and "digital understanding" to foster public engagement (Miller et al. 2018, p. 6; Müller-Peters 2020, p. 128) and people's "data sovereignty" (Kitchin 2021, p. 223). Scholars have also argued that digital literacy programs should move away from individualistic approaches and should rather "find ways to highlight the societal implications" of the structural levels of datafication (Turow et al. 2018, p. 475). Already in 2015, Turow, Hennessy and Draper succinctly summarised what is needed:

> We need initiatives that will give members of the public the right and ability to learn what companies know about them, how they profile them, and what data lead to what personalized offers. We also need to get people excited about using that right and ability. (2015, p. 21)

In a similar vein, others have called for a "broad campaign of popular capacity-building" that builds competences for an informed debate about datafication by enabling "people to form considered opinions and debate the issue in a factually informed way" (Grzymek and Puntschuh 2019, p. 11). These authors further suggest a "Bundeszentrale für algorithmische Kompetenz" (German for: Federal Agency for Algorithmic Literacy), a public institution that works towards informing and educating citizens about algorithmic systems (ibid., p. 32). Moreover, Iliadis and Russo emphasise that educating people about data practices in fact constitutes one of three basic principles of Critical Data Studies: "the identification of social data problems, the design of critical frameworks for addressing social data problems, and the application of social solutions to increase data literacy" (2016, p. 5). Based on Aristotle's Nicomachean Ethics, they refer to the notion of "education for the common good", which, they argue, deeply informs Critical Data Studies (ibid.). In their view, this entails that scholars from this field should contribute to data literacy efforts and provide individuals "with the necessary tools for becoming more informed and the ability to organize efforts around data justice issues" (ibid.). Thus, it can be said that responsibilities to foster better understanding of data practices are seen to lie not only with governments and public institutions, but also with academia.

More Knowledge = More Concern?

In recent years, a growing number of studies has examined the relation of people's knowledge about datafication and their concern about data practices, in other words: does more knowledge and understanding entail a more concerned attitude? Some studies have compared the levels of concerns of more and less knowledgeable internet users and have found that those who are more knowledgeable are "more likely to have negative attitudes" towards data uses (Kennedy et al. 2021b, p. 9) and demonstrate "higher privacy concerns and were more likely to take privacy protection strategies on Facebook" (Xie and Karan 2019, p. 10). This suggests that "change is needed, because when people know about data uses, they don't like what they know" (Kennedy et al. 2021b, p. 9). These findings are strengthened by several before-and-after studies, which found that the *mere mention* of privacy in newspaper articles led to less disclosure of personal information, arguing that people's privacy concerns may be dormant and only manifest when asked to think about privacy (Marreiros et al. 2017, pp. 3; 10); or that Facebook users who learned about the platform's curation algorithm showed lasting changes in their usage patterns, an increased "algorithmic awareness", and felt overall more in control (Eslami et al. 2015, p. 153).

Some studies have further identified diverse effects of educating about data practices. My own previous small-scale longitudinal study examined the effect of online critical data literacy resources on university students' privacy concern and behaviour (Sander 2020a). The findings demonstrated a nearly unambiguous increased concern for privacy and distinctly more privacy-sensitive internet usage one week after the intervention, and diverse developments after eight months, with some participants showing concern only about *some* aspects of privacy, one 'defaulting back' to their original attitude and behaviour, and two others showing a *persistent and even growing* increase in privacy concern and behaviour (ibid., p. 5ff). Pangrazio and Selwyn's study with young social media users, on the other hand, found diverse attitudes of the participants regarding different areas of data use (2018). While participants developed "clearer understandings" and new concerns on how their data is used, they were less concerned about text and image analyses and their attitudes to targeted advertising hardly changed (ibid., p. 5f). This last finding is somewhat contrary to a British nationally representative study by Worledge and Bamford, who observed distinct changes in people's perceptions of online advertising and its strategies, with 43% viewing these practices as unacceptable after learning more about how they work (14% before intervention) (2019, p. 19).

Overall, these studies strengthen the notion that critical data literacy efforts can be effective in educating internet users, and that for many internet users, more knowledge about data practices leads to more concern and feelings of uneasiness. While the findings regarding effects on people's *concerns* differ slightly in the different studies, the results on participants' altered *behaviour* – for some even in the longer term – seem consistent. Although more research on the relation between knowledge, concern about data and behaviour is needed, these first studies clearly support the calls for more education on datafication outlined above and reemphasise the importance of literacy in this field.

2.1.4 Conclusion

This chapter reviewed key literature from the Critical Data Studies field, which outlines the societal transformation processes and risks related to datafication. Moreover, studies that highlight citizens' lacking knowledge on these processes and risks were presented along with initial findings that suggest that more knowledge on data practices can lead to more concerns and a more empowered internet usage. In light of this, many scholars have called for more and better education about data technologies in recent years, and many new data literacy conceptualisations have been suggested.

2.2 Educating about Data: (Critical) Data Literacies

This chapter reviews existing approaches to (critical) data literacy and offers a tentative categorisation of such approaches. Calls for more education about data practices are increasing and educational responses have even been put forward as not only the dominant, but also the "most plausible and successful strategy to combat the challenges of datafication" (Pangrazio and Sefton-Green 2020, p. 212). Scholars further highlight that education about datafication should be seen as a key component or even prerequisite of legal and tactical responses to datafication (ibid., p. 218).

These claims correlate with an upsurge of data literacy conceptualisations, initiatives, projects, networks and curricula in recent years.[1] However, while the term data literacy may seem self-evident, a closer examination of the data literacy discourse reveals great disparities regarding how data literacy is understood and

1 For examples, see introduction chapter.

what educational objectives are being followed, highlighting that the term "rests on competing definitions" (Pangrazio and Sefton-Green 2020, p. 212). In light of this, some researchers have called for a unified terminology of data literacy (Koltay 2015), whereas others have argued that finding a single definition of literacy is "in fact [...] not desirable" in light of the multiple different skills and competences that are required (Fotopoulou 2020, p. 4). An examination of current literacy discourses quickly shows that the majority of data literacy concepts originate from data science tradition and follow an instrumental, skills-based approach, aiming at fostering people's technical skills to use and manage data (as highlighted by, e.g., Raffaghelli and Stewart 2020; Seymoens et al. 2020; Pangrazio and Sefton-Green 2022). Raffaghelli and Stewart, for example, conducted an extensive literature analysis of data literacy approaches with a focus on higher education faculty development, and found that the majority of literacy definitions "lean towards an instrumental framing", focussing mainly on the development of technical skills (2020, p. 447). The authors argue that while some analysed approaches aim for learners' empowerment, most do not support such "holistic idea of data literacy" and lack "acknowledgement of the emerging debates on data and ethics, minorities, privacy, agency and empowerment" in datafied societies (ibid., p. 444; 447).

In line with these findings, my study's review of the literature found that critical data literacy conceptualisations that aim for understanding and critical reflection of data systems are far less common than instrumental approaches. Yet, during the time of my engagement with the data literacy field, critical approaches to data literacy have increased significantly. When first reviewing research on data literacy as part of my Master's dissertation in early 2018, critical perspectives were rare and the few that could be identified almost all took a combined practical and critical approach. As I continued my research in the field during a research fellowship in 2019 and prepared two publications on "critical big data literacy", several new critical conceptualisations had emerged, including some that placed a strong focus on a broader reflection of datafication (see Sander 2020c; Sander 2020a). This trend continued while conducting my initial literature review for this study in early 2020 and was observed again when revising this chapter in 2023. Particularly in these two years, a large increase of critical data literacy publications was identified, signifying the growing importance of this field. This can also be illustrated by the texts referenced in this chapter: while the first version from early 2020 reviewed only 33 (critical) data literacy conceptualisations, this final version of the chapter provides an overview of a total of 75 publications.

This chapter thus draws on insights from my ongoing reviews of data literacy literature throughout the last five years and aims to provide a comprehensive – yet not exhaustive – overview of the diverging definitions of (critical) data literacy. Moreover, reflecting on the findings of these ongoing literature reviews, the chapter suggests a tentative categorisation of literacy approaches. According to this, data literacy concepts can be broadly categorised into three overlapping categories that are located on a spectrum between practical-instrumental and critical-reflective literacy understandings (see fig. 1). The 'traditional' understanding of data literacy as data science skills as well as creative approaches to using data constitute the first category of *practical-instrumental literacy understandings*. The second category aims to *foster critical perspectives through the active use of data* and includes concepts that place a varying focus on practical data usage skills while also promoting critical reflection. Finally, some authors suggest that critical data literacy should focus on supporting *understanding and critical reflection of the wider, structural-level implications* that come with the datafication of our societies. Although all approaches to data literacy can offer useful insights, the concepts included in this last category are of particular relevance for the theorisation and further conceptualisation of critical datafication literacy in my study as well as for informing my empirical research.

Figure 1: Categorisation of (critical) data literacy concepts along a spectrum from practical-instrumental to critical-reflective approaches.

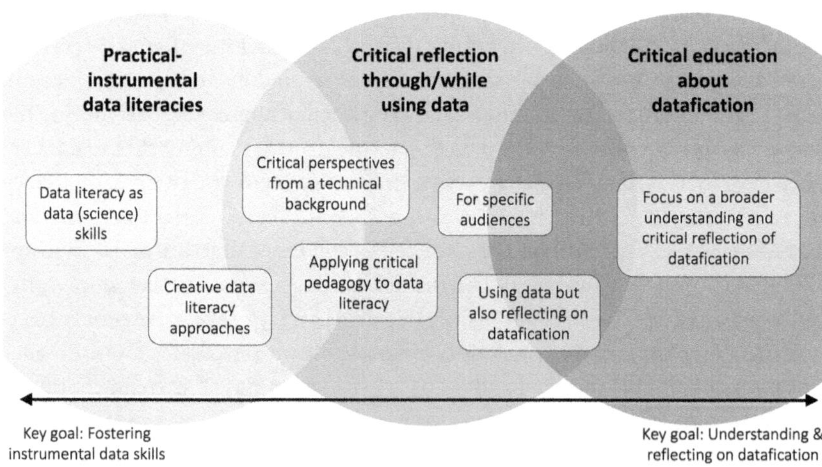

Yet, it should be clarified that this categorisation constitutes a tentative order, aiming for a structured overview of the field of data literacy concepts rather than a fully developed typology of data literacy approaches. The categories are not distinct or exhaustive in nature and many of the presented concepts include aspects that fit in more than one of these proposed categories. Moreover, as mentioned above, the (critical) data literacy research field evolved significantly during the course of my study, and in 2019, very few literature analyses of data literacy concepts had been published. One early example is Maybee and Zilinksi's 2015 study, which identified eight key frameworks for data literacy in a literature review. Similar to my categorisation, they found predominantly data usage skills, but also "awareness: understanding data and its role in society" (2015, p. 2).

Between 2020 and 2022, several new categorisations of (critical) data literacy conceptualisations that make similar distinctions as mine were published. For example, Yousef et al.'s analysis of data literacy as a "multidimensional concept" found practical uses of data such as research data management or learning analytics as key areas of data literacy concepts, but also identified goals such as an informed citizenry, awareness of datafication and citizen participation (2021, pp. 26f, 30). In a German-language examination of critical data literacy approaches, Dander differentiated critical data literacy concepts by eight levels, such as their audiences and educational contexts, but also (relating to the same differentiation in data activism projects) their pro- or reactive nature (2021). Finally, Raffaghelli analysed nine higher education data literacy initiatives and identified four dimensions, which range from using data in pedagogical or open data settings to fostering understanding of the role data play in society and a postcolonial perspective on data (2020, p. 15). While using different terminologies and developing different categorisations of data literacy concepts, what these studies have in common is that they identify very diverse goals of data literacy approaches, ranging from active data usage skills to awareness and reflection. This chapter details the diverse objectives and characteristics of existing (critical) data literacy concepts, outlining parallels and key lines of argumentation in the field as well as highlighting differences and gaps of research.

2.2.1 How Is Data Literacy 'Traditionally' Understood?

Data Literacy as Data (Science) Skills

As outlined above, the most 'traditional' understanding of data literacy can be broadly summarised as a practical, skills-based approach that aims to teach how to *use data and datasets*. In their overview of previous data literacy research, Gray et al. summarise this understanding as: "being able to access, analyse, use, interpret, manipulate and argue with datasets in response to the ubiquity of (digital) data in different fields" (2018, p. 2). A similar definition is suggested by Wolff et al., who define data literacy as "the ability to ask and answer real-world questions from large and small data sets through an inquiry process", which includes the abilities to "select, clean, analyse, visualise, critique and interpret data" as well as using data to communicate stories and in design processes (2016, p. 23). Schüller et al.'s "data literacy charter" emphasises data literacy's role as a "key competence for all people in the 21st century" as it is "key to systematically transforming data into knowledge and actions" (2021, p. 2). This highlights the core objective of many 'traditional', instrumental data literacy understandings: to enable and motivate people to actively use data, deal confidently with their own and other people's data and to "use new drivers and technologies such as Big Data, Artificial Intelligence or Internet of Things" (ibid.).

Frank et al. follow a similar understanding and add that they view data literacy as a "recent addition to a growing band of literacies such as numerical literacy, statistical literacy and IT literacy" (2016, p. 5). Others equally highlight the overlap or connection between these concepts, arguing that, given the "greatly amplified role that data now play in our lives", statistical literacy should be updated to include data literacy (Gould 2017). Other suggestions state data literacy should be incorporated into information literacy programmes (Calzada and Marzal 2013) or propose a combined "data information literacy" (Carlson et al. 2011). Similar to the data literacy discourse, also statistical literacy concepts have broadened in recent years, developing from a narrow technical understanding to "a broader meaning including critical, ethical-political aspects" (François and Monteiro 2018, p. 3). The "Data Revolution Group", a United Nations Secretary-General's Independent Expert Advisory Group, similarly called for a "global data literacy" that includes statistical literacy but also aims to enable citizens to "fully participate in initiatives to foster citizenship in the information age" (2014, p. 20). Other approaches to data literacy focus on business and employability perspectives through data literacy (Gummer and Mandinach 2015; Wolff and Kortuem 2015). Thus, even among instrumental, practical data literacy concepts, a variety of goals and approaches can be identified, and no single definition has emerged so far. Yet, the one defining characteristic of these approaches is that they aim to encourage learners to actively use data (analytics) for their purposes.

Creative Data Literacy Approaches

Several scholars have built on such skills-based data literacy approaches but have added a focus on creativity. D'Ignazio, for example, has suggested a "creative data literacy" as an approach for "non-technical learners" who may need "an alternative to the traditional quantitative approach to working with data" (2017, pp. 6; 7). Tactics for this include working with "community-centered data" or making data "messy" (ibid., p. 8, 11). Together with Bhargava, D'Ignazio has further proposed a "data mindset" that supports the "ability to think both creatively and critically" about opportunities to use data to answer questions and gain insights (2018). Here, they also clearly differentiate this "critical and creative mindset" from the "technical skills, statistical techniques, or particular software packages" that instrumental, skills-based definitions of data literacy such as the ones introduced above focus on. Thus, although they also aim for practical use of data, D'Ignazio and Bhargava clearly regard data literacy as an approach that should foster critical perspectives and work towards *empowerment* (e.g., D'Ignazio 2017, p. 6) This becomes even clearer in their 2015 concept, which will be outlined in more detail in section 2.2.3.

A similarly creative and critical data literacy understanding is suggested by Ahlborn et al. who suggest fostering data literacy through "critical making" and through using data, coding and artificial intelligence in creative play scenarios (2021, pp. 21; 32). Despite this focus on practically using data, their goal for data literacy is for learners to gain new perspectives on how social, cultural, political and economic processes are affected by data and to become empowered to participate in datafied societies in an informed manner (ibid., p. 34).

These critical and creative approaches to data literacy already show strong overlaps with the next category: concepts that aim to *foster critical perspectives through or while using data*. While purely instrumental, skills-based data literacy concepts constitute the most common and established understanding of data literacy, they are only of limited relevance for the conceptualisation of critical datafication literacy in my study. Although statistical and data analysis skills can also support better understanding of datafication, these competences can shed little light on questions such as "how are my data used to profile and score citizens" or "what is the influence of algorithms on my daily life?". Therefore, data literacy needs a "more complex" approach "than simply learning to access, use, analyze, or create data through statistics or comprehending data visualizations and data calculations" (Markham 2020, p. 230). Moreover, research has found that fostering technical skills alone, without also promoting understanding and critical reflection, is a "problematic strategy" and can lead, "directly or indirectly, to more exposure [of children] to online risks" (Livingstone et al. 2021a, pp. 21; 22).

In line with this, it has been argued that the uncritical use of data, such as everyday data-related practices in education, can lead to "'data (il)literacy' – an uncritical, one-dimensional understanding of data and datafication" (Mertala 2020, p. 1). According to Mertala, when learners are introduced to data as "direct measurements" instead of the "imperfect proxies and indicators" they are, a subconscious outcome – or "hidden curriculum" – of this could be that they "overestimate the accuracy of data and build excessive trust in datafied systems" (ibid., p. 14). For these reasons, critical education about data is required.

2.2.2 Fostering Critical Perspectives Through the Use of Data

When examining the history of different literacy concepts, a common trend emerges: often, initial understandings of literacy are of instrumental, narrow nature, describing predominantly practical skills. Over time, broader and more critical and reflective literacy understandings emerge. This "gradual expansion" has been traced in digital literacy concepts (Pötzsch 2019, p. 235; see also chapter 3.1) as well as in concepts of statistical and mathematical literacy (François and Monteiro 2018, p. 3). The data literacy field shows a similar development: while the instrumental, skills-focussed data literacy concepts outlined above still constitute the most established understanding of data literacy in many contexts in- and outside academia, calls to include more critical perspectives have emerged in recent years. Many new data literacy conceptualisations that include critical perspectives aim to *combine data usage skills*, for example analysing and visualising data, with *critical and ethical reflections* for example on the "protection of privacy, surveillance, epistemic manipulation and exploitation of data-related labour" (Špiranec et al. 2019). This combined approach has also been described as connecting "data literacy goals", such as collecting, analysing, examining and communicating with data, with "critical literacy goals", for example uncovering social inequalities with data, addressing data ethics or envisioning "new public spaces with data" (Louie 2022, pp. 4–6). The following sections provide an overview of different combined practical and critical data literacy approaches.

Critical Perspectives Originating from a Technical Background

Despite the dominance of instrumental, skills-based data literacy understandings, suggestions for critical data literacy approaches are increasing and have even come from technical backgrounds. One example is the already mentioned article by François and Monteiro whose concept originates from a statistical and mathematical literacy background and constitutes a very practical data literacy approach that nevertheless is "explicitly connected with ethical and political aspects" and aims for "constructive, concerned and reflective citizens" (2018, p. 1). Despite the technical background of their literacy concept, the authors clearly emphasise that today's citizens "must be able to understand the processes behind and to value the powers and limitations of Big Data" in order to achieve active citizenship and be prepared for the "data-driven society in which they live" (ibid., p. 5).

Similarly, Koltay et al. build on very practical definitions of data literacy that aim for learning to access, manage, handle and understand data, yet at the same time they emphasise the importance of a "critical assessment of data" and call for a "profound understanding of the big data phenomenon" (2015, pp. 403; 407). Although the authors place a great emphasis on practical skills such as learning to read graphs or drawing conclusions from data, they also aim to support learners in recognising when data are used misleadingly or inappropriately, and they see critical thinking as "one of the most important goals of data literacy education" (ibid., p. 407). A more recent publication by Verständig further describes critical data literacy as best located at the intersection of computer science and media education, and reports on a higher education course project, in which problem-based learning was applied to foster both students' data science skills and critical reflection of data phenomena (2021).

Applying Critical Pedagogy to Data Literacy Approaches

Another popular approach is to combine skills-based data literacy conceptualisations with the Freirean critical pedagogy that aims to empower learners and address questions of power in relation to data technologies. Indeed, the field of critical pedagogy with its pioneer Paulo Freire provides a highly relevant approach for educating about data that many critical data literacy conceptualisations have built on (for overview, see Špiranec et al. 2019) and that will be examined in more detail in chapter 3.3. An early example of a practical data literacy approach with a strong critical pedagogy perspective is Philip et al.'s "Big Data Literacy" (2013). Besides a pronounced focus on data science related objectives, their framework also includes two distinctly critical objectives. It aims to enable students to understand that "data are never neutral or objective" but always premised on certain assumptions and that they (re)produce forms of power in society, and aims to encourage students to see the generation, analysis and work with data as "powerful ways to understand and address societal issues as well as issues that affect their lives and the lives of people in their communities" (ibid., p. 114f). Philip et al. ground their framework within sociocultural theories of learning and critical pedagogy perspectives that "situate learning within its larger historical, social, political, and economic contexts" (p. 112).

Moreover, Dasgupta and Hill's concept of "critical algorithmic literacies" is rooted in Freire's critical pedagogy (2021, p. 5). Through practically engaging and experimenting with real-world datasets, they aim to encourage children to not only understand technical concepts around algorithms but also to "understand and critique the algorithmic systems that affect their lives" and evaluate their societal implications (ibid., p. 5; 2). Tygel and Kirsch place an even greater emphasis on Freire's influence and develop a "Freirean Inspired Critical Data Literacy" (2016, p. 113). Besides data processing, data communication and data production, their literacy concept promotes the skill of "data reading", which "starts with understanding how the data was generated [and] also includes understanding who produced it, in which context and why", and positions data as "the output of a social process" rather than an objective fact (ibid., p. 117).

Practical and Critical Approaches for Specific Audiences

As the empirical findings in this study will demonstrate, it is important to consider the audience that a (critical) data literacy intervention addresses. In line with this, some data literacy conceptualisations are developed for specific audiences, such as high school students or teachers, whereas others address the general public. Koltay's already mentioned data literacy concept, for example, addresses students but also academics or "data librarians" and aims to fulfil "the mission of the contemporary academic library" (2015, p. 401). Fontichiaro et al. equally target "librarians and their classroom colleagues" in their practical guidebook for "data literacy in the real world", which aims to foster practical data usage skills as well as awareness of data collection and reflection of ethical questions and "unintended consequences" of big data (2017, pp.ii, 255).

Hautea et al. focus on working with youths and suggest "possible strategies for engaging youth in critically thinking about the role of data in their lives and in their world" (2017, p. 920). In their understanding of critical data literacy, the authors follow an instrumental skills-based data literacy definition by the Oceans of Data Institute but also emphasise that "the term 'critically' is central" in their critical data literacy approach, building – again – on Paulo Freire's already mentioned critical pedagogy (ibid.). Another data literacy concept that addresses a very specific audience is Fotopoulou's "critical data literacies for civil society organisations" (2020). While she also considers "citizens more generally", the author focusses on collective actors: civil society organisations that need to "make sense of data, communicat[e] in ways that are relevant to broad audiences, and us[e] data for the social good" (ibid., p. 1). Fotopoulou builds on D'Ignazio and Bhargava's 2015 definition of big data literacy (see 2.2.3), but argues for "literacies in the plural", framing data literacies as "agentic, contextual, critical, multiple, and inherently social" (ibid., p. 4). Particularly relevant is the author's emphasis on criticality, stressing the "importance of raising awareness about the ideological and power aspects of data" (ibid.). Similar to other combined practical and critical approaches, Fotopoulou argues that this critical awareness "can be developed gradually and in parallel to developing certain technical competences" (ibid, p. 15).

Concepts That Begin to Consider Datafication as Part of Active and Practical Approaches

Finally, the literature review identified several examples of data literacy concepts that take a practical and skills-based approach while at the same time aiming for *critical reflection of how data and datafied systems change our lives and our society.* While still advocating for practical data skills and fostering critical understanding *through using data*, these concepts place a greater emphasis on the systemic and societal implications of datafication. Nevertheless, the lines between this tentative sub-category and the previous and following sub-categories are blurry and overlaps may occur.

What the concepts presented in this section have in common is that they, similar to those presented in the first section, aim to foster various practical skills that can be summarised as "reading and working with datasets" (Gray et al. 2018, p. 8), for example "data collection, data cleaning and rendering and visualisation" (Davies 2022, p. 158); interpreting, navigating, collecting and presenting data (Seymoens et al. 2020, p. 103); or giving people access to their own data through apps or hackathons (Pybus et al. 2015). However, these data literacies do not stop at this practical level, but also aim for critical reflection both of the data analysis and of the way data practices affect our lives and societies. For example, Davies suggests that learners should gain a critical perspective on how flawed and misleading data collection, analysis and representation can be, aiming for "social scientific critical analysis of strengths and weaknesses of quantitative data" that should be connected to goals of data justice (2022, p. 158). Seymoens et al., relating to a Data Literacy Competence Model that was developed by the Flemish Knowledge Centre for Digital and Media Literacy,[2] similarly highlight that besides *using* data, individuals should also *understand* data, for example by observing how it is used, analysing individual and social consequences of data practices, and evaluating and reflecting on the impacts of these consequences (2020, p. 103). Thus, this framework is oriented towards learners "critically and consciously understanding the role of data in society [and] personal life" (ibid., p. 104).

These definitions already point at a stronger focus on understanding and critically reflecting the implications of data systems. Apart from that, some combined practical and critical-reflective approaches to data literacy aim to *highlight potential negative consequences* of data systems and *empower* citizens in datafied societies. Nguyen, for example, argues that data literacy "offers paths to holistic strategies" for addressing the challenges of datafication and should be seen as a "tool of empowerment" that is important for "retaining agency and enabling inclusion as well as resistance in the digital society" (2021, p. 212). Pybus et al. suggest a "holistic data literacy" that aims to foster the ability to "question how meaning is constructed and (re)presented from the data", but also encourage learners to "unpack those opaque material processes" and to participate in "the active (re)shaping of data infrastructures" (2015, p. 4). In addressing these goals by giving learners access to their own data, the authors hope to promote "empowerment that comes from gaining access to what we collectively generate" (ibid., p. 8).

A similarly early data literacy conceptualisation by Crusoe agrees that data literacy should emphasise that "algorithms are opaque", "utilize stereotypical user models", may determine what the individual "gain[s] or lose[s]", and can lead to discrimination (2016, p. 40). Besides knowledge of "what data are, how they are collected, analyzed, visualized and shared", Crusoe suggests that data literacy consists of "the understanding of how data are applied for benefit or detriment, within the cultural context of security and privacy" (ibid., p. 38). While equally a combination of practical and critical goals, Gray et al.'s "data infrastructure literacy" goes one step further and aims to

> promote critical inquiry into datafication, into how datasets are created with certain purposes in mind as well as opening up "infrastructural imagination" (Bowker 2014) about how they might be created, used and organised differently (or not at all) – and the tensions that emerge between these two. (2018, p. 3)

---

2 As no original English-language publication of this framework could be found, Seymoens et al.'s text constituted the most suitable source for this framework.

Despite this very broad and critical objective, Gray et al.'s literacy concept is grounded within data, science, technology and human-computer interaction studies and includes a strong emphasis on practical data skills. Similarly, a systematic literature analysis that aimed to identify critical dimensions in data literacy approaches concluded that critical data literacy can be understood as a "critical approach to data and our data realities" that encourages learners to problematise and transform the "oppressing and unjust conditions of life produced by exclusionary, exploitative, invasive and manipulative uses of data" (Špiranec et al. 2019).

Overall, it seems that the combined approach of fostering practical skills as well as critical reflections is a relatively common approach in (critical) data literacy conceptualisations. These concepts provide many relevant insights for a more in-depth conceptualisation of critical datafication literacy in my study, for example by suggesting different understandings of 'critical reflection of data'. Many of these concepts aim for critical reflection that is directly related to data usage, including questions around critically considering the origin and context of datasets, the way they are used and for what purposes, where and how securely data are stored or how they affect individual privacy. However, in light of the increasing complexity of algorithms and data structures, such critical perspectives in the sense of "*what* do the data tell us" are not enough and a critical attitude towards data needs to also reflect on how data powers affect our actions and experiences in life, asking: "*how* do data take effect?" (Leineweber 2021, p. 147f, own translation, emphasis in original). In addition, the majority of these concepts still places the focus on fostering the skills to practically use data. Yet, as van Audenhove et al. put it, "*using data* and *understanding data* are different competences that both need attention", and a broader discussion beyond skill-based data literacy understandings is needed (2020, p. 2, emphasis in original). This reiterates findings from the NGO Doteveryone that argue at there is "a big difference between having skills – knowing how to use the internet – and having understanding – knowing the implications of using the internet" (Miller et al. 2018, p. 5).

While some of the presented concepts already touch on critical reflection of how data and datafied systems change our society, and there is certainly overlap between the different categories that are suggested, what has been missing thus far are critical conceptualisations of data literacy that *place critical thinking and reflection at their core* and focus on promoting a broader critical reflection of the *structural and systemic levels of datafication* that are becoming deeply engrained into today's societies and *how to effectively challenge them*.

2.2.3 Towards Critical Understanding of Datafication

In recent years, a small but growing number of concepts have emerged that focus on exactly this distinctly critical and reflective understanding of data literacy. These approaches emphasise that "digital understanding is not about being able to code, it's about being able to cope", and focus on improving people's understanding of the "impacts of technologies – how they shape people's lives and society as a whole" (Miller et al. 2018, pp. 5; 8). The terminology, as usual, differs widely from, for example, a "'manifesto' for the 'public understanding of big data'" that connects concerns around big data to the "broad multidisciplinary fields of public understanding of science (PUS) and public engagement with science and technology (PEST)" (Michael and Lupton 2016, p. 105); to different variations of data literacies as well as calls for an "algorithmic literacy" that aims to enable "people to form considered opinions and debate the issue in a factually informed way" (Grzymek and Puntschuh 2019, p. 11). Markham even speaks of "X_literacy, [...] ('X' meaning whatever we want to call it)" (2020, p. 229). What the concepts presented in this next section have in common, however, is that they place scrutiny and critical reflection at their core, aiming for, among others, "deep curiosity" and "critical orientation" that lead to "a level of comprehension and critical awareness that, once we have it, keeps us asking new questions" (Markham 2020, p. 229). In other words, they call for an understanding of "how algorithmic processes can turn otherwise harmless-seeming data into valuable information" and reflection of "the critical perspectives around these practices" through data literacy (Bilstrup et al. 2022, p. 226). The following section details a small number of concepts and frameworks from this final category that are most relevant for my study.

An Extended Definition of Big Data Literacy – D'Ignazio and Bhargava

The earliest concept in this section that has influenced many critical understandings of data literacy that were developed later on (e.g., Fotopoulou 2020) is D'Ignazio and Bhargava's "extended definition of Big Data literacy" (2015). The authors highlight four problematic issues of big data: big data's lack of transparency, extractive collection, technological complexity, and control of impact, and argue that these problems are "ones of 'data literacy'" (ibid., p. 2). To address these issues, D'Ignazio and Bhargava suggest a big data literacy that – again – builds on Paulo Freire's work on "empowerment through literacy education", aiming for technical skills as well as "emancipation [...] through the literacy process" (ibid., p. 2; 5). Besides practical skills of working with data, their extended big data literacy hopes to encourage learners in:

- Identifying when and where data is being passively collected about your actions and interactions.
- Understanding the algorithmic manipulations performed on large sets of data to identify patterns.
- Weighing the real and potential ethical impacts of data-driven decisions for individuals and for society. (ibid., p. 3)

Such distinct critical understanding and reflection is unusual for data literacy concepts from this time. A working paper from Bhargava and others from the same month further argues for a "literacy in the age of data", which aims to enable citizens to "constructively engage in society through and about data", and which can evolve and expand over time in light of the continuously changing requirements of an increasingly datafied society (Data-Pop Alliance and Internews 2015, pp. 26; iv). This flexible nature of data literacy as well as the authors' focus on empowerment and emancipation constitute relevant insights for my study's conceptualisation of critical datafication literacy.

Educator's Data Literacy – Raffaghelli

Again highlighting potential overlap between the tentative categories suggested in this chapter, Raffaghelli's literacy understanding is developed out of a context of *educator's* data literacy (2022). Despite this specific context, her conceptualisation of data literacy provides novel insights and unusual approaches for addressing the wide-reaching implications of datafication on our societies through a literacy-angle. The author's goal is to "support educators' reflection and organic action" and develop a "bigger picture" of data literacy (ibid., p. 82). Based on a review of critical data literacy literature and 12 interviews with different educators, Raffaghelli develops a complex conceptual scheme for data literacy that builds on "the proactive and reactive dispositions towards data" identified by data activism research (see chapter 2.1), aiming to "strike a balance" between these perspectives (ibid.). This scheme presents data literacy as a "complex puzzle" that includes traditional, instrumental understandings of data literacy; "critical and participatory approaches" that aim to empower learners through gaining access to, creating and using their own data; as well as data literacy approaches that call for "activism against datafication and algorithmic biases" by applying media education principles to data (ibid., p. 92). Thus, Raffaghelli's conceptual scheme for data literacy highlights the interplay between data activism, data science and media education in (critical) data literacy approaches, emphasising the variety of skills and understandings that citizens need to navigate datafied societies in an informed and empowered manner.

Critical Digital Literacy – Pötzsch

Another very relevant concept that aims to foster citizens' understanding of datafication is Pötzsch's critical digital literacy (2019). Despite using the term "digital literacy", this approach provides manifold insights into fostering critical awareness and reflection of the impacts of datafied systems. In contrast to many literacy concepts presented thus far, Pötzsch does not consider data skills to be an integral part his literacy understanding. In contrast, he emphasises that neither digital technologies nor expensive software are required for critically educating about digital technologies and datafied systems (ibid., p. 227; see also section 2.2.4). This constitutes a clear dissociation from combined practical and critical concepts that aim to promote critical awareness through the active use of data. While Pötzsch acknowledges instrumental user skills, he rather places his focus on *critical thinking*, aiming to foster "the ability to critically assess, appropriate, and, if need be, replace, repair, or resist such [digital] technologies" in order to form "a self-determined future citizenry" (ibid., p. 236).

This critical thinking about 'the digital' takes "structural aspects of the technology into account", while using the "widest possible contextualisation of technology", which, importantly, includes issues of "exploitation, commodification, and degradation in digital capitalism" (Pötzsch 2019, p. 221). To achieve such "critical awareness of digital technologies' wider societal, political, economic, cultural, and environmental implications", the author argues that "blackboxed technologies need to be opened up, contextualised, and critically questioned" with a view on "capitalist dynamics, environmental ramifications, and individual empowerment" (ibid., p. 235; 236; 222). Pötzsch's distinct goals of a self-determined citizenry and a wide-angle perspective on the impacts of technology, including structural transformations in society, constitute novel approaches that have informed this study's development of a critical datafication literacy framework.

Information Literacy in the Digital Age - Polizzi

Like Pötzsch, Polizzi also uses the term "critical digital literacy" to describe a very relevant literacy understanding for this chapter (2020b). Polizzi emphasises that critical digital literacy, or "information literacy in the digital age", needs to go beyond a focus on digital content such as evaluating online information, and rather foster a broader understanding of digital infrastructures (ibid., p. 1). He criticises that research thus far has overlooked the importance of understanding the digital environment for "civic and political engagement" and calls for literacy in the sense of "an ensemble of critical abilities, knowledge and interpretations that are essential in the context of democratic participation and social inclusion in the digital age" (ibid., p. 7; 2). Similar to Pötzsch, Polizzi argues that critical digital literacy should foster understanding of the socio-economic structures of digital technologies and embedded power structures, revealing "democratising potentials" as well as "structural constraints" (ibid., p. 16). To achieve this, Polizzi – similar to my arguments in chapter 3.2 – sees value in connecting literacy perspectives from media studies with insights from political research and democratic theory (ibid., p. 13). This distinguishes this literacy approach and makes it particularly relevant for this study's development of a theoretical framework for critical datafication literacy.

Data Citizenship - Carmi, Yates et al.

The third relevant concept, the "data citizenship" model, is developed in several publications by the "Me and My Big Data" project at the University of Liverpool (Carmi et al. 2020; Yates et al. 2020; Yates et al. 2021). While the authors' journal paper focusses on the connection of data literacies "to disinformation, misinformation and malinformation" (Carmi et al. 2020, p. 1), this particular context is not specified in the two reports. Nevertheless, this specific context of data literacy should be kept in mind when examining the data citizenship model. The authors aim to address gaps in existing data literacy frameworks by exploring "links between 'data, power, and positionality'" and encouraging citizens to have "critical and active agency" (Yates et al. 2020, p. 10; Carmi et al. 2020, pp. 1; 10).

The data citizenship framework revolves around three areas (Yates et al. 2021, pp. 14–25). First, "Data Doing" addresses 'traditional' data literacy skills around using and managing data but doing so in "an ethical and critical manner" (ibid., p. 19). The second domain, "Data Thinking" takes a more reflective approach (ibid.). It should be noted that the definition of this domain showed distinct changes between the initial and the final research report, from a focus on *using data* to think (critically) about data (see Yates et al. 2020, p. 10) to a strong emphasis on critical understanding of the data economy and critical reflection in the sense of Paulo Freire's "conscientização – or a critical consciousness"[3] as goals for data citizenship (Yates et al. 2021, p. 19f). Particularly this newly strengthened critical focus makes data citizenship a highly relevant model for informing my study.

The last domain, "Data Participation" also takes a distinctly critical perspective to educating about data, as it "seeks to address the problem of citizens' feelings of disempowerment in data-driven environments and the unequal power dynamics" by highlighting the "importance of citizens' proactive engagement" (Yates et al. 2021, p. 21). Building on data activism and data literacy research in combination with "ideas from digital citizenship and democratic education", the authors understand data participation as "civic and/or collective action", encouraging learners to "exercise their digital / data human rights" (ibid., p. 22). This interdisciplinary combination hints at what will be demonstrated in more detail in chapter 3: how much critical data literacy conceptualisations can learn from more established fields such as citizenship education or Paulo Freire's critical pedagogy. However, the connection between the concept of "data citizenship" to data literacy and education scholarship is sometimes blurry, and the context of dis-/mis- and malinformation is not always clear.

Moreover, several suggestions for promoting data citizenship in practice are made. While the authors stress the need for "proactive citizens" instead of "passive consumers", they nevertheless warn against merely shifting the responsibility to the individual, which may "potentially remov[e] the onus from regulatory bodies, institutions or the state" (Carmi et al. 2020, pp. 9; 15). If the responsibility to be data literate lies with the individuals, the authors warn, "we can expect socio-economic

3 See chapter 3.3 for a detailed definition.

inequalities to influence their ability to have access and resources to such education programmes" (ibid., p. 12). Furthermore, the authors emphasise the need to consider different populations and "address different social contexts", particularly of marginalised communities, arguing that "a 'universal' one size fits all solution" for data literacy is not possible (ibid., p. 11). Moreover, data literacies should go beyond the individual and instead work with people's "networks of literacy", including the people they engage with and the different media they use (ibid., p. 12). Finally, the authors – similar to Pötzsch (2019) – highlight that data literacy does not need to utilise digital methods but should be expanded "outside the 'digital' realm" and regarded as a "more holistic and networked experience" that includes online and offline spheres (ibid., p. 17). All of these valuable considerations have informed several methodological decisions of the empirical research conducted in my study (see chapter 4).

Critical Digital and Data Literacies – Pangrazio et al.

The work of Pangrazio and co-authors proposes several literacy concepts for promoting critical reflection of the datafication of our societies. This section will outline four key conceptualisations by Pangrazio and others: the concept of "critical digital literacy" (Pangrazio 2016), "personal data literacies" (Pangrazio and Selwyn 2019), research on "the social utility of data literacy" (Pangrazio and Sefton-Green 2020), and on "critical data education" (Pangrazio and Selwyn 2020). Despite their different terms and some variations in authorship, all these approaches provide highly relevant insights for an extended framework for critical datafication literacy.

First, an early publication by Pangrazio suggests a *critical digital literacy* concept that examines "broader issues associated with digital media use", such as how such technologies "reinforce issues of social class, race and gender and what might be done to challenge and overturn exploitation and inequality" (2016, p. 169). This literacy intends to "cultivate a dispassionate, critical disposition in a context that invests deeply in the personal and affective" and work towards a "nuanced understanding of power and ideology within the digital medium" (ibid., p. 168). The goal and challenge for such literacy is to encourage "the individual to move between these mindsets (i.e., critical and technical) as part of their digital practices" (ibid., p. 170). By placing this strong focus on a broad and structural understanding as well as critical reflection, this literacy already distinctly differs from most digital and data literacy conceptualisations at the time.

A key concept that informed my study's theoretical framework for critical datafication literacy and the empirical research that was conducted is Pangrazio and Selwyn's *personal data literacies* (2019). The authors suggest to "see personal data as a 'text' in the New Literacies sense" instead of seeing it as "information to be managed" (ibid., p. 427). In taking this perspective, they go beyond data skills and rather "foreground[...] 'personal data' as a social practice and tool for action" (ibid.). Moreover,

Pangrazio and Selwyn's personal data literacies framework places a strong emphasis on critical thought. It aims to foster understanding of the sociocultural context around data and the ideologies that underpin them, and to cultivate the "metaphorical 'space'" to reflect critically on the implications of data and the "inherently political nature of the broader data assemblage" (ibid., p. 426).

Of the five domains that make up Pangrazio and Selwyn's personal data literacies framework – "(1) Data Identification, (2) Data Understandings, (3) Data Reflexivity, (4) Data Uses, and (5) Data Tactics" (2019, p. 428) – particularly the third and fifth provide valuable new insights for my study. These aim to support citizens' critical understanding of the "profiling and predictions that are made from processed personal data" and their ability to employ "tactics of resistance and obfuscation" (ibid., p. 429; 431). Overall, the authors place a strong emphasis on fostering the individual's "capacity to understand and control one's personal data", which they see as "a crucial part of living in contemporary society" (ibid., p. 419). Yet, Pangrazio and Selwyn nevertheless criticise a shift of "the burden of time and responsibility" to the individual in other literacy approaches and clarify that their focus lies on *supporting* citizens "to engage critically with their personal data, so they have a sense of understanding, control and agency within the data assemblage" (ibid., p. 425; 426). This careful balance between empowerment and responsibility distinguishes this framework's novel approach to data literacy.

Moreover, the authors make suggestions for practically implementing personal data literacies. Similar to Carmi et al. above, they recognise that people have "varied capacities" and therefore "unequal agency" in engaging with data, and argue that such "data inequalities" need to be considered by data literacy frameworks (Pangrazio and Selwyn 2019, 433f). The authors further suggest two "areas of obvious application" for their framework: "public education and academic research" (ibid., p. 431). They highlight that critical data and digital literacies are "sorely missing from education", and that they should be strengthened in both formal education and in "informal educational initiatives more appropriate for adults" (ibid., p. 431; 432). Moreover, they call "IT providers and government agencies" to action (ibid., p. 431). Both the authors' novel framework and these suggestions for a practical implementation provide numerous valuable insights for my study's theoretical and empirical analyses.

A third key publication by Pangrazio and Sefton-Green examines the *social utility of data literacy*, reviewing recent models of data literacy, which are categorised as "formal, personal and folk pedagogies of data" (2020, p. 208). The article criticises that although literacy is often "posited as the ideal response" to challenges of datafication, how such literacy is understood is often vague and "there is certainly an absence of practical models" (ibid., p. 211). The authors suggest that data literacy should foster "critical understandings of the technological infrastructure and the political economy of digital platforms" and should provide citizens with the "skills required to have agency in a datafied world" and to protect their privacy (ibid., p. 214). Such literacy, they argue, can "protect individuals from being manipulated by datafication processes" and is central to democratic processes, together with an "optimisation of both legal and tactical responses" (ibid., p. 218).

Apart from this relevant definition, Pangrazio and Sefton-Green raise a number of novel considerations that have informed my study. They provide a clear argumentation for the suitability of the term "literacy" for educating about datafication, arguing that the educational dimension of literacy suggests that individuals can have sufficient literacy to participate while at the same time being "continuously involved in processes of self-improvement" (2020, p. 217). Moreover, they differentiate between operational and critical literacy, whereas the latter comes with "a host of 'higher order' questions, including the ability to challenge, ask questions and reflect" (ibid., p. 213). This literacy understanding resembles the German concept of "Bildung" (see chapter 3.2) and strongly informed my study's critical datafication literacy framework (see chapter 3.4). Another significant point the authors raise and that strongly informed my study's empirical approach is that "without viable alternative data practices, critical awareness might actually increase feelings of anxiety and apathy", a problematic issue that also emerged in my prior empirical work (ibid., p. 218; see also Sander 2020a; Sander 2020c). Therefore, data literacy interventions should always include "a set of practical strategies and tactics that individuals can experiment with in order to operationalise their newfound awareness and understanding" (Pangrazio and Sefton-Green 2020, p. 218).

Pangrazio and Selwyn further suggested a *critical data education* concept based on the findings of three empirical research projects (2020). Similar to the literacy frameworks outlined above, this concept aims for a broad and critical understanding of datafication and its social, political and economic implications as well as fostering data protection strategies. However, it places a particular focus on "the social injustices associated with datafication" and on "revealing structural inequalities" that data systems create and strengthen, clearly arguing that a "critical approach" is "the most appropriate way to fully address issues of datafication" (ibid., p. 5). Moreover, this article provides a number of valuable insights for practically implementing critical data education (see section 2.2.4).

Overall, the four publications by Pangrazio and co-authors suggest novel and highly relevant literacy concepts that provide many insights for the critical datafication literacy framework developed in my study and have strongly informed the study's empirical research. In particular, the authors' strong focus on a broad critical perspective on the social, political and economic dimensions of data and the structural changes through the datafication of our society constitute key novel insights.

Own Initial Conceptualisation: Critical Big Data Literacy

Finally, I have suggested an initial conceptualisation of a so-called *critical big data literacy* in my prior work. This literacy aims for an awareness, understanding and ability to critically reflect upon big data collection practices, data uses and the possible risks and implications that come with these practices, as well as the ability to implement this knowledge for a more empowered internet usage (Sander 2020a; Sander 2020c). Importantly, this critical reflection does not contain a certain set of beliefs or attitudes as its outcome, meaning it does not necessarily entail a negative stance towards data practices. Rather, critical big data literacy aims at empowering citizens to question and scrutinise the socio-technical systems of big data practices and to form considered opinions on current debates around data analytics. This would allow citizens to make informed decisions on personal choices such as which data to share or which services to use, and it would enable them to engage in public debates around datafied systems. Nevertheless, it is important to emphasise that – similar to previous concepts – the goal of this literacy is not to "merely shift responsibility to individuals" (Sander 2020c, p. 5). Instead, providing learners with constructive advice is intended to empower them and to counteract a potential resignation in learners that may arise when learning about the ubiquitous collection and analysis of personal data in our datafied worlds.

Preliminary Conclusion: Insights and Shortcomings of Existing (Critical) Data Literacies

Overall, this chapter has demonstrated that although the 'traditional' instrumental and skills-based understanding of data literacy still dominates academic discourses, many critical data literacy approaches are emerging. Particularly the last five years have shown a strong increase of critical perspectives on educating about data. While the authors of such critical concepts agree that data literacy needs to go beyond data usage skills and should include critical perspectives, they take different stances on the extent to which technical skills of using, interpreting and manipulating data should still be involved in critical data literacy as well as what the 'critical' in critical data literacy should look like. Some focus on critical reflection during handling data or of digital content, whereas others call for a broader perspective, aiming for critical understanding of political, societal and economic impacts of datafication and data infrastructures. The latter critical-reflective and empowering understanding of data literacy as an approach for critically educating about datafication constitutes the most relevant approach for this study's development of a theoretical framework for critical datafication literacy.

However, some scholars also question the suitability of literacy as a concept for educating about data or highlight the shortcomings of existing (critical) data literacy approaches. Fotopoulou, for example, despite suggesting a new critical data literacies concept, also argues that "the term 'literacy' has been deemed too basic and indeed counterproductive" (2020, p. 5) and she instead considers "expertise" or "socially distributed expertise" as developed by Bassett (2015). A comprehensive analysis of different alternative terms and concepts to literacy is provided by Pinney, who highlights that literacy as a term can be problematic because it has different meanings and is embedded with different notions of power for different people (2020, p. 229). She therefore concludes that literacy can be useful as a concept but not so much as a term, especially when addressing audiences outside of academia (ibid., 2020).

Moreover, a limitation of many data literacy conceptualisations is that they focus on "individualised rather than collective forms" (Hintz et al. 2022, p. 149). In instrumental literacy concepts, this focus is evident as they foster technical skills and competences for the individual. However, critical data literacy approaches also tend to focus on promoting the skills to better protect one's own data and to avoid data disclosure, thus shifting the responsibility of addressing problematic issues around datafication to the individuals. Similarly, digital privacy is often framed as individual responsibility (Kazansky 2015, p. 193). This "responsibilisation" in which users "enter into a dependent relationship with opaque technologies and are effectively left no choice but to deal with ensuing threats individually" is problematic since notions of informed consent, notice and choice have been called into question (ibid.; see also Forbrukerrådet 2018; Larsson et al. 2021). Thus, recently, calls for more collective approaches have increased, and some critical data literacy scholars have recognised and addressed the tension between an empowering literacy in contrast to a shift of responsibility to citizens (e.g., Pangrazio and Selwyn 2019; Carmi et al. 2020).

Finally, the "seeming[...] 'neutrality'" of existing data literacy concepts has been criticised (Jansen 2021, p. 1). Jansen argues that the "mere act of centring data in a literacy approach is political and value ridden" and that a "(re)politicization of data literacy" is needed (ibid.). This could take place by "politicizing the learner" who should not only learn about risks and opportunities of data but also "gain competencies to be able to influence political processes and challenge existing power structures" (ibid., p. 5). Moreover, Jansen contends that the "practice of data literacy in itself needs to be politicized" and its "blind spots related to structural inequality and power" should be reflected (ibid.). Thus, a (re)politicised data literacy takes a "bottom-up approach to dismantling power structures, understanding inequality and promoting political participation" and should learn from pedagogical approaches that aim for "democratic engagement, dismantling power structures, policy reform and activism" (ibid., p. 1; 8). Several of Jansen's criticisms have been addressed in my study, which learns from political education (chapter 3.2) and critical pedagogy (chapter 3.3) and suggests a critical datafication literacy framework that aims for broad, systemic understanding of datafication as well as enabling citizens to become active (see final framework in chapter 7).

2.2.4 Practically Implementing Critical Data Literacies

Apart from the theoretical conceptualisations of (critical) data literacies that have been outlined in the chapter thus far, academic research has also made many suggestions on how best to implement critical education about data in practice. As will be argued in more detail in chapter 3.4, my study's framework for critical datafication literacy focusses on a theoretical literacy conceptualisation, identifying key goals and objectives for critical education about data. However, my study's empirical research examines one way to practically implement critical data literacy: online educational resources about datafication. For this research, much could be learnt from reviewing recent suggestions for a practical implementation of critical data literacy. The following section aims to provide a concise overview of key advice from other scholars and practitioners on how best to critically educate about datafication.

Scholars have highlighted that it is difficult to implement literacy objectives into a practical model, but that different approaches are suitable: formal education, personal pedagogies of data, folk pedagogies of data – i.e., "open, public programmes [...] raising awareness and critical understanding of data" (Pangrazio and Sefton-Green 2020, p. 217) as well as artworks (Stark and Crawford 2019). As already mentioned above, a first key recommendation by the literature is that there is no one-size-fits-all-approach to literacy but that different audiences need different approaches (Carmi et al. 2020, p. 11). Thus, data literacy promotion should "involve providing multiple pathways" for people with different needs and capacities (Data-Pop Alliance and Internews 2015, p.iv), and educators should be aware that it may not be possible to reuse educational resources outside their intended context (Jansen 2021, p. 8).

Moreover, several suggestions are made in regard to the content of critical data literacy approaches. A common recommendation is to emotionally engage learners by using data or hypothetical data scenarios that are relevant to them and reflect their realities (D'Ignazio and Bhargava 2015; Tygel and Kirsch 2016; Markham 2019; Agesilaou and Kyza 2021; Bilstrup et al. 2022). This could, for example, be achieved by showing learners what data is stored about them by comparing mainstream and alternative services (Pötzsch 2019, p. 233), or by using relevant real-life case studies (Fontichiaro et al. 2017, p.v). Further concrete suggestions include using metaphors to describe data systems (Windeyer 2019, p. 318) or using popular culture (Pötzsch 2019, p. 235) to foster learners' imagination of datafication, which is often limited (Pangrazio and Selwyn 2020, p. 11). Importantly, educators should not try to convince learners that certain data practices are good or bad (Fontichiaro et al. 2017, p.v; Markham 2019, p. 758), but rather act as "problem posers" that encourage students to act as "active agents" (Aliakbari and Faraji 2011, p. 80). Critical reflection should be promoted, for example by prompting learners with good questions (Markham 2020, p. 231f), historicising technology (Pötzsch 2019, p. 232) or by showing learners ways in which data are used that are undesirable to them (Bilstrup et al. 2022, p. 233). In order to not leave learners feeling frustrated or resigned after gaining such information, it is key to provide "adequate pathways forward" (Jansen 2021, p. 7) and show learners "how they can take the first steps to call for change" (Bilstrup et al. 2022, p. 234). In doing so, it is crucial to not reinforce the responsibilisation critiqued above.

Academic research further makes a number of relevant suggestions on useful formats to foster critical data literacies. Importantly, scholars have highlighted that (critical) data literacy does not necessarily need to be fostered using digital formats but that traditional teaching methods and embodied and tangible approaches may even be better suited to promote critical reflection of datafication (Pötzsch 2019; Windeyer 2019; Bilstrup et al. 2022). Apart from that, applied and participatory approaches are recommended (D'Ignazio and Bhargava 2015; Iliadis and Russo 2016; Markham 2019) as well as using data in creative play scenarios (Ahlborn et al. 2021, p. 34). While some authors also advocate for gamified approaches (Agesilaou and Kyza 2021, p. 464), others found that tools that were "too fun" made it difficult to evoke critical reflection (Pangrazio and Selwyn 2020, p. 11). A clear call was identified to materialise the intangible world of data in order to break down complex issues and foster understanding (Windeyer 2019, p. 329; Pangrazio and Selwyn 2020, p. 9f). This could, for example, be achieved by using visual approaches (D'Ignazio and Bhargava 2015, p. 4), such as data visualisations. These further "have the potential to evoke empathy, pity, sorrow, shame and other emotions" (Kennedy and Hill 2018, p. 843), which reiterates other scholars' emphasis on the role of emotions when discussing data and its implications for learners' own lives (Bilstrup et al. 2022, pp. 226; 233).

2.2.5 Conclusion

This chapter highlighted how many conceptualisations of (critical) data literacy already exist, how diverse they are, and which parallels can be identified. A tentative categorisation of literacy approaches from practical-instrumental to critical-reflective was suggested, which highlighted a strong dominance of instrumental data literacies. Critical approaches that go beyond practical data usage skills or critical reflection during data handling or of digital content are still rare. Yet, a final category of literacies that aim for broad critical understanding and reflection of political, societal and economic impacts of datafication and data infrastructures was identified. These literacy approaches proved most relevant for my study and provided manifold insights for the development of a theoretical framework for critical datafication literacy. Nevertheless, many of the analysed critical data literacy concepts focus on individualised approaches, thus potentially leading to a 'responsibilisation' of individuals, and they often come with little theoretical grounding, which can leave them disconnected from insights of traditional critical education scholarship. Scholars have further argued that data literacy needs to be 're-politicised' to address questions of power and inequalities and to promote political participation. Particularly in this regard, much can be learnt from traditional education scholarship.

My study builds on the existing critical data literacy conceptualisations that were analysed in this chapter and aims to address gaps in research by developing a theoretically and empirically grounded framework for critical datafication literacy. Chapter 3.4 presents a preliminary outline of this framework and discusses how it has been informed and shaped by insights from this chapter and from the three traditional educational approaches that are analysed in the next chapters. In addition to these theoretical findings, this chapter also highlighted that scholarly research has made many useful suggestions on how to implement critical education about data intro practice, which have informed this study's methodological decisions (see chapter four) and will be discussed in more detail in chapter six.

3. Theoretical Framework

Introduction

This chapter aims to contribute to the theoretical framework for critical datafication literacy that is being developed in my study by analysing what can be learnt from selected traditional educational approaches. The field of education and pedagogy provides countless well-established and theoretically grounded approaches that can provide valuable insights into ways to address the challenges of datafication through an educational lens. Traditionally, education aims to increase people's "development of critical thinking" (Barrow 2014, p. 258) and prepare young people to become future citizens who are able to "live and function in such a [democratic] society" and to "come to some understanding of it" (Wringe 2012, p. 5). It is exactly this broader societal perspective that is still often overlooked in existing data literacy approaches, yet that offers particularly relevant insights given the wide-reaching societal implications of new data technologies. The fact that in recent years, this picture has begun to shift, and more broad and critical data literacy approaches are emerging emphasises the necessity of such perspectives.

Education is often "seen alongside other social institutions as working to create and maintain a stable society" (Bartlett and Burton 2016, p. 28). This important role of education in our democratic societies is also emphasised by the inclusion of the right of individuals to "an educational program that respects their personality, talents, abilities, and cultural heritage" in various international agreements, including the 1948 Universal Declaration of Human Rights (Lauwerys et al. 2019, no page number). Importantly, education not only includes private or state-regulated schooling, but also many forms of "parallel or supplementary systems of education often designated as 'nonformal' and 'popular'" (ibid.). In light of the implications data systems have on the way our societies are "ordered, decisions are made, and citizens are monitored" (Hintz et al. 2019, p. 2f), it can thus be argued that fostering understanding and critical reflection on data systems should be an integral part of education.

What is Education (Not)?

Before outlining how the field of education was approached in this study, however, a brief introduction is necessary in order to answer the fundamental question of "What is education?". In the field of education and pedagogy, there are not only many terms connected to education that are all associated with different meanings, but also the concept of education itself is seen by most scholars as "an essentially contested concept" (Barrow 2014, p. 256). Because of its "inherently evaluative" nature, Barrow argues, education is "inevitably going to be differently interpreted according to the changing values of time and place" (2014, p. 256).

In my study, education is understood as oriented "towards the human being as subject" (Biesta 2012, p. 586), and, as already highlighted above, seen as a preparation for the future lives of pupils as members of their particular society" (Wringe 2012, p. 2). In this sense, education is differentiated from *training* (Biesta 2012, p. 586), a mere "passing of the *facts*" (Wringe 2012, p. 2), or "being '*clever*'" (Barrow 2014, p. 257). Education is further differentiated from *pedagogy*, which describes the "study of teaching methods" (Peel 2017, no page number). Despite some blurry uses of the term, pedagogy generally does not describe the ends of learning, but rather the "ways in which such goals may be achieved" (ibid.). Thus, this field can offer useful insights for implementing critical education about data into practice.

In contrast to training, learning or pedagogy, but also to terms such as qualification, socialisation or subjectification (see Biesta 2012, p. 584), education is usually understood as broader knowledge and understanding of the world. More specifically, education relates to "bringing up or developing the individual in way that we regard as desirable, but with particular reference to knowledge and the mind" (Barrow 2014, p. 257), while at the same time "always anticipat[ing] the freedom of those being educated" and not treating students simply as "material to be moulded or as objects to be trained" (Biesta 2012, p. 585). Importantly, education is less focused on a repertoire of skills and "knowledge how to", but rather aims for an understanding of "the reason why of things" and the "development of critical thinking" (Barrow 2014, p. 257f). This "deeper" perspective on education was in part shaped by Peters, a renowned scholar of education in the 1960s and 70s (e.g., 1966), who argued that education "involved a linking of concepts by the learner to gain a wider understanding of the world" (Bartlett and Burton 2016, p. 24). Such understanding of education is particularly relevant for my study, and it bears resemblance to the German "Bildung" which will be discussed in chapter 3.2.

Importantly, the understanding of education that my study follows is not one that necessarily aims to "reproduce in the next generation the society in which they currently work" (Wringe 2012, p. 2). Instead, learners should be encouraged to "'cope with', to make something of, the world in which they will lead their adult lives", either by aiming to "reform or change the current pattern of things" or by "stoically grinning and bearing what cannot yet be altered" (ibid.). Teachers thus "often aspire to make the next generation in some way better than the last" and desire to "build a better – more virtuous, more powerful, juster, or in our own day simply more affluent – society" (ibid.). Therefore, Wringe argues, a teacher cannot teach "without reference to the wider social and political context" and thus cannot leave "social and political considerations to others" (ibid., p. 3). Although Wringe mostly seems to relate to formal education in a school context, these objectives can be easily transferred to other areas of education, and they clearly demonstrate the relevance of the education field as a theoretical framework for critical datafication literacy. With the increasing datafication of our societies, gaining understanding of one's society as well as being able to live and function in an informed manner *must* include some awareness and understanding of the data systems that already shape and govern so many areas of our lives. Moreover, the potential of education to lead to a "determination to reform or change the current pattern of things" (Wringe 2012, p. 2) provides valuable lessons for more empowering education about datafication.

In order to develop a more grounded theoretical framework for such critical datafication literacy in my study, I selected three educational approaches as most relevant: 1. *education about (digital) media*; 2. *the German concept of "Bildung"* (including "politische Bildung" / political literacy); and 3. *critical pedagogy* according to Paulo Freire. These educational approaches were selected on several grounds. Firstly, each of these constitute well-established, internationally recognised educational approaches with strong theoretical groundings. Secondly, these approaches follow a broad understanding of education similar to the one outlined at the beginning of this chapter. They aim to foster understanding of the (mediated) world we live in and empower learners to form their own opinions and critique this world instead of understanding education in the sense of 'training' or a mere passing of knowledge. Thirdly, each of the three fields has already been connected to education about data, which emphasises their relevance and how much can be learnt from these approaches for a theoretically grounded conceptualisation of critical datafication literacy.

However, the following subchapters do not provide a comprehensive review of the three fields of educational research. Considering how well-established these fields are, this alone would constitute an additional multiyear study. Instead, a small number of key texts for each field was carefully chosen and analysed. These texts are examined in regard to *key insights* that *help fill the gaps* in data literacy research by suggesting approaches to *educate about structural changes in our society* (rather than a focus on media content or digital skills) and to *foster critical thinking*. This includes a) canonical texts that represent recognised key conceptualisations of the respective educational approach; b) secondary literature that provides additional framing and understanding as well as suggestions for implementation; and c) a selection of relevant publications that have already adapted the respective educational approach to education about data. The texts are selected both from international and from the German-language academic discourse. The reason for this is less my own German background, but rather the long and rich history of German research on education and the strong academic discourse in the field even today. Concepts such as "Bildung" or "politische Bildung" (political literacy) originate in Germany but are internationally recognised and offer important insights for the (critical) data literacy field (see chapter 3.2).

3.1 Education about (Digital) Media

The first field of education research, education about (digital) media, constitutes one of the key predecessors of data literacy with a long history. However, it is a highly diverse and contested field. In order to represent this diversity, a rough outline of historical and disciplinary developments in media education research will be presented. Embedded in this outline, three key texts that are particularly relevant for my study will be examined: a 'classic' approach to media literacy, an extended and broader perspective, and finally a concept that already draws connections to data literacy by suggesting that education about media should include education about (big) data.

3.1.1 Introduction – Terms, Concepts and Background of the Field

While many terms and concepts are employed in this field, for example media skills, media education, media pedagogy, or media criticism; the key relevant concept here is *(digital) media literacy*. While the term literacy traditionally referred to "alphabetisation and the ability to use language in reading and writing" (Pötzsch 2019, p. 222), a wider understanding of literacy developed in the 1990s (see below). One example is media literacy, which originates in pedagogical discourses and whose "theoretical traditions [can be traced] from the language theory of Noam Chomsky through Jürgen Habermas to Dieter Baacke" (Gapski et al. 2017a, p. 21, own translation). After initially following the intention to protect children from harmful content and negative consequences, more ideologically critical and radical approaches to media education started to emerge in the 1960s and 1970s (Niesyto 2018, p. 59). Later, media pedagogy understanding moved towards the ability to critically perceive and decode media messages, and the field was increasingly institutionalised in the 1980s and 1990s (Buckingham 2018, p. 47ff). In the 1990s, the emergence of new media led to increasing calls for new media competences (Gapski et al. 2017a, p. 18f). While media literacy was a somewhat vague concept from the beginning, many scholars argue that the concept always included both instrumental approaches and reflective and critical components, educating, for example, about the production contexts and political economy of media (Sander 2017, p. 130; Livingstone et al. 2021b, p. 222). This is also evident in a well-known 'classic' approach to media literacy: the work of the German media pedagogy scholar Baacke.

3.1.2 Baacke: A 'Classic' Approach to Media Literacy

Baacke's understanding of media literacy (German: Medienkompetenz) is well-established in the German field of media pedagogy and is often referenced as one of the key early conceptualisations of the term (e.g., Gapski et al. 2017a; Moser 2018; Niesyto 2018). Baacke's concept is developed throughout a number of publications, but the key argument remains that media literacy should consist of four dimensions: 1) *media criticism* ("Medienkritik"), 2) *media knowledge* ("Medienkunde"), 3) *media usage* ("Mediennutzung"), and 4) *media design* ("Mediengestaltung") (Baacke 1997, p. 98f).

Table 1: The four dimensions of Medienkompetenz according to Baacke, 1997, p. 98f, own translation.

The four dimensions of Medienkompetenz by Baacke		
1) *Media criticism* ("Medienkritik")		
a) analytical	b) reflective	c) ethical
2) *Media knowledge* ("Medienkunde")		
a) informative	b) instrumental-qualifying	
3) *Media usage* ("Mediennutzung")		
a) receptive	b) interactive	
4) *Media design* ("Mediengestaltung")		
a) innovative	b) creative	

The first and most relevant dimension for my study, *media criticism* ("Medienkritik"), is further differentiated into an analytical, a reflective and an ethical layer. Baacke argues that media literate users should be able to a) *analytically* apprehend problematic societal processes (e.g., concentration trends); b) *reflectively* apply the analysed knowledge to their selves and their actions; and c) take an *ethical* perspective by understanding analytical thinking and "reflective referring back" as socially responsible (1997, p. 98, own translation). In addition to becoming aware of concentration trends, knowing that private channels are funded through advertising and reflecting on the effect this has on the channel's structures and content is mentioned as an example for this dimension of media criticism (Baacke 2001).

As a second dimension, Baacke suggests *knowledge* about today's media and media systems ("Medienkunde"), that should include an *informative* (e.g., "How do journalists work?", "How can I use a computer for my purposes?") as well as an "*instrumental-qualifying*" layer, meaning the ability to use new technologies, for example familiarising oneself with new software (ibid., p. 99). Baacke's third dimension, *media usage*, includes the *receptive* use of media (e.g., being able to use specific software) and the *interactive* use of media (responding while using media, e.g., teleshopping). Finally, the last dimension of *media design* can also be seen in a twofold manner, as this dimension aims for *innovative* media design: "changing a media system within its inherent logics", as well as *creative* media design: "emphasis of aesthetical variants, going beyond communicative routines" (ibid.).

Despite having been developed at the time of analogue media – when mass press and the wide popularity of television were current issues – Baacke's concept remains valuable and insightful also in times of digital media, the internet and big data (Moser 2018, p. 77f). Particularly its goals of economic critique and self-reflective action constitute valuable approaches in times of digital capitalism (ibid, p. 78). Moreover, although several of Baacke's dimensions seem to focus on abilities the individual media user ought to gain, the author emphasises that media literacy should not be restricted to a subjective-individualistic level, but should rather be implemented at a supra-individual, societal level and should foster a public discourse (1997, p. 99). These objectives are highly relevant for education about datafication. Furthermore, besides a somewhat instrumental nature – aiming for the practical skills to use media or create content – Baacke's concept also attaches great importance to media criticism. This is unusual as 'traditional' media literacy is often understood as practical and skills-based, and even when critical reflection is included, this reflection often only concerns critical readings of media *content*, rather than a consideration or critique of media *structures* (see e.g., Zorn 2015; see also below). This correlates with developments in the data literacy field, which is similarly predominantly of instrumental nature, and where critical perspectives are included, they often relate to digital content or data handling (see chapter 2.2).

It is this focus on fostering critical reflection of societal processes related to media, including a self-reflective and an ethical component, that makes Baacke's concept so very valuable for this theoretical framework. Moreover, also today's media scholars most often discuss this critical aspect when referring back to Baacke's media literacy. Niesyto, for example, argues that Baacke's dimension of media criticism is somewhat "transverse" to his other three dimensions (2018, p. 65). He further emphasises that Baacke vehemently disagreed with the normative control and youth protection objectives that had until then often been associated with media literacy, as they regarded children and youths as passive recipients of media content (ibid.). Similarly, Moser points out that media criticism is placed as the first of the four dimensions in Baacke's framework and argues that Baacke regarded critical media education as a central task for media pedagogy (Moser 2018, p. 77). Thus, Baacke's 'classic' media literacy already provides meaningful insights for an extended theorisation of critical datafication literacy. This traditional media literacy approach has also been adapted to our digital times, for example by adding a fifth dimension that includes fostering media and internet policy competences (Oberle 2017, p. 190f). Dander even developed a model of "data critique" that builds on Baacke's model in combination with Ganguin and Hobbs, and aims for the ability to recognise, decode, analyse, critically reflect on and evaluate data and data practices as well as fostering citizen's agency and civic participation (2014, pp. 10–12, own translation).

3.1.3 Developments and Controversies in Media Literacy Concepts

Over the years, the field of media pedagogy and media literacy gained wider recognition. Although media scholars still criticise the lacking implementation of media education in school curricula, the field has nevertheless become more established and institutionalised (Gapski et al. 2017a). Yet, as already highlighted above, media literacy remains a contested concept with various different understandings. My review of the field further found that common points of disagreement between media literacy scholars bear significant resemblances to the differences in data literacy understandings that were identified in chapter 2.2. Some of these contested issues have already been mentioned in relation to Baacke's concept above. One key issue is that media literacy is located between the poles of, one the one hand, working towards reflection, responsibility, character development and potentially empowerment, and, on the other hand, the goal of technical or instrumental qualifications (Gapski et al. 2017a, p. 21f). Perhaps in part due to the terms' linguistic origins – literacy coming from reading and writing; competence often referring to skills, qualifications or abilities – there is an ongoing discussion about the extent to which media literacy should be understood in an instrumental and practical manner or should rather aim for understanding and critical reflection of media. Many scholars argue that the problematic challenges especially of digital media cannot be solved through practical abilities of using (digital) media alone (e.g., Gapski et al. 2017, p. 19; Sander 2017, p. 130f).

Moreover, traditional media literacy approaches usually focus on media texts – in other words, media content. Thus, even when media literacy concepts include a critical perspective, this often addresses only the content of media, encouraging questions about the intended message of a media text or potential alternative readings. While these are important critical considerations for media users, a broader perspective on underlying technologies and structures of media is necessary in order to understand current developments in the media landscape (Zorn 2015, p. 20). This issue is amplified when considering the challenges of digital media and the internet, and the wide-reaching influence these technologies and their underlying structures have on today's citizens and our societies in general.

Another tension evident in many media literacy approaches, which Baacke also identified, is the recurring criticism of subjectification. Sometimes media literacy can be (mis)understood as shifting responsibility to the individual rather than working towards necessary social structural changes (Gapski 2019, pp. 26; 28). As already argued in regard to data literacy in chapter 2.2, this raises unreasonable expectations for individuals and leads to an unequal distribution of responsibility. While citizens require certain abilities and knowledge to participate in our digital societies and should ideally be able to critically reflect on current media developments, it should not be their responsibility alone to address challenges related to digital media and the datafication of our societies.

Considering these tensions, it is particularly media literacy concepts that a) are focussed on knowledge and critical reflection rather than practical skills; b) go beyond media content and also aim for understanding of media structures; and c) are careful not to merely shift responsibility to the individuals, that are particularly relevant for the critical datafication literacy framework developed in this study. One example for such media literacy approach is presented in Mihailidis' 2018 paper on "civic media literacies".

3.1.4 Mihailidis: Critically Reflecting Media Structures and Enabling Agency

In contrast to Baacke's more traditional approach, Mihailidis clearly distances his work from "media literacy's long-standing approach to critical inquiry through reasoned deconstruction and the creation of media texts" (2018, p. 1). While "not diminishing their [these frameworks'] impact" but rather building on these foundations, Mihailidis outlines five points of criticism in prior media literacy frameworks: their need for critical distance from media; transactional nature (prioritising skill attainment); focus on deficits; emphasis on creation or critique of content; and their prioritisation of individual responsibility (ibid., p. 4f). These points of criticism are in line with the tensions between different approaches to media literacy outlined above and highlight this concept's relevance for my study. As argued in prior chapters, when it comes to critically educating about datafication, critical distance is often impossible; practical skills are insufficient; a focus solely on deficits could lead to resignation; content is less relevant than understanding structures; and it is important to not place too much responsibility on individuals.

In going beyond these five points, Mihailidis suggests that media literacy "must be reimagined as intentionally civic" and reframed as "relevant to the social, political, and technological realities of contemporary life" (2018, p. 1). Relating to Boyte's work (2014), Mihailidis argues that there is a "gap 'between concern and capacity to act'" (2018, p. 7). This "agency gap" must be addressed so that people are able to "translate their capacity to understand media with taking deliberate civic actions to improve, reform, or re-imagine media's role in our civic systems" (p. 8). It is these goals of civic participation and agency that highlight the novel nature of Mihailidis' literacy concept. In order to "reframe media literacy interventions towards civic intentionality", Mihailidis suggests that future media literacy initiatives should aim at

> enabling agentive action-taking, evoking a caring ethic, inspiring critical consciousness, developing persistent engagement, and creating conditions for emancipatory communication, where people are able to work together to respond to social problems that prevent progress from taking place. (ibid., p. 11)

Overall, Mihailidis' concept of civic media literacies provides a highly relevant approach to media education for this theoretical framework, pointing out key weak points of prior concepts that should be considered and suggesting ways to overcome the "agency gap" to better support citizens to take action. In some instances, the author even addresses issues related to datafication, arguing that "people are increasing[ly] subjected to algorithmic advertising, personalized information, and targeted content that is designed for the extraction of data" (2018, p. 6). Thus, he argues that instead of focusing on media content, media literacy initiatives should consider the "platform or modality relationships to information and communication" and the impact of "algorithms, platforms, and abundant information flows across a myriad of loosely affiliated networks" (ibid., p. 4f).

3.1.5 Digital Literacy

With the ever-growing importance of digital technologies in society, many new concepts have emerged that specifically focus on fostering citizens' literacy in relation to digital media. In the German academic context, many scholars called for changes in existing concepts of Medienkompetenz in order to include digital media (e.g., Helbig 2016). A number of new concepts emerged as well, using terms such as "Digitalkompetenz" (digital competence) or "Digitale Souveränität" (digital sovereignty) (Gapski et al. 2017a, p. 19). In the English-language academic discourse, "digital literacy" constitutes the most common term. However, defining digital literacy has "proven complicated" and it remains a "contested term" today (Pangrazio 2016, p. 163; Pangrazio et al. 2020, p. 445). To add to the confusion, there is "significant overlap between digital literacy, information literacy and other fields such as technological literacy" (Leaning 2017, p. 118f) and the distinction between media literacy and digital literacy can be blurry. Generally speaking, digital literacy can be understood as "the technical, cognitive, and sociological skills needed in order to perform tasks and solve problems in digital environments" (Shade and Shepherd 2013, no page number).

Similar to the field of media literacy, the academic discourse around digital literacy started from an instrumental understanding but has seen increasing calls for more critical perspectives instead of an "overly technocratic and acritical framing" for several years (Hinrichsen and Coombs 2013, p. 1). Pötzsch provides a detailed review of recent work in the field of digital literacy (2019). Examples for critical perspectives include scholars who have connected digital literacy with Paulo Freire's critical pedagogy and its goals of critical consciousness, democratisation and civic participation (e.g., Hammer 2011; Garcia et al. 2015), or who approach digital literacy from the perspective of traditional humanities, fostering a critical "Bildung" in a Humboldtian understanding (Simanowski 2018). Both of these educational theories will be discussed in more detail in the next chapters.

Moreover, several scholars have suggested a distinct *critical digital literacy*. Such concepts often focus on the "critical consumption of digital forms", "the personal experiences of the individual", or "critical skills in specific digital contexts" (Pangrazio 2016, p. 164f). Thus, similar to the media and data literacy discourse, there is a predominance of objectives regarding technical skills, content creation or critique of content. However, some concepts also aim for a broader critical understanding of the implications of digital technologies and for fostering citizen involvement. For example, Shade and Chan's "digital privacy policy literacy" promotes understanding of digital policy processes, the political economy of digital technologies and technological infrastructures as well as supporting citizens' participation in "policy-making processes [...] to formulate their right to privacy" (2020, pp. 327, 336). Furthermore, the critical digital literacy concepts by Pötzsch (2019) and Pangrazio (2016), discussed in detail in chapter 2.2, foster similarly broad and critical understanding.

3.1.6 Aßmann et al.: Big Data Practices as a Challenge for Media Education

Finally, some media literacy approaches have been identified that directly relate to the challenges of datafication and call to include into media literacy critical reflection of big data structures and the influence of datafication on our societies. A key text here is a position paper by a group of seven German media literacy scholars, who outline problematic issues related to datafication, highlight key areas to be addressed by media pedagogy (and argue why this is needed), and give suggestions on how to implement their calls into practice (Aßmann et al. 2016).

Aßmann et al. outline five key areas of responsibility that media pedagogy should address in relation to datafication: 1) making visible and understandable the invisible and complex technical, economic, social and ethical implications of datafication; 2) fostering citizens' agency regarding the use of their data and their involvement in decision-making on new data systems; 3) demanding diversity and denouncing discrimination, for example through algorithms; 4) supporting citizens' self-determination and fostering public debate about datafication; and 5) fostering critical reflection and enabling productive and societally desirable forms of usage (2016, p. 4ff). While all five calls constitute novel approaches to media literacy – especially at the time of publication – particularly the fourth point provides a highly relevant insight for my study. The authors urgently call to support citizens' self-determination while at the same time emphasising that this cannot be individualised but is dependent on a civic framework for action that allows for self-determination. What such a framework for action could look like for citizens of datafied societies will be further discussed in chapter six.

In order to work towards these five areas of responsibility, the authors of the position paper call for interdisciplinary work (Aßmann et al. 2016, p. 6) as the complexity of datafied societies can only be addressed through the collaboration of media pedagogy with legal, political, technical, economical, and media and communication studies discourses. Moreover, a permanent and sustainable implementation of media pedagogy in school curricula and other educational institutions is needed. The authors make very clear that understanding the structural processes of datafication and its political implications constitutes a necessary prerequisite for participating in societal debates and enacting one's right to informational self-determination and must therefore be included in educational policies (ibid.). Overall, the authors of the position paper make several highly relevant arguments for the conceptualisation of critical datafication literacy. Although the paper was published in 2016, several of the authors' claims are still not yet sufficiently considered in today's (critical) data literacy approaches. In particular, the strong foci on making ethical issues transparent, empowering citizens, and on working towards more diverse and democratic data societies have significantly informed this study's theoretical framework.

Two co-authors of the position paper have further published their own suggestions on how to address media pedagogy in light of new data systems. Gapski argued that existing media literacy approaches focus too much on media texts and content, and that, considering the "media catastrophe" that digital society faces, media education needs to de-mystify big data, educate about opportunities, limitations and risks, and, importantly, go beyond an instrumental and individualised approach to media literacy (2015, p. 63). Similarly, Zorn clearly states that media pedagogy has the responsibility to study big data's implications on education, personal development, the protection of equal opportunities and the promotion of a self-determined life, as well as to develop educational concepts that approach these issues (2015, p. 20). In doing so, media pedagogy should collaborate with other fields and with practitioners but should avoid individualisation and resignation while fostering critical reflection of data structures and promoting data protection abilities.

In the same edited volume as these two texts, other contributions also make suggestions for an update of media literacy approaches to include concerns around datafication (Brüggen 2015; Grimm and Kimmel 2015; Koska 2015; Sieben 2015), or suggest a connection of the English-language discourse around data literacy to German media pedagogy (Dander and Aßmann 2015). Newer publications make similar arguments, suggesting that "algorithm literacy instruction" (Brodsky et al. 2020, p. 55) or "conceptual understanding of technology – of which data literacy is a constituent part" should be incorporated into media literacy (Knaus 2020, p. 13). Others call for a "media-grounded data literacy" (Claes and Philippette 2020, p. 26).

3.1.7 Conclusion

The theoretical framework that is being developed in my study contributes to these discourses, learning from established and theoretically grounded models such as media literacy and connecting them to current conceptualisations of (critical) data literacy. The analysis of selected key texts of the German- and English-speaking media and digital literacy discourse in this chapter already provided manifold relevant insights for the conceptualisation of critical datafication literacy. Novel insights for the framework development included the analysed literacy approaches' strong focus on *understanding* media structures and on *critical reflection* and a critique of (digital) media. Moreover, their goal of using education *for societal change* and increasing citizens' *agency*; their emphasis on *interdisciplinary* approaches; and their *warnings against individualisation* strongly informed my framework for critical datafication literacy.

3.2 The Concept of (Politische) Bildung

3.2.1 Humboldt: The Original Concept of Bildung

A second highly relevant approach to education for this study's theoretical framework is "Bildung", a German concept in educational theory. While sometimes used interchangeably with "education" in the German language and in translations of German texts, Bildung in fact constitutes a very specific understanding of education. For clarity, I use the original German term Bildung (and a small number of other specific original terms) to refer to the specific, narrow concepts they describe, similar to other scholars who use Bildung as a foreign word in their English-language texts (e.g., Lovlie and Standish 2002; Nordenbo 2002).

There are a number of scholars that have had great influence on the theoretical discourse around Bildung, such as Kant (1783 /1964), Herder (1774) and Klafki (1991). One particularly influential text, however, is a fragment written by Humboldt more than two hundred years ago, that has coined today's understanding of the term Bildung and is still referenced frequently by today's scholars. In 1793 or 1794, Humboldt wrote his "Theory of Bildung" (printed among others in 1986) – a surprisingly concise and, from today's perspective, somewhat convoluted text considering its influential nature. In it, Humboldt argues that at their core, humans are interested in learning about and understanding the world around them; to "expand the sphere of [their] knowledge and [their] activity" and to seek to "grasp as much as possible and bind it as tightly as [they] can to [themselves]" (von Humboldt 2000, p. 58, translated by Horton-Krüger). Thus, the goal of humans is to connect their selves with the world. This objective is also described in the following quote, which is often viewed as the key sentence of Humboldt's text, and which summarises his theory of Bildung:

> It is the ultimate task of our existence to achieve as much substance as possible for the concept of humanity in our person, both during the span of our life and beyond it, through the traces we leave by means of our vital activity. This can be fulfilled only by the linking of the self to the world to achieve the most general, most animated, and most unrestrained interplay. (ibid.)

According to Humboldt, this substance and the linking of the self to the world – in other words, Bildung – does not require a "heightening of [one's] powers and the elevation of [one's] personality", but he rather states that "every business of life can exercise on our inner Bildung" (ibid., p. 60). No matter what one does in one's daily life, any business can "give the mind its own, fresh view of the world and through this its own, fresh self-determination" when approached with the right mindset (ibid.). Through "deep reflection and unceasing observation" of one's self, and by "proceeding step by step and finally surveying the whole, one can reach the point of explaining completely to oneself how human Bildung manages to progress evenly and endure" (ibid., p. 61).

In order to fully comprehend Humboldt's theory of Bildung and its influence on educational discourses, it is helpful – if not essential – to consult secondary literature. As mentioned above, Humboldt's text was written in 1793 (or 1794) as a "fragment".[1] Earlier, in a letter written in November 1793, Humboldt had "remarked on the absence of anything more than an embryonic theory of Bildung", for which his fragment develops a number of general principles (von Humboldt 2000, p. 57, translated by Horton-Krüger). Sander provides a concise English-language synopsis of Humboldt's 1793 text (2019). The author summarises the Humboldtian Bildung as the linking of the self to the world "in the sense of an interaction" (2019, p. 23). Thus, Bildung is not "a simple adaption of the individual to a predetermined order of the

1 Published under the title: "Theorie der Bildung des Menschen. Bruchstück" (Theory of the Bildung of humankind. Fragment).

world" but rather about *reciprocity* between the individual and the world around them (ibid.).

A key aspect of Humboldt's understanding of Bildung is his idea of individual's inner *forces*, or *strengths* – today we would rather speak of "potentials inherent in a person, which he or she can develop through experiences of the world" (Sander 2019, p. 23). According to Humboldt, humans by nature aspire to deal with objects outside of them in the world and thereby develop their "strengths". Thus, Bildung in Humboldt's understanding is not concerned with the passive acquisition of knowledge or attaining practical skills, but rather relates to the development of an individual's potential, which is revealed "not only in their inner experience, but also in their activity in the world" (ibid.). For this reason, Humboldt sees a close connection between the development of the individual and the development of the entire nation (Sander 2018, p. 100). The origin of Humboldt's understanding of Bildung lies in the pedagogical theory of neo-humanism, for which it constitutes an "ideal type" (Vogel 2008, p. 123). Humboldt's Bildung represents a dissociation from the rather unassuming concepts of the bourgeois lifestyle and upbringing in the German enlightenment and rather aims at decreasing social differences through general humanistic education, as Humboldt saw a deep commonality between all societal classes (ibid., p. 123; 125).

However, it should be clarified that Bildung is neither an exclusively German concept, nor was it 'invented' by Humboldt. Rather, the "topic of the educated mind" is central in "most educational theories and philosophies in various cultures, languages, and epochs" (Reichenbach 2014, p. 86). Nordenbo, for example, outlines how the ideas behind Bildung date back to ancient Greece (2002). Similarly, Sander argues that the concept of Bildung has been around since pre-Christianity, and he relates it to Socrates' philosophical practices such as the "productive effect of doubt" and the "importance of the art of using targeted questioning" in order to promote independent thinking and critical scrutiny (2019, p. 24). Nevertheless, German literature has been prolific in the discourse around Bildung (Reichenbach 2014, p. 86), and the modern conceptualisation of Bildung has been strongly influenced by Humboldt in particular (Sander 2019, p. 20). Moreover, Humboldt's influence expands beyond theoretical considerations, as he developed the basis for the humanistic grammar school as a new school form as well as a new model for universities based on the concepts of "freedom of research" and "unity of research and teaching", which are still widely followed in many parts of the world today (Sander 2018, p. 97ff).

3.2.2 Developments and Today's Understandings of Bildung

Despite Humboldt's relevance to today's discourses of Bildung, his ideas have been "disputed or declared as outdated time and again" (Sander 2019, p. 20). In the 1960s and 1970s, Bildung was increasingly replaced with terms borrowed from sociology and psychology such as "socialisation" and "learning", prompting a heated debate, with more than 300 publications with the term Bildung in the title within ten years in German journals alone (Siljander 2014, p. 327). More marginalisation followed (ibid.) and the concept still remains contested today. Some call to "abandon the concept of Bildung" as it has "lost the possibility of functioning as a point of resistance and critical principle" (Masschelein and Ricken 2003, p. 139), whereas others argue that even today, Humboldt's ideas "represent an important point of reference for theories of education" (Sander 2019, p. 20), because "the concept of Bildung extends to areas of human activity that the candidates for equivalency fail to grasp" (Siljander 2014, p. 328). In the last two decades, there have been increasing attempts to link Bildung to current debates, such as new media (Bauer 2003, p. 135), and it has attracted interest in the English-speaking area and Scandinavia, where Bildung is now used as a foreign word (ibid.; Sander 2019, p. 20). The Scandinavian concept of "digital Bildung", for example, constitutes another relevant approach for this study's theoretical framework, referring to an "overall intercultural competence" that goes beyond aspects such as online etiquette but rather aims for "insight into ethical issues and participation in the digital and democratic society" (Gran et al. 2019, p. 24; Gran 2019, p. 104).

Despite its long history, defining Bildung can be somewhat "cumbersome" (Reichenbach 2014, p. 88). The term is often used in "a very broad and unspecific way", so that it "tends to lose its distinct quality (Bauer 2003, p. 135),[2] or even as a "container-word" (Lüders 2007, p. 186). Nevertheless, a number of modern definitions have outlined Bildung's specific nature and thus highlight the relevance of the concept for my study. For example, Pleines characterises Bildung as a state or process of mind, as "a permanent task", and "as human's self-fulfilment in freedom" (1989, pp. 12–38, translation by Reichenbach 2014, p. 87). Others have similarly highlighted Bildung's nature as a "spontaneous, emergent and never ending process" (Bauer 2003, p. 134) without "defined goals in a utilitarian sense", but continuing throughout life (Sander 2019, p. 19). Moreover, Bildung constitutes a "critical and emancipatory enterprise" (Masschelein and Ricken 2003, p. 140) that aims for maturity, the development of personality, the ability to make judgements, and reflective understanding of experiences of the world" (Sander 2019, p. 19). Finally, scholars outline that Bildung is a normative concept (Vogel 2008, p. 125; Siljander 2014, p. 329), but can also be seen as "non-affirmative" (Siljander 2014, p. 329).

Thus, despite being suggested over 200 years ago, the Humboldtian Bildung still provides numerous relevant insights for my study's conceptualisation of critical datafication literacy. Particularly Bildung's emancipatory nature and its goals of

2 This vagueness was also observed when preparing chapter 3.1, as the German media literacy discourse often uses the term "Medienbildung" (media Bildung) somewhat interchangeably with "Medienkompetenz" (media literacy) or "Medienpädagogik" (media pedagogy).

maturity or self-determination as well as the ability to reflectively understand one's experiences of the world and, based on this, to make judgements, are extremely valuable goals for citizens of increasingly datafied societies. Moreover, understanding education – or Bildung – about datafication as more than "mere" acquisition of knowledge but as a lifelong endeavour is a highly useful approach in light of continuously changing technology landscapes.

3.2.3 Politische Bildung – Origin, Developments and Key Text by Autorengruppe Fachdidaktik

What is Politische Bildung and Where Does It Originate?

A specific form of Bildung constitutes the concept "politische Bildung", another German 'specialty' that is usually translated as "political literacy", "citizenship education" or "civic education" (see below). In this chapter, I will use the original term "politische Bildung" in order to avoid mistranslations and confusion between the various English terms that describe the same concept. The history of politische Bildung has been traced back until before the French revolution (see Detjen 2013, pp. 13–208), and the concept constitutes an encompassing research field today (overviews of research can be found in Detjen 2013; Pohl 2016; Sander and Pohl 2022). The German scholar Lange provides a valuable concise English-language summary of the origin and key developments of politische Bildung (2008). The author links today's understanding of politische Bildung back to post-war Germany in 1945, when the National Socialist regime was toppled (ibid., p. 89). As the German population had very limited awareness of democratic processes and principles after Hitler, the Allies started a re-education programme, with the belief that the democratisation of Germany "could only succeed if its society was made up of citizens who had proficient grasp of democratic concepts" (ibid.). Although only a few re-education measures worked well and were sustainable, this early form of politische Bildung "gave vital momentum to the idea that democracy should not only be fostered as a form of government, but also as a way of life" (ibid.).

The early stage of politische Bildung was strongly influenced by the school of American pragmatism, particularly the philosophy of education following John Dewey, and the concept of civics, which "sought to democratize a public that was first and foremost obedient to authority" (Lange 2008, p. 89f). During these first phases of development, politische Bildung was "derived from the closely related fields of education and political science", only expanding into a "didactics of politische Bildung" in the 1960s (ibid., p. 90). The 1970s were then marked by a polarization of the field between critical rationalism, aiming to "help citizens make rational judgements", and critical theory, attempting to "teach citizens how to emancipate themselves from those who might seek to seize power" (ibid.). Both sides were drawn together by the so-called "Beutelsbacher Consensus", an important directive for politische Bildung still today. It includes the prohibition against "overpowering" students, the imperative to represent controversy in the classroom, and the empowerment of learners to represent their interests politically (Autorengruppe Fachdidaktik 2016, p. 16). Today, politische Bildung is "firmly integrated in Germany's educational landscape" through a specific subject in school curriculums in every German state (Lange 2008, p. 93).

"What Is Good Politische Bildung?" - Key Text by Autorengruppe Fachdidaktik

The key text for this section was published by a group of eight established scholars and authors in the field of politische Bildung in Germany, who aim to support teachers with a guideline for 'good' politische Bildung (Autorengruppe Fachdidaktik 2016). They provide a concise and coherent definition of politische Bildung that describes the *core* of politische Bildung as regarded by this group of established authors in the field and outline the key notion of "Mündigkeit" (usually translated as responsibility or autonomy) in detail. These definitions constitute highly valuable starting points for understanding politische Bildung. Thus, the group of authors offer the following definition:

> Politische Bildung is based on human's "Mündigkeit" [responsibility / autonomy] and fosters the power of judgement of the democratically sovereign individual. It improves the ability to orient oneself in the social world. It develops the ability to evaluate and criticise societal phenomena. It promotes the competence to political participation and civic involvement. (Autorengruppe Fachdidaktik 2016, p. 7, own translation)

These few sentences clearly communicate the key idea of the concept. The core idea behind politische Bildung is the goal of Mündigkeit, which will be further discussed below. The goal of this educational approach – informed citizens who are able to navigate their social world in an autonomous and critical manner and participate politically – is reemphasised in the next paragraph, in which the authors highlight "the promotion of power of judgement and critical thinking as well as the enabling of participation" as the *core* of politische Bildung (ibid., p. 8, own translation).

As the point of departure and goal of politische Bildung is the Mündigkeit of citizens (see below), the "subjects of politische Bildung do not derive from its disciplines of reference" (Autorengruppe Fachdidaktik 2016, p. 8, own translation). Instead, the objects of learning change, as they are determined by current challenges to Mündigkeit and democratic self-determination. This flexibility in combination with its overarching democratic and social objectives make politische Bildung particularly relevant for informing my study's conceptualisation of critical datafication literacy. If politische Bildung aims to work towards an autonomous and informed citizenry, democratic self-determination and political participation, and to educate about whatever challenges these values, then it seems self-evident that politische Bildung should educate about the societal challenges surrounding datafication.

Moreover, the authors highlight that 'the political' of politische Bildung is not directly related to political science but rather takes an interdisciplinary, or transdisciplinary approach (Autorengruppe Fachdidaktik 2016, p. 8). The authors argue that the political aspect of the concept relates to the "public creative force" of autonomous citizens and that it represents the "aspiration and the ability of learners to understand, evaluate, criticise and change the social world" (ibid., p. 8, own translation). The concept of politische Bildung is not only implemented in school and classroom settings, but has a broad area of application, including adult and further education, but also more informal educational settings.

Finally, it is crucial to consider the often-mentioned Mündigkeit in more detail. This notion derives from Immanuel Kant's ideas during the enlightenment (Autorengruppe Fachdidaktik 2016, p. 13). Thus, Mündigkeit can be seen as consisting of the individual's ability to sustain oneself in the society and as the goal of one's actions, as well as a goal of education and Bildung more generally. In the context of politische Bildung, this notion describes the "ability to grapple with society, politics and economy in an independent, informed and interest-based manner, to act self-determined and self-efficacious in these areas, and to justify one's actions transparently" (ibid., p. 15, own translation). In practice, these imperatives can be implemented by teaching about Mündigkeit, as well as by applying principles of Mündigkeit to one's teaching methods (ibid., p. 19). The authors emphasise that "teaching oriented towards Mündigkeit differentiates cause, concern and responsibility, courses for action and real potentials for influence" (ibid., p. 21, own translation). By including many references to the learners' daily lives and presenting them with alternative visions, politische Bildung aims to support the learners' Mündigkeit as they "develop the ability for critique, contradiction and resistance" (ibid., own translation). This makes Mündigkeit a highly relevant concept and a suitable goal also for critical datafication literacy, which, one could argue, aims to increase citizen's Mündigkeit in datafied societies.

Other authors in the field of politische Bildung similarly argue that an informed, responsible and "mündig" citizenry constitutes the goal of politische Bildung (e.g., Gesellschaft für Politikdidaktik und politische Jugend- und Erwachsenenbildung (GPJE) 2004, p. 9; Lange 2008, p. 91; Gapski et al. 2018, p. 44; Waldis 2020, p. 59). Politische Bildung's goals of Mündigkeit and enabling citizens to "live self-determined lives in an increasingly complex society" (Lange 2008, p. 91) highlight how much the conceptualisation and implementation of critical datafication literacy can learn from this established field of research and practice. In our datafied societies, it becomes increasingly difficult for citizens to orientate themselves; to make informed decisions, for example on which data technologies to use; and to engage in public matters, such as debates around datafication. Therefore, it can be argued that critical approaches to educating about datafication should learn from the established field of politische Bildung; but also that politische Bildung – given its flexibility in learning objects – should educate about the challenges to self-determination and Mündigkeit that come with the datafication of our societies. The following section briefly outlines a number of texts that take exactly this perspective.

3.2.4 (Politische) Bildung about Big Data

Bildung about Big Data

Both the more general concept of Bildung and the specific notion of politische Bildung have been adapted to the challenges that arise with new data technologies. Besides calls to "digitise" Bildung, which usually aim for using digital teaching methods or fostering learners' digital skills, a number of scholars have also emphasised the need to understand and critically reflect on the datafication of our societies through Bildung. Two relevant examples will be outlined briefly. The first is the "Frankfurt-Dreieck" ("Frankfurt-Triangle"), an education policy declaration by several authors on how to approach Bildung in times of digitisation, that constitutes a reaction to a prior "Dagstuhl-Erklärung" by different authors and aims to fill the gaps left by the first declaration (Brinda et al. 2019). The "Frankfurt-Triangle" mentions a number of relevant aspects related to data. The authors warn about risks of universal compatibility of data (ibid., p. 6); and argue that Bildung in times of digitisation should include a "technological-medial" perspective that aims at understanding underlying principles and structures of digital systems and their implications as they emphasise that data and algorithms are never neutral (ibid., p. 9f). Furthermore, they call for a "societal-cultural perspective" on Bildung, which analyses and reflects on interactions between individuals, society and digital systems, and considers questions of responsibility as well as risks around data traces and profile building (p. 11f).

Besides this general policy declaration, the 2018 report on "Bildung für und über Big Data" ("Bildung for and about big data"), part of the "ABIDA (Assessing Big Data)" project, makes a more in-depth connection of Bildung with topics of datafication (Gapski et al. 2018). This extensive 188-page research report presents theoretical and empirical findings as well as recommendations for action for a variety of audiences. This includes a clear call to incorporate issues around datafication into Bildung, offering suggestions on how to achieve this. The report not only highlights gaps in the education policy discourse in relation to big data (chapter 3.1.2 and 5.2.1), but also outlines key challenges of big data and how Bildung should address these (ibid., p. 11ff). For example, the individual and social implications of information and power asymmetries should be highlighted, the workings and decision-making processes of algorithms explained, and learners empowered to lead a self-determined and socially responsible life in a digitised world (ibid., p. 18f).

Based on this, the report presents concrete educational and learning goals for Bildung about big data (Gapski et al. 2018, p. 118f). These include a "reflexive evaluation of the social and socio-political implications of big data"; an understanding that data is never neutral and of the economic forces around big data; the realisation of one's options for action, including self-data protection; and, eventually, a "sovereign position and self-determined choice of options for action in data worlds" and an "awareness of the factual and possible future scope for action" (ibid., own translations). With these considerations and suggestions, the ABIDA report constitutes an original contribution for conceptualising how Bildung about datafication could look like.

Media Literacy as a 'Classic Goal' of Politische Bildung

Moreover, the concept of politische Bildung has been connected to challenges surrounding digital technologies. The most common perspective taken in this context is to see media literacy as a 'classic goal' of politische Bildung and extend this media literacy to include issues around datafication. A key text for this perspective is the edited volume "Media literacy: a challenge for politics, politische Bildung and media education" (original: "Medienkompetenz: Herausforderung für Politik, politische Bildung und Medienbildung", Gapski et al. 2017b). The editors argue that media literacy has been a key goal of politische Bildung even before digitisation and that dialogue between the fields should be intensified (Gapski et al. 2017a, pp. 22; 24). In digital times, they continue, this should not just include the active usage of media, but also the ability to comprehend and evaluate the technological and (attention-)economic conditions of the media system, including understanding of algorithms, filter bubbles and other data-related phenomena (ibid., p. 23). Thus, in their view, politische Bildung has the responsibility to establish a new discussion culture about the implications of digital technologies (ibid., p. 24).

Several other chapters in the edited volume confirm this perspective and provide further arguments. Herzig and Martin, for example, outline the structural commonalities and interdependences of media literacy and politische Bildung and argue that both ultimately work towards societal participation (2017, p. 126f). Especially in light of new challenges surrounding digital technologies, they argue that citizens need to be media literate in order to participate in society politically and culturally. Oberle's text in the edited volume further details how media literacy as a goal of politische Bildung should be addressed in today's digital societies: politische Bildung should foster critical reflection of new media and its (also political) uses and enable citizens to shape digital media's underlying conditions (2017, p. 191). Similarly, Manzel argues that media literacy is needed in order to reach Mündigkeit – the underlying goal of politische Bildung – in today's digitised societies, as well as to be able to use reason, make political evaluations and act politically (2017, p. 208). Thus, although the boundaries between disciplines are blurry and the responsibilities not always clear, scholars of politische Bildung as well as of media literacy have already made evident the need to educate about structural aspects of big data and datafication.

Politische Bildung about Big Data

The texts outlined so far give a good idea of why politische Bildung should or even needs to educate about challenges related to the datafication of our societies. However, only few texts seem to exist that explicitly bring together the concept of politische Bildung and the goal of critically educating about big data. One possible explanation could be that the discipline of Critical Data Studies is not yet as pronounced in the German discourse as it is internationally. However, the research presented so far calls this suggestion into question, as many German publications distinctly relate to challenges of datafication and call for a critical perspective on these issues. Another reason could be the blurred boundaries between the fields, with media education often using the term Bildung (although not always in its original meaning); media literacy approaches aiming for civic involvement; and politische Bildung including media literacy as one of its key goals – and all these fields including some calls for critical reflection of datafication.

An additional, and perhaps the most likely explanation might be that the inclusion of issues related to datafication into approaches of politische Bildung is self-evident for many scholars and is therefore not directly addressed. As outlined above, concepts of politische Bildung clearly argue that the objects of learning of politische Bildung vary depending on the current challenges to citizens' Mündigkeit. It is possible that practitioners of politische Bildung already address topics of datafication of their own accord, and that at least some scholars include issues around datafication when they outline the tasks of politische Bildung in times of datafication, without necessarily mentioning data technologies directly. For example, scholars have highlighted politische Bildung's responsibility to "take up and simplify digital developments in relation to societal regulations and democratic decision-making" (Waldis 2020, own translation), and to identify possible implications and risks of digitisation "as a problem area of societal coexistence and put them to debate" (Sander 2017, p. 144, own translation). Others have highlighted specific challenges of digital technologies that should be considered by politische Bildung, such as subjection to algorithms, the power of Google and Facebook, and the need to protect democratic elections from manipulation (Goll 2018, pp. 217; 219).

3.2.5 Conclusion

Thus, scholars of politische Bildung are clearly (becoming) aware of issues around datafication and are beginning to consider them as a crucial component of politische Bildung in today's societies. Moreover, some English-language publications make suggestions for critical education about datafication that resemble the discourses portrayed in this chapter, without necessarily using the terms Bildung or politische Bildung. For example, they aim to involve individuals continuously in "processes of self-improvement" and to work towards "full and complete participation in wider society" (Pangrazio and Sefton-Green 2020, p. 217), or they suggest that critical digital literacy approaches should learn from and be connected to political and civic education approaches (Polizzi 2020b). These examples as well as the publications and arguments presented throughout this chapter clearly highlight how productive a (politische) Bildung approach to education about datafication could be, and how much can be learnt from this field for the conceptualisation of critical datafication literacy in my study.

3.3 Critical Pedagogy according to Paulo Freire

3.3.1 The Field of Critical Pedagogy

The third relevant established educational approach examined in detail in this theoretical framework is the notion of "critical pedagogy". This "multi-voiced field and movement" defines education as an "inherently political practice that shapes how we think about and move within the social world" (Vossoughi and Gutiérrez 2016, pp. 140; 142). Critical pedagogy (CP) aims for "transforming relations of power which are oppressive and which lead to the oppression of people" (Aliakbari and Faraji 2011, p. 77). CP is most associated with the work of the Brazilian educator and activist Paulo Freire (ibid.), and particularly his seminal work "Pedagogy of the Oppressed", which galvanised theoretical, pedagogical and political traditions (Vossoughi and Gutiérrez 2016, p. 140). Freire's ideas, which will be analysed in detail below, were taken up by later scholars, who "laid the foundation for an educational model of communication characterized by favouring participation, empowerment, and consciousness-raising to generate individual and collective transformation" (Barbas 2019, p. 75).

Scholarship in critical pedagogy draws on "Hegelian-Marxist philosophy and the European tradition of Critical Theory" (Vossoughi and Gutiérrez 2016, p. 142). Particularly the principals of critical theory of the Frankfurt school, which pursue the idea of a "just society in which people have political, economic, and cultural control of their lives" can be seen as starting point and main source of critical pedagogy (Aliakbari and Faraji 2011, p. 77). Scholars of CP argue that teaching and learning are never neutral, and that schooling can never be understood "outside of its historical, social, political, and economic contexts" (Philip et al. 2013, p. 113). Besides offering powerful analyses of the relationship between education, oppression and power; CP articulates an alternative, suggesting that schools become "transformative spaces" where students and teachers together work towards developing a deepened awareness of the social conditions and their capacities to change them (Vossoughi and

Gutiérrez 2016, p. 142). This transformative understanding of education that aims for learners' critical consciousness has been applied in many different contexts, including feminist work in the 1960s and 1970s, the prominent Italian social theorist Antonio Gramsci, and Scandinavian Participatory Design (Markham 2019, p. 755). In recent years, CP seems to have "gained momentum" (Aliakbari and Faraji 2011, p. 77), and has even begun to be applied to approaches to data literacy (see 3.3.3).

3.3.2 Paulo Freire's Work on Critical Pedagogy

Life and Work of Paulo Freire

In order to comprehend Freire's approach to education, it is necessary to understand the very particular context in which it was created. Freire was a Brazilian educator who worked in the northeast region of Brazil in the 1960s, where the "illiteracy rate – percentage of adult people who could not read or write – reached 72.6%" (Tygel and Kirsch 2016, p. 109). Freire believed in "education as a way of liberating poor oppressed people", characterising the process of literacy education "both as technically learning how to read and to write, and as the emancipatory process of understanding and expressing oneself in the world" (ibid., p. 108f). He aimed to empower individuals to transform their social realities and believed that through "genuine education grounded in democratic praxis, even the most oppressed learners could lead self-determined lives and shape their own destiny (Mihailidis 2018, p. 10). This emancipatory perspective originated not only from intellectual analyses but rather was grounded in Freire's own experiences of poverty and class differences, which "led, invariably, to Freire's radical rejection of a class-based society" (Macedo 2014, p. 13).

After Freire's first large-scale application of his literacy method in 1963, he was invited by the president of Brazil to organise a "National Literacy Plan", aiming for "teaching more than 2 million people to read and write" (Tygel and Kirsch 2016, p. 110). Although these plans had to be cancelled due to a civil-military coup, which eventually led to Freire's arrest and exile, Freire nevertheless became "worldwide famous for his critical pedagogy", and in Latin America, the "history of education cannot be told without the name of Paulo Freire" (ibid., p. 109). His approach to support "critically conscious individuals – radically curious, politically aware, and empowered to intervene" (Mihailidis 2018, p. 10) is applied in educational contexts beyond merely teaching to read and write, and Freire's work continues to influence many educators all over the world (Tygel and Kirsch 2016, p. 108). While Freire's critical pedagogy provides highly relevant insights for a number of educational contexts – including critical education about datafication – its very specific context of origin, namely "teaching poor peasants how to read and write", should always be taken into account (ibid., p. 109).

Key Text – Pedagogy of the Oppressed

In his influential 1970 work "Pedagogy of the Oppressed", Freire criticises the way education is normally carried out (in his historical and geographical context) – with students as passive recipients of knowledge provided by the teacher. Freire speaks of the "'banking' model of education", in which "those who consider themselves knowledgeable" merely deposit knowledge onto "those whom they consider to know nothing" (2017, p. 45). Freire argues that this form of education supports oppression, explaining that the oppressed are "fearful of freedom" as they have "internalized the image of the oppressor" and have "adapted to the structure of domination in which they are immersed, and have become resigned to it" (ibid., p. 21). Despite the different context, this description of people's adaption or resignation bears strong resemblance to today's citizens' resignation towards data collection (see chapter 2.1).

In order to surmount this situation of oppression, Freire calls for a "pedagogy of the oppressed", a pedagogy which "must be forged *with*, not *for*, the oppressed (whether individuals or peoples)" (Freire 2017, p. 22, emphasis in original). The goal of this pedagogy is for the oppressed to view their "reality of oppression not as a closed world from which there is no exit, but as a limiting situation which they can transform" (ibid., p. 23). Therefore, it "makes oppression and its causes objects of reflection" by the oppressed and, so Freire argues, "from that reflection will come their necessary engagement in the struggle for their liberation" (ibid., p. 22). While the language of "oppression" and "the oppressed" originates from the very specific context of Freire's considerations, the goal of *working together with the learners* and to empower them to *reflect on societal structures that limit their freedom* as well as to view this reality as a situation that can be *transformed*, constitute highly relevant approaches to critical education about datafication.

According to Freire, when oppressed learners have unveiled the oppression around them and committed themselves to its transformation, the pedagogy of the oppressed turns into a "pedagogy of all people in the process of permanent liberation" (2017, p. 28). In such "liberating education", teachers must be "partners of the students" and regard them as "conscious beings", thereby resolving the "teacher-student contradiction" and replacing it with "dialogical relations" (ibid., p. 48; 52). Instead of "depositing" knowledge onto the students, teachers must pose "problems of human beings in their relations with the world" and aim for dialogue with the students (ibid., p. 52). Only such "problem-solving education" that overcomes the teacher-student contradiction can, according to Freire, "fulfill its function as the practice of freedom" (ibid., p. 53). These suggestions already highlight the value of CP for educating about the challenges of datafication, which affect – and potentially oppress (see chapter 2.1) – citizens in their daily lives. In the following, I will consider three interrelated key aspects of Freire's pedagogy in more detail: *dialogue, critical thinking*, and "*conscientização*".

Key Relevant Aspects of Freire's CP: Dialogue, Critical Thinking and "Conscientização"

Through *dialogue*, Freire aims to dissolve the traditional roles of teacher and students and turn students into "critical co-investigators" (2017, p. 54). The role of the teacher – or, "problem-posing educator" – is to present "the material to the students for their consideration" and to reconsider their own earlier considerations as the students express theirs (ibid.). Thus, through dialogue, both sides learn about each other's perspective, and realise that "their view of the world, manifested variously in their action, reflects their *situation* in the world" (ibid., p. 69, emphasis in original). With students being increasingly confronted with "problems relating to themselves in the world and with the world", Freire argues, they "will feel increasingly challenged and obliged to respond to that challenge" (ibid., p. 54). As they understand these challenges "not as a theoretical question" but in their wider context, the "resulting comprehension tends to be increasingly critical and thus constantly less alienated" (ibid.) This argument constitutes a highly relevant suggestion for educating about datafication: that to enter into dialogue and present real-world problems within their wider context could solve the difficulties people seem to have with imagining concrete negative consequences of data systems, as expressed for example by participants in my prior study (Sander 2020a).

Moreover, Freire contends that "only dialogue, which requires critical thinking, is also capable of generating critical thinking" (2017, p. 67). *Critical thinking* – which is at the same time goal and method of Freire's critical pedagogy – constitutes another highly relevant aspect of Freire's pedagogical approach for my study's conceptualisation of critical datafication literacy. The scholar emphasises that "true dialogue cannot exist unless the dialoguers engage in critical thinking", and he defines engaging students in "critical thinking and the quest for mutual humanization" as a key goal of his liberating pedagogy (ibid., p. 65; 48). Freire defines critical thinking as:

> Thinking which discerns an indivisible solidarity between the world and the people and admits of no dichotomy between them – thinking which perceives reality as process, as transformation, rather than as a static entity – thinking which does not separate itself from action, but constantly immerses itself in temporality without fear of the risks involved. (ibid., p. 65)

This quote highlights not only the parallels between CP and Bildung, which will be further detailed below, but also illustrates that for Freire, thinking and transformative actions are closely interwoven. This is confirmed by secondary literature that outlines that for Freire, thinking is "not an object lesson in test-taking, but a tool for self-determination and civic engagement" (Giroux 2010, p. 716). Similar to (politische) Bildung, Freire views pedagogy as a way to empower students towards "reading the world critically" and "intervening in the larger social order as part of the responsibility of an informed citizenry" (ibid.). Freire's CP aims for learners to realise "their own power as critically engaged citizens" (ibid., p. 717), and to encourage them to "act as active agents" with a critical consciousness that "helps them evaluate the validity, fairness, and authority within their educational and living situations" (Aliakbari and Faraji 2011, p. 80). These goals of encouraging learners to think critically and become empowered citizens constitute highly relevant objectives for critical datafication literacy as well.

The notion of critical consciousness, or *conscientização,* constitutes the third particularly relevant aspect of Freire's critical pedagogy for my theoretical framework. Conscientização is a concept developed by Freire throughout his work. Simply put, Freire argues that dialogue and critical thinking help students develop a certain consciousness of themselves and their situation in the world (see e.g., 2017, p. 42f). This consciousness cannot be reached through propaganda or "implanted" by leadership, but it can only emerge through dialogue and critical thinking "by means of which people discover each other to be 'in a situation'" (ibid., p. 41; 82). Through this critical consciousness, an "authentic transformation of reality" takes place, in order "to humanize women and men" (ibid., p. 156). Despite Freire's very specific context, the concept of critical consciousness can easily be adapted to the issue of datafication. In today's societies, it is similarly necessary that people become aware of their situation in our datafied world – i.e., how datafication affects their lives and our societies – and to critically reflect this situation. Many scholars and activists further argue that people, rather than corporations, should own their data – similar to the way Freire emphasises that workers need to be the owners of their own labour (ibid.).

Parallels to Bildung and Digital and Data Literacy

Similar to Bildung, Freire's critical pedagogy understands education as "an ongoing activity" and views humans continuously "in the process of *becoming*—as unfinished, uncompleted beings in and with a likewise unfinished reality" (Freire 2017, p. 57, emphasis in original). In order to prepare students "for a self-managed life" (Aronowitz, 2009, p.ix), and to improve this unfinished reality and work towards a "more socially just world" (Giroux 2010, p. 717), Freire argues that critical pedagogy "must begin with the human-world relationship" (Freire 2017, p. 58). As outlined in the previous chapter, Bildung is similarly always concerned with this relationship, and similarly works towards empowered, independent citizens.

Apart from this, Freire highlights that critical pedagogy can help with people's *resignation* in light of seemingly overwhelming power structures by developing a "deepened consciousness of their situation" that allows them to apprehend their situation as "an historical reality susceptible of transformation" (2017, p. 58). Through such consciousness, resignation can be replaced with a drive for transformation and inquiry as learners feel more in control of their situation in the world (ibid.).

As outlined in chapter 2.1, resignation in light of powerful digital companies and a wish for more control over one's data are key challenges in datafied societies. Thus, critical datafication literacy can learn much from CP in terms of how to fight resignation with critical consciousness and empowerment. Moreover, Freire developed an "emancipatory theory of literacy" together with his colleague Donaldo Macedo (1987, p. 6). The authors view their critical literacy as "inherently a political project", aiming to develop "democratic public spheres" (ibid., p. 7; 2). Freire and Macedo's literacy aims to empower citizens and to give them "a voice in both shaping and governing their society", thus promoting "democratic and emancipatory change" (ibid., p. 2; 141). Further, they highlight that literacy should not be "approached as merely a technical skill to be acquired", but rather as a "necessary foundation for cultural action for freedom, a central aspect of what it means to be a self and socially constituted agent" (p. 7). Thus, this understanding of literacy not only shows resemblances to the concept of Bildung but also reemphasises the need for critical literacies that go beyond instrumental skills, strengthening the key argument of chapters 2.2 and 3.1.

Overall, Freire's understanding of education and literacy, while developed within a very specific historic and geographic context, offers many relevant insights and connection points to various education contexts, and has had considerable influence on the field of education in Latin America and beyond. Freire's work has been particularly popular in the Southern hemisphere and "most totalitarian states" (Macedo 2014, p. 12), but has also influenced many educators and academics in the Western world. Although Freire's acceptance in the West has been "more problematic" than in societies that are struggling with "colonialism and other forms of totalitarianism" (ibid., p. 15), and some scholars argue that his ideas are not yet appropriately appreciated or understood by Western academics and educators (ibid.; Shaull 2014), others consider his texts a 'classic' and argue that since the 1980s, there has been "no intellectual on the North American educational scene who has matched either his theoretical rigor or his moral courage" (Giroux 2010, p. 718).

Moreover, the cited scholars agree on the relevance of Freire's critical pedagogy for today's societies. They highlight that CP's emancipatory nature (Aliakbari and Faraji 2011, p. 77) and its focus on the "relationship between democracy and pedagogy" make Freire's work in fact "more relevant today than when [it was] first published" (Giroux 2010, p. 717). Besides Freire's specific context of education, the parallels of his situation to today's societies "should not be overlooked", particularly in relation to digital technologies, as "our advanced technological society is rapidly making objects of most of us and subtly programming us into conformity to the logic of its system" (Shaull 2014, p. 33f). Applying Freire's language to today's context, Shaull continues to state that "the young perceive that their right to say their own word has been stolen from them" and emphasises the importance of "the struggle to win it back" (ibid.). It is this struggle of empowering citizens in increasingly datafied societies for which CP can offer highly valuable insights.

3.3.3 Applying Freire's Critical Pedagogy to Data Literacy Approaches

It seems that other scholars agree with CP's relevance for educating about digital and data technologies, as there are a number of digital and data literacy concepts that build on Freire's work. In fact, Špiranec, Kos and George's systematic critical review of 99 critical data literacy publications found that authors almost exclusively turn to Freire's CP as a pedagogic approach for critical data literacies (2019). The following section presents key relevant Freirean critical data literacies and analyses what can be learnt from these for the conceptualisation of critical datafication literacy.

Data Literacy Based on Freire – A Popular Approach

Many authors see particularly Freire's notion of a critical consciousness as fruitful for educating about digital and data technologies, arguing that such consciousness is needed for navigating today's complex digital societies (e.g., Hammer 2011; Garcia et al. 2015), or drawing their definition of 'critical' from Freire's work (Hautea et al. 2017). Others propose to connect Freire's critical consciousness to data activism approaches (e.g., Milan 2017), thus fostering "resource mobilization and critical conscious making" (Meng and DiSalvo 2018, p. 1). Freire's approach of empowering learners through literacy education has also been applied to big data's "empowerment problem", such as in D'Ignazio and Bhargava's "big data literacy" (2015, p. 5). Moreover, Philip et al. have argued that technology or knowledge about big data alone will not suffice to "address fundamental issues of equity and justice in society" but that "self-transformation, dialogue, and political struggle" in the sense of Freire's work are "more likely avenues for change" (2013, p. 112).

These few examples – out of an extensive corpus of Freirean-inspired approaches to educating about digital and data technologies – already highlight that CP offers many useful insights for critical data literacies. Two publications have been identified as particularly relevant for my theoretical framework as they examine parallels and points of connection between Freire's critical pedagogy and approaches of critical data literacy in detail.

Tygel and Kirsch: Contributions of Paulo Freire to Critical Data Literacy

Firstly, Tygel and Kirsch's "critical data literacy" was already presented in chapter 2.2. However, besides suggesting a new literacy concept, Tygel and Kirsch also provide an in-depth analysis of parallels between Freirean literacy and data literacy. The authors identify four stages of Freire's literacy method: An investigation, thematisation, problematisation, and systematisation stage, which they then apply to data literacy (2016, p. 111f). As figure 2 shows, the four stages can be easily adapted to goals of data literacy. However, it should be noted that the authors follow an understanding of data literacy that predominantly focusses on *using* data, aiming for the skills to use and deal with data sets, as well as learning to critically view these data sets, question where they came from, what they represent and which potential biases they might include. Thus, the goals of data literacy depicted in figure 2 mostly focus on the (critical) use of data, and broader issues such as problematising the implications of datafication on people's lives and our society are not necessarily considered.

Figure 2: The four stages of Freire's critical pedagogy applied to data literacy (from Tygel and Kirsch 2016, p. 113).

Stage	**Literacy**	**Data Literacy**	**Result**
Investigation	Understanding of educand's context, and discovery of socially relevant themes in that reality		Survey of vocabulary universe: source for generative themes and thematic axes.
Thematisation	Coding and decoding of words and understanding of its social meaning	Coding of the themes into existing (or not) data, and decoding for understanding realities	Generative theme and thematic axis coded as images, film or data
Problematisation	Finding contradictions surrounding the decoded themes, and demystifying the realities	Discovering non-neutrality in data: which aspects are exposed by data, and which are hidden?	Critical view about the themes
Systematisation	Organization, interpreting, and presentation of the lived experience	Organizing and interpreting reality through data, and communicating discoveries	Communication products

Nevertheless, Tygel and Kirsch's adaption of the Freirean literacy approach to the field of data literacy provides relevant insights for this study's theoretical framework. Most relevant here is the third stage, in which the "non-neutrality" and lacking transparency of data is problematised and the authors call to "unveil what is behind the scenes" (2016, pp. 113; 116). Although the main focus still lies on data skills and learning to "use data with critical consciousness", this stage also includes broader, potentially societal, perspectives as the authors urge to problematise the non-neutrality of data "in a critical perspective of data literacy education" (ibid., p. 116). While the examples they provide mostly relate to the use of data sets, questions around the non-neutrality and lacking transparency of data can easily be transferred to critical education about broader issues around datafication.

Moreover, again building on Freire, Tygel and Kirsch emphasise the "emancipatory character" of their suggested data literacy concept (2016, p. 113). They argue that their literacy concept can be "analysed in two dimensions: the technical abilities and the emancipation achieved through the literacy process" (ibid.). In this context, they observe that "there seems to be a natural tendency for this [technical] dimension to suppress the emancipatory one" (ibid.). The authors argue that given the high technical complexity of data manipulation and the many technical skills that individuals need to master, there might be a tendency for learners to "leave behind the critical reflection about the social meanings of data in the world, and therefore the emancipatory perspective may be put in background" (ibid., p. 113f). This is in line with the findings of chapter 2.2, which highlighted the strong focus on instrumental data literacy approaches in the literature – suggesting that this tendency exists not only with learners but also with scholars and practitioners of data literacy. Overall, Tygel and Kirsch's analysis of contributions of Paulo Freire to critical data literacy and their "Freirean inspired critical data literacy" clearly demonstrate how many parallels and connection points exist between Freire's CP and critical datafication literacy.

Markham: "Critical Pedagogy as a Response to Datafication"

The second key relevant text is Markham's adaption of CP to the challenges of datafication (2019). While also drawing parallels from Freire and CP to data literacy, Markham does not provide a fully developed theoretical conceptualisation of a "Freirean inspired data literacy" like Tygel and Kirsch's paper. Instead, Markham's article constitutes "more of a manifesto", which argues that "critical pedagogy, combined with a strong qualitative orientation, can challenge quantification, datafication, and computational logics" and which provides suggestions on how to implement such "critical data pedagogy" (2019, pp. 759; 754; 755). Markham, in contrast to Tygel and Kirsch, takes a broad and decidedly critical approach to data literacy, omitting data skills in her literacy approach and rather aiming for critical reflection of the growing datafication of our societies. Her article exemplifies her suggested "*critical pedagogy of the digitally oppressed*" by an ongoing research project and suggests ways to implement such pedagogy, which combines "the strengths of critical approaches and qualitative epistemologies" and aims for "understanding and critically analyzing data, datafication, and other aspects of the digital era" (ibid., p. 755, emphasis added; p. 754).

In her ongoing research project, Markham has been taking a CP approach and training youth in self-reflexive ethnographic analyses of their own social media experiences since 2012 (2019, p. 755). The author criticises the usual instrumental, skills-based approach to digital literacy and instead sees critical theory as the "foundation for anything we might call literacy" (beyond "knowing how to read and write") (ibid., p. 757). Instead of letting her student participants read about critical theory, however, Markham encourages them to actively apply critical theory through watching or having an experience (ibid.). She further argues that students should not be convinced that "big data are bad or wrong" but should rather be supported "to learn for themselves that they are being tracked and calculated as data in ways they cannot see or don't notice" (ibid., p. 758). As a side benefit, Markham points out, her students "begin to pay attention to how this might serve others' interests more than their own", and they can "begin to see the flaw in the idea that we simply trade privacy for convenient access" (Markham 2019, p. 758). Moreover, Markham aims to "raise questions and cause a chain reaction whereby participants raise their own questions and ask their parents, siblings, friends, and colleagues to also raise questions" (ibid., p. 756). All of these approaches are very much in line with Freire's CP, and they offer novel insights on how to learn from CP for critical education about datafication.

The findings of Markham's ongoing research project further show that her participants are "highly reflexive and show clear signs of consciousness raising", with many using "a critical lens to analyze their social media use" (Markham 2019, p. 756). For some participants, this made them initially feel bad about themselves or even led them to believe that they "should stop using social media altogether", but "most of this self-negativity wore off" as participants realised the complexity of the situation (ibid.) – a similar finding as in my own prior study (Sander 2020a). These findings of increased critical reflection and a more in-depth understanding of datafication highlight the promising potential of applying Freire's CP to critical data literacy research.

3.3.4 Conclusion

Overall, this chapter demonstrated that despite its very different context of origin, much can be learnt from Freire's CP for the conceptualisation of critical datafication literacy, and there is good reason that this pedagogy has been adopted to data literacy so often in the past. The empowering, emancipatory nature of Freire's pedagogy constitutes a highly valuable approach in light of the new power imbalances and citizens' resignation that arise with the datafication of our societies. CP's focus on critical thinking further offers a much-needed counterbalance to the prevalence of instrumental approaches in data literacy scholarship and practice. Finally, CP's use of dialogue and real-world problems helps address the complexity of many topics related to datafication. However, the use of CP for digital and data literacy conceptualisations has also been criticised. Polizzi summarises key points of criticism, arguing that CP has "perpetuated the idea of social action as necessarily critical of dominant ideologies", and has encouraged citizens' critique of such dominant representations while "only sporadically emphasising the importance of understanding media structures and the broader digital environment where information circulates" (2020b, p. 6). Such risks and limitations should be taken into consideration when taking Freire's critical pedagogy out of its original context and applying it to new contexts such as critical education about datafication.

3.4 Preliminary Framework for Critical Datafication Literacy

This chapter aims to bring the findings of the preceding theoretical chapters together and draw conclusions from them in order to develop a preliminary framework for critical datafication literacy. As already outlined in the introduction chapter, the overarching goal of this study was to develop an in-depth theoretical framework for critical education about datafication. This framework takes not only existing critical data literacy conceptualisations into consideration but also learns from established educational approaches as well as practitioners of critical data education. The first two steps of this framework development took place throughout the previous chapters. After reviewing, analysing and categorising existing (critical) data literacies in chapter 2.2, the chapters 3.1 to 3.3 examined key texts from the three selected established educational approaches (digital) media literacy, (politische) Bildung, and critical pedagogy in detail. Each approach was analysed with regard to what makes this educational approach unique and what can be learnt from this approach for critical datafication literacy.

After these most relevant aspects were identified, they were visualised in a thematic map, and patterns and parallels between the different educational approaches were investigated. These key points and patterns make up my study's theoretical findings and the theoretical core of the developed literacy framework. Thus, the previous chapters went beyond a mere review of the literature, but rather constituted a detailed analysis and transfer of the selected educational concepts to the field of critical data literacy. In doing so, my study aims to contribute to a "more complete theorisation" of critical data education that is urgently needed (Pangrazio and Sefton-Green 2020, p. 208).

3.4.1 The Terminology

As outlined throughout the last chapters, many different terms can be applied to the practice of educating about data technologies. While most English-language approaches use some variation of the term "literacy" even when aiming for critical perspectives, in the German language discourse, "literacy" is often associated with skills-based approaches. Here, reflective and critical approaches tend to use terms such as "*Bildung*" (education), "*Souveränität*" (sovereignty), or "*Mündigkeit*" (responsibility/autonomy). All these concepts provide new and useful insights to the conceptualisation of critical datafication literacy, but particularly the German "*politische Bildung*" strongly influenced the development of this preliminary framework for critical datafication literacy. Politische Bildung aims to promote civic involvement by enabling citizens to orient themselves in the social world and to evaluate and criticise societal phenomena – thus ultimately striving for Mündigkeit (see e.g., Autorengruppe Fachdidaktik 2016). These goals provide useful guidance in defining the goals of critical datafication literacy, as they aim to empower individuals without simply shifting responsibility to citizens (see also below). Therefore, the concept of (politische) Bildung constitutes a strong influence for this preliminary framework.

However, also regarding the term literacy, the theoretical analyses of the previous chapters have provided new insights. As highlighted in chapter 2.2, the term *literacy has been criticised as problematic* because literacy has different meanings for each person, and different notions of power are embedded in different populations' implicit understandings of literacy (Pinney 2020, p. 229). Thus, particularly when working with vulnerable populations, the term literacy can be problematic (ibid.). Scholars have further highlighted that a single definition of critical data literacy may not be possible or even desirable (Fotopoulou 2020, p. 4), whereas others have criticised the "literacification of everything" in light of the emergence of many new literacy concepts (Hug 2019, p. 151). Moreover, as the term literacy is applied to "an ever-increasing variety of practices", some argue that its specific meaning has sometimes gotten lost and it has become "a metaphor for 'competence', 'proficiency' or 'being functional'" (Lankshear and Knobel 2011, p. 21).

Nevertheless, other scholars have argued that literacy as a concept remains useful despite these criticisms because it allows to account for sociocultural factors and it enables people to ask critical questions about power relations and inequality (Pinney 2020, p. 227). Pangrazio and Sefton-Green make a strong case for the *usefulness of data literacy as a term*, arguing that literacy always possesses a "learning or pedagogic dimension" and is "usually understood as a process", making the term a "useful modifier" as it aims to establish normative principles and enable individuals to participate in society (2020, p. 217). In fact, they argue that literacy has moved from being a technical process of learning (such as learning to read and write) to "a way of ensuring full and complete participation in wider society" (ibid.). Thus, they understand literacy as "a useful shorthand to explain how individuals are able to make sense of complex underlying patterns and to relate them to commonly shared and understood theoretical insights" (ibid., p. 213). It is this definition of literacy that informs the use of the term in my study. However, as Pangrazio and Sefton-Green further highlight, "data literacy requires a more complete theorisation if it is to stand as a meaningful response to datafication" (ibid., p. 217). As outlined above, the framework for critical datafication literacy being developed throughout my study aims to contribute to such in-depth theorisation.

Another terminological consideration concerns the *grammatical form of the term literacy*. As highlighted in chapter 2.2, some scholars have argued for the plural form of "literacies" when conceptualising critical data education. Reasons for this include an understanding of literacies "as always socially and culturally situated" (Pangrazio and Selwyn 2019, p. 426), or the wish to highlight the "multiplicity and interconnection of data literacy practices with other literacies" (Fotopoulou 2020, p. 4; see also Golden 2017).[3] Others have argued that different audiences need different literacies and that the use of the singular term may suggest a "homogeneous understanding of the learner and their needs" (Jansen 2021, p. 9). However, I made a conscious decision in my study to differentiate between the *theoretical concept* of critical datafication literacy and the *practical implementation* of this framework (see 3.4.4). Similar to educational concepts such as (politische) Bildung, I argue that the literacy developed in my study consists of specific *educational objectives*, which are then adapted to different *educational contexts* and *groups of learners*. The theoretical concept of critical datafication literacy can thus be seen as the connecting element between the countless educational settings in which critical education about datafication can be fostered – providing guidance on the educational objectives to follow and to adapt to each setting. For this reason, working with a singular literacy term is most appropriate for this framework.

The final terminological decision concerns the *term "data"* in critical data literacy conceptualisations. As highlighted before, I have developed an initial "critical big data literacy" concept prior to this research project (Sander 2020c). While this concept's objectives are still valid and are being refined and extended in this study, the term "big data" is less suitable now than it was in 2018, when I first started working on this initial conceptualisation. Today, the term is more prevalent in the economic sector than in critical research, and its use in the critical data studies research field seems to have been replaced by the term "datafication". As defined in the first chapter, datafication describes the transformation processes in society prompted by the increasing use of data technologies. Thus, this term suggests a reflection of the broader societal implications of digital technologies and is therefore more appropriate for a framework for critical education about datafication than "data" or "big data". For these reasons, I decided on selecting the term "*critical datafication literacy*" for the literacy concept that is being developed throughout my study.

3 A more in-depth discussion of the plural use of literacies is offered by the research field "New Literacies Studies" (e.g., Street 1997; Gee 2005; Lankshear and Knobel 2011). This field was also analysed as part of this research project, but an extensive discussion had to be omitted from the book due to space constraints. Nevertheless, insights from this field have informed my research.

3.4.2 The Goals

An initial guideline for potential goals of critical education about datafication was provided by my previous concept of critical big data literacy, which aimed at awareness, understanding and ability to critically reflect upon big data collection practices, data uses and the possible risks and implications that come with these practices, as well as the ability to implement this knowledge for a more informed internet usage (Sander 2020a; Sander 2020c). These goals have been refined, revised, extended, and theoretically underpinned by the findings of the theoretical analyses conducted throughout the previous chapters.

One key goal that has emerged is that critical datafication literacy should contribute to an ongoing process of learning, aiming at *reflective understanding* of datafication. Instead of focussing on the passing of specific knowledge, critical datafication literacy should rather empower citizens' *critical thinking*, aiming for reflective understanding, or "critical consciousness", of the datafied world around them, as well as enabling citizens to *imagine alternative data futures*. Besides this critical understanding, such literacy should aim to empower citizens to an informed societal and political participation and greater *agency*, ultimately aiming for *Mündigkeit* – the ability to grapple with society, politics and economy in an informed and self-determined manner – and thus fostering an empowered and informed citizenry in datafied societies. According to Milioni and Papa's user typology, critical datafication literacy would thus aim for an "*enlightened user*", who has the opportunity to turn into a "resisting" or "emancipated user" – if they choose to do so (2019, p. 6f).

What is important in this context is that while this preliminary understanding of critical datafication literacy aims for self-determination and empowerment of citizens, which might also include fostering people's abilities to protect their data, it recognises that it is crucial to *not merely shift responsibility to the individuals.* This can not only discourage citizens and may lead to resignation, but it is also a fallacy as not all areas of data collection and usage can be controlled by individuals' actions. It is therefore necessary to find a balance between encouraging people to protect their data, while not making them feel as if it is solely their responsibility to address the risks and challenges that come with the datafication of our societies.

3.4.3 The Content

The theoretical analyses of the previous chapters further identified several key findings in terms of the content of critical datafication literacy. Based on this, it can be said that critical datafication literacy – as defined in this preliminary framework – should educate about the *process of datafication* and its *implications* on individuals as well as wider political, societal and economic impacts. To provide a basis for this awareness and understanding, it is likely necessary to foster *understanding* of how data is collected about citizens, and about the *non-neutrality* of data and algorithms. This should not be too technical or specific to one medium, but should rather aim at making complex principles comprehensible, using concrete examples, and connecting to wider societal or political issues.

Moreover, based on the approach of politische Bildung, there should be no set of specific topics for critical datafication literacy, but its *objects of learning should rather be determined by current challenges* to democratic self-determination deriving from data systems. In line with this, the focus should lie on understanding of the *(infra)structural changes* in society through datafication rather than on topics around the content of digital media. Finally, based on the literature analysed in the previous chapters, critical datafication literacy should include *constructive advice* to avoid resignation, for example fostering citizens' ability to protect their data – while considering the balance outlined above.

3.4.4 The Implementation

Finally, the theoretical findings of the previous chapters made some suggestions on how to practically implement critical datafication literacy. To start with the key finding here: Scholarship on critical data literacy highlighted that *no one-size-fits-all approach* to literacy is possible, and that different audiences require different approaches (see e.g., Carmi et al. 2020). This also suggests that no generic guidance for the implementation of a theoretical concept such as critical datafication literacy should be included in this framework, as the framework's goals and content should rather be adapted to each group of learners based on their abilities and needs as well as the specific educational context. However, some broader recommendations can be made based on the literature.

Several educational concepts analysed in the previous chapters highlighted that education about data should take place *with* the learners, aiming for dialogue and treating the learners as equals by supporting them in forming their own opinion rather than telling them what to think. This could, for example, be implemented by confronting learners with *real-world problems* (e.g., Freire 2017, p. 54) or using *interactive and participatory* approaches (e.g., Iliadis and Russo 2016; Agesilaou and Kyza 2021). Moreover, it was highlighted that critical education about datafication *does not need to take place through digital technologies*, but that many creative analogue alternatives exist as well (e.g., Pötzsch 2019). When using digital methods, they should be chosen with care, as they can come with a "hidden curriculum" (Mertala 2020). Finally, it was suggested to consider people's "*networks of literacy*" (Carmi et al. 2020), aiming for a "chain reaction" of critical thought, in which one person's awareness and critical understanding is fostered and this person can pass this critical thinking about datafication on to many others in their social networks (Markham 2019, p. 756).

Overall, the theoretical analyses of the previous chapters provided many insights for the development of this preliminary framework for critical datafication literacy. The two literature review chapters highlighted the need for more education about datafication and a stronger theoretical foundation for such literacy, but also revealed how much scholarship on critical approaches to data literacy already exists that this framework can build on. The following analyses of the three selected educational approaches then demonstrated not only how much the critical data literacy field can learn from these more established educational fields, but also that there are many parallels between these different educational notions. All three fields thus provided highly valuable and novel insights for the terminology, goals, content and implementation of critical datafication literacy. The preliminary framework that was developed based on these findings and was presented in this chapter will be further refined and substantiated through the empirical findings of this study, and the final framework for critical datafication literacy will be presented in chapter seven.

4. Methods

4.1 Introduction and Project Design

The empirical research in my study examined online educational resources about datafication and how they are created as well as applied by educators as one way to teach about datafication. Although these resources constitute one of the longest-standing and most established approaches to critical data education, they have been examined in very few studies thus far. Little is known about their objectives, educational strategies, their creators' considerations, and their use by educators. My study addresses these gaps in research and aims to learn from these practices in order to develop a theoretically and empirically grounded framework for critical datafication literacy. In line with this, the empirical research took three different approaches, which examined three key research questions:

a) What is the range, shape and focus of *online critical data literacy resources*?
b) What are the goals, strategies, and experiences of *creators* of online critical data literacy resources?
c) What are *educators'* experiences with the topic of datafication and what do they need and wish for from a critical data literacy resource?

The research design of the study took a mixed methods approach, combining qualitative methodologies such as expert interviews and a qualitative survey with more quantitative methods such as a content analysis. This mixed methods approach helped to address the different research questions of my study and allowed insights into critical data literacy practice from different perspectives. The expert interviews were able to complement the '*what*' (do online resources look like?) of the content analysis with a '*why*' (are they created this way?). Combining qualitative with quantitative methods can help in locating a target population (in this study the online critical data literacy resource creators); can increase the generalisability, validity and reliability of research; and, importantly, it can provide more robust understanding of research results by triangulation of methods (Hesse-Biber 2010, p. 465f). Triangulating seeks to "find convergence" or validate research findings by comparing results from different methods (ibid.). In my study, the triangulation of methods allowed for a more complete picture of critical data literacy – through identifying parallels as well as contradictions between different findings. As will be outlined throughout this chapter, one key characteristic of my study was that the different stages and methodologies continuously built on and informed each other. These reciprocal influences are illustrated in figure 3.

Moreover, as outlined in the introduction chapter, my study included a collaboration with the NGO Privacy International. The NGO and I closely collaborated in the final knowledge mobilisation project (see chapter 4.5); but the NGO also acted as an advisor throughout conducting the research, and knowledge exchange in the form of online meetings and email communication with PI executive director Dr Gus Hosein took place in the different stages of the research.[1] During this exchange, Dr Gus Hosein provided feedback on many of the study's methodological decisions. While this feedback and the NGO's considerable experience in practically educating about datafication constituted a very valuable second perspective, which helped to inform my methodological decisions, it should be clarified that the NGO never tried to exert influence over how the project was designed, or the research conducted. The final say in all methodological decisions was mine and the NGO was not involved in the analysis or interpretation of the findings. The following chapter will discuss the study's methodological considerations and highlight the NGO's involvement in this process.

1 In person meetings were originally intended but were not possible in the first 2.5 years of the research project due to the ongoing COVID-19 pandemic.

Figure 3: Visualisation of the project's mixed methods approach and its reciprocal influences.

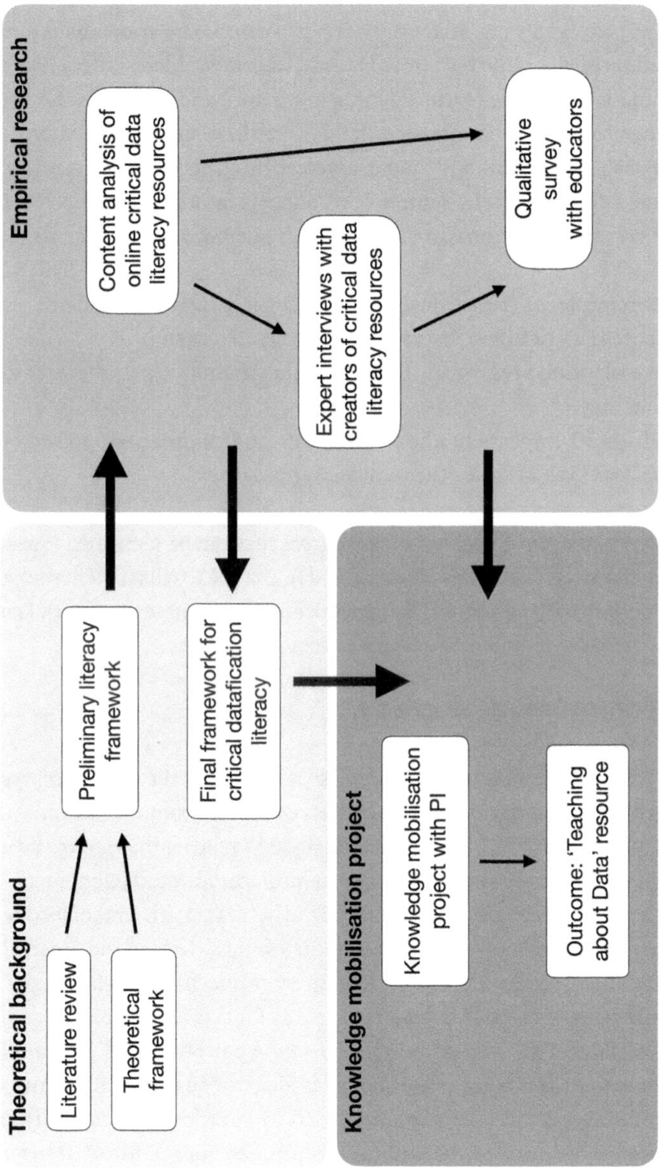

4.2 Identifying, Analysing and Selecting Online Critical Data Literacy Resources

In order to gain better understanding of how critical education about datafication is fostered through online resources (such as websites, videos, interactive tools and others), and what can be learnt from their creators and educators for the further development of critical datafication literacy, the first step consisted of gaining an overview of such resources and their characteristics. This was also necessary to make an informed decision on the sample of resource creators for the expert interviews. Thus, the research questions for this first stage of empirical research were:

1) What examples of critical data literacy resources can be identified?
2) What are their defining features and who created them?
3) Are the identified resources in line with the preliminary framework for critical data literacy?
4) Which (best) implement the ideas, goals and approaches presented in this framework? Which take other, unusual approaches?

In order to systematically record the resources that can be identified (question one) and their characteristics (question two), and to analyse to what extent they are in line with the preliminary theoretical framework (questions three and four), I conducted a content analysis of online critical data literacy resources.

4.2.1 Content Analysis as a Method

Content analysis is a research technique that allows for the "objective, systematic, and quantitative description of the manifest content of communications" (Berelson 1952, p. 147). The method was originally designed to "bring the rigour and authority of 'natural' scientific inquiry to the study of human and social phenomena" (Deacon et al. 2007, p. 118). However, despite its goal of a "systematic and objective analysis of any particular text" by "essentially counting things" (Davies and Mosdell 2009, p. 98), content analysis does not provide entirely "value-free insights to the study of content" (Deacon et al. 2007, p. 118). One reason for this is that content analysis is "a directive method; it gives answers to the questions you pose" (ibid., p. 119). Nevertheless, the method's ability to "count things" is ideal to "quantify salient and manifest features of a large number of texts" (ibid.). Its key purpose is to "identify and count the occurrence of specified characteristics or dimensions of texts" (Hansen 1998, p. 95) – in this case, to record and count characteristics of a large number of online critical data literacy resources. Although originally developed for "the analysis of textual materials, namely newsprint, in social research", the method can easily be adapted to other forms of media – such as online educational resources about datafication – and has been used for "nearly any cultural artifact" (ibid.).

Content analysis can be seen as a "hybrid technique" between quantitative and qualitative methods, bridging "statistical formalism and the qualitative analysis of the materials" (Bauer 2000, p. 132). One key strength of the method is its ability to reduce the complexity of a collection of texts in a systematic manner, thereby "distil[ling] a large amount of material into a short description of some of its features" (ibid., p. 132f). This ability to produce "a big picture" (Deacon et al. 2007, p. 119) makes content analysis an ideal method to gain an overview of the key characteristics of a large number of online critical data literacy resources that have been hardly researched so far. Further strengths of the method include its "systematic and public" approach, that it "mainly uses 'naturally' occurring raw data", "can deal with large amounts of data", and offers a set of "mature and well-documented procedures" (Bauer 2000, p. 147). Bauer further describes content analysis as "far from being the last word" but argues that it "may be the first step in ordering and characterizing materials in an extended research effort" (ibid., p. 148), which ideally describes the way content analysis is applied in my study.

Limitations of Content Analysis

One key challenge of content analysis has already been outlined above: it can only provide answers to the questions the researcher poses, thus harbouring the risk of overlooking unexpected findings. Moreover, it "tends to focus on frequencies, and so neglects the rare and the absent" (Bauer 2000, p. 148). In my study, this was addressed by including a variable asking for unusual approaches (see below). Content analysis is further "not well suited to studying 'deep' questions about textual and discursive forms" (Deacon et al. 2007, p. 119), or to "interpret the wider social significance or meaning of the quantitative indicators" it generates (Hansen 1998, p. 123). These aspects, Hansen continues, need to be "drawn and developed from the theoretical framework" of one's study (ibid.), which is the case in my study. Related to this, a common fallacy of content analysis is to make inferences about "particular intentions or understandings from the text alone", as "intentions and reception are features of the communicative situation and do not depend on the text alone" but are "co-determined by situational variables" (Bauer 2000, p. 145). My study addressed this limitation by combining the content analysis with qualitative interviews with the resource creators.

A further key challenge of content analysis is the accurate quantification of variables as content analysis does not work reliably "when coders are required to 'read between the lines' to get at latent structures of meaning" (Deacon et al. 2007, p. 124), or when "a considerable degree of interpretation by the coder" is needed (Hansen 1998, p. 115). To overcome these challenges, a detailed codebook (including example cases) was created, and a pilot study conducted.

4.2.2 Conducting the Content Analysis

Sources and Sampling

The total range of content, or *population*, that this study's content analysis examined consisted of English- and German language online resources that educate about datafication. Resources in both languages were considered in order to reach a wider population and because I speak these two languages fluently. The individual resource, such as a website, an online series, a short video or an interactive game was the *sampling unit*, and its characteristics in terms of format and content were the *units of measurement*.

As a first step, a "set of decisions [...] to identify systematically which units of [my] sample fall within the remit of [my] study" was necessary (Deacon et al. 2007, p. 125) – in other words: what counts as an "online resource that educates about datafication"? First, I decided that "online resource" would be understood in very general terms, encompassing *any resource that is available online*, also including, for example, PDF brochures or websites that provided print-out material for educational simulation games. The second question was more difficult to determine: how can resources that "educate about datafication" be defined? To make systematic decisions on this, I defined three qualifying criteria for critical data literacy. These were developed based on this study's theoretical framework and findings from my prior research (2020c), and they aimed at defining critical data literacy resources in the broadest way possible: the resources needed to 1) educate about datafication (the transformation of our societies through data technologies); 2) foster critical reflection of the implications of datafication; and 3) should not require any prior knowledge (see also below).

After specifying this, a decision needed to be made on what sample size of the population to analyse in order to "construct a credible, representative sample" (Deacon et al. 2007, p. 121). Since little research has been conducted on online critical data literacy resources so far, no list of such resources existed and also data on their use and popularity was scarce. Therefore, no sampling frame existed, and a truly representative sample was not possible. Instead, "sampling validity" – finding a sample that "represents the whole body of the text" (Bauer 2000, p. 144) – was considered by identifying a sample that is as broad, diverse and comprehensive as possible, yet feasible in the given time frame.

In order to reach such sample, a variety of sources for critical data literacy resources were examined, including my prior publications (Brand and Sander 2020; Sander 2020c; Sander 2020b); all resources in the database by the Critical Big Data and Algorithmic Literacy Network as of 07.05.2021;[2] resources that were recom-

2 An international network of critical data literacy scholars and practitioners I co-founded in 2020 and that provides an online database of online resources that critically educate about

mended by the project partner Privacy International or during the 2021 Data Justice Conference; and all resources on a list of potential critical data literacy resources that I had maintained for two years prior to starting the content analysis, which included all online resources that I came across or that others had recommended and that, on first glance, seemed to be educating about datafication. In addition, a small number of resources were identified via other, already examined resources. A detailed description of the sampling process and an overview of the numbers of resources identified through each of the sources can be found in the "methodology annotations" (appendix I, section I.I.I).[3]

After all sources listed above were examined, 250 resources were identified in total. Of these, 75 met all three qualifying criteria and were thus fully coded. While the sample was not representative, it consisted of a broad and diverse selection of critical data literacy resources. This was further confirmed by the coding, which highlighted a large variety of the resources' creation contexts and formats. For these reasons, the sample size was considered sufficient for my study. However, the analysis later demonstrated that some characteristics prevailed in the sample. For example, a predominance of resources with a German background was identified. This could be traced back to the high 'success rate' of the German sources of the sample in comparison to the international sources: the two sources through which most critical data literacy resources were identified were 1) the database by the Critical Big Data and Algorithmic Literacy Network, which has many very active German members; and 2) an online collection of German critical data literacy resources that I created as part of my prior work.

Codebook and Coding Sheet

Deciding on "what to count" is a crucial step in any content analysis (Deacon et al. 2007, p. 119). In this regard, my study's interconnection between theory and practice proved useful. The preliminary framework for critical datafication literacy (chapter 3.4) as well as my small previous study of online critical data literacy resources (Sander 2020c) provided a thorough grounding for the content analysis and reduced the risk of asking the "wrong" questions or overlooking relevant aspects and helped to ensure semantic and construct validity (see Bauer 2000, pp. 148; 144; 145). Based on these considerations, the codebook and coding sheet for the content analysis were

datafication and that were recommended by network members. For more information on the database and the resources it includes, see appendix I.I.I.

3 These annotations provide detailed descriptions of the execution of different methodological approaches in this study. This aims to ensure transparency and replicability of the study's methods, which often needed to find novel and creative approaches due to a lack of sampling frames and generally little existing information on online critical data literacy resources.

developed (see appendix III). As described in more detail in the methodology annotations (see appendix I.I.II), the variables were categorised into four sections: section A recorded the resource and its sampling source; B tested for the qualifying criteria for the analysis; C described the resource and its creator; and D examined to what extent a resource was in line with the preliminary critical datafication literacy framework. Section D consisted of five variables: interactive design, different audiences, practical advice, individual responsibility, and real-life examples. These represented key aspects of the preliminary literacy framework and key findings on implementing such literacy into practice. Only if a resource met *all three* of the qualifying criteria, sections C and D were coded.

The variables in section C were either open text fields (e.g., creator name) or gave several answer options (including "other"). If no information on a variable could be found (e.g., publication date), the field was omitted. Moreover, if a resource older than 2015 was identified, it was excluded as it would likely be outdated and not include current issues around datafication.[4] Section D then used the same three answer options for each variable: variable somewhat met, met, or met very well (see appendix I.I.II for further details). As most variables in this section required some amount of interpretation or judgement, "very clear interpretation guidelines" for these variables (Hansen 1998, p. 115) as well as concrete examples were included in the codebook. Finally, the last variable, '19. Special category' intended to highlight resources that take an unusual approach (content or format). Particularly in light of how under-researched the resources are, this helped to balance the content analysis' focus on frequencies, which can sometimes neglect "the rare and the absent" (Bauer 2000, p. 148). Moreover, this focus on unusual approaches helped to avoid a 'self-fulfilling prophecy' in the further development of the literacy framework, and it allowed for an open-minded selection of diverse resources for the next empirical step.

Coding took place using an Excel table to save time and prevent errors (see appendix I.I.II for more details), and a logbook was used to record coding solutions for unexpected cases (see Deacon et al. 2007, p. 130). Being the only coder further minimised reliability challenges, such as inter and intra-coder reliability (see Bauer 2000, p. 143f.).

Piloting

A pilot study was conducted to prepare the content analysis. This "test coding of a small sub-sample of the material [...] helps to reveal inadequacies and/or inconsistencies in the category systems of the coding schedule" (Hansen 1998, p. 118). The pilot was conducted with 20 resources, which were deliberately not taken from sources

---

4 The sample thus included resources created between 2015–2021, along with some resources for which no publication date could be identified.

related to my prior research as this had informed the development of the variables in the first place. The pilot confirmed the usefulness of coding in an excel-sheet and led to a number of smaller changes in the order of variables, the way some variables were coded, and solutions for uncertainties in coding (for details, see appendix I.I.III).

Finally, the analysis of the variables consisted of counting frequencies, calculating total numbers and percentages, comparing results, and creating tables and graphs for data visualisation.

4.3 Learning from the Experts

The next stage of empirical research investigated the inspirations, ideas, and strategies behind the online critical data literacy resources that were analysed in the first stage and examined their creators' underlying understanding of critical data literacy. Expert interviews with ten creators of such resources were conducted in order to learn from them for the conceptualisation of critical datafication literacy and for ways of implementing such literacy into practice.

4.3.1 Qualitative Interviewing and the Special Case of Expert Interviews

Interviews are a commonly used research method in social science research and other research fields. The expert interviews conducted in my study consisted of semi-structured interviews, which are defined by their "flexible and fluid structure" (Mason 2004, p. 1020). Semi-structured interviews are usually organised around a topic list or interview guide rather than using a sequenced script of standardised questions (ibid.). This allows for an open conversation that can be shaped by the interviewee's understandings and the researcher's interests and ensures flexibility in changing the order of questions or reacting to unexpected aspects, while still addressing all questions and themes necessary for the research question (ibid.). Criticisms that semi-structured interviews produce data that cannot be compared are misplaced because they use "a logic where comparison is based on the fullness of understanding of each case, rather than standardization of the data across cases" (ibid., p. 1021). However, semi-structured interviews alone can only produce "partial interpretive understandings" (ibid.), and can therefore usefully be supplemented by other methods, as is the case in the method triangulation of my study. Moreover, interview research always comes with complex power dynamics that need to be considered (Edwards and Holland 2013, p. 78; see also below).

Expert Interviews

Expert interviews are "qualitative semi-structured or open interview[s] with a person holding 'expert knowledge'" (van Audenhove and Donders 2019, p. 179). This "systematic and theory guided process" (ibid., p. 181) has "long been popular in social research" (Bogner et al. 2009, p. 1). The literature differentiates between different types of expert interviews based on the kind of knowledge that is produced. The expert interviews conducted in my study can be categorised as a mix of "systematizing interviews", producing "process knowledge" about the *process of creating critical data literacy resources*, and "explanatory interviews", producing "explanatory knowledge" about my *interviewees' understanding of critical data literacy* (van Audenhove and Donders 2019, p. 183ff).

Strengths and Weaknesses of Expert Interviews

Key advantages of expert interviews are that experts are often relatively easy to access as they are usually embedded in organisational structures (Bogner et al. 2009, p. 2), and that they are confident in their knowledge and opinions so that exclusive knowledge can be created in a comparatively reliable way (van Audenhove and Donders 2019, p. 181). Talking to an expert can further be an "efficient and concentrated method of gathering data", in part because the interviewer and the interviewee often "share a common scientific background or relevance system", which makes "quickly obtaining good results" more likely (Bogner et al. 2009, p. 2). This "shared understanding of the social relevance of the research" together with experts' "professional curiosity", their "desire to help 'make a difference'", and their interest in sharing their "thoughts and ideas with an external expert" can further "increase the level of motivation on the part of the expert to participate" (Bogner et al. 2009, p. 2). Such shared interest in, in this case, educating about datafication often emerged during my interviews.

Nevertheless, expert interviews also come with some methodological weaknesses. As expert interviews are very time consuming, most authors recommend using them only when knowledge is "otherwise difficult to generate" (van Audenhove and Donders 2019, p. 182). Moreover, the "naïve image of the expert as source of objective information [...] has long been problematic" (Bogner et al. 2009, p. 5). Especially when the interviews aim to reconstruct "latent content of meaning", they require "careful validation and a solid theoretical basis" (ibid., p. 5f), which, as outlined above, is the case in my study. Furthermore, expert interviewees can have their own agenda on the topic that is discussed, making it crucial for the researchers to maintain a critical distance. Expert interviews also come with complex power dynamics, as while the interviewer is the one who "defines the situation and who frames the topic and course of the interview" (Edwards and Holland 2013, p. 78), the expert interviewee holds exclusive knowledge and thus has the "power of defining the situation" that they are interviewed about (Meuser and Nagel 2009, p. 18). Therefore, power positions can shift around in expert interviews (Edwards and Holland 2013, p. 78).

Finally, it can be difficult to identify who is an expert, and some authors argue that with an increasing specialisation of expertise, experts can become "mere representatives of specialized knowledge" (Bogner et al. 2009, p. 5). However, Meuser and Nagel provide a useful definition of experts in the context of scientific research, arguing that an individual is defined as an expert "because the researcher assumes – for whatever reason – that she or he has knowledge, which she or he may not necessarily possess alone, but which is not accessible to anybody in the field of action under study" (2009, p. 18).

According to this definition, it is primarily the "exclusive realm of knowledge" that constitutes an expert, and it is this knowledge that the expert interview aims to discover (Meuser and Nagel 2009, p. 18). Thus, the term "expert" is decoupled from "holding a formal position in a hierarchy of occupational status positions", and also, for example, citizen groups or NGOs can be seen as experts (ibid., p. 25). This last argument is particularly relevant for the expert interviews in my study as the interviewees held different formal positions, but all were active participants in the process of creating critical data literacy resources, and this experience and expertise constituted their "exclusive realm of knowledge" for this study.

4.3.2 The Sampling Process and the Final Sample

Purposive Sampling

In order to find the right experts for a study, different strategies can be applied, such as screening specialised literature in the field or using a snowball sampling approach (van Audenhove and Donders 2019, p. 189). However, particularly when different groups or stakeholders are involved, "purposive sampling representing the different perspectives/groups" is recommended (ibid., p. 190). Purposive sampling is a "non-probability form of sampling", in which participants are sampled "in a strategic way, so that those sampled are relevant to the research questions that are posed" (Bryman 2016, p. 408). Often, the goal of purposive sampling is to reach variety in the final sample, with participants "differ[ing] from each other in terms of key characteristics relevant to the research question" (ibid.). As outlined below, this was the case in my study. Thus, while purposive sampling does not lead to a strictly representative sample and does not allow for generalising findings, it can lead to a diverse sample that is relevant to the individual study's research questions. It is therefore particularly suitable when, as in my study, not much is known about the population that is to be interviewed, and the researcher is interested in understanding different perspectives.

Specifically, my study took a sampling approach that has been called "generic purposive sampling" (Bryman 2016, p. 412). In this sampling approach, the researcher initially "establishes criteria concerning the kinds of cases needed to address the research questions" and identifies appropriate cases (ibid. p. 413). Based on this initial sample, the researcher then "samples from those cases that have been identified" (ibid.). In a mixed methods study, this process can be implemented by using the findings of a survey "as the basis for the selection of a purposive sample" (ibid., p. 414). This describes my study's sampling process very well, with the 75 resources identified in the content analysis constituting the initial sample, which constituted the basis to select resource creators for the expert interviews (see below).

Sample Size

Moreover, an appropriate sample size had to be determined. The literature on qualitative interviewing highlights that it is difficult to establish at the outset of a study how many interviews will be necessary (e.g., Bryman 2016, p. 416ff; Malterud et al. 2016). However, there are some guidelines to determine a suitable sample size. As expert interviews are a time-intensive method and the interviews in my study aimed at "generating fine-grained data" rather than making comparisons between groups, a small sample size was appropriate (Bryman 2016, p. 416f). Moreover, Malterud et al.'s notion of "information power" helped to identify a suitable sample size for my study (2016, p. 1753). As the aim for my study's expert interviews was *specific and narrow*; the sample specificity was *dense*; there was a *strong theoretical background*; the study aimed for an *in-depth analysis of a few, selected cases*; and the *quality of dialogue* was expected to be satisfactory due to a strong common interest between participants and researcher, Malterud et al.'s guidelines suggest that the sample held substantial information power (ibid.). Furthermore, the population of interest for my study was very specific and likely small. Based on these methodological considerations, I decided to conduct ten expert interviews, and to reconsider this number as needed during the course of the research based on the knowledge gathered in the interviews.

Sample Selection Process

As a next step, an informed selection of ten creators from the 75 analysed resources had to be made. This selection, on the one hand, aimed at selecting resources that are *in line with the preliminary framework for critical datafication literacy* and are thus particularly relevant for my study. On the other hand, the selection intended to *ensure diversity* as there is no one-size-fits-all approach to literacy and different people need different approaches (see e.g., Carmi et al. 2020, p. 43; chapter 3.4), and in order to gain new insights for the further development of the framework and avoid a self-fulfilling prophecy. The goal was thus to balance these two objectives rather than selecting the 'best' ten resources for the expert interviews.

In addition, two crucial findings from the literature were considered in the selection process. First, the selected resources should include *constructive advice*. This is important to encourage learners to take action and for avoiding learners' resignation (Pangrazio and Sefton-Green 2020, p. 218; Sander 2020c, p. 13; Bilstrup et al.

2022, p. 234). Second, the resources should *not convey the idea that it is up to the individual to address the challenges of datafication* (for example through self-data protection). Such shift of responsibility to the individuals is highly problematic as it can be discouraging and may lead to resignation, but also because citizens' agency to control the collection and use of their data is limited (Aßmann et al. 2016; Mihailidis 2018; Pangrazio and Selwyn 2019; Carmi et al. 2020). A detailed description of how I implemented these considerations and objectives in the multi-level selection process and selected the final ten resources in cooperation with the project partner Privacy International can be found in appendix I.II.I.

The Final Sample

The final sample for the expert interviews then consisted of ten resources, which were produced in six different countries (Canada, France, Germany, Switzerland, United Kingdom, United States), addressed different target groups (adults in general, teenagers, kids, parents, educators, activists, policymakers and technologists), and applied a variety of different design formats (see table 2). Moreover, the creator backgrounds varied, with three civil society actors, two journalistic creation contexts, two resources created by researchers or private individuals, one by a public institution, one by a museum, and one by a commercial actor. Thus, it can be said that the goal of reaching a diverse sample was achieved.

Table 2: The final sample of ten resources, including the interviewed creators and the different design formats the resources applied.

Nr.	Resource Name and URL	Creator / Interviewee	Format(s)
1	Anna. Das vernetzte Leben https://www.annasleben.de/	Ludwig Reichers-torfer	Website, including videos, podcasts, short stories and downloadable dossiers
2	Automating NYC https://automating.nyc/	Akina Younge, Deepra Yusuf, (Elyse Voegeli), Jon Truong	Interactive website
3	Center for Humane Technology https://www.humanetech.com/	David Jay	Website, including videos, podcasts, teaching material, data protection toolkits and recommendations for further resources

4	Clear Your Tracks https://www.clearyourtracks.org/	Ed Parkes	Website
5	Datak – A game about personal data https://www.datak.ch/	Julien Schekter	Online serious game
6	Do Not Track https://donottrack-doc.com/en/	Brett Gaylor	Interactive web series
7	Lehrmittel Big Data https://www.mfk.ch/bigdata/	Carmen Siegenthaler	Website and teaching material, including videos and recommendations for further resources
8	Lernparcours Big Data http://bigdata.jfc.info/lernparcours.html	Esther Lordieck	Website, including teaching material, videos and recommendations for further resources
9	Me and My Shadow https://myshadow.org/	Fieke Jansen	Website, including teaching material, videos and data protection toolkits
10	My Data and Privacy Online https://www.lse.ac.uk/my-privacy-uk	Mariya Stoilova	Website, including videos and recommendations for further resources

4.3.3 Developing the Interview Guide

As outlined above, the expert interviews in my study were organised around an interview guide. The key goal was to understand the creators' *idea of literacy* and the *strategies* they applied to foster this literacy with the users of their resource.

Cooperation with the "Civic Participation Project" by the Data Justice Lab

In a first step, a preliminary interview guide was developed and tested in preliminary interviews. This took place in cooperation with a research project called "Towards Democratic Auditing: Civic Participation in the Scoring Society" by the Data Justice Lab, Cardiff University.[5] One way in which I cooperated with this project was

5 This project was closely interrelated with my research, and I participated in the workstream of the project by informing the literature review on data literacy, co-developing and co-publishing a guidebook on "Critical data literacy tools for advancing data justice" together with Jess Brand (Brand and Sander 2020), and conducting and analysing expert interviews together. A first summary of these findings can already be found in a project report (Hintz et al. 2022, p. 145–160), and more detailed findings are presented in this study (chapter 5.2).

by conducting and analysing expert interviews with creators of critical data literacy resources together with Jess Brand in May and June 2020. These preliminary expert interviews acted as a pilot study for my research project. We asked all interviewees if they agreed to a follow-up interview one year later and all agreed. Despite the Civic Participation project's slightly different perspective on critical data literacy – examining ways to foster critical data literacy *for public sector workers* – three resource creators interviewed in these preliminary interviews were part of my study's final interview sample: Akina Younge and Deepra Yusuf (*Automating NYC*), Brett Gaylor (*Do Not Track*), and Fieke Jansen (*Me and My Shadow*). Thus, my interviews with these creators were conducted as follow-up interviews,[6] allowing me to inquire further about aspects that were mentioned in the first interview and to ask questions specific to my project focus and the findings of my content analysis.

Developing the Final Interview Guide

These preliminary expert interviews helped refine the focus of this study's expert interviews and informed the development of the interview guide. After my study's theoretical framework had identified *scholarly insights for critical datafication literacy*, the content analysis had examined *existing educational resources about datafication*, and the preliminary interviews in cooperation with the Civic Participation project focussed on the *practical process of creating* such resources and their *strengths and limitations*; the expert interviews in this study aimed to close gaps in understanding. Therefore, the goal was to analyse the creators' *understanding of literacy* and their *idea of an empowered datafied citizen* as well as their *strategies* in reaching such literacy and empowerment. Besides the cooperation with the Civic Participation project, the collaboration with Privacy International informed the development of the interview guide, with PI providing valuable insights and open questions on the process of creating educational resources about data.

The final interview guide then consisted of four sections (see appendix VI): The first section served as an introduction, asking general questions about the creator's *background and their resource*. The second section asked about the *strategies and approaches* that were used to reach the creators' educational goals, including one question about findings of the content analysis in regard to the specific resource. The third section then inquired about *practical considerations*, including more sensitive questions, for example about finding funding. This section was particularly informed by Privacy International's experience and the challenges they encountered in their resource creation. Finally, the last section invited interviewees to reflect freely on their field of expertise and provide *final comments*. The design of the interview guide took recommendations from the methodological literature into account, such as asking sensitive and very open questions later in the interview; not forcing

6 Two follow-up interviews were conducted as virtual face-to-face interviews and one via email.

the order of questions but rather leaving room for flexibility and open conversation; adapting the interview guide to each interviewee; and avoiding leading questions (Warren 2004; Meuser and Nagel 2009; van Audenhove and Donders 2019). Moreover, some *optional questions* were included, which were omitted in the question list sent to the interviewees, as they were not key to answering the research question but focussed on specific additional aspects or helped to clarify when an interviewee misunderstood a question (highlighted in grey font, see appendix VI).

After the English interview guide was developed, it was translated into German as the literature recommends conducting expert interviews in the native language of the interviewee (Littig and Pöchhacker 2014). Since I am fluent in both languages and all my interviewees were fluent in either of these languages, with the majority speaking English or German as their native language, this considerably helped the interviewees to "express themselves freely and without the constraints arising from the use of a foreign language" (ibid., p. 1086). My own "cultural experiences" in the United Kingdom and Germany and my familiarity with the academic discourse in both languages allowed for a smooth translation process and accurate translation of key terms (ibid., p. 1092). This further enabled me to conduct the interview analysis bilingually, working with the original transcripts in both languages, and English-language themes – thus keeping the data as original as possible.

4.3.4 Preparing and Conducting the Interviews

After the interview guide was finalised and translated, potential interviewees were contacted via email with a short summary of the research project. Upon positive response, they were sent a comprehensive information sheet and a consent form, providing details on their participation, the use of their data, and giving participants the opportunity to choose if they wanted to remain anonymous (see appendix IV; V). These documents as well as the invitation email and the study's overall research plan were reviewed and approved by the Cardiff University's School of Journalism, Media and Culture Ethics Committee before contacting the interviewees. All ten interviewees indicated in their written consent forms that they wished to be quoted by name. Interviewees were given the choice to be interviewed via telephone or video call. If they chose the latter – which all did – they were further given the choice of their preferred platform (such as Zoom, Teams, Jitsi, Skype or others). This ensured convenience for the interviewees and minimised the likelihood of technical problems, yet it required a certain 'privacy pragmatism' from my side (for more details, see appendix I.II.II).

Considering the context in which the interviews took place (June-September 2021, amidst the ongoing COVID-19 pandemic with social distancing regulations and travel restrictions) and the different locations of the experts (Canada, Germany, Netherlands, Switzerland, UK, US), in-person face-to-face interviews were not an option. Virtual face-to-face interviews further came with several benefits, such as flexibility in terms of geographical locations and scheduling and greater control for participants (Hanna and Mwale 2017, p. 259ff). The normalisation of video calling for work and for staying in touch with loved ones during the COVID-19 pandemic likely contributed to a smooth interview experience. However, many people experienced a "Zoom fatigue" in light of too many video calls in 2021 (cf. Brown Epstein 2020; Bailenson 2021). Furthermore, technical problems and poor internet connection that impact the quality of conversation constitute challenges of virtual interviews. Having already conducted several expert interviews in person, via telephone and through video calling in research projects in the past helped me navigate the process and its challenges. As recommended in the literature, all interviews were audio-recorded with participants giving consent in written form as well as verbally (see e.g., van Audenhove and Donders 2019, p. 192).

Given the qualitative nature of the interviews and the interviewees' passion and interest in the topics of conversation, many interviews were very extensive. Overall, the 12 interviews (including preliminary and follow-up interviews) lasted on average 55 minutes, with two shorter interviews of 26 and 34 minutes, and the ten others ranging from 45 to 81 minutes. This extensive dataset together with my first impression of the interview contents suggested that saturation was reached.

4.3.5 Analysing the Interviews

After conducting the interviews, each interview was transcribed in full. This is recommended for expert interviews, as already the transcription itself is "a reduction of the information available" (van Audenhove and Donders 2019, p. 193). I transcribed some interviews myself and used a professional transcription service for others – all applying the intelligent verbatim style. In total, the interviews produced a significant amount of 192 pages of textual, qualitative data: 142 pages of transcripts and 50 pages of additional documents. The additional documents were provided by the interviewees and included, among others, project concepts and reports on the development of the resource as well as adult learning principles and other methodologies that were applied in creating the resource.

This data was analysed in a thematic analysis using the software NVivo. Thematic analysis "involves the searching across a data set [...] to find repeated patterns of meaning" (Braun and Clarke 2006, p. 15). This method of analysis focusses on "identifying and describing both implicit and explicit ideas within the data" (Guest et al. 2012, p. 10), which are identified by first developing codes from the data and then aggregating these into themes. This makes thematic analysis "the most useful in capturing the complexities of meaning within a textual data set" and a common method of analysis for qualitative interviews (ibid., p. 11). Thematic analyses are particularly useful for *expert* interviews because these typically consist of thematic units –

"passages with similar topics which are scattered about the interviews" (Meuser and Nagel 2009, p. 35). Sequentiality within an individual interview is less relevant than the overall context of the expert's position, which is taken into account for assessing the meaning and significance of every expert statement (ibid.).

Inspired by Polizzi's study on digital literacy (2020a), the thematic analysis conducted in my study combined inductive and deductive approaches and can be described as a mix of the "conventional content analysis" and a "directed content analysis" (Hsieh and Shannon 2005, pp. 1279; 1281). The directed content analysis is applied when "existing theory or prior research exists about a phenomenon that is incomplete or would benefit from further description" (ibid.). The goal of this method is thus to "validate or extend conceptually a theoretical framework or theory" (ibid.) – in this case my preliminary framework for critical datafication literacy. This approach uses a more deductive and structured approach than conventional content analysis, which helps in supporting, extending, or questioning existing theory, but this also means that the researcher approaches the data "with an informed but, nonetheless, strong bias" (ibid., p. 1283). Yet, as inductive elements played a by far greater role in my study's thematic analysis than deductive approaches, this limitation could be mitigated.

After a preliminary step of developing some categories and nodes deductively, the thematic analysis followed the guidelines by Meuser and Nagel (2009) in combination with Braun and Clarke (2006). I first paraphrased the transcripts and then coded them into 332 initial codes. After this, I revised the codes, identified initial themes, and reviewed the initial thematic framework in several rounds of revision (including the 680 extracts for all themes in NVivo). Through this process, I developed a final thematic framework of 12 main themes and 45 subthemes and visualised this in a mind map. While the three categories that were developed deductively proved helpful in sorting the codes and themes, the analysis demonstrated that an inductive, bottom-up approach worked better to identify themes in the data, and the final thematic framework thus only included few deductive themes. A detailed description of how the thematic analysis was conducted and how it combined deductive and inductive approaches is provided in appendix I.II.III.

4.4 Learning from the Educators

In the third and last empirical stage of my study, a qualitative online survey with educators was conducted. The key goal here was to understand educators' expectations, requirements and wishes when it comes to critical data literacy resources, complementing the prior foci on the resources themselves and their creators' intentions. Thus, I was interested in the educators' experiences in teaching about datafication and in the materials and resources they use for this. The term "educators" is used very broadly here, encompassing people who teach, train and raise awareness about datafication in a number of educational contexts.

4.4.1 Qualitative Online Surveys

The challenge in this empirical stage was the scope and the diversity of the education field, as educators in a number of different professions may already educate about digital and data technologies. An appropriate method for reaching a wide and diverse audience while still allowing for qualitative insights was needed. Based on these considerations, I decided to conduct a qualitative online survey.

Advantages of Self-Administered Online Questionnaires

In contrast to qualitative interviews, questionnaires – especially self-administered online questionnaires – can be distributed to a large sample at the same time and are thus particularly suitable when the population is large and geographically dispersed (Clark et al. 2021, p. 212). Further advantages include low financial costs; low time effort; considerably less risk of interviewer effects or social desirability bias; and the ability to customise the appearance of the questionnaire (Regmi et al. 2017, p. 641; Clark et al. 2021, pp. 212f, 222). Finally, online questionnaires are convenient for respondents as they have greater control over the time and place where they answer the questions and complete the questionnaire at their own pace, taking as much time as they need, and potentially completing it over several sessions (Couper 2004, p. 506; Regmi et al. 2017, p. 641; Clark et al. 2021, p. 213).

The Special Case of Qualitative Online Surveys

Although the survey is a "familiar tool in social research", qualitative surveys are less widely used, potentially because of the very limited methodological literature available (Braun et al. 2021, p. 1). These surveys typically use open-ended questions as they seek "nuanced, in-depth and sometimes new understandings of social issues" (ibid.). Thus, they "*can* provide richness and depth, when viewed in their entirety, even if individual responses might themselves be brief" (ibid., p. 2, emphasis in original).

The key advantage of qualitative surveys in contrast to other qualitative methods is their "wide-angle lens" through which a "diversity of perspectives, experiences, or sense-making" can be captured (Braun et al. 2021, p. 3). This is particularly useful when the topic is under-explored, the population of interest is large, geographically dispersed, and diverse, or when "perspectives from different groups within a wider population are sought" (ibid.). All of this was the case in my study, making a qualitative survey the ideal method of study. It allowed for hearing a range of "'within-group' voices" rather than treating one person as a "spokesperson" for their background or group – thus enabling "diversity rather than typicality" (ibid.). Further advantages of online qualitative surveys include their openness and flexibility towards different research questions; that they can give a voice to those who would not be able or willing to take part in an interview; that they can "feel anonymous"; come with less social pressure and potentially more social comfort than face-to-face settings; are less burdensome for respondents; and less risky for researchers (ibid., pp. 2; 4–6).

Limitations and Challenges of Qualitative Online Surveys

Limitations of surveys include that they do not allow researchers to prompt or probe to avoid misunderstandings or inquire further (Clark et al. 2021, p. 213f). Furthermore, some complex questions are difficult to ask, and the number of questions is limited because of the possibility of "respondent fatigue" (ibid.). Online surveys in particular can come with representational issues as certain literacy (ability to read and write), digital equipment and internet access are required to participate (Couper 2004, p. 506; Braun et al. 2021, p. 4; Clark et al. 2021, p. 214). Moreover, response rates in online surveys can be lower and the researcher cannot be certain if the questionnaire was completed by the intended respondent (Clark et al. 2021, p. 213f). These limitations were considered in the questionnaire design. The common critique that the depth of data is lost in a survey, however, is, according to Braun et al., "falsely based on imagining what qualitative surveys cannot offer, and an idealization of what interviews will offer" (2021, p. 4). The authors argue that "while an individual response may lack the meandering detail of an interview transcript", the dataset as a whole, when executed properly, "will be likely be rich and complex" and able to "deliver rich, deep and complex data" (ibid.).

4.4.2 The Survey Sample

The goal for this survey was to reach educators from different backgrounds who are interested in teaching about digital and data technologies and might even have already done so in the past, potentially using online critical data literacy resources. In order to reach this population of interest, I contacted large numbers of educators with my survey, specifying that "any educator who is interested in teaching about digital technologies and (big) data is invited to take part in my study".

Aiming at Diversity rather than Representativeness

As there exists no list of educators with this particular interest, no sampling frame was available and a probability sampling not possible. This was not very problematic for my study as my interest in hearing from a diverse range of voices stemmed – as is typical for qualitative researchers – from the goal of "gaining rich(er) insights into the topic of interest, not generating a sample that achieves statistical representativeness and allows simple claims of generalizability" (Braun et al. 2021, p. 3).

Braun et al emphasise that "this diversity of voices matters" – for "quality and validity of knowledge"; for "what knowledge might inform practice" and also from a "social justice and inclusion point of view" (ibid., p. 3f). When no sampling frame is available and representativeness is not a significant concern for the researcher, online surveys provide useful possibilities of reaching a diverse sample, such as posting "an invitation to answer a questionnaire on a relevant message board, email it to suitable mailing lists, or share it on websites and social media" (Clark et al. 2021, p. 186). While this will lead to a sample of unknown representativeness and response rate, it allows the researcher to "target groups that have a specific interest or form of behaviour" (ibid.). This, together with its cost-effectiveness, makes this approach an "attractive means of contacting sample members" (ibid). Moreover, Braun et al. highlight that also in a sample that is not statistically representative, "wider inferences may be drawn" (2021, p. 3).

Finding the Sample

The next step was to identify how the population of interest for the online survey could be reached. First, specific groups of educators were identified as likely most relevant for this survey: teachers, student teachers, teacher trainers, higher education lecturers, adult educators, media education centres and trainers in civil society. In order to further narrow down this large population, I decided to focus on three (supra)national contexts: Germany, the United Kingdom and the European Union. I selected these areas because they a) are addressed by common educational programmes and frameworks (for example "DigComp", EU Science Hub – European Commission [no date]); b) correspond to the scholarly literature that was analysed in my study's theoretical framework; c) offer existing connections to educators interested in the topic of datafication through the collaboration with Privacy International and several projects and research networks I am involved in; d) as English and German are widely spoken by educators in these places, limiting language barriers.

As a second step, I identified communication channels – mailing lists, social media accounts, organisations and well-connected individuals – to reach this population. This included large mailing lists by, for example, the European Communication Research and Education Association (ECREA), but also smaller groups that specifically address educators who are interested in learning more about digital technologies. In identifying these channels, also the project partner Privacy International's connections were useful. The full list of contacted organisations and individuals can be found in appendix VII. Moreover, a detailed discussion of the sampling process, including challenges, strategies in reaching a diverse sample, and a reflection on how successful the different communication channels were in reaching the survey's sample can be found in the methodological annotations in appendix I.III.I. Overall, it can be said that information about the survey reached several thousand people (particularly through large mailing lists by different organisations), although likely only a small fraction of these was part of the survey's target population: educators interested in teaching about digital and data technologies.

The Final Sample

As the literature emphasises, it is difficult to determine an appropriate sample size for a survey (Freedman 2004, p. 988; Braun et al. 2021, p. 9). Qualitative online surveys in particular will likely have larger samples than typical for qualitative studies but smaller samples than typical for quantitative and representative online surveys (Braun et al. 2021, p. 9). The appropriate sample size is determined by the following factors: "the scope of the study and breadth of the topic; the research question [...]; the characteristics of, and diversity within, the population; the motivation of participants; and, relatedly, the depth and detail of the individual responses" (ibid.). Braun et al. further stress that not all of these factors can be anticipated in advance, and "dataset richness and ability to address the questions" are more important than reaching an exact number (ibid.). For these reasons, a sample size was not determined before conducting the survey, but the goal was rather to reach a wide and diverse sample and achieve data richness.

In total, 265 people opened the link to my survey in the three months it was open (25.11.2021 – 25.02.2022), but only 102 began completing the questionnaire. This gap is likely explained by the very specific population that the survey addressed and that was highlighted on the survey's landing page: educators "interested in teaching about digital technologies and (big) data". As these topics are not yet routinely covered in many curricula, it is likely that not many educators teach about topics of digital technologies and datafication yet. Of the 102 people who began completing the questionnaire, 44 aborted when they saw the first open question asking about their experience. This effect is described in the literature and was therefore expected (see 4.4.3). All of these as well as one participant who clicked through the questionnaire without completing any field were excluded from the final sample. Of the remaining participants, the majority completed the full questionnaire, but some (10) omitted parts of it. I decided that all participants who completed over half of the questionnaire would be included in the final sample. Thus, a final sample of 57 participants was determined.

Before closing the survey, I examined the sample's breadth and diversity in terms of different areas of education (such as pre-school, school, teacher education, vocational training, and many others) and nationalities. Both showed great variety (see chapter 5.3 for a more detailed discussion of the sample's demographics), and even several non-European educators participated in the survey. While these were not specifically addressed in the sampling, their answers were nevertheless included in the analysis as they added more diversity and novel insights. Moreover, data richness could be achieved as participants often provided extensive answers to the open questions, which generated extensive qualitative data. Therefore, I decided that 57 participants was an appropriate sample size.

4.4.3 Developing the Questionnaire

Methodological Considerations about Questionnaire Design

The wording, type and order, and layout and length of questions in the survey were informed by methodological literature on (qualitative) online surveys. All questions were worded carefully, aiming for open, but short, clear and unambiguous questions and avoiding making any assumptions (Braun et al. 2021, p. 8). At times, I provided examples as guidance for participants (ibid.). Qualitative surveys typically use open-ended questions, which allow participants to type their responses in their own words and can produce the "rich and complex accounts of the type of sense-making typically of interest to qualitative researchers" (ibid.). This further allows researchers to access their participants' language and terminology (ibid), and tends to lead to a much more diverse set of answers than by using close-ended questions (Reja et al. 2003, p. 159).

However, open-ended questions also need extensive coding and have higher rates of non-response, and participants are most likely to abandon a questionnaire in the middle of a series of open-ended questions (Reja et al. 2003, p. 159; Crawford et al. 2001 in Clark et al. 2021, p. 187). Therefore, Clark et al. suggest minimising the number of open-ended questions in self-completion questionnaires (2021, p. 187). Taking these considerations into account, I decided to include both closed and open-ended questions, aiming for a balance between convenience for the respondents – and thus hopefully high response rates – while still collecting rich and in-depth data about the key questions of the survey (see below). As recommended by Braun et al., all closed questions further included an "other – please specify" or "not applicable" option to ensure no perspective is left out (2021, p. 7).

The questionnaire was kept as short as possible, began with closed, easy demographic questions before the first open-ended questions were introduced, and an honest estimate of the required time was provided on the starting page. Subsequently, closed questions alternated with open-ended questions, while clustering questions on similar aspects and of a similar format together in distinct and coherent sections, always keeping questions and answer options close together and providing clear instructions how to respond and the opportunity to skip questions (Regmi et al. 2017, p. 642; Braun et al. 2021, p. 8; Clark et al. 2021, p. 220). The layout and design of the questionnaire was further as user-friendly, easy to follow and visually attractive as possible (Regmi et al. 2017, p. 641). Key terms of each question were underlined, and a progress indicator was used to help participants navigate the questionnaire.

Applying a user-friendly design was considerably aided by using an online survey platform. This decision further protected against the loss of data, facilitated data transfer and eliminated transcription errors, improving the "reliability and validity of the data collection process and the collected data" (Regmi et al. 2017, p. 642). However, it is important to take care when selecting an online survey platform as particularly free platforms have been found to compromise confidentiality (Regmi et al. 2017, p. 642). Thus, considerable effort was put into identifying a secure and privacy-sensitive platform. The platform that was used, soscisurvey.com, was developed by communication scholars for academic surveys (SoSci Survey GmbH [no date]). It places a high value on data security (with servers located in Germany); is adapted specifically for academic research with a wide range of possible question formats and individual survey settings; and is free for non-commercial research. Moreover, ethical considerations influenced the design of the questionnaire. Based on recommendations from the literature on informed consent, the landing page of the survey included important participant information (Regmi et al. 2017, p. 642; Braun et al. 2021, p. 8f). It explained what participation meant, that it was voluntary and participants could withdraw at any point, and how data would be handled: that the survey data would be entirely anonymous, participants could not be identified, and all precautions for data security within the requirements of the General Data Protection Regulation would be taken.

Translation of the Questionnaire

Although online surveys give respondents the opportunity to read questions several times and take as much time as needed for answering, they should still ideally be conducted in a language the respondent speaks fluently. For this reason, my survey was offered in two languages – English and German – hoping that most European educators would feel comfortable enough in either language to complete an online questionnaire. Survey translation is not as straightforward as might be expected, as small changes in wording can make a difference and words can have several or ambiguous meanings, might not exist in another language and it can be difficult to translate gendered or gender-neutral language (Harkness et al. 2004, p. 456ff). Translation should further only take place once a "common source questionnaire" is finalised and comparability needs and concept operationalisations should be kept in mind (Behr 2018, pp. 7; 17). Translators should keep the content of the questions semantically similar, use the same question format and range of response options, and should aim to capture the "intended *sense of the question*" (Harkness et al. 2004, pp. 456; 462, emphasis in original; Harkness et al. 2010, p. 117f). In light of these challenges, translators of surveys should be "bilinguals, professional translators, people who understand empirical social science research, or some combination of these" (Harkness et al. 2004, p. 463). My bilingualism, my familiarity with both cultures and the fact that I am both the researcher and translator of the study therefore facilitated translation. Moreover, the questionnaire was piloted in German and in English to test the question wording, spot ambiguously worded questions and check for further issues around comprehensibility.

Pilot Study

It is generally recommended to carry out a pilot of questionnaires with potential participants (Regmi et al. 2017, p. 642; Braun et al. 2021, p. 9). Pilot studies can lead to unexpected findings and can help "ensure the adequacy of the questions" and the question order; test comprehensiveness; ensure clear instructions; and check for technological problems (Regmi et al. 2017, p. 642). Typical pilot sizes consist of 5–20% of the anticipated sample (Braun et al. 2021, p. 9). I decided on a pilot size of 10 participants, which would likely lie in the range between 5% and 20% of the final sample.

In order to test the questionnaire in both languages, 5 German and 5 international[7] pilot testers were selected. All testers were personal or professional acquaintances who were part of my target population – educators interested in teaching about digital technologies – and worked in a variety of educational sectors.[8] Some of these were well-versed in the field of critical data studies, whereas others had no experience in this field. This helped to ensure that any educator would understand the questions, regardless of their experience with these topics. Piloting the questionnaire with this very diverse set of pilot testers proved extremely valuable. The pilot testers provided detailed and extensive feedback and constructive suggestions. Changes made to the questionnaire after piloting included small changes in wording and refining some translations; changes to some answer options; breaking up long open questions; and adding examples in order to clarify the question or the answer options (for a detailed description of changes, see appendix I.III.II).

Final Questionnaire

Apart from these methodological considerations, the development of the questionnaire was strongly influenced by my study's previous theoretical and empirical findings. The survey aimed to investigate if these findings corresponded with educators' daily lived experience. To achieve this, seven specific goals for the survey were identified, such as investigating if the educators know and use the resources examined in this study's content analysis, which formats they find useful and if they agree with the 'best practice' approaches to educate about datafication that are suggested by

7 British, Dutch, Bulgarian, Israeli, and American. Some were native, some non-native speaker, but all fluent in English.

8 The pilot sample included one student teacher, one primary school teacher, two secondary school teachers, one teacher and media pedagogy trainer, one teacher trainer, three higher education lecturers (from different fields and countries), and one civil society trainer.

previous findings of this study and other scholars' findings (for more details, see appendix I.III.III). Moreover, feedback from the project collaborator Privacy International was considered when developing the final questionnaire.

The final questionnaire consisted of three thematic sections (see appendix VIII). It began with a landing page that provided information about the study and on participation and data handling. Moreover, the estimated completion time for the questionnaire was stated, giving a realistic estimation, as recommended in the literature (Clark et al. 2021, p. 187). The first thematic section of the questionnaire then consisted of a short demographics section that aimed at understanding the educational contexts in which aspects of datafication might already be covered, but also discovering if the survey was successful in reaching diverse educators from different fields and countries.

The second section examined educators' experience with topics around digital technologies. It included several rating scale questions (5-point scale, "not applicable" (N.A.) option provided), which tested how well-equipped and experienced the educators felt about four broad topical areas around digitisation and datafication (for more details on these topical areas and the methodological considerations behind the questionnaire design, see appendix I.III.III). In addition, open questions asked about educators' experiences, the topics they covered, their goals and methods, and challenges they encountered.

The third section then addressed educational resources about datafication. Open and rating questions were used to examine how educators find information and teaching material on digital and data technologies, how satisfied they are with this, and how useful they find different design formats. Moreover, one question tested agreement with ten statements about how best to educate about these topics – developed based on my study's previous findings and the literature (see appendix I.III.III). Finally, an open question invited participants to provide final remarks and comments. As Braun et al highlight, this can often generate "unanticipated and useful data" (2021, p. 8). After participants submitted their answers, the survey ended with a final thank you-page, which further invited the participants to contact me via email if they were interested in testing and providing feedback on a new educational resource that was being developed with Privacy International as part of my study.

4.4.4 Analysing the Educator Survey

After closing the survey, the survey data was exported and cleaned, and the final sample of 57 participants determined (see above). Subsequently, all closed questions and the short, single-line open questions (e.g., country of origin) were analysed in Excel, and the open question data analysed through a qualitative thematic content analysis similar to the one applied in the expert interview analysis.

Analysing the Closed and Single-Line Questions

For the multiple-choice questions, the frequencies were counted; percentages and totals calculated; and the data visualised in tables and graphs. Single-line questions first had to be coded manually. This was sometimes straightforward (e.g., nationality and country of residence), and sometimes more complex (e.g., the positions participants worked in). The coding for the latter question was conducted in a more detailed rather than too broad manner to provide maximum accuracy; and stringent coding decisions were followed. Finally, the rating questions were analysed by counting the frequencies of responses (including N.A. and missing responses); calculating percentages and totals (using the total number of valid answers for each answer option) as well as cumulative percentages (agreement versus disagreement) and average agreement; comparing results across topics and across questions; and finally visualising the data in tables and graphs.

Thematic Content Analysis of the Open Survey Questions

To analyse the seven long form open questions in the survey, a thematic content analysis was conducted using the software NVivo. In total, these seven questions produced 26 pages of qualitative textual data – on average half a page per respondent. This is a significant amount of writing, which highlights many respondents' passion for the topics the survey addressed (which some also emphasised in their comments, see chapter 5.3). As suggested in the literature on qualitative surveys, this data was not summarised by each question as this "typically results in an impoverished and underdeveloped qualitative analysis" (Braun et al. 2021, p. 10). Instead, the data was treated "as one cohesive dataset" and the coding was conducted one participant at a time, which allowed for "develop[ing] analytic patterns across the entire dataset" (ibid.). Throughout the analysis, it became clear that this was the right decision, as participants often referred to the same aspect – such as the topics and goals in their teaching – across different questions, and they sometimes referred back to something they wrote for an earlier question.

The steps of the analysis were similar to the interview analysis (see section 4.3.5; appendix I.II.III). Based on the experiences with the interview analysis, the survey data was analysed inductively, taking a bottom-up approach to identify patterns. Furthermore, paraphrasing the data was omitted as participants had already submitted succinct arguments. The first step of the analysis thus consisted of a detailed coding, leading to 416 initial codes. Subsequently, these were sorted into initial categories that were identified inductively; the initial codes and categories were revised; and initial themes identified. Three of the six categories that were identified collected more 'straightforward' data, such as information on where educators search for material (e.g., "internet", "literature" etc.). These were represented in subthemes only as no overarching main themes could be identified. For the remaining three categories, main and subthemes were identified and reviewed in several rounds of revision. During this revision, it was decided that subthemes which were only mentioned rarely but showed strong parallels to the interview findings would be kept in order to highlight these parallels. The final thematic framework then consisted of nine main themes and 42 subthemes (in the three key categories). This framework was visualised in a mind map, which used different colour shades to highlight the different frequencies of the (sub)themes for reasons of transparency.

4.5 Knowledge Mobilisation: Developing the "Teaching about Data" Resource

After the empirical research was conducted and analysed, the findings of this study were mobilised in a knowledge mobilisation project in cooperation with the NGO Privacy International. As outlined in the previous subchapters, the NGO acted as an advisor throughout my study, with knowledge exchange taking place in the different stages of the research and the NGO providing feedback on a number of methodological decisions based on their practical experience. In this final stage, however, a close collaboration took place and an online learning resource for educators who are interested in teaching about data technologies was co-created. In the following, the methodological grounding of this co-creation project and its outcome in the form of an online resource will be outlined. Details on the goals for the resource, its target audience, the rationale behind design and content decisions as well as a detailed description of its creation process and a presentation of the resource itself can be found in a report on the cooperation with Privacy International in appendix IX.

What is Knowledge Mobilisation?

In the past, academic research has often been criticised for taking place in an "ivory tower" – distinct and disconnected from the real-life challenges of society (Gontcharov et al. 2021, p. 39). When this "gap between discovery and implementation" was highlighted as "a social problem", the proposed solution was that academic knowledge should increasingly be translated and transferred into other societal sectors in order to facilitate its implementation into everyday products and services (ibid., p. 35). However, as scholars argue, "30 years later, the gap is still there" (ibid.), and the academic knowledge production process "has failed consistently to move the most credible evidence from practice and research into improved outcomes" (Naidorf 2014, p. 15). Education research equally experiences a significant "gap between research, practice and policy", which is "mainly associated with the hiatus between knowledge producers (academic researchers) and knowledge users (teachers)" (Flores 2018, p. 622). There are many calls to address these gaps as well as a "growing recognition of the importance of the use of research to inform practice and to enhance teacher professionalism" (ibid., p. 621).

In this context, several new approaches that aim to better integrate research and practice have been developed. Examples include "*socially relevant research; knowledge mobilization; research impact; innovation*; and *university priorities*" (Naidorf 2014, p. 1, emphasis in original). A detailed analysis of the contexts and consequences of these different approaches can be found in Naidorf's 2014 paper. One term that is increasingly used in recent years and is of particular relevance for my study's goal of connecting research and practice is the term *knowledge mobilisation*. As Naidorf outlines, knowledge mobilisation differs from mere dissemination of research findings in that it "actively creates linkages and exchanges between producers and users of data, information and knowledge to engage in value-added activities" (2014, p. 15). While dissemination mainly describes the distribution of research results, for example in academic journals and at congresses, knowledge mobilisation "makes knowledge ready for service or action" by making it "more useful, proactive and applied" (ibid., p. 16).

Moreover, knowledge mobilisation goes beyond what is understood as "knowledge transfer". According to Gontcharov et al., the concept of knowledge mobilisation "emerged as a critical response to the overall ineffectiveness of the knowledge transfer paradigm" in closing the gap outlined above (2021, p. 35). While knowledge *transfer* or *translation* aims at "communicating a message from academia to other fields of research, sectors of the economy, policy makers, and the public", they explain that knowledge *mobilisation* "seeks to reimagine the very relationship between science and society" (ibid.). In doing so, it intends to "trigger deeper structural changes" in academia and in "*knowledge society* in general, a society in which 'academic science' is an embedded social institution" (ibid., emphasis in original).

To achieve these goals, Gontcharov et al. argue that "actual change needs to take place on the ground", with research institutions and individual researchers adopting innovative and reflexive research practices (2021, p. 38). The authors provide a number of suggestions on how individual researchers can promote knowledge mobilisation in their work, which Privacy International and I tried to follow in our project. First and foremost, they highlight that the process by which "engaged researchers" work should be "both *critical* and *reflexive*" (ibid., p. 33, emphasis in original). Researchers should implement ideas such as "*knowledge co-creation, citizen science, community-initiated studies,* and cooperation with alternative knowledge systems" and should think about how to provide open access to their research data (ibid., p. 39, emphasis in original). They should therefore rethink the public "from passive *informants/end users* to *collaborators/co-researchers*" and engage in "ongoing dialogue" (ibid., p. 39, emphasis in original). In doing so, the authors suggest that knowledge mobilisation projects should "exercise curiosity" and "accept a plurality of approaches to knowledge production" (ibid., p. 39). Thus, knowledge mobilisation can create "stronger meaningful links between academia and a knowledge society" (ibid., p. 39). The detailed report on the cooperation with PI provides more details on how these ideas and goals were implemented in our knowledge mobilisation project (appendix IX).

Mobilising Findings on Critical Data Literacy

The prior sections highlighted an overall need for more knowledge mobilisation in academia. In critical data literacy research specifically, the interconnection of research and practice could also be improved. Critical data literacy scholars Pangrazio and Sefton-Green have highlighted that translating the abstract objectives of academic concepts of critical data literacy "into a practical model that can be operationalised by educators is challenging" (2020, p. 215). While many "folk pedagogies of data" exist – programmes that aim to raise public awareness and critical understanding of data – replicating these approaches "in an educational setting requires further experimentation" (ibid., p. 217). Similarly, media pedagogy scholar Zorn has called for more support for educators who aim to teach about topics around big data and data protection (2015, p. 23). In line with these calls, my study intended to not only call for more critical data literacy, but to actively support educators in fostering this literacy by creating an online learning resource for "Teaching about Data" (Privacy International et al. 2022).

This resource, which was created between January and September 2022, is available at https://privacyinternational.org/learning-resources/teaching-about-data-resource-educators. It aims to provide educators with everything they need to foster critical data literacy in their educational setting – based on academic research findings and the practical experiences of educators and advocates. It addresses educators of any background: any person who wants to educate others about data and datafication but may not have the knowledge or material to do so. The resource intends to raise educators' own awareness and critical understanding of datafication, and to enable them to educate about datafication by providing best practice advice and research findings on suitable pedagogical approaches along with access to teaching material. These goals are addressed in five chapters, which each include a short video summary and many external links for further information. More details on the considerations behind the resource's content and design and on the creation process are provided in the report on the collaboration in appendix IX.

4.6 Conclusion

Overall, my study applied various methodological approaches throughout its different empirical stages. An overview of the methods that were used, the samples, and the time spans of conducting the research is provided below (table 3). Due to the limited research that exists on online critical data literacy resources thus far and a lack of sampling frames, the study often had to find novel and creative approaches to researching these resources. Particularly the triangulation of methods and the mixed methods approach – combining qualitative methodologies such as expert interviews and a qualitative survey with more quantitative methods such as a content analysis – proved very helpful in improving the study's quality, validity and reliability. This approach further allowed for a more complete picture of critical data literacy, as the different methods complemented each other: after the *'what'* (do online resources look like?) of the content analysis, the expert interviews addressed the *'why'* (are they created this way?), and the qualitative survey added a *'how'* (do educators perceive and use these resources?). The next chapters present the findings of the three empirical approaches and highlight parallels and contradictions between the different findings.

Table 3: Overview of research methods applied in the study.

Method	**Sample**	**Time span of data collection**
Content analysis	250 resources examined; 75 fit the qualifying criteria and were fully coded and analysed.	April – May 2021.
Expert interviews	10 interviewees (10 initial and three follow-up interviews were conducted).	Preliminary interviews in May and June 2020; Final interviews from June – November 2021.
Qualitative online survey	57 participants.	November 2021 – February 2022.

5. Findings and Analysis

The following chapters present my study's empirical findings. The three chapters are structured along the three research questions of my study (see chapter 4). At the end of each chapter, a brief summary and discussion of key findings is provided. As many common themes between the three empirical perspectives were identified, each findings chapter includes only a brief discussion of key arguments, and chapter six then provides more detailed discussion, in which the findings of all three chapters are interwoven and discussed in relation to the academic literature.

5.1 Online Critical Data Literacy Resources

This chapter presents the findings of my study's first empirical perspective, addressing the research question: What is the range, shape and focus of online critical data literacy resources? The content analysis demonstrated that many online educational resources about datafication already exist. The 75 analysed resources applied diverse design formats and came from diverse and international creation backgrounds. The analysis further revealed that *some* aspects of this study's preliminary theoretical framework for critical datafication literacy are already addressed by the majority of analysed resources, whereas others, such as the importance of not shifting responsibility to individuals, are only considered by a minority. Altogether, the analysis provided new knowledge on the under-researched field of online critical data literacy resources, led to new insights for the further conceptualisation of critical datafication literacy throughout this study, and allowed for an informed selection of the ten most suitable resource creators for the expert interviews.

5.1.1 Identifying Online Critical Data Literacy Resources

In a first step, 250 potential critical data literacy resources were identified and examined. Of these, 75 resources met the study's qualifying criteria and were fully coded and analysed in a quantitative content analysis.[1] The qualifying criteria for this sampling described critical data literacy resources in the broadest possible definition: resources that 1) educate about datafication; 2) foster critical reflection of the implications of datafication; and 3) do not require any prior knowledge. The most common reason for exclusion was that resources did not *educate about datafication*, for example because they only covered specific aspects such as data protection or the use of data systems in particular areas (e.g., in the education sector or by the police). Only 97 resources met this qualifying criterion.

The two other criteria were met considerably more often: 142 of the 250 resources fostered critical reflection of data technologies and 156 required no prior knowledge. Resources that did not meet these criteria and were therefore excluded from further analysis would, for example, highlight only the benefits of data technologies; foster an instrumental data literacy (data usage skills only) without addressing more critical questions; or cover specific and complex issues such as the implications of data technologies in political advertising, or bills on facial recognition without providing any introductory knowledge. Already this first selection prior to conducting the content analysis thus provided insights on the landscape of online educational resources about data, highlighting that many existing resources focus on specific aspects or perspectives on data technologies, and that a broader critical consideration of datafication is less common in the examined resources.

5.1.2 Characteristics and Origins of Critical Data Literacy Resources

International and Multilingual Resources

The goal of the content analysis was to examine the range, shape and focus of online critical data literacy resources – including to what extent they are in line with the preliminary framework for critical datafication literacy. First, the analysis of the resources' countries of origin revealed that over half of the resources originated in Germany (41 of 75), whereas only 15 were created in the US, 8 in the UK, 5 in Switzerland, 4 in the Netherlands and 3 in Canada. Apart from that, one resource originated in each Brazil, France, Austria and Italy. Finally, one resource was coded as European: a series of short explanatory videos by the "Project Sherpa", a decidedly European research project with stakeholders and team members from several European countries (R67, see appendix II). This distinct dominance of resources with a German origin is likely not representative but can be explained by the study's sample and its sources (see chapter 4.2.2).

The resources' languages showed a similar German predominance. In total, 45 of the 75 resources were available in German and only 36 in English. The sample included any resource that would fit the qualifying criteria and was available in at least

1 For a full list of the 75 resources, see appendix II.

English or German. Yet, the analysed resources were offered not only in these two languages, but 17 different languages in total were identified in the sample. This included not just widespread languages such as English, Spanish, French or German but also less widespread languages such as Persian, Burmese, Amharic or Welsh (see table 4). Moreover, several languages from the Global South were included although most countries of origin were located in the Global North. However, a closer look revealed that only a small group of 18 of the 75 resources was multilingual, whereas the rest were provided in only one language. The high number of languages thus resulted from very few resources that were offered in many different languages. For example, the "Surveillance Self-Defense" resource, a website offering "Tips, tools and how-tos for safer online communications" by the NGO "Electronic Frontier Foundation" was available in 12 different languages (R12).

Table 4: All languages identified in the resources and how often they appeared in the sample.

German	45	Turkish	2
English	36	Amharic	1
Spanish	7	Burmese	1
French	6	Dutch	1
Arabic	4	Persian	1
Portuguese	3	Thai	1
Russian	3	Vietnamese	1
Italian	2	Welsh	1
Rumanian	2		

Diverse Creator Backgrounds

To get a clearer picture of the societal sectors and actors that create online educational resources about datafication, I further examined the background of the resource creators. As suggested by the literature, civil society emerged as a strong actor in this context (see below). In total, 29 resource creators were coded as civil society actors, 15 as journalists or media producers (such as television producers), 15 resources were created by researchers, and 15 by governmental or public institutions. As with all other figures in this chapter, these numbers include duplicates, since several resources were produced by more than one creator. While civil society and journalism and media constitute creation contexts that were also identified in previous studies on critical data literacy resources (Sander 2020c; Young and Pridmore Forthcoming), identifying researchers and public institutions as resource creators constitutes a novel finding. In line with previous studies, the content analysis further identified eight commercial companies, six private individuals and two educational institutions (a publishing house, R48, and an online competence centre for teachers, R52). Moreover, one museum was identified as a creation context: the museum for communication in Bern, Switzerland, developed an entire package with teaching material about big data, including animated videos, lesson plans and assignments (R39, see also chapter 5.2).

Figure 4: Creator backgrounds with number of resources identified in each field.

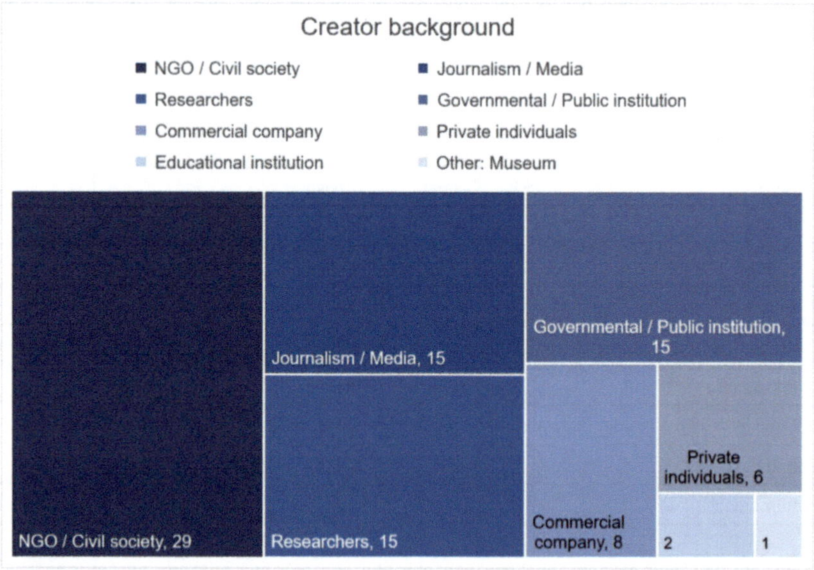

Various and Unusual Formats

The analysis of the resources' formats identified short videos (43) and websites (35) as most common formats (see fig. 5). Apart from this, 24 resources were coded as "online courses". This included short tutorials and MOOCs (Massive Open Online Courses) that learners can work through individually. However, the majority of resources in this category consisted of teaching material, such as lesson plans for teachers or work assignments for pupils. Several examples are outlined in more detail in chapter 5.2. This relatively large amount of existing critical teaching material on topics around big data and datafication represents a contrast to the focus on instrumental data literacy approaches and calls for more teaching material (see chapter 2.2; Pangrazio and Sefton-Green 2020, p. 211). Yet, later findings of my study suggest that at least some educators seem to be aware of this "abundance" of material (see chapter 5.3.4).

Moreover, a high number of games was identified (10). Five of these were analogue games such as simulation games or card games, for example the "Fairdata" game as part of the "Dataselfie" resource (R20), and five were online games. These included short games that could be played within a few minutes, such as the browser game "Data Clash" as part of the "Your Data Your Rights" website (R19), as well as more extensive so-called "serious games", such as the "Datak" game that is outlined in more detail in chapter 5.2 (R41). Since the development of games is time-consuming and expensive (especially when it comes to digital games), ten games in a sample of 75 resources can be seen as a high number. Particularly serious games constitute an increasingly popular approach to learning as they offer "motivating and engaging experiences" for learners (Anastasiadis et al. 2018, p. 139).

Figure 5: Identified resource formats with number of resources applying each format.

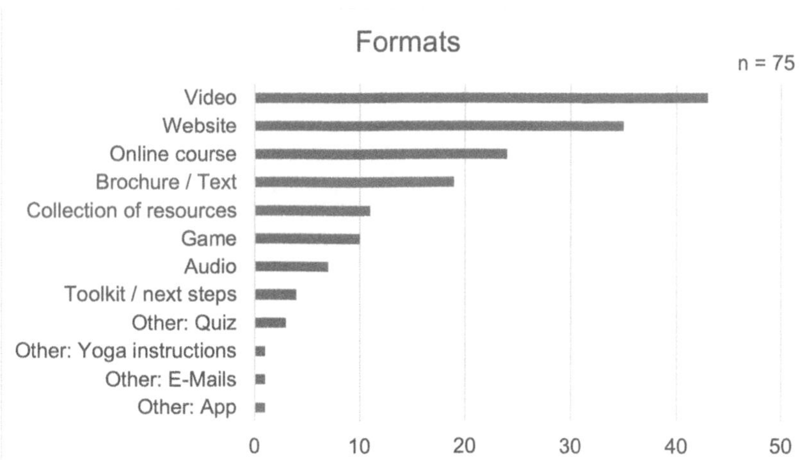

Finally, the analysis of the resources' formats revealed new formats that were not included in the coding sheet. Apart from three quizzes, the research identified one app that educates about datafication. The "Stadt Land DatenFluss" app, a gamified course on a large variety of topics around data was created by the Volkshochschule in Germany (Adult Education Association) (R54). Moreover, one resource used an email newsletter format in combination with a podcast series: The "Privacy Paradox" Newsletter provided subscribers with daily insights on data and privacy and a daily "challenge" on how to protect one's data, sent on five subsequent days alongside its five-part podcast series (R4). Even yoga instructions were used to educate about datafication: the "Coveillance: Watching the watchers" website offered "Countersurveillance Yoga" (R74).

The (No) One-Size-Fits-All Approach

The content analysis further investigated if the resources recognise the need for different approaches for different audiences or if they follow a "one-size-fits-all" approach (see Carmi et al. 2020, p. 11). This is a key aspect of this study's preliminary critical datafication literacy framework (see chapter 3.4). The content analysis examined this in two ways: a) the target group(s) of the resources were coded and b) a second question tested whether the resources recognised the need for different approaches for different audiences (see codebook, variable 13 and 15, appendix III). As outlined in the methods chapter, both variables were difficult to code and, to some extent, a matter of interpretation.

Figure 6: Identified target groups of the resources.

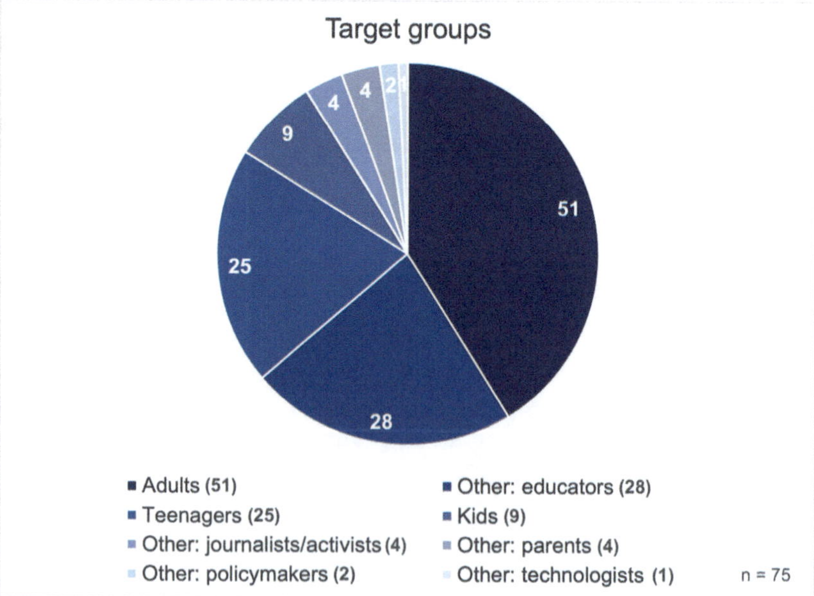

The first variable was coded based on the overall content and style of the resource as well as, if available, information on the resources' intended use. This was the case when a website included specific sections, for example for "youth, parents and educators", "policymakers" and "technologists" (R62); or specifically stated its target audience, such as the "Digital Defense Playbook" by "Our Data Bodies" (R31, p. 12). Further examples for resources that were very clear about their audience included the infographic "Dein Tag in Daten" (your day in data) by "Watch Your Web" that clearly addresses kids and teenagers, as the data that is portrayed includes "arriving at my school" and "checking how long I need to wear my braces" (R29); the "curriculum materials" by Mijente for educators (R61); and the video courses on privacy by Privacy International on the "Advocacy Assembly" website for activists who want to gain better skills in advocacy (R5). If no target group could be identified at all, the variable was omitted.

The overall distribution of identified target groups within the sample is shown in figure 6. Apart from many resources addressing adults and teenagers more generally, the large number of 28 resources targeting educators stands out. This corresponds with the large amount of teaching material in the sample that was outlined above. Apart from that, some resources seemed to address specific groups such as journalists or activists (4), parents (4) and the already mentioned policymakers (2) and technologists (1). With the exception of the target group "educators", however, the number of resources addressing specific groups was very small in contrast to the large majority of resources addressing broader groups such as "adults".

This is in line with the findings for variable 15 that tested for "different audiences". This variable examined if resources recognise the need for providing different approaches for different audiences, for example by addressing a specific target group or by offering adaption possibilities for different needs of their audiences. All examples outlined above met this variable. Further examples include the "Watching You" website with material for pre-school children (R58) or websites with sections for different target groups, such as "Klicksafe" (R28) or the "My data and privacy online" toolkit (R2). Overall, five resources were coded as meeting the criterion "different audiences" very well, 12 as meeting it, and 12 as somewhat meeting it (see fig. 7). Thus, 29 resources in total considered different audiences at least in some way. However, this also means that the majority of resources did not specifically cater to the needs of different audiences but rather seemed to take a 'one-size-fits-all' approach. This represents a contrast to the strong emphasis on the importance of catering for the needs of different learners in critical data literacy research and general education literature (e.g., Brüggen 2015, p. 16; Aßmann et al. 2016, p. 15; Carmi et al. 2020, p. 43). However, it is possible that some of these resources were indeed designed for specific audiences and their needs, without making this transparent in the resource itself.

5.1.3 How Do the Resources Implement Critical Data Literacy?

The content analysis further examined if – apart from the different audiences – other key aspects of the preliminary theoretical framework for critical datafication literacy developed in this study could be found in the resources. Figure seven shows all five variables in this section, with the different shades of blue representing how well each variable was met by how many resources. Again, this differentiation into three stages is to some extent a matter of interpretation. However, given the diversity of the analysed resources and the size of some of the websites, the goal here was to give at least some idea *to what degree* a resource was, for example, interactive, and to differentiate between resources using one interactive element, such as the "Daten, Daten, Daten" website that includes a short online game (R16), and others that are profoundly interactive in their entire design, such as the "How normal am I?" online video experiment (R66). A resource was also coded as "somewhat interactive" if the resource itself was not interactive, but it was intended for an interactive use, such as simulation games or work assignments for students, as for example the case in the "Unbias Fairness Toolkit" (R32).

Figure 7: Variables testing for resources' alignment with the preliminary theoretical framework.

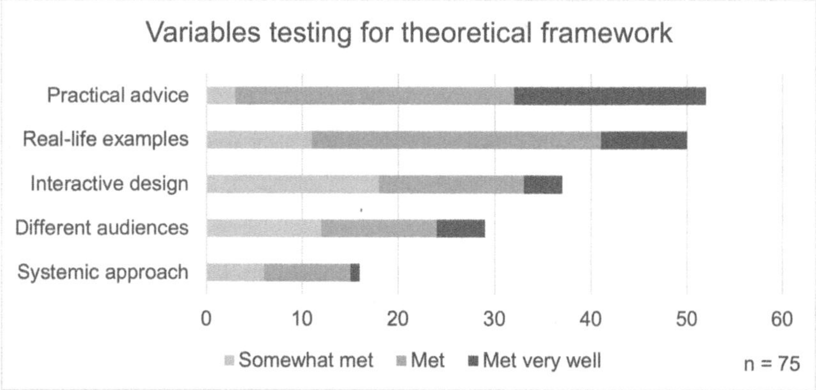

Many Popular Characteristics Identified

Of the five variables that tested for different aspects of my preliminary literacy framework, the variable that was met by most resources was *practical advice* (52 of the 75 resources), which in figure seven summarises any kind of advice provided (detailed analysis below). *Real-life examples* were nearly as common and were found in 50 resources. The third most common characteristic that was tested – *interactive design elements* – was met by 37 of the 75 resources. This is high considering the additional effort and time and financial resources required to develop interactive online tools. Both of these approaches – using real-life examples and interactive formats to educate about datafication – correlate with calls from participants of my previous study (Sander 2020c), with other critical data literacy scholars (e.g.,

D'Ignazio and Bhargava 2015; Iliadis and Russo 2016), and with critical pedagogy's approach of entering into dialogue with learners and presenting them with real-world problems (see chapter 3.3).

Practical Advice for Data Protection – (Too much) Individual Responsibility?

The variable "practical advice" tested not only if a resource provided practical or constructive advice for users, but also *what kind of advice* it suggested. As figure eight shows, the different types of advice tested for showed a very different distribution within the sample. *Data protection advice* was by far the most common form of practical advice. In total, 36 of the 75 resources included suggestions on how to better protect one's data online, for example by installing ad and tracking blockers, turning off location tracking, using a VPN, changing social media settings or using secure passwords. Related to this, 21 resources recommended using *alternative services*, such as privacy-sensitive independent or non-commercial messaging apps, search engines or email providers.

While steps towards more data protection online and using alternative services are easy to suggest and often also to implement, these are not final solutions for the problems surrounding datafication. There are many controversial issues, such as risks of discrimination related to data systems, the use of automated decision-making systems in increasing societal areas, or risks of surveillance through smart technologies (for more details, see chapter 2.1), that cannot be addressed by individuals changing their behaviour online. For this reason, many scholars argue that critical data literacy approaches should not shift responsibility to the individuals by conveying the impression that it is up to the individuals to solve these issues through an altered internet usage (e.g., Pangrazio and Selwyn 2019; Carmi et al. 2020).

In order to examine whether existing online critical data literacy resources recognised this shift of responsibility to individuals as problematic and suggested broader, more systemic approaches instead of, or alongside, individual solutions, the content analysis further tested for a *systemic approach*. One resource that met this variable very well was the "Lernparcours Big Data" by the youth media centre "jfc Medienzentrum" (R18). In its section "Becoming active" (original: "Aktiv werden"), the website writes:

> Learning about this topic [big data] can often lead to feelings of helplessness and powerlessness. This is understandable, as we are experiencing a profound technological and societal transformation through digitisation. Big commercial and governmental interests are fuelling this development. It is characterised by global entanglements and high technological dynamics. Individuals and the civil society are initially in a weak position. (jfc Medienzentrum [no date], own translation)

Following this statement, the website takes different options of "becoming active" into consideration. For example, it argues that abstinence is not an option as this restricts social participation. Some tips for "digital self-defence" are offered, but the website highlights that these steps require certain knowledge along with self-discipline, and that they can still be subverted by the companies behind the internet services. Thus, the website concludes, what is needed is *awareness-raising*, as this helps users become aware of data collection and its risks, such as discrimination, as well as *becoming politically active*. The website clearly calls for political action and asks readers to become active in political parties, via consumer advice centres and in civil society.

However, this elaborate and sophisticated practical advice is unusual in the sample. In total, only 16 resources met the variable "systemic approach": one resource met it very well, nine met it and six somewhat met it (see fig. 7). Further examples include the "Klicksafe" website's section "What can we do" that calls for privacy-by-design and for becoming politically active (R28), and the "Mathwashing" website that urges users to think critically and to "demand to know how 'what is good' [in an automated decision-making system] is decided upon. In a democracy we decide this together. You should have a say" (R68). The "Digital Defense Playbook" further includes a "community defense toolkit" and activities to move "from paranoia to power" and for people to "recognize their collective strength in identifying and practicing alternatives to oppressive, unjust data collection and data-driven systems" (R31, p. 70).

Other Types of Practical Advice

These examples not only clearly met the variable testing for a systemic approach, but they also constitute ideal examples for *political / societal activism* as a form of practical advice (see fig. 8). This form of advice was comparatively rare and was only identified in 16 of the 75 resources. It was often provided in combination with other forms of advice.

The third most common form of advice in the sample – after advice on data protection and alternative services – was coded as *networks of literacy* (18 resources in total, see fig. 8). Resources in this category actively asked users to share their new knowledge and awareness with others, thus establishing "networks of literacy" (Carmi et al. 2020, p. 12), or starting a "chain reaction" of critical thought (Markham 2019, p. 756) as discussed in the academic literature. In practice, this could mean asking users to share their knowledge with their friends and family, such as the "Dataselfie" website that asks users to "share your knowledge!" on the bottom of each page (R20), or providing material that can be used to inform others about datafication.

One less common type of advice in the sample consisted in fostering the *imagination of alternatives*. Again, this is discussed and recommended in the academic literature (see chapter 2.2; 3.4) but was identified in only eleven resources. Two resources that met this category very well were the "Do Not Track" video series (R9) and the simulation game "Future Influencer" (R46). In the game, secondary pupils act out a fictional future, in which they decide how much and what data is collected by a smart bracelet that is mandatory for all pupils. In the Do Not Track series, the last episode "To Change The Future, Click Here" brings together different arguments made throughout the series and finally offers three possible imaginations of the future: "Big Brother", "Big Business" or "Big Win" (Gaylor et al. 2015). All three future scenarios are detailed in short stories that start from the present (at the time the resource was developed in 2015) and detail key developments around datafication until 2021–2024.[2] The reader is thus shown different imaginations of the future: one full of surveillance, where liberty is sacrificed for security; one of the "glory days of big data" and the companies behind it; and one in which the internet is governed internationally and with the interest of citizens in mind and where "a balance is struck between privacy and the rule of law" (ibid.). These detailed imaginations are very much in line with calls to foster people's "critical imagination" (Milan 2017, no page number) or "infrastructural imagination" in relation to data systems (Gray et al. 2018, p. 3).

Figure 8: Different types of practical advice identified in the resources.

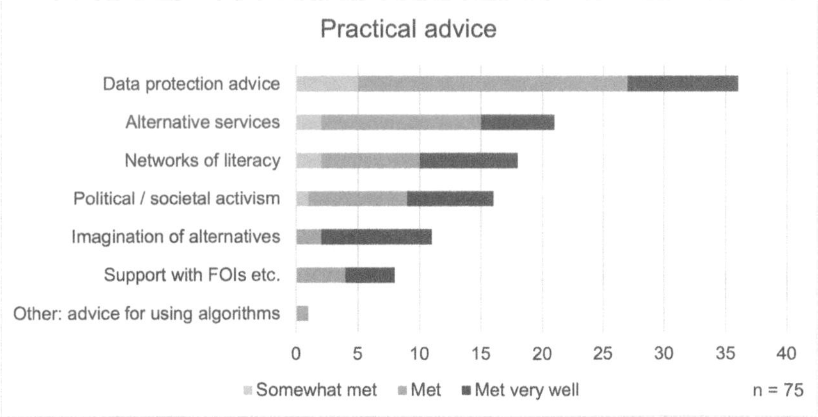

Another rare form of advice was *support with Freedom of Information requests (FOIs)*, which was identified in eight resources. While most combined this with other forms of advice, one resource focussed entirely on this type of advice: a short documentary on how to access one's data through Freedom of Information requests (R21). Finally, one resource provided practical advice that was not included in the coding sheet and was thus coded as "other". The "Mathwashing" website offers three steps of practical

2 However, this example also highlights how quickly these resources can become outdated, as today's users are likely confused by "future" scenarios that take place between 2021–2024.

advice (two are already outlined above), of which one addresses people who apply data systems: "If you're deploying algorithmic systems, learn about their limitations. Hire an ethics expert to do an algorithmic audit" (R68). This direct call to action is unusual and was not found in any other resource in the sample.

Appealing Visualisations

As explained in chapter four, the coding sheet included a "special category" variable which was intended to highlight resources that take an unusual approach (content or format); fit the project focus extremely well; or came especially recommended by established practitioners. Most of these aspects predominantly aimed to support a selection of diverse expert interviewees. Yet, some novel findings were identified: only 17 of 75 resources used *appealing visualisations*. This appears to be a small number considering that using visualisations of data systems is an approach that is often suggested in the literature as one way of materialising complex topics around data technologies (D'Ignazio and Bhargava 2015; Windeyer 2019; Pangrazio and Selwyn 2020). However, it should be noted that this variable is difficult to code and, to some extent, a matter of interpretation. More details on the reasoning behind using visualisations emerged in the interview findings and will be discussed in chapters 5.2 and 6. A small selection of data visualisations from the sample are displayed below (figure 9–11).

Figure 9: Visualisation of the "Datenkraken" (data octopuses) by the teaching material "Lehrmittel Big Data", R39.

Illustration: Nina Christen, Team Tumult, © Museum für Kommunikation, Bern.

Figure 10: Visualisation of the "Chupadados, the Datasucker" monster (Felizi and Varon [no date]), R6.

Figure 11: "Toy algorithm" that visualises how different variables affect the outcome of an algorithmic calculation included in the website "Automating NYC", R33.

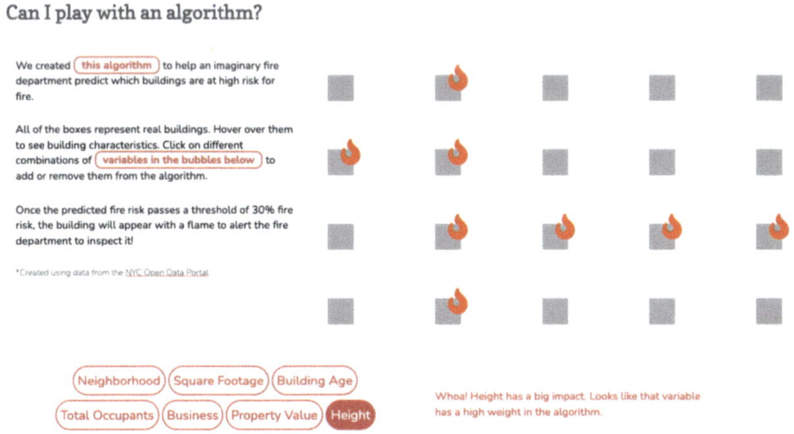

5.1.4 Conclusion and Discussion

Introducing the Topic of Datafication

The first question the content analysis aimed to address asked about the range of online critical data literacy resources that could be identified. 75 different and diverse resources might seem like a large number that could be identified and analysed. However, since 250 resources were examined in total, this also means that 175 did not meet my study's qualifying criteria. This seems high considering the broad nature of the criteria for inclusion – the resources should educate about datafication, foster critical reflection and require no prior knowledge. A common reason for exclusion was that resources lacked a general introduction to datafication and jumped directly to specific topics such as data protection, digital rights or police surveillance. These resources could be very valuable for people who already understand the basics of datafication and want to learn more about specific aspects. However, considering citizen's fragmented and incomplete knowledge about datafication (see chapter 2.1), a general introduction to datafication should be a key part of critical data literacy resources.

Novel Findings regarding the Resources' Origins and Formats

The content analysis further examined the creation backgrounds and defining features of online critical data literacy resources. The analysis revealed *international* and *multilingual* resources in *diverse formats* and from *diverse creators*. The 75 analysed resources originated from ten different countries and were available in 17 languages. However, both of these characteristics were distributed unequally throughout the sample and were likely affected by the sample's sources. The majority of resources originated in Germany or English-speaking countries (US, UK or Canada), and only 18 were available in more than one language. Overall, a higher proportion of multilingual resources would be desirable in order to reach different audiences and offer them resources in their preferred language. However, the sample of my study is by no means representative or comprehensive, and it is possible that many resources in other languages exist. Moreover, if the sample's resources' target groups were primarily native German and English speakers, the predominance of these languages would be appropriate.

In line with previous research, the most common *formats* were websites and short videos, and the most common *creators* came from civil society and journalism and media production (Sander 2020c; Young and Pridmore Forthcoming). However, many resources were also developed by researchers and public institutions. Thus, it seems that Iliadis and Russo's call for critical data literacy scholars to contribute to data literacy efforts and provide individuals "with the necessary tools for becoming more informed and the ability to organize efforts around data justice issues" is being implemented (2016, p. 5). Moreover, the analysis identified a large number (nearly a third of the analysed resources) of online courses or teaching and training material. This might be explained by a growing general awareness of topics around data technologies or by changing curricula. For example, one of the Swiss resources was created as a reaction to the new Swiss school subject "media and informatics" (interview with Siegenthaler, see chapter 5.2). The amount of educational material on datafication identified in this analysis further reinforces scholarly calls for supporting "networks of literacy" and a "chain reaction" of critical thought as it enables individuals to easily spread their knowledge and educate others about datafication (Markham 2019; Carmi et al. 2020). Moreover, the great variety of formats that was identified supports the "no one-size-fits-all" argument (Carmi et al. 2020; chapter 2.2), as different formats take different approaches – textual, visual, audio-visual or interactive – which correspond with different learning types, thus helping different learners to approach the topic in a way that works for them.

Parallels between the Theory and Practice?

Finally, the analysis explored to what extent the identified resources aligned with the preliminary framework for critical datafication literacy. Strong parallels that could be identified included that more than two-thirds of the analysed resources provided (different forms of) practical or constructive advice; that two-thirds incorporated real-life examples and that about half of the resources used interactive elements. Thus, the majority of resources corresponded with scholarly calls for applied and participatory approaches (D'Ignazio and Bhargava 2015; Iliadis and Russo 2016; Markham 2019); for connecting people's real-life experiences with data (Freire 2017; Fontichiaro et al. 2017); and for including "practical strategies and tactics" (Pangrazio and Sefton-Green 2020, p. 218).

However, other characteristics of the preliminary literacy framework were less common. While the sample included many different formats, which help cater to different learner types, only 29 resources seemed to recognise the need to provide different approaches for different audiences, and the large majority seemed to address the general population. Although it is not always possible to recognise the intended target group of a resource without talking to the creators, this nevertheless demonstrates that a "one-size-fits-all approach" seems to be more widespread than recommended by the literature. Moreover, only few resources addressed the difficult balance between empowering individuals through data protection advice but not merely shifting responsibility to individuals but rather promoting a systemic approach. While 16 of the 75 resources openly communicated this intricacy and called for, among other approaches, societal and political action, six others took a contrary position and clearly *urged individuals to take responsibility* for their data. They would, for example, demonstrate to users that their data are "the new gold" and argue: "It is therefore up to each individual to become active and protect their privacy" (R24, p. 2, own translation). Both challenges – addressing different audiences and finding a balance between empowerment and responsibility – will be discussed in more detail in chapter six based on findings from the next two empirical perspectives.

Overall, the answer to the third guiding question of the content analysis can only be: the analysed resources are *somewhat* in line with my preliminary literacy framework. While some characteristics were identified in the majority of the sample, others were rare in the analysed resources. Yet, the content analysis identified a small number of resources that offered elaborate and sophisticated approaches to critically educate about datafication, cater to different audiences – without requiring any prior knowledge – and provide detailed constructive advice – without shifting responsibility to the individuals. Moreover, a number of novel approaches were identified. These provided valuable new insights for the further development of this study's framework for critical datafication literacy, and informed both the expert interviews with resource creators and the qualitative survey with educators.

5.2 Goals, Strategies and Challenges of Critical Data Literacy Resource Creators

The goal of my study was to learn from practitioners of critical data literacy: creators of online educational resources about datafication, and educators who might use these resources to foster critical understanding of data systems through their educational work. In order to learn from the resource creators, ten diverse resources were selected based on the previous content analysis and 12 expert interviews (ten initial and two follow-up interviews) with their creators were conducted and analysed along with additional material (see chapter four). The interviews demonstrated that while the interviewed resource creators may not necessarily use the concept of "literacy", they all had specific educational goals they wanted to achieve with their resource. Key goals included fostering systemic understanding of datafication, promoting critical thought, and empowering learners to become active – both individually and collectively. Moreover, the interviews led to novel findings on how these objectives can be reached through the format of online resources, for example highlighting strategies to create personal involvement and develop engaging and entertaining resources. Finally, challenges around the funding of resources, evaluating them and keeping them up to date were discussed. This chapter presents key findings on these themes, which include strong parallels but also some diverging opinions among the different interviewees. Overall, the expert interviewees provided numerous new insights for the further development of critical datafication literacy in this study.

5.2.1 Creation Contexts of Critical Data Literacy Resources

As outlined in more detail in chapter three, the multistage selection process for this analysis led to a final sample of ten diverse resources (see table 5). This sample included a variety of design formats, such as websites, collections of teaching material, interactive video experiences, an online game, short videos, podcasts, data protection toolkits and several brochures. The ten resources were produced in six different countries (Canada, France, Germany, Switzerland, United Kingdom, United States) by creators from various backgrounds.

Table 5: The ten selected resources and the creators who were interviewed for the study.

Reference (see appendix II)	Resource Name	Interviewee(s)
R17	Anna. Das vernetzte Leben	Ludwig Reicherstorfer
R33	Automating NYC	Akina Younge, Deepra Yusuf, Jon Truong
R62	Center for Humane Technology	David Jay
R75	Clear Your Tracks	Ed Parkes
R41	Datak – A game about personal data	Julien Schekter
R9	Do Not Track	Brett Gaylor
R39	Lehrmittel Big Data	Carmen Siegenthaler
R18	Lernparcours Big Data	Esther Lordieck
R10	Me and My Shadow	Fieke Jansen
R2	My Data and Privacy Online	Mariya Stoilova

This variety in the resources' creation backgrounds and thus the diversity in my expert interviewees' vocational contexts was one of the first findings from the interviews. Three of the interviewees created the resources as part of their work in non-governmental organisations such as the *Tactical Technology Collective* (Jansen);[3] the *iRightsLab*, formerly NGO, now think tank (Reicherstorfer); or the *Center for Humane Tech* (Jay). Two others worked in journalism and media production: Gaylor as a documentary filmmaker and Schekter as a producer journalist for the *Swiss National Radio*. Further roles included working as a media pedagogue at the youth media centre *jfc Medienzentrum* (Lordieck) or as a research fellow at the *Department of Media and Communication* at the London School of Economics (Stoilova). The interview sample further included some more unusual backgrounds for critical data literacy resource creators. Parkes, for example, has a consultancy for "data innovation and data transformation projects in the public sector" (Parkes Interview, 2021), and created "Clear Your Tracks" (R75) together with his colleague Jemma Venables as part of his freelancing work. Equally unusual is the background of "Automating NYC" (R33): It was

3 Jansen was involved in the development of "Me and My Shadow" (R10) and many other resources by the Tactical Technology Collective but did not work at the organisation anymore when the interview was conducted.

created by Akina Younge, Deepra Yusuf, Elyse Voegeli and Jon Truong as part of their Master's Thesis on Public Policy at the *Harvard Kennedy School*. Finally, the "Lehrmittel Big Data" (R39) was created by Carmen Siegenthaler, a museum communicator and former teacher, and her colleagues at the *Museum for Communication* in Bern.

Thus, this short introduction of my interviewees and the contexts in which they developed the different online educational resources on datafication already provides a first valuable finding: critical data literacy resources can be created in a variety of contexts by a variety of actors. As the further analysis throughout this chapter shows, this variety can also be found in the funding and the target audiences of the examined resources. Nevertheless, many common goals and strategies were identified among the interviewees – along with some significant controversies.

5.2.2 Critical Data Literacy Resource Creators' Goals

Overall, twelve main themes were identified in the analysis (see fig. 12). These were structured along three categories. The first, *goals of the resource*, describes the resource creators' idea of a 'literate' or empowered citizen, or, in other words, their practical understanding of critical data literacy: What should people know, understand or do after using their resource? The second category, *creators' strategies and principles*, represents the 'how': How did the creators try to reach their goal of a 'literate' citizen? How did they decide on the resources' format, design and content? The third category finally addresses *challenges and practical considerations*. This category summarises key challenges that repeatedly emerged across the different interviews together with the creators' considerations on using their resource in educational settings.

The main themes that are shown in figure 12 constitute the key findings for each category – the key answers to the research question. However, the most interesting findings could often be found in the subthemes of each main theme. These provide the (sometimes controversial) answers to open questions and dilemmas that had emerged in the prior stages of my study, such as: What exactly does a 'critical reflection' of data technologies entail? How can abstract issues around datafication be made tangible? Which actions should people take? Should citizens' digital skills be fostered or does this only shift responsibility to the individuals? Thus, it is these subthemes that show many parallels to key findings from the theory chapters and chapter 5.1, and that highlight diverging opinions between the expert interviewees' perspectives. For this reason, the subthemes identified in the analysis are not only outlined and discussed throughout this chapter but are also visualised for each category (see fig. 13, 14 and 15).

Figure 12: Categories and main themes identified in the expert interview analysis.

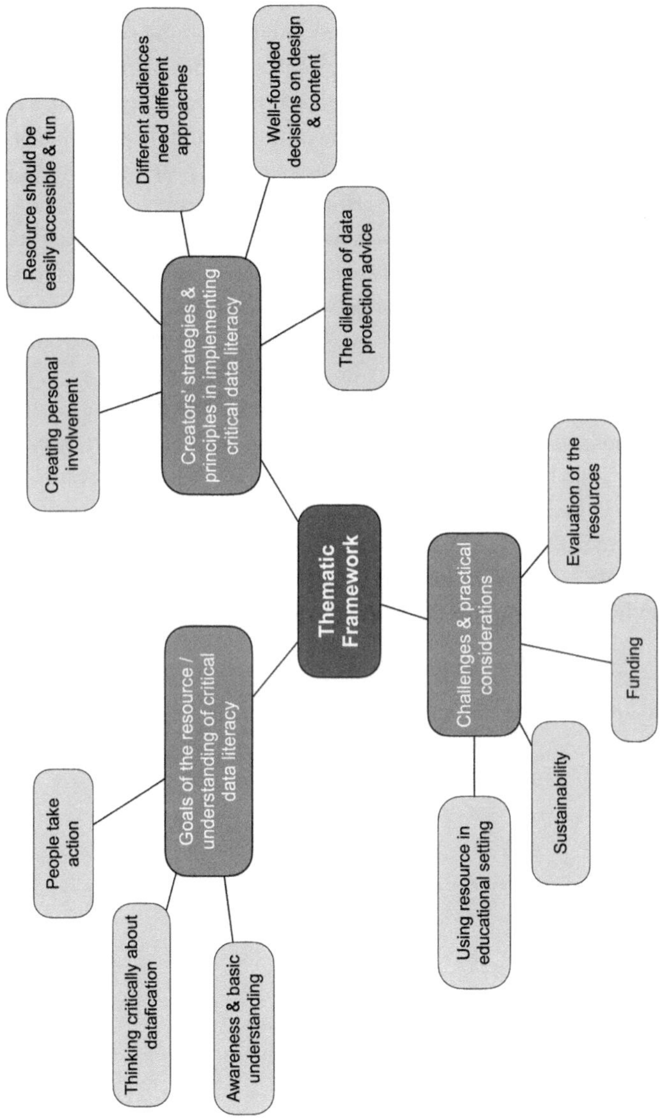

Awareness and Basic Understanding

The creators' goals for their resources and their practical understanding of critical data literacy could be condensed into three main themes. Figure 13 displays these three main themes and their related subthemes. The first main theme that was identified was awareness and basic understanding. Particularly considering citizen's lacking awareness of the use of algorithms (e.g., Grzymek and Puntschuh 2019; Hitlin and Rainie 2019) and their "major understanding gap" when it comes to the business model of the internet (Doteveryone 2018, p. 5), *raising awareness* about data systems is an expectable goal of critical data literacy resources.

However, the interviewed creators wanted to go beyond awareness: they wanted to demystify technology. Eight of the ten interviewees stated that one goal of their resource was for people to gain an *understanding of how the technology around them functions*, including its *shortcomings* and the "assumptions baked into the product development process" (Jay Interview, 2021). Brett Gaylor even specified such "visceral understanding of the way that their data is used online" as the key goal – or the "big hairy audacious goal, so BHAG" – of his resource Do Not Track (Gaylor Interview, 2020). Apart from technologies' shortcomings, some of the creators also aimed for people to *learn about opportunities* of data and technology. This represented somewhat of a contrast to the overall critical perspective of the examined resources. Yet, including how people can "save the world through big data" (Siegenthaler Interview, 2021) could also help with the issue of fear and resignation, which is further discussed below.

Figure 13: Main themes and subthemes in the category "goals of the resource" in the expert interview analysis.

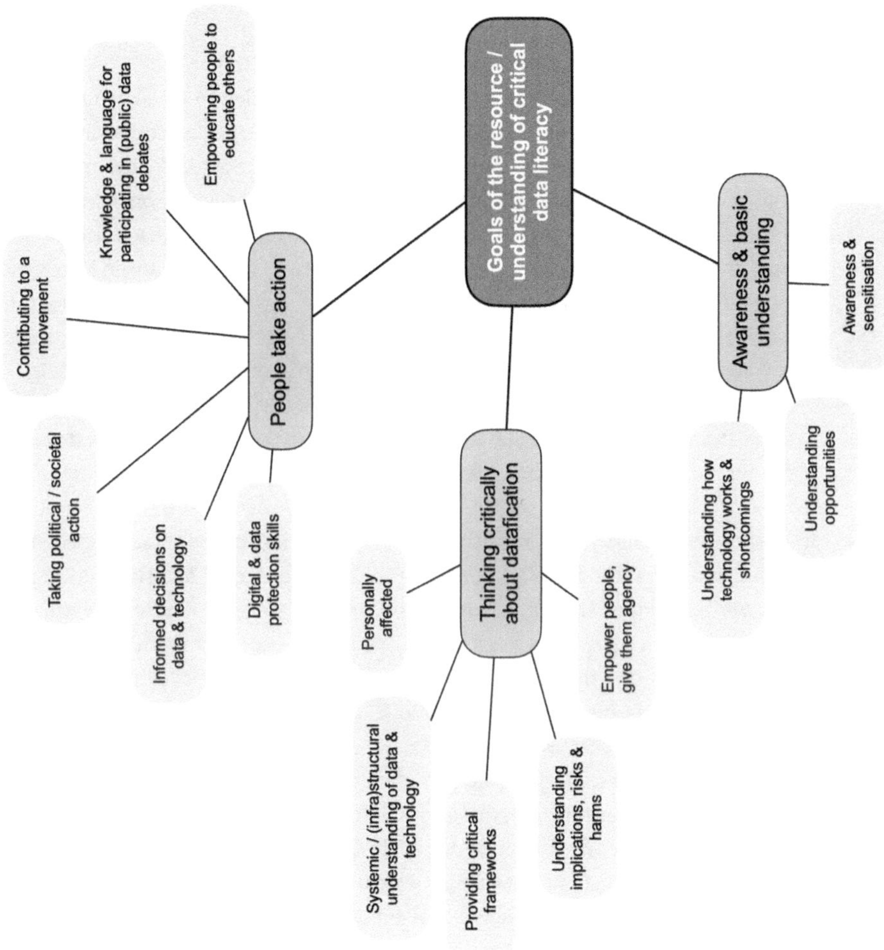

Thinking Critically about Datafication

The second main theme identified as a key goal of the creators was to encourage users to think critically about datafication. This goal was expected since critical reflection was one of the qualifying criteria for selecting the resources in the prior analysis (see 5.1). However, examining *how* exactly practitioners envision this critical reflection to take place and how they try to foster it led to novel insights. One goal that many interviewed creators highlighted was to provide people with *critical frameworks* to think differently about digital technologies. Some, like the creators of Automating NYC, wanted to "give people a conceptual framework from which to enter" (Truong Interview, 2021). Others aimed for their resource to teach people how to apply "their own social and political frameworks" to technology (Jansen Interview, 2020). Either way, many hoped to change the way people think about technology, to encourage them to critically reflect on technology and to "continuously ask questions" and "think outside what they know so far" (Siegenthaler Interview, 2021).

Related to this, many creators wanted the users of their resources to gain *systemic or (infra)structural understanding of data and technologies*. Such broader understanding – not just of how data technologies function, but also of the process of datafication and its implications on individuals and wider political, societal and economic impacts – is currently still missing from many critical data literacy concepts in academia (see chapter 2.2), but is a key aspect of the critical datafication literacy framework developed throughout my study (see chapter 3.4). The interviewed creators described this perspective as "helping people have a systemic view on how this technology is limiting their agency" and "reveal[ing] the systemic forces underneath [social media]" (Jay Interview, 2021); or as a "sociological, societal understanding" (Younge Interview, 2021).

To foster people's critical reflection of data technologies, the majority of creators aimed to educate about the *risks and harms* that come with datafication and to make people realise *how they themselves are affected* by issues around data and technologies. They aimed for people to understand "how data about you can impact your life online and offline" (Gaylor Interview, 2020) and to create "personal involvement" (Reicherstorfer Interview, 2021). Specific strategies on how to reach this involvement are discussed in section 5.2.3 below. Apart from feeling that they are personally affected, the creators further wanted to make people *feel empowered* and to give them "real agency" (Stoilova Interview, 2021). This leads to the third key goal of the interviewed creators: they wanted learners to take action.

People Take Action

In light of the common criticism that critical data literacy and other awareness-raising efforts do not specify what comes after increased awareness, this third theme was particularly significant. The uncertainty of unclear steps after awareness also came up in the interviews: "the question is then always: What now? Knowledge is the one thing, knowledge transfer is the one thing, but what results from this?" (Reicherstorfer Interview, 2021). Brett Gaylor further pointed out that people ask the question of "what can I do? [...] almost every time" they watch a documentary or hear about a societal issue, but, he argues, "that's not the right question to ask about systemic issues. You probably can't do that much" (Gaylor Interview, 2021). Another creator, Carmen Siegenthaler, took a similar stance from another perspective, stating that changing the behaviour of her resource's users is in her view a goal that is too big and unrealistic (Siegenthaler Interview, 2021).

Despite this uncertainty about whether it is possible to get people to take action, and whether this action would lead to any significant changes to the problems around datafication, all resources aimed at people taking action in one way or another. Two common goals were to increase people's *digital and data protection skills* and to enable them to *make informed decisions* about the technologies they want to use in the future. This reiterates findings of the analysis of resources in chapter 5.1, which also found a strong focus on advice on data protection and alternative services. The interviewed creators for example outlined that they wanted to give users "better control" of their data and help them develop healthier habits in their use of digital technologies (Stoilova Interview, 2021); that they hoped to create the "prerequisite for self-responsibility" (Reicherstorfer Interview, 2021); and aimed to empower people to make "enlightened choices. If you give your data, just know what you are doing, that's the main goal" (Schekter Interview, 2021). Enabling people to make informed choices rather than telling them what to do is a strategy several interviewees followed and that will be further discussed below. However, as already touched upon above, practical advice and the idea of "enlightened choices" were also controversial among the interviewees, as some argued that the technology is too sophisticated and the issues are too systemic, which makes actual enlightened choices impossible. This dilemma around data protection advice will be further discussed below.

Beyond taking individual and technical steps to protect one's data, several interviewees hoped the users of their resources would become active on a societal level. For example, four creators outlined that they wanted to enable people to *take part in public debates* about data technologies by providing them with the necessary knowledge and the appropriate language. The aspect of requiring a "data language" in order to participate in public debates was discussed in detail by Akina Younge, Deepra Yusuf and Jon Truong. They criticised the "expectation that everyone needs to have technical expertise" and the "gatekeeping nature" of this expectation (Younge Interview, 2021). Akina Younge further stated:

> I wish it weren't the case, that people didn't need this, I don't think this should be the case, I don't think that's the way the world should work. I believe the political education stuff is way more important and I understand that the contextual reality is that they're going to be dismissed if they don't say some of the right words. (ibid.)

This argument of needing the "right" language in order to be able to participate in public debates about data systems and to be taken seriously represents a crucial aspect of critical data education that does not receive much attention in the literature as yet. Others similarly wanted to "create a shared vocabulary" (Jay Interview, 2021), and give people a language to "articulate … [their concerns about facial recognition] through a lived experience" (Gaylor Interview, 2021). Some interviewees hoped that enabling more people to make their voices heard in personal and public discussions about data, would help "shift the frame around which problems with technology are discussed" (Jay Interview, 2021).

Several interviewed creators articulated even more ambitious goals and wanted to empower people to *take societal or political action* – an approach that was already identified in the content analysis of resources (see chapter 5.1) – or even hoped to *contribute to a movement*. Esther Lordieck very clearly argued that changing one's device settings is not enough, but that political action is needed. She aimed to empower young people to form their own opinion and make it heard, for example by contacting political parties about data issues (Lordieck Interview, 2021). Mariya Stoilova took a similar stance, wanting to make "children more active participants and citizens in a digital environment" (Stoilova Interview, 2021). Although some admitted that "we're not going to turn everyone into activists" (Parkes Interview, 2021), three interviewees outlined that they saw their resources as "someone's first step into a broader movement" and hoped that for some people, the educational resource "will be a journey into more leadership in the movement" (Jay Interview, 2021). Deepra Yusuf further specified that she thinks "we are really just at the cusp of starting that movement", in which the knowledge trickles from academia to creators of critical data literacy resources and "hopefully then following that, you really have the on the ground movement" (Yusuf Interview, 2020).

These very ambitious and political goals of the creators are unusual in critical data literacy scholarship but resemble "re-active data activism". This form of activism aims to educate about data technologies and fight against the datafication and its problematic implications (see chapter 2.1). Data activists encourage citizens to carry out "practices of resistance", such as "self-defence, civil disobedience and disruption" (Milan and Gutiérrez 2015, p. 122; Milan and van der Velden 2016, p. 67). Thus, re-active data activism represents a similarly politically activist stance as my interviewees, albeit possibly with a more disruptive focus in contrast to my participants' idea of citizens enacting their democratic rights.

Finally, some interviewees specifically wanted to start a snowball effect of education, hoping to *empower people to educate others* by publishing teaching material, curricula and public speaking material as part of their resource. This correlates with scholarly calls to support learners to foster reflection and literacy for those around them (Markham 2019, p. 756; Carmi et al. 2020, p. 12). Nevertheless, other interviewees also highlighted that comprehensive, systematic data education cannot be provided by small non-governmental organisations and other critical data literacy resource creators but that a literacy strategy should be developed by governments (Jansen Interview, 2020).

5.2.3 Creators' Strategies and Principles for Implementing Critical Data Literacy into Practice

The analysis of the expert interviews further revealed novel findings regarding the strategies and principles for implementing critical data literacy into practice. Five main themes were identified in total: Creating personal involvement; resource should be easily accessible and fun; different audiences need different approaches; well-founded decisions on design and content; and the dilemma of data protection advice (see fig. 14). Many of these reiterate theoretical findings and academic discussions on critical data literacy (see chapter 2.2), such as the aim for a low threshold, the "no one-size-fits-all" approach or considerations around providing practical advice while not shifting responsibility to individuals. The interviewees further provided many suggestions on how these approaches can be implemented in practice, including some parallels to academic discussions as well as a number of controversial issues among the interviewed creators.

Figure 14: Main themes and subthemes in the category "creators' strategies and principles in implementing critical data literacy" in the expert interview analysis.

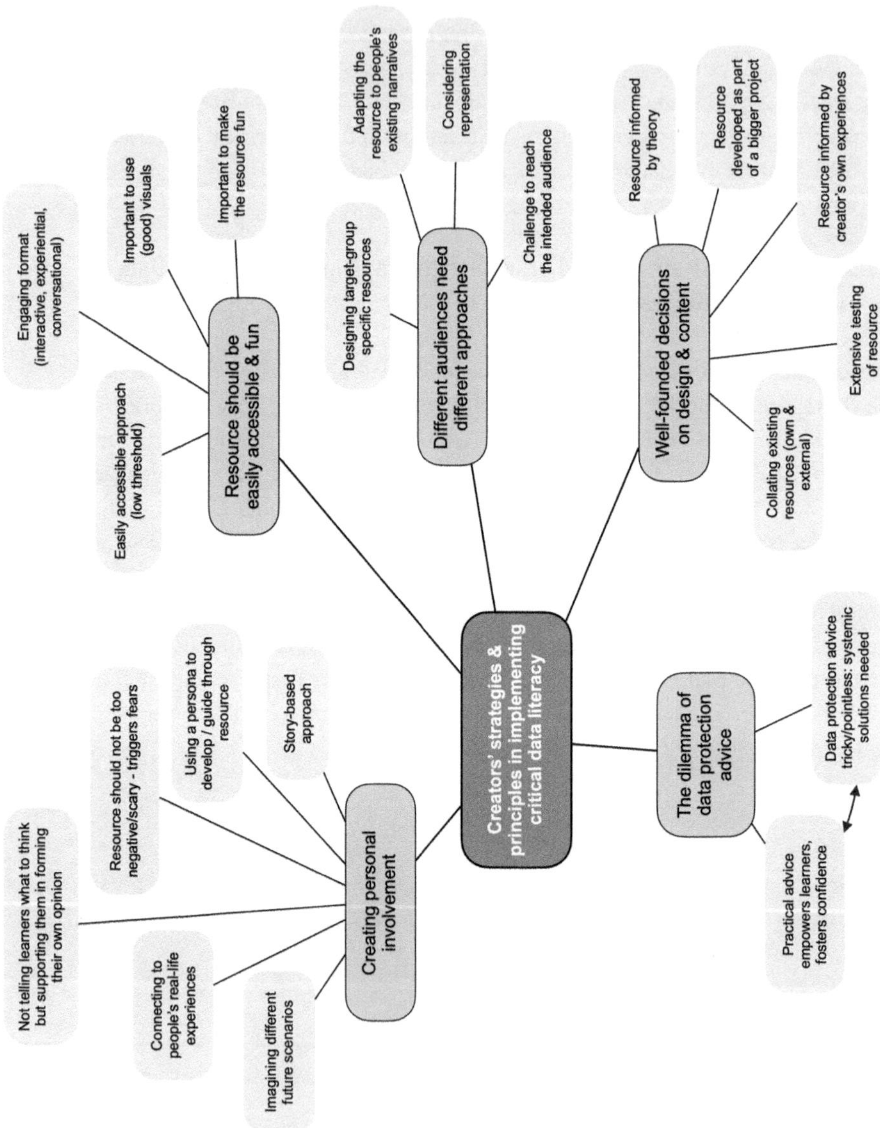

Creating Personal Involvement

As already highlighted above, many interviewees aimed to create a sense of personal involvement through their resources, to make people realise that issues around the datafication of our societies affect them personally. According to the interviewed experts, this is necessary because of "issue fatigue" (Yusuf Interview, 2020) in society, with too many problematic issues that citizens could or should be concerned about. Critical data literacy resources should therefore try to move issues around datafication into people's "circle of worry", which includes issues they are concerned about, such as "am I going to have a job; is the earth going to explode; am I going to get Covid-19?" (Gaylor Interview, 2020). All interviewees agreed that a sense of personal involvement should be created to demonstrate to people why they should care about issues around datafication. The creators applied several strategies to reach this personal involvement. Some of these were already identified in the prior analysis of online resources (chapter 5.1), but also some entirely new approaches emerged.

A very common strategy among the interviewed creators was to connect their resources to *people's real-life experiences* with technology. One way to implement this that was also identified in the previous analysis of 75 resources was to include real-life stories in the resource. One example is the story of Porfirio, the owner of a bodega (a small type of grocery store common in New York City), who was nearly put out of business due to a faulty fraud detection algorithm (see R33). The Automating NYC website uses this story as an "entry point" and common thread throughout the resource in order to make the "immaterial and abstract" issues around automated decision-making systems more tangible (Truong Interview, 2021). Other approaches for connecting to people's lives were to demonstrate that data technologies already affect nearly every area of life and "I am confronted with this every day" (Reicherstorfer Interview, 2021); to encourage people to talk "about their own experiences and the experiences of their friends and the harms showing up in their life and in their community" (Jay Interview, 2021); to include real-life dilemmas in the resource (Schekter Interview, 2021); and to make the resource itself experiential (see below). The Datak game (R41) even included a real-life impact: if users entered their real phone number they would receive an automatic call by a masked number one hour later, which first tried to trick the users and then admitted that "it's just a machine, but you have played Datak and maybe you should think twice next time you put your real number wherever on the web" (Schekter Interview, 2021).

A second very common strategy to create personal involvement that was suggested by the majority of creators was *to not tell people what to think*, but to support them in forming their own opinions. Several interviewees emphasised that critical data literacy resources should try "not to be moral" and not tell "that's wrong or that's good" (Schekter Interview, 2021). Instead, they should educate about advantages and risks and empower learners to "form your own opinion and make it heard" (Lordieck Interview, 2021). This could be achieved by including "philosophical thought experiments", which suggest different data scenarios to learners and encourage them to imagine how they would handle data in each scenario (Siegenthaler Interview, 2021). Another approach is to prompt people with questions rather than imposing answers, which, according to Truong and Younge constitutes "good pedagogy" (Truong Interview, 2021). They deliberately used questions as headers to allow readers to "lean into something that you might disagree with" (Younge Interview, 2021), and often tried to foster people's critical reflection "without telling people the answer, which I think is a really important part of education" (Truong Interview, 2021).

Related to the question of morality highlighted above, the question of how negative or scary a resource should be kept emerging in the interviews. While some interviewees admitted that fear gets people's attention, most agreed that *critical data literacy resources should not be too negative*. Using fear to educate, they argued, means that "right away you'll lose a bunch of people because they'll be like [...], I don't want to think about that" (Gaylor Interview, 2020). They further stated that fear "does not help anyone" as it does not offer solutions (Reicherstorfer Interview, 2021), and that it is the "worst way to learn because if you scare people, they stop learning" (Jansen Interview, 2020). Instead, many agreed that educational resources should be "colourful and fun" (Jansen Interview, 2020; see also below). However, others believed that "a certain amount of fear is useful" for particular groups of people (Parkes Interview, 2021), or argued that people can be reached "through a negative emotion" (Jay Interview, 2021). Lordieck tried to find a balance between these positions, arguing that there is a "thin line" as resource creators often feel strongly about datafication, but they still want their resource to not be too negative (Lordieck Interview, 2021). Thus, it can be said that the interviewed creators did not agree on a common stance toward a fear-based approach to critical data literacy but rather expressed divided opinions. This is in line with the student users of critical data literacy resources in my prior study, who had in part stated that they wanted to be "scare[d] into it" and that this is "always necessary", and in part argued that scaring people is "not the right approach" and people should not do "the right thing because they're scared" (Sander 2020c, p. 12).

Besides these discussions, the interviewees provided further concrete suggestions on how to create a sense of personal involvement. For example, many creators placed a great emphasis on the use of stories in their resources. Brett Gaylor explained the *importance of stories* to foster specific narratives in critical data literacy resources:

> The thing is if you want people to move towards a narrative, it's not necessarily that you just tell them that. [...] you have to drop all these little breadcrumbs, so you can tell a story that promotes that narrative. Narratives have a protagonist; they have

> an emotion that they generate and they have an ending which is a happy ending or an unhappy ending. (Gaylor Interview, 2020)

Similarly, Carmen Siegenthaler argued that stories help learners to critically reflect on issues and form their own judgement, without a moral perspective of "you have to behave like this, this or this" (Siegenthaler Interview, 2021). Other creators equally found that stories are the best way to reach people and to communicate complex issues (Yusuf Interview, 2020), and that stories are popular, with Ed Parkes' testing audience demanding: "why don't you just tell us what it is, tell us a story about what actually happens" (Parkes Interview, 2021).

Another approach that could easily be connected with a story-based strategy was to foster people's *imagination of different data futures*. Presenting different future scenarios and "articulat[ing] the steps that we need to get there" was seen as a cheap and effective way to motivate people (Gaylor Interview, 2021), and foster people's imagination (Siegenthaler Interview, 2021). Similar calls for different future imaginaries have been made in academic critical data literacy approaches, for example in Gray et al.'s concept of "data infrastructure literacy" that includes the goal of "infrastructural imagination" (referring to Bowker 2014) about how datasets "might be created, used and organised differently (or not at all)" (Gray et al. 2018, p. 3). Yet, this approach was only identified in eleven of the 75 resources analysed in the previous chapter.

Finally, some interviewees suggested to use *personas* in the design of their resource – either visibly, to guide through the resource, or as an invisible personification of their target audience. A visible persona, such as "Anna" in "Anna. Das vernetzte Leben" (R17) functions as an identification figure, that, like the resource's audience, navigates life in a digital society (Reicherstorfer Interview, 2021). However, a persona can also serve as an invisible personification that represents the resource's target audience and guides decisions on design and content along this audience's needs. This was the case in Automating NYC, where Yusuf's mother served as an embodiment of the 'typical' New York citizen (Young and Yusuf Interview, 2020).

Resources Should Be Accessible and Fun

As a second main theme, nearly all interviewees agreed that resources should be easily accessible and fun. They highlighted the importance of an *easily accessible approach*, for example by using friendly and lay language and avoiding technical or too academic definitions; by not using too much text, modularising it into chapters or making it 'skimmable' through headers; and by considering people's convenience when deciding on a format or design. However, an easily accessible approach should not only affect the resource's format, design, and language, but also its content. One way to implement this is through a 'step by step' approach, that begins with basic information that does not require any prior knowledge, and slowly offers more advanced knowledge for those who are interested, such as extensive dossiers on each topic (Reicherstorfer Interview, 2021). Nevertheless, several interviewees highlighted that the balance between technological accuracy versus accessibility, for example when it comes to technical terms, remained a challenge.

Moreover, many expert interviewees agreed that it is good to use an *engaging format* for critical data literacy resources. Mariya Stoilova, for example, conducted workshops with children that informed the development of the "My Data and Privacy Online" toolkit (R2). These revealed that the children most enjoyed using engaging and interactive resources, and they also liked to "find the loopholes" and "outsmart" the resources, whereas "if they just have to sit and watch something, they were like I know this, I don't want to be doing that" (Stoilova Interview, 2021). This reiterates findings of my prior study, in which university student users clearly called for interactive resources (2020c), and strengthens scholarly calls for participatory approaches (e.g., D'Ignazio and Bhargava 2015; Iliadis and Russo 2016).

Other interviewed creators called for interactive resources that constitute a "conversation" or let users have a "tiny little experience" of what it means to be affected by data systems (Gaylor Interview, 2021). The outcome of such an experiential approach, which was also the "overarching strategy" of Siegenthaler, is that learners reach "an essence, an insight" (Siegenthaler Interview, 2021). The popularity of an analogue, black-story-style game included in Siegenthaler's resource further shows that this approach does not necessarily have to be implemented digitally. This experiential rather than 'only' interactive approach was not something I had come across in the academic literature before, but it constitutes a significant finding considering the immateriality of issues around datafication, which often make them difficult to grasp for learners.

As another way to reach people, many interviewed creators highlighted the *importance of using visuals* to illustrate abstract concepts and to offer another way of understanding (Lordieck Interview, 2021). Some examples of this were already illustrated in the previous chapter. However, as Fieke Jansen emphasised, it is crucial to avoid stereotypical visualisations of data systems and instead use images that people can relate to:

> We wanted to be material because if you type in privacy or digital security on Google, you will get padlocks, you get matrix, you get all of these images, but these are images people don't relate to, like it doesn't stick in their heads. So, we wanted to be material, so tangible and relatable. (Jansen Interview, 2020)

Finally, seven of the ten expert interviewees called for *colourful and fun resources*. The entire resource, they argued, should be approachable, playful and entertaining and this should be represented in its visual style. This is particularly important for resources targeting adults, as they "must want to learn" and thus "interest and conversation" must be sustained throughout a training or educational resource (Tactical

Technology Collective 2018, additional material, p. 1f). Similarly, Gaylor argued that "people should enjoy the experience, [...] you should laugh" (Gaylor Interview, 2020). In Do Not Track, he aimed to include an interactive feature in the first 30 seconds of each episode, and he emphasised that especially these interactive tasks should be entertaining and resource creators should always ask themselves: "the thing that you're asking the person to do, is it fun at all?" (ibid.). Others equally stated that they aimed for fun and interesting (Jansen), entertaining (Schekter) and playful (Siegenthaler) resources.

Different Audiences Need Different Approaches

Another main theme that emerged in all interviews – that different audiences need different approaches – was already identified in the literature on critical data literacy (e.g., Carmi et al. 2020) and in the previous chapter. The interviews further revealed that several creators had defined very different and often specific audiences, such as educators, children, teenagers, young adults, parents, "Generation X", activists or advocates, journalists, lawyers, technologists, New York City residents, people who often use the internet, or people who are open to taking action. However, also some broader groups were mentioned, such as all Germans (Reicherstorfer Interview, 2021) or "people who watch TV" (Gaylor Interview, 2021, speaking about his resource "Internet of Everything"). Several creators further found it *difficult to reach the intended audience* for their resource, such as audiences beyond Europe and the US (Jansen Interview, 2020), or beyond the "digital rights communities" in order to not just "preach to the converted" (Gaylor Interview, 2020).

Despite these difficulties, the majority of interviewees emphasised the *importance of target-group specific resources*. In practice, this could mean developing a resource specific for a location (e.g., Automating NYC, R33), creating location-specific versions of a resource (Do Not Track, R9); deciding on a format based on your intended target audience (e.g., podcasts for "senior leaders in tech", Jay Interview, 2021); combining different formats and approaches in one resource to cater to different learning types (Reicherstorfer Interview, 2021); or to collaborate with social media influencers to reach a young target audience (Schekter Interview, 2021). Several creators further emphasised that identifying your audience is "the first thing that you do because decisions will cascade from that" (Gaylor Interview, 2020). Targeting a broad audience was seen as "a big challenge" (Reicherstorfer Interview, 2021) and some interviewees highlighted that it is "probably impossible to make one tool that can reach everyone" (Younge) or that a "product for everyone is a product for no one" (Jansen, additional material, 2020). However, they also argued that "public literacy tools could and should reach everyone" (Younge Interview, 2020).

One way to reach different people through critical data literacy resources is to adapt a resource to *people's existing narratives*. Jansen highlights this when she explains that issues around datafication have "so many dimensions", from technical, social, political to economic, and that there are "different hooks that make people tick and you have to try to find these hooks and build on them" (Jansen Interview, 2020). Gaylor similarly stated that:

> I think what you need to do is you need to understand the narratives that people already have in their head around these issues. [...] They might hold in their head a narrative that you as the maker might consider unhealthy, or that you actually want them to hold a different narrative in their head, like that's part of your goal and that kind of thinking and that kind of persuasion and propaganda is pretty explicitly different than enabling literacies for people. [...] how receptive are those people to different messages? (Gaylor Interview, 2020)

This quote highlights a crucial point: that enabling literacies is a fundamentally different approach than trying to persuade people to adopt a certain opinion. Instead, enabling literacies should mean empowering people to form their own opinion and act on it. To achieve this, people's different points of departure and their existing narratives should be considered, and the resource adapted accordingly. This is in line with Younge and Truong's argument above, which suggested prompting people with questions rather than providing answers in order to invite them to lean into perspectives they might otherwise disagree with.

A final approach to more target-group specific resources that the interviewed creators suggested was that it is important to *consider representation*. Jansen, for example, stated that she deliberately did not use "representations of people because it's very difficult if you work in a global context, what skin colour do you use, what gender do you use, what sex do you use and it always ends up looking horrible" (Jansen Interview, 2020). Several other creators did use a visual persona in the resource (see also above) but refrained from assigning the main characters in their resource a gender (Schekter), or chose a mixed-race person "of indeterminate gender, a non-binary person" (Parkes Interview, 2021). In contrast, Ludwig Reicherstorfer explained how his main character Anna, although she has a defined age, gender, relationship status and living environment, was intended to create a high degree of identification for users through the different scenarios from her life that are depicted in the resource. He stated:

> No matter how old I am, which gender I have, which profession I may have, which training, which level of education etc. – all scenarios apply to me in one way or another. So I am Anna, we all are Anna. (Reicherstorfer Interview, 2021)

Thus, it can be said that several creators considered questions of representation and highlighted its importance for target-group-specific resources, although they drew very different consequences for their resources.

Well-Founded Decisions on Design and Content

The next main theme that was identified concerns the background and development processes of critical data literacy resources. The analysis revealed that the interviewed creators made well-founded decisions on the design and content of the resources. Many explained that their *resource was developed out of a bigger context*, such as an academic research project (Stoilova); a Master's Thesis project including a collaboration with a think tank (Younge, Yusuf and Truong); a user research project with a user-centred design focus (Parkes); a radio show with a number of investigative journalism pieces (Schekter); a new permanent exhibition in a museum for communication that is interconnected with the resource (Siegenthaler); or the creator's practical experiences in giving workshops on data-related issues (Lordieck; Jansen). Some resources were also *informed by theory*. This could be academic theory, as with "My Data and Privacy Online" (R2), which was informed by a "typology of privacy" and "three different notions of data" developed throughout the creators' own research as well as additional media literacy frameworks (Stoilova Interview, 2021). However, it could also be adult learning principles (Jansen) or a model of big data that was developed by the resource creators themselves to make sense of the different levels on which data systems affect our society ("Cassata-model", Siegenthaler Interview, 2021).

Apart from this, many resources were informed by the creator's personal interests in the topic or their *personal experiences* with data technologies. Moreover, several creators stated that one intention to develop their resource was to *collate existing resources* in one place. This could be a collection of their own already existing resources – "a place where we could park a lot of the answers and practices that we developed" (Jansen Interview, 2020), as Schekter, Lordieck and Jansen explained. Or it could be "a way to lift up the people around us" (Jay Interview, 2021), and to collect and recommend existing resources by others, as Stoilova, Siegenthaler and Jay pointed out.

Finally, the analysis demonstrated that some of the interviewed creators conducted *extensive testing of the resource*, often with their target audience. Carmen Siegenthaler, for example, reported testing her teaching material with teachers and in two classrooms with different age groups. Similarly, Julien Schekter also tested his game in two classrooms with different ages. Ed Parkes tested a first prototype of his resource with the use of a professional recruitment agency. Akina Younge, who reported testing with friends, family and fellow students, said: "one of the things that we probably wish we had done more is more extensive user testing" (Younge Interview, 2021).

The Dilemma of Data Protection Advice

A final key finding on the creators' strategies and principles for implementing critical data literacy concerned the dilemma of data protection advice that was already touched on in previous chapters (see chapter 3.4, 5.1). It describes the difficult balance between the importance of providing constructive next steps when educating about datafication to avoid resignation and to encourage learners to become active, while not merely shifting responsibility to individuals (see e.g., Pangrazio and Selwyn 2019, p. 425). Without me actively bringing it up, this dilemma came up in many of the interviews and seemed to be something that many of the interviewed creators faced when developing their resources.

On the one hand, many highlighted that *practical advice on data protection can empower people and foster their confidence*. Ludwig Reicherstorfer argued that it is important to include constructive advice into a resource in order "implement users' understanding into actions" and so that citizens can "feel safe in a digital society" because they can make informed decisions on which services to use. Akina Younge argued further that a certain amount of technical knowledge can "empower people and encourage them and instil the confidence" that they need to articulate their experiences with data, and that it also makes "you seem legitimate to someone else" (Younge Interview, 2021). Esther Lordieck outlined that practical advice on "concrete, tangible things to do" can help to not feel "overrun by a feeling of powerlessness" (Lordieck Interview, 2021). Despite using different terms, these arguments strongly correspond with academic research on resignation and with findings of my previous study, in which participants argued that easy-to-follow practical advice could help against resignation. However, Lordieck also emphasised that it was important to her to not give users the impression that "if you adjust your devices' settings the right way, everything is fine, but I think it is necessary to talk about this on a societal, political level" (ibid.).

This hints at the counterarguments to including practical advice that many interviewees brought up: that *data protection advice is tricky or even pointless because systemic solutions are needed*. The creators brought up different arguments for this perspective. One line of argumentation was that today's technology is "so sophisticated" and there is "so much asymmetric power" that "it's not on us as individuals to use them in a way that's balanced and healthy for us" (Jay Interview, 2021). Suggesting individual solutions thus only "allows them [the big companies] to play on their terms", when what is really needed are "systemic solutions instead of these individual ones, which won't amount to anything" (Gaylor Interview, 2021). This reiterates recent academic research that examined YouTube videos on surveillance resistance. The authors, whose findings will be further discussed in chapter six, argued that while "personal protection can superficially make people feel better", this "small bandage approach to systemic problems feeds into post-privacy mindsets" and "perpetuates a feeling of helplessness beyond individual action" (Young and Pridmore Forthcoming). When calling for systemic solutions to datafication, several interviewed creators further compared challenges of datafication to the issue of climate change, which is a similarly complex and systemic issue that is often approached through individual solutions, such as using reusable bags for shopping or cycling to work instead of driving.

Apart from being pointless, many interviewees further argued that individual solutions to datafication shift responsibility to the individuals. Similar to academic scholars (see above), they emphasised that "putting that burden on the individual" is the "wrong approach" (Gaylor Interview, 2021) and that instead of "shifting everything to the consumers, the legislator has to step in" (Reicherstorfer Interview, 2021). In her own research, interviewee Stoilova even found that "technical skills on their own [...] can actually increase the risk for children and the harmful outcomes" if they are not fostered along with critical reflection (Stoilova Interview, 2021; see also Livingstone et al. 2021a). Only when children learn technical skills together with critical thinking, she explained, can this lead to "better outcomes for children and reduces risk" (ibid.). Jansen further stressed that this education cannot be provided by individual actors such as NGOs, but that "a good data literacy strategy would be something that is offered [...] in the system so that governments prescribe [it] in educational packages" (Jansen Interview, 2020).

Overall, the question of data protection advice remains a dilemma. The interviewed creators in my study did not agree on a common stance towards whether or not, how much, and what type of practical advice should be included in critical data literacy resources. Often, the interviewees themselves saw both sides of the issues, highlighting the advantages of practical advice as well as the risks that come with it. Thus, the inclusion of practical advice remains challenging when implementing critical data literacy into practice.

5.2.4 Challenges and Practical Considerations in Developing Critical Data Literacy Resources

Apart from the already discussed dilemma of data protection advice, several other challenges and practical considerations in developing critical data literacy resources were identified in the analysis. Three key challenges kept emerging in the different interviews along with considerations on an educational use of the resources.

Figure 15: Main themes and subthemes in the category "challenges and practical considerations" in the expert interview analysis.

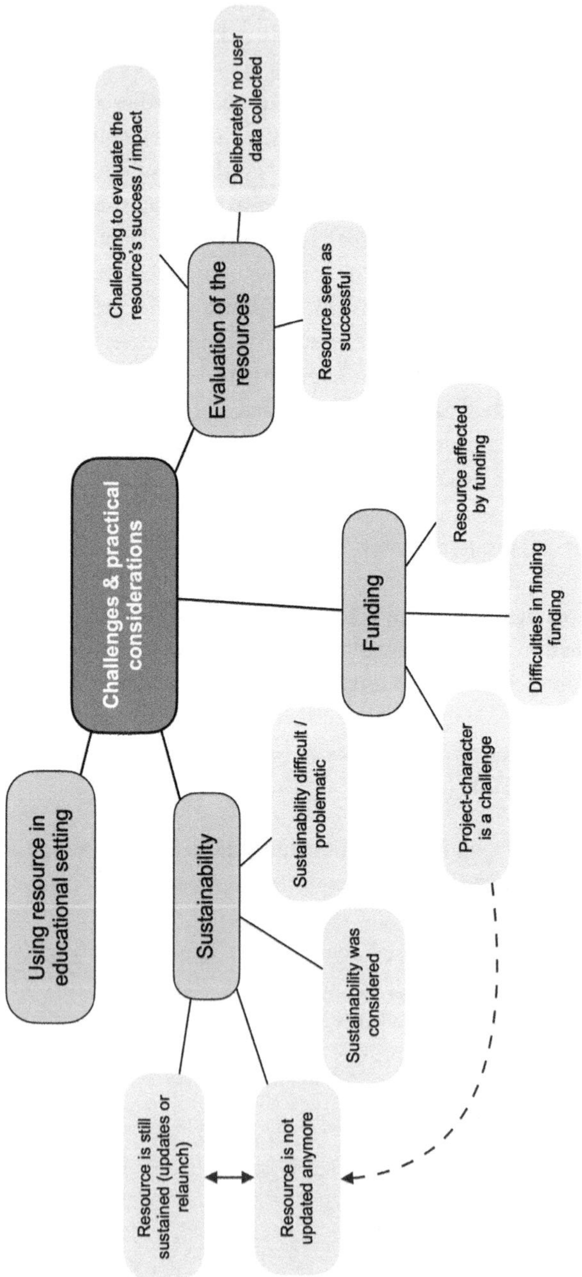

Dilemma: Evaluating Resource While Protecting User Data

The first of the three key challenges that was identified relates to two different statements by the creators. First, they argued that it is generally a *challenge to evaluate a resource's success or impact*. Even if statistics about the resource's use are measured – for example through collecting user statistics or generating conversion rates (e.g., how many website clicks lead to how many email newsletter sign-ups) – one of the creators, Stoilva, argued that this does not say much about the learning effect that the resource had for its users. This uncertainty about the resource's use and impact is for her "one of the biggest shortcomings" of her project (Stoilova Interview, 2021).

The second challenge was that many interviewees wanted to lead by example and *deliberately did not collect any user data* in order to protect their users' privacy. In most cases, this meant not being able to make any statements on the resource's use or success. While many interviewees were happy with this decision, one creator stated that he would be "less extreme and a bit more pragmatic" if he designed another resource since he has "no idea whether anyone has looked at it" (Parkes Interview, 2021). In other words, this creator would create a less privacy-sensitive resource in the future in order to gain some knowledge on its use. Another interviewee found a compromise in this dilemma: Julien Schekter outlined how his project team put considerable effort into finding ways to measure their resource's use while at the same time protecting their users' data. He explained the elaborate technical solutions they implemented to collect user statistics in an entirely anonymous manner.[4]

Overall, however, most interviewees *saw their resource as successful*, which was usually based on anecdotal feedback they received from users or educators. Considering the dilemmas around evaluating a resource and protecting user data, anecdotal feedback was the main or only form of success evaluation for most creators. Two interviewed creators further mentioned that their resource was "critically [...] very well received" (Gaylor Interview, 2020) and that they were nominated for and won several awards and prizes for their resource (Gaylor, Schekter). Yet, this finding is not without contradictions as another creator stated he was unhappy with the success of his resource because his privacy-protecting measures made it difficult to reach a large audience (Parkes Interview, 2021).

Funding of Resources

The interviewed creators further highlighted funding as a major challenge for developing critical data literacy resources. The interviewees spoke about the diverse funding avenues for their resources, including state and national programmes and

4 They erased the five last digits of each IP address, getting only a rough area (e.g., country) for each player; their game respected the "do not track" setting in people's browsers; any data that users entered was deleted; and they used the local storage in people's browsers to allow users to continue a game they had started without using any cookies or a log in.

organisations,[5] Federal and State Ministries,[6] foundations, broadcasters, city governments, and private donors. Diverging statements were made on whether the interviewees' *resources were affected by the funding*. While some outlined how the funding influenced the way their target group was set (Stoilova), the topic and contents decided (Lordieck, Parkes) or which format was used (Gaylor); others reported they were given complete freedom from the funders for developing their resources (Reicherstorfer, Siegenthaler).

Overall, many interviewees reported on *difficulties in finding funding*. Some were mostly self-funded (Younge, Yusuf, Truong) or had minimal funding and thus were unable to hire external designers or developers (Stoilova), which impacted their resources. Ed Parkes further argued that when he was working with open data in the public sector, he could "never get anyone to fund a public literacy programme around data" (Parkes Interview, 2021). In his view, not many funders would want to foster people's literacy and data transparency, but he rather thinks that "it's in a lot of people's interest that that doesn't happen" (ibid.).

A specific issue with funding that kept occurring in different interviews was that the *project-character is a challenge*. Often, funding comes in the form of a project with finite financial and time resources. While this can give flexibility to the creators (Parkes Interview, 2021), several interviewees argued that this project-character had a detrimental effect on their work and their resource. They emphasised that the short time frame presented a constant challenge and, in some cases, did not allow for any testing of the resource. Moreover, the project character often meant that keeping the resource updated was impossible as the project is finished, and it is "easier to get new money for new products than it is to update old products" (Jansen Interview, 2020) – an issue that will be discussed in more detail below. Therefore, the creators called for permanent funding for critical data literacy resources.

Sustainability

This leads to the next main theme identified in the analysis: several interviewees highlighted how *difficult it is to keep an online resource up to date* since the "web is increasingly changing" (Gaylor Interview, 2021), and the resource should be "relevant to the discussions that are happening at the moment" (Stoilova Interview, 2021). Moreover, when other resources are recommended, there is a risk that they expire or the links

5 E.g., Swiss state federal programme "Youth and Media"; Canada Council for the Arts; British Columbia Arts Council; National Fund Switzerland; German Federal Agency for Civic Education; UK Information Commissioner's Office.

6 E.g., German Federal Ministry for Justice and Consumer Protection; North Rhine-Westfalia Ministry for Children, Families, Refugees and Integration; North Rhine-Westfalia Ministry for Culture and Science.

change and thus they have to be checked regularly (ibid.). If the resource is interactive, some parts of it might also stop working for technical reasons: "every few months, there's different aspects of it that break and we have to fix them" (Gaylor Interview, 2021). This maintenance requires time and effort, which, due to the project-character of many resources, often has to take place in the creators' spare time.

For this reason, some of the interviewed creators explained that they already *considered questions around sustainability* during the development of their resource. For example, Younge and Truong decided against building a very interactive resource because they knew they would not be able to provide the long-term maintenance (Younge and Truong Interview, 2021). Others purposely included no current real-life examples but set their resource in a fictional future to prevent it from outdating too quickly (Reicherstorfer Interview, 2021), or contacted the creators of other resources they recommended to ask how long their resources would be online (Siegenthaler Interview, 2021). Finally, Jansen explained that another way to ensure longer sustainability is to include more generic rather than detailed content in the resource, although this, on the other hand, reduces the "added value" of the resource (Jansen Interview, 2020).

Apart from these valuable recommendations on how to consider sustainability when designing a resource, I was interested in finding out how many of the resources were still updated. Overall, five creators stated that their resources are *not updated anymore* (usually due to their project-character) and four explained that they are *still updating their resource*. This could be by adding new content and making sure the resource works on a technical level (Schekter), by regularly checking all recommended links and examining if the content is still up to date (Siegenthaler), adding new recommendations (Stoilova) or even planning a relaunch of the resource (Lordieck). Yet, one creator questioned if sustainability should even be desirable for such resources. In his view, these resources are "un-updatable" as they represent "a snapshot of a moment in time of the way that the web worked and we built something with that set of assumptions" (Gaylor Interview, 2021). Because the internet is changing continuously, but also because he as an artist would rather focus on new projects than having "the burden of maintaining these for the rest of my career", Gaylor sees updating these resources as undesirable and rather argues that an appropriate way of archiving digital works is needed. This demonstrates that there are many open questions and dilemmas regarding the sustainability of online critical data literacy resources.

Interest in Using Resource in an Educational Setting

A final main theme was that many of the interviewed creators expressed explicit interest in a use of their resource in educational settings. Overall, eight of the ten interviewees reported interest from educators in their resource. Particularly teachers often reached out to the interviewed creators to express their interest, to share feedback that they found the resource useful in their teaching, or to ask for further material. These perspectives on critical data literacy resources by educators will be investigated in more detail in the next chapter (5.3). While some creators stated that their resource was not necessarily created for use in a formal education setting, others described this as the "dream use case" for their resource (Younge Interview, 2021). In this context, Esther Lordieck further highlighted a relevant point, arguing that creators of critical data literacy resources require both expertise in understanding datafication as well as pedagogical expertise (Lordieck Interview, 2021). This again highlights the crucial work of resource creators in this field, constituting an intermediary between academic knowledge and educational settings.

5.2.5 Conclusion and Discussion

In total, twelve main themes in three different categories were identified in the analysis of the resource creator interviews. Some findings constituted strong, relatively homogenous themes that most or all interviewees seemed to agree on, but the analysis also revealed several contradictions. In some cases, the themes represented dilemmas rather than a coherent opinion: the interviewed creators did not necessarily agree on a solution, but the same issue (e.g., fear-based approaches or sustainability) kept emerging for nearly all of them. Apart from that, issues that are debated controversially in academic research also appeared to be controversial for the interviewed creators (e.g., the dilemma of data protection or the challenge of designing target-group specific resources). Overall, the expert interviewees agreed on the importance of educating about datafication and they called for more critical data literacy resources, for more research on education about datafication, a stronger public debate on these issues and for systemic solutions that go beyond the individual approach of fostering people's literacy.

Goals: What Does a 'Critically Data Literate' Citizen Look Like?

Although it was highlighted that literacy is a never-ending process and a 'fully literate' person does not exist, the interviewed creators voiced many specific goals for their resources – outlining their understanding of critical data literacy. They aimed not just at raising people's awareness of data systems but wanted to demystify technology and foster understanding of how data systems work. A key goal of the interviewees was to encourage critical thinking. Through their resources, they wanted to provide people with frameworks to think critically about datafication, the risks and harms that come with it and how this might affect them, and to support learners in gaining deeper understanding of the systemic forces and structures behind processes of datafication. Such systemic, structural understanding is a key aspect of the critical datafication literacy framework that is being developed throughout my study and is a perspective that, as argued in chapter 2.2, does not yet get enough attention in existing academic critical data literacy concepts.

Apart from understanding and critical reflection, the creators wanted users of their resources to take action. A common criticism about literacy approaches is that there is no clear idea of what follows once someone is 'literate'. For the interviewed creators, literacy included the goal of taking action and they outlined many specific actions they wanted their users to take. In part, this included common approaches such as advice on how to better protect one's data online or how to make informed decisions on which services to use, that are also suggested by critical data literacy scholars (e.g., Pangrazio and Sefton-Green 2020). However, many interviewees recognised the limitations of such individual steps and of citizens' agency, and promoted approaches that go beyond the individual level. Several encouraged their users to take political or societal action or wanted to contribute to a movement. These constitute unusual approaches, which are rarely found in academic concepts of critical data literacy but recall the goals of (re-active) data activism that educates about as well as fights against the datafication of our societies (see chapter 2.1). However, while data activists encourage "practices of resistance" such as "self-defence, civil disobedience and disruption" (Milan and Gutiérrez 2015, p. 122; Milan and van der Velden 2016, p. 67), the interviewed creators aimed to support citizens in enacting their democratic right to make their voices heard.

The interviewees further argued (and, in part, criticised) that citizens need the "right" language in order to take part in public debates and to be taken seriously. For this reason, several interviewed creators aimed to provide people with such "data language" through their resource. This approach to empowering citizens of datafied societies is not very present in the critical data literacy literature but constitutes a key insight on how to engage citizens in public data debates. Another goal of the interviewees was to enable citizens to educate others. This is in line with scholarly calls for starting a "chain reaction" of critical thought (Markham 2019, p. 756) and supporting "networks of literacy" (Carmi et al. 2020, p. 12).

Strategies and Principles for Implementing Critical Data Literacy into Practice

When analysing the creators' strategies and principles for implementing critical data literacy into practice, several divergent findings emerged. However, there were also approaches that all interviewees seemed to agree on: for example, that it is important to create personal involvement to overcome people's "issue fatigue" (Yusuf Interview, 2020). Ways to achieve this included connecting to people's real-life experiences, using personas and supporting people in forming their own opinion rather than telling them what to think. These approaches correspond with scholars who argue that educators should not try to convince learners that certain data practices are good or bad (Fontichiaro et al. 2017; Markham 2019), but rather act as "problem posers" (Aliakbari and Faraji 2011, p. 80), who present learners with real-world problems and enter into dialogue with them (Freire 2017). Concrete implementation examples by the interviewed creators included using open questions or including stories that promote a certain narrative rather than simply telling learners that narrative. Moreover, some creators called for presenting users with different future scenarios of a datafied society to create personal involvement. Similar calls for different future imaginaries have been made by academic scholars, for example Gray et al., who aim for "infrastructural imagination" about the creation and use of datasets (2018, p. 3).

Similar to the student users in my prior study (Sander 2020c), the interviewed creators expressed divergent opinions on how negative or scary a resource should be and if fear should be used to get people personally involved. Although some creators admitted that fear does get people's attention, most agreed that scaring people was not the right approach but that critical data literacy resources should rather be colourful and fun. A main theme that was identified, and that was in line with the literature, was that resources should be easily accessible and engaging, for example by using interactive and playful approaches (e.g., D'Ignazio and Bhargava 2015; Iliadis and Russo 2016; Markham 2019; Ahlborn et al. 2021). Moreover, the interviewees' call to use tangible, non-stereotypical visualisations to materialise the intangible world of data matches scholarly findings (e.g., D'Ignazio and Bhargava 2015; Windeyer 2019; Pangrazio and Selwyn 2020). A novel finding in this context was further that several creators suggested that a critical data literacy resource should constitute an "experience" in itself, which leads people to new insights.

Apart from that, most creators emphasised the importance of developing target-group specific resources and to adapt the resource to people's narratives. In this context, one interviewee defined literacy as explicitly different from persuasion or propaganda since it considers people's different existing narratives, adapts to these and empowers people to form their own opinions (Gaylor Interview, 2020). This focus on people's existing narratives constitutes a highly relevant approach to literacy that is not much discussed in critical data literacy scholarship. The general need for target group specific resources, however, aligns with scholarly research on critical data literacy, which has emphasised the need to consider different populations and "address different social contexts", particularly of marginalised communities, and has argued that "a 'universal' one size fits all solution" for data literacy is not possible (Carmi et al. 2020, pp. 16; 11). However, the interviewed creators also reported on the difficulties of implementing this into practice – for example when addressing a large audience – and of reaching their intended audience. Moreover, the analysis demonstrated that many resources originated from larger background projects, such as a research project or a journalistic investigation; were informed by theory; or applied extensive testing – all leading to well-founded decisions on content and design.

Finally, the question of providing data protection advice remained a dilemma. Although, or possibly because, it could not be solved here, this dilemma constitutes one of the most significant findings of this analysis. Already in chapters 3.4 and 5.1, the difficult balance between empowerment versus a shift of responsibility was outlined. Although I did not bring up this dilemma in the interviews, many interviewees acknowledged the issue and discussed it in detail. Several interviewees stressed that they did not want to shift "the burden of time and responsibility" to the individual, as expressed by scholars Pangrazio and Selwyn (2019, p. 425), and they further highlighted that the individual citizen's agency is limited, and systemic solutions for issues around datafication are needed. This correlates with academic research, for example by Young and Pridmore, who argue that "personal protection can superficially make people feel better" but is a "small bandage approach to systemic problems" (Forthcoming). In the same context, several interviewees drew parallels to individual solutions in the area of climate activism – a comparison that may also be fruitful as a metaphor when educating about datafication. On the other hand, many interviewees highlighted that data protection advice can empower people, foster their confidence, and help against feelings of powerlessness, as also suggested in the literature (e.g., Bilstrup et al. 2022).

Challenges and Practical Considerations

As a first key challenge, the expert interviewees reported that it is generally difficult to evaluate a resource's 'success', but it is even more difficult if its creators want to lead by example and develop a privacy-sensitive resource that protects its users' data. For this reason, most interviewees' assessment of their resource's success was based on anecdotal feedback. Secondly, funding for critical data literacy resources can be difficult to find; can sometimes affect the resource's content or format; and – most crucially – often comes in the form of time-limited projects with tight deadlines and little opportunity for extensive testing or long-term maintenance. Related to this, the third major challenge was the sustainability of critical data literacy resources. Although several interviewees outlined that they considered sustainability in the design of their resource and provided valuable advice for keeping a resource up to date, half of the resources in this sample were not updated anymore and will likely be outdated soon. However, one creator also called the goal of sustainability into question and instead called for better archiving opportunities. This open question as well as the other controversies that emerged in the interview analysis will be further discussed in chapter six.

Finally, although not all resources were intended for usage in formal education settings, many creators reported interest from educators in their resource. In particular, many had received feedback from teachers who liked using their resource in the classroom. This highlights the value of online critical data literacy resources not just for reaching individual citizens, but also for supporting educators in addressing topics around datafication in their teaching. The next chapter will provide more details on educators' experiences with the topic of datafication as well as their needs and wishes for critical data literacy resources.

5.3 Teaching about Data – Educators' Perspectives, Experiences and Needs

In order to investigate and learn from educators' experiences with the topic of digital technologies and datafication and their needs and wishes for critical data literacy resources, a qualitative survey with 57 participants from a variety of educational backgrounds was conducted. The survey demonstrated that educators already address a wide range of topics around digital and data technologies in their educational practice, and that they often follow similar goals and methods as identified in the previous chapter. Moreover, many surveyed educators found resources such as the ones examined in chapter 5.1 useful. Novel and, in part, divergent findings were identified on the practical skills the survey participants aimed for, the way they combined critical with practical approaches, and their stance towards shocking learners to engage them. The participants further highlighted several challenges for educating about digital technologies and using online critical data literacy resources. In particular, the interplay of open and closed questions in the survey led to new findings on educators' perspectives on teaching about data that complemented my study's previous two empirical perspectives and provided valuable insights for the further development of the critical datafication literacy framework.

5.3.1 Learning from Educators from Different Backgrounds

The first finding of the survey was that topics around digital technologies and datafication are already being addressed by educators from a variety of backgrounds. As intended by the sampling (see chapter four), the survey included educators from many different areas of education and nationalities. In total, 18 nationalities and countries of residence were represented, with the majority of participants living in Germany (24), 14 in the UK, eleven in other European,[7] and seven in non-European countries.[8] Gender and age also showed a diverse and even near-equal distribution, with 30 female and 23 male participants (4 preferred to omit their gender), and between 11–18 participants in each of the 10-year age spans between "30-39" and "over

---

7 In order of numbers of participants: Austria, Netherlands, Hungary, Spain, Cyprus, Switzerland, Turkey, Italy, Denmark.

8 In order of numbers of participants: Argentina, Nigeria, Colombia, Saudi Arabia, Australia, US, Canada.

60" (only one participant was younger than 30). These findings begin to highlight the diversity of educators interested in teaching about digital and data technologies.

However, the most relevant finding in this context concerned the professional background and the subject area of the surveyed educators. As illustrated in figure 16, the sample showed a strong predominance of educators working in formal education and specifically in higher education (34 participants). While this may be an adequate representation of the areas of education in which data topics are already covered, it may also be explained by the study's non-representative sample. Either way, this predominance of formal education fields should be kept in mind when interpreting the survey findings. Yet, it should be noted that many participants who indicated that they worked in higher education *also* worked in other educational areas, such as teacher training or adult education.[9] The second most common area represented was the school (primary and secondary, 18 participants), closely followed by "teacher education / training" (17) and "adult / further education" (14). Fewer participants worked in the non-formal education sector (8), civil society (6) or vocational training (4). Three indicated additional areas such as "business leaders, leaders in the public sector", one participant worked in a library, and one in a pre-school.

Figure 16: The surveyed educators' areas of education.

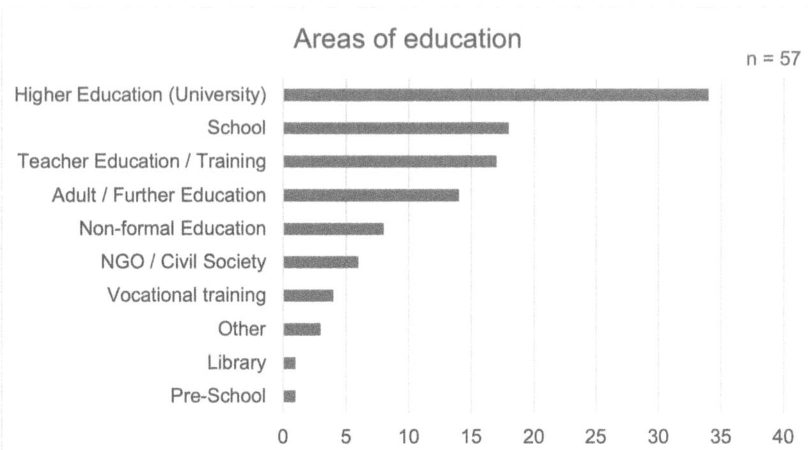

Moreover, a total of 22 different roles – from professor to high school teacher to privacy trainer – was identified, and many participants used an open text field to

9 All numbers and figures in this chapter include such duplicates, e.g., participants working in several areas (such as higher education and teacher training).

specify the context in which they taught about data and digital technologies. This revealed a number of specific contexts, such as teaching in a school with a digital skills pathway, providing further training for kindergarten staff on digital and data technologies, or giving courses on journalism or screenwriting. The participants' subject contexts also differed widely and included, among others, media education, informatics, politics and economics, Italian, Greek, and even religion. These novel findings highlight that educators in various educational settings already educate about digital and data technologies. This diversity is at the same time an opportunity to establish critical data literacy approaches in a variety of subjects and fields, and a challenge as all of these different contexts require different approaches in practically fostering such literacy.

5.3.2 Educators' Experiences and Goals for Teaching about Digital and Data Technologies

Teaching about Different Aspects of Digital Technologies and Datafication

A key goal of the survey was to learn about the topics that educators cover when teaching about digital and data technologies, and their goals for this education. Among others, the survey tested whether the surveyed educators' topics for their teaching were in line with imbalances in academic digital and data literacy approaches. These discourses show a predominance of general topics around the use and content of digital technologies (e.g., "Where can I find information online?") and attempts to promote a more secure internet usage (e.g., "How do I recognise safe websites?") in contrast to more complex topics around (big) data systems and algorithms (e.g., "How do algorithms work?") or the way they affect society (e.g., "How is my data used online?").

The findings demonstrated that the majority of surveyed educators felt very or extremely well-equipped (77%) and experienced (61%) to teach about *digital technologies generally*, and nearly as many felt well-equipped (70%) and experienced (61%) to teach about *societal implications*. This represents a contrast to scholarly approaches to digital and data literacy, which only rarely address societal implications of digital and data technologies. Educators' confidence in fostering reflection of digital technologies constitutes a significant finding, particularly as the survey's sampling did not specifically address educators with critical perspectives. However, it should be noted that it is unclear which implications educators addressed, and this could range from more basic aspects such as how digital media have changed our personal communication to more advanced questions around the consequences of automated decision-making systems.

Only about half of the educators (52%) felt very or extremely equipped to teach about *data security*, and this topic emerged as the one that the least educators felt very or extremely experienced in (32%). This stands in contrast to the literature and the analysed resources, in which a more secure internet usage and protection of one's data was a common theme (see chapters 2.2 and 5.1). Finally, and corresponding to the literature, the topic of *(big) data systems and algorithms* reached comparatively low numbers, with 42% indicating that they felt very of extremely well-equipped, and 39% feeling very or extremely experienced in this topic.

Figure 17: Total numbers of surveyed educators indicating how well-equipped they feel to teach about the four given topics.

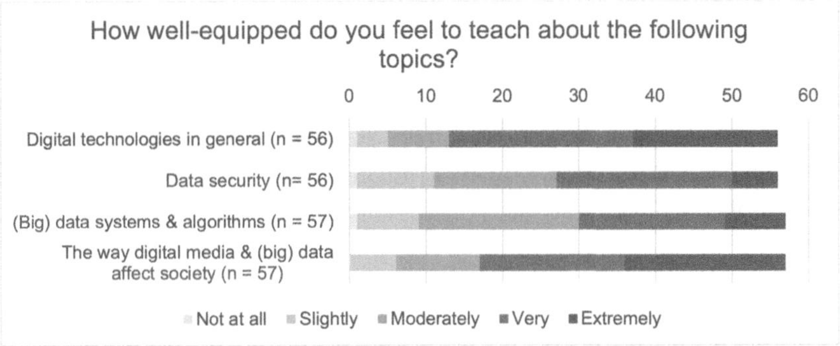

Figure 18: Total numbers of surveyed educators indicating how experienced they are in teaching about the four given topics.

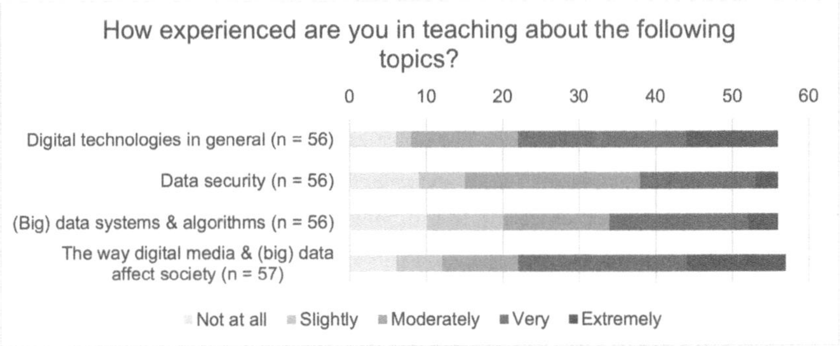

On average, across all topics, only 13% of the surveyed educators felt not at all or slightly equipped, and 25% felt not at all or slightly experienced in teaching about digital and data technologies. Thus, the educators overall felt fairly well-equipped (average per topic between 3.4 and 4 on a scale of 1–5), and also well, but a little less experienced (average per topic 2.9 to 3.6). These are positive findings as they suggest that of those educators who are interested in teaching about digital and data technologies, many feel that they to have the knowledge, resources and experience to do so. However, distinct differences between topical areas could be identified and the surveyed educators highlighted a number of challenges in teaching about digital and data technologies (see section 5.3.4).

Topics and Goals of the Educators

Apart from asking about pre-defined topical areas based on the literature, the survey also invited educators to expound on the topics and goals of their teaching in several open questions. Several of the themes and the three categories that were identified resembled the findings of the previous chapter: topics and goals; methods and approaches; and challenges, needs and wishes. However, due to the open nature of the survey, participants covered very different aspects in their answers and some themes were much more common than others. To illustrate this and improve transparency, the data visualisations in this chapter use different colour shades that represent the number of participants who were found to support each subtheme (see fig. 19, 21, 23).

Overall, the participants clearly provided most information on the first category: topics and goals. Nearly every participant expressed some perspective on their topics and goals, and nearly 200 codes were identified in this category. The first finding when analysing these was that "teaching about digital and data technologies" can include an extremely wide range of topics: from a general understanding of the internet to the psychological mechanisms in digital technologies and the attention economy; from identifying fake news to understanding data privacy laws; from using office software to applying data analytics. This wide range of topics on the one hand shows why it is so difficult to develop succinct definitions of digital or data literacy and why implementing these literacies into practice and into curricula is challenging. On the other hand, it also highlights how many different skills and understandings citizens need to navigate our digital and datafied societies and why digital and data literacies are so urgently needed.

In total, three main themes and 18 subthemes were identified in relation to the educators' topics and goals (see fig. 19). While many of these showed remarkable similarities to the creator interviews, it is important to keep in mind that some themes were only brought up by a small number of participants. Not being able to make assertions about how the rest of the educators in the sample feel about these subthemes is a limitation of the qualitative survey approach. However, in some cases this limitation could be addressed by combining these results with the data derived from the closed questions.

Figure 19: Main themes and subthemes in the category "topics and goals" in educator survey.

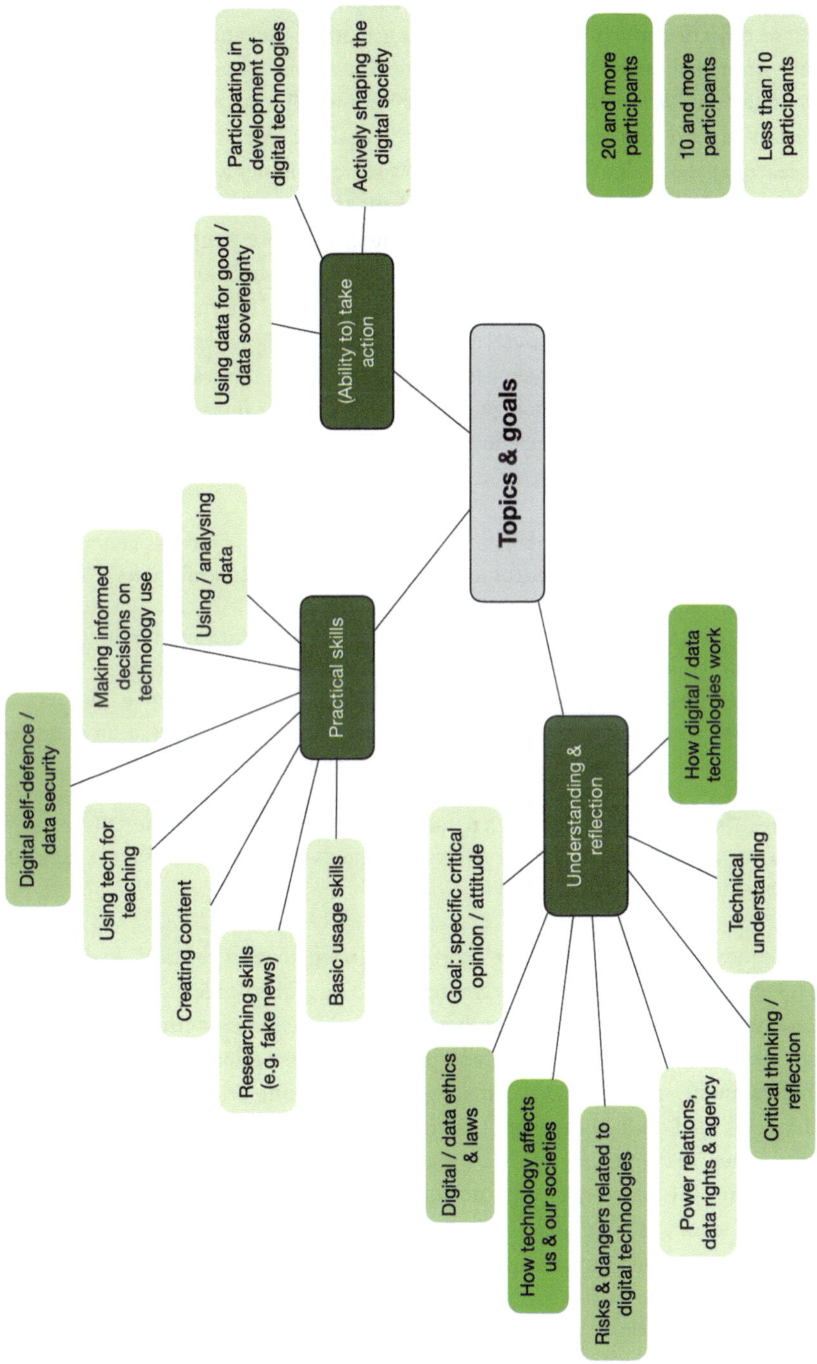

Key Goal of Educators: Understanding and Reflection of Digital Technologies

A large majority of 46 of the 57 educators emphasised some aspect of understanding or reflection as a goal for their teaching about digital and data technologies. A first strong subtheme that could be identified was that educators wanted learners to understand *how digital and data technologies work*. This was highlighted by 27 educators in total, and encompassed both technical and infrastructural aspects, such as learning about algorithms, big data, how search engines work, how data is used, the "myth of objective knowledge" (participant 209), or the business models behind digital services (mentioned by five participants). But more complex topics were also mentioned, such as "educational and communications policy around digital media" (345), the "economy of attention" (209), understanding "the social factors shaping technology" (202) or that "societal decisions on technology affect all of us" (122, own translation).[10] These aspects show strong similarities to the resource creators' goal of understanding how technology works and unpacking shortcomings, which was detailed in chapter 5.2. Some educators further provided detailed elaborations on the kind of understanding that learners need:

> Firstly, I believe the learners must understand that data practices and narratives are various and represent a complex problem. There are several orders of elements imbricated that must be disentangled.
>
> Firstly, the several beliefs and dispositions around data stem from the philosophical problem of an external reality that can be perfectly and objectively captured. The discourses about metrics and data as source of objective information are not new, and have been the drivers of what we see nowadays as an excessive hope on what AI systems and data-driven technologies can do for us.
>
> Secondly, I believe they must understand that we live in a post-digital society. Therefore, it is not enough to understand the digital as it is, but it is relevant to engage with the techno-structure, with the data infrastructures that shape our experience as users [...]. (209)

This educator's third point – that "this type of engagement is political" – will be discussed below. These statements represent a thoughtful attitude to educating about data, which strongly correlates with goals for my preliminary critical datafication literacy framework and shows strong parallels to the creators' goals of a 'systemic understanding of data and technology' and 'promoting critical frameworks' (see chapter 5.2). Beside these comprehensive or systemic types of understandings, some educators aimed for a *technical understanding* of digital and data technologies, for example of "how encryption works" (339) or of "secure communications and data collection, storage and sharing" (316). These technical understandings were not common among the interviewed creators or in academic approaches to critical

10 All originally German quotes in this chapter were translated into English.

data literacy, again emphasising the wide variety of topics that can be covered by education about digital technologies.

Another strong subtheme that was identified was that educators aimed to teach about *how technology affects us and our societies*. In total, 23 educators emphasised this goal. They highlighted general objectives such as educating about the "social, political and economic implications of digital media and (big) data" (226), or how digital technology affects different societal sectors (e.g., work, consumption or communication). Yet, specific aspects were also mentioned, including how digital technologies affect democracy and "how they are used in political communications" (196), or teaching about "media effects research (physical, psychosocial and cognitive implications of screen media)" (102). Moreover, a small number of educators highlighted implications of digital technologies on teaching and learning themselves. These educators aimed to teach about "changes in learning and thinking through the use of digital media" (229), "the limits of educational technology" (345), and the "effect of [the] EdTech sector on education policy" (102). This is a significant finding as these topics are not commonly considered by critical data literacy scholarship – although considerable critical research on the datafication of education exists (e.g., Williamson 2017; Hartong and Förschler 2019; Manolev et al. 2019). Nonetheless, it is understandable that this is a perspective that is of interest for educators.

Related to this, a number of educators specified that they aimed to educate people about *power relations in digital technologies as well as their agency and data rights*. While this was only mentioned by six participants, it constitutes an important novel finding as this does not get much attention in critical data literacy scholarship, nor in the analysed resources (see previous chapters). Yet, these educators seemed to have very specific ideas for teaching about power in relation to technology, for example that learners should "understand how society shapes technology and how technology shapes society, and what role power and agency play in these things" (301). Others mentioned teaching about people's "own data rights" (181) and "what they can do but also how what they do is small compared to the change that's needed" (321). This last aspect constitutes a significant finding, as it again highlights the need for systemic solutions, which has already been identified in the interview analysis. However, as will be further discussed below, several other educators nevertheless saw individuals as responsible to protect their own data.

Two further common goals of educators were to teach about *risks and dangers of digital technologies*, and – related to this – to foster *critical thinking or reflection*. Apart from risks to people's privacy, some educators mentioned very specific aspects such as "danger of personalisation for forming an opinion" (122), the "digital divide" (292), "ability to recognise bias" (289) or "understand how software/ algorithms can discriminate" (202), demonstrating an advanced knowledge level. Many of these educators further specifically highlighted critical thinking, ethical thinking or critical reflection as key goals. Some emphasised that "technical perspectives" and skills are less important to them than "analytical-reflexive abilities" (174) and "social scientific perspectives as well as understanding the bigger picture" (172). These positions stand in contrast to academic data literacy concepts, which show a clear dominance of practical-instrumental approaches, as well as to studies that have identified a predominantly "instrumental and technical approach" to data topics in educational institutions (Raffaghelli and Stewart 2020, p. 448). This is a particularly significant finding when considering that the survey sample – in contrast to the interview sample – did *not* specify that educators should be interested in fostering *critical* perspectives to digital and data technologies. However, these positions are very much in line with this study's preliminary critical datafication literacy framework.

One educator further provided details on their approach to fostering critical thinking:

> I prefer to combine critical media scholarship on big data with analytical applied ethics studies. [...] Rather than a principled debate, a process oriented balancing discussion is encouraged to promote critical thinking. [...] I also prefer this process oriented debate so that the students are prepared for an ethical thinking on unforeseeable yet emerging technologies. (282)

This is a particularly relevant approach as it not only encourages learners to form their own opinions through critical thinking and discussion, but it also invites learners to apply this critical thinking to future developments of digital technologies. Considering the fast-changing landscape of digital and data systems, this approach could provide a more sustainable solution. Moreover, this correlates with approaches of politische Bildung, which emphasise continual adaption of topics to address current societal challenges (see chapter 3.2). Furthermore, twelve educators indicated that they teach about *digital and data ethics and laws*. This is another topic that is not common in academic critical data literacy approaches, nor was it identified in the creator interviews. The educators detailed several legal aspects they covered in their teaching: media law, copyright law, privacy law, media ethics and data ethics. Particularly the last three constitute relevant topics for critical datafication literacy in the sense of systemic understanding and critical reflection of the datafication of our societies.

Finally, some educators aimed to promote a *specific critical opinion or attitude* in their teaching. For example, two educators, referring to the use of educational technologies, wanted their learners to understand about "data assemblages, false promises and broken dreams" (209) and that the "use of digital media/content does not replace pedagogical decisions of the educators" (229). Others specified that they wanted learners to criticise the "individualisation" of digital technologies (102), to see the "dangers of a cybernetic control society" (174), or to understand "the necessity of a political-societal design of new technologies" (233). By aiming for learners to take a specific stance towards digital and data technologies, these educators seem to take a normative approach in their teaching. Although the goals themselves are similar to other themes outlined above, this normative approach somewhat contradicts prior findings of letting learners form their own opinion (see chapter 5.2). However, one educator who took this normative stance also wondered how they can balance "sober informational description and charged room for interpretation (through science fiction, drastic examples)", yet also take a position themselves (174).

From Basic Usage Skills to Digital Self-Defence: Educators Aim for Practical Skills

Besides promoting understanding and critical reflection, a second key goal of the educators was to foster their learners' practical skills. In total, 33 of the 57 educators indicated aiming for practical competences in some form. However, what kind of skills the educators fostered differed widely among the survey participants. Moreover, some contrasts between participants' goals *in terms of understanding* and their goals *in terms of skills* were identified. For example, participant 249 teaches digital and web design as well as website administration – very practical usage skills that do not indicate a particularly critical or reflective attitude. However, the participant detailed critical reflection, engaging with surveillance capitalism and with surveillance through digital technologies as key goals for their teaching. This important finding highlights that critical and reflective perspectives can also be included in teaching that is very practical and focussed on technical skills, and that educators who teach usage skills do not necessarily endorse an unreflecting, enthusiastic use of digital technologies.

This finding further helps to interpret the fact that many educators aimed for practical usage skills. Several indicated fostering *basic usage skills* for digital technologies, such as using office technologies or aiming for "basic facility in accessing and using technology" (345). This is another example for the importance of understanding the data in its context, as participant 345 continues:

> but my primary aim would be to do with CRITICAL digital literacy, based on a conceptual understanding of how these media are used to communicate, how they are produced and used, and how they represent the world. (345)

This again emphasises the above finding that teaching technical skills can go hand in hand with a critical perspective. A similarly usage-focused goal of educators was to foster learners' *researching skills*, such as using "technologies for news gathering" or being able to "detect fake news" (148). Other educators wanted to support learners in *creating content*, promoting, for example, "production skills for social media" (319), "social media strategy" (112), "thinking creatively" and "writing for the web" (141), or "online community management" (319).

A small number of educators also aimed to foster skills of *using and analysing data*, such as "statistical literacy" (289) or data visualisation. One also taught "skills to anal[y]ze school related data (e.g., general achi[e]vement data, competence measur[e]ment, etc.)" (186). This highlights another novel finding: several educators wanted to foster skills for *using technologies for teaching*, such as "using ICT in classroom, LMS [Learning Management Systems], analysing general educational data" (186), or using "learning analytics [and] AI in primary education" (270). Many of the indicated practical skills stand in contrast to the strong emphasis on critical reflection outlined above. This controversy might be explained by divergent opinions of different educators; however, it is also possible that these educators – as highlighted above – aim for practical skills as well as a critical perspective.

Besides the basic usage skills outlined thus far, the second most common skill that educators wanted to foster was *digital self-defence or data security*. Thirteen educators in total indicated this goal. The educators' responses included different dimensions of data protection, from data security, the "correct and secure use of IT products" (206) and the "technical details of password selection and protection" (339), to aiming for a more critical and empowered use of digital technologies. This included "digital selfdefense (ethi[c]al tools, alternatives to big tech)" and learners taking "control of their own data [and] avoid[ing] tracking and surveillance and manipulation" (341) – similar approaches to those suggested by the examined online resources.

Finally, and related to the prior theme, some educators aimed to support their learners in *making informed decisions on technology use*. One educator summarised this goal under the term "tech intuition":

> Tech intuition: the ability to make confident decisions about technology due to an understanding of social impact even if lacking a full understanding of the nuts and bolts of every tool or system. (316)

This definition constitutes a novel and particularly relevant approach to educating about data systems as it admits to a common problem in this education: the functional workings of these systems are often unknown and impossible to uncover. Aiming for an 'intuitive' approach to make informed decisions based on social impact constitutes a valuable solution to this issue. Others aimed for "critical consumption" (173) or, likely relating to educational technologies, wanted people to "choos[e] a digital tool based on pedagogical criteria" (256). Especially these last two themes – the goals of data protection skills and informed decisions – show strong similarities to my prior findings from the content analysis and the expert interviews, and to my preliminary framework for critical datafication literacy.

Supporting Learners in Taking Action

Finally, some educators also aimed for learners to take action – a theme that was very common among the interviewed creators. Most of the ten educators who indicated this goal wanted to support their learners in *actively shaping the digital society*. One educator, whose elaborate definition of critical data education was already quoted above, detailed:

> Thirdly, that this type of engagement is political. To be a citizen in the post-digital society is to engage in participatory processes to decide and control about the data extraction, classification, label[l]ing, and of course usage, particularly if there is monetisation of our data. (209)

This understanding of citizenship in modern societies is reminiscent of academic definitions of "data citizenship" (Carmi et al. 2020, p. 3) or of "digital citizenship in a datafied society" (Hintz et al. 2019, p. 19). Other educators made similar points, emphasising the goal of "actively helping to shape the digitising society" (218) and highlighting that "in society, decisions are made that affect all of us [...] willingness and interest [are needed] to engage with societal challenges" (122). These arguments and goals, which are supported by a closed question on the importance of political and societal action (see below), correspond with the creators' goals outlined in chapter 5.2.

A related goal of the surveyed educators was to enable learners to *use data for good and support people's data sovereignty*. This is a novel finding that has not come up much in the prior analyses. These educators wanted to show learners "how to empower themselves with their data", taking "a proactive approach", which includes "data sovereignty, Open Data for learning, [and] Open scholarship and open data" (341). Another novel theme that emerged was that a small number of educators aimed for learners to *participate in the development of digital technologies*, hoping that learners could take part in "user-centric development" and could "critically evaluate" suggestions in this process (96).

Overall, the educators outlined a wide range of topics that they cover in their teaching about digital and data technologies. Many parallels to prior findings emerged, particularly in regard to educators' goal of understanding and critical reflection of digital technologies. However, some novel approaches and divergences from the previous findings could also be identified, such as different ideas of skills and actions that learners should take. The next section analyses the ways in which educators try to reach their educational goals.

5.3.3 How Do Educators Teach about Digital and Data Technologies?

Educators' Access to Information and Educational Material

Overall, the survey identified many parallels between the educators' preferred methods and approaches to teaching about digital and data technologies, and the previous findings of my study. The findings on how educators inform themselves and find teaching material were encouraging. After literature, which 35 participants indicated as a source for information, the second most common source was the internet (22 participants); followed by colleagues, friends or communities of learning (15); educational formats such as courses, workshops or talks (13); and news media (10). Less commonly mentioned sources of information were institutions or organisations (6 participants), participants' own research (6); videos, movies or documentaries (5); surveying the technology or industry landscape and discourses (3); podcasts (2) and museum exhibitions (1).

Overall, these findings show that choosing an open design for this question and coding it afterwards was the right approach, as these answers include several options I could not have foreseen. This included that educators read "policy materials" (295) and "trade regulations" or "reports from inquiries, commissions, regulatory investigations, thinktanks" (196); that they survey the technology industry discourses; and that they use museum exhibitions as a source of information. Moreover, the predominance of literature rather than the internet as the most common source of information was a significant finding considering the fast-changing landscape of digital technologies. Equally, I underestimated the importance of learning from one's colleagues, which reemphasises the already highlighted approach of "networks of literacy" (see prior chapters and Carmi et al. 2020).

Particularly the findings on how educators find teaching material offered valuable insights: most surveyed educators who provided information on this found materials online (17 participants), followed by literature (12). The popularity of the internet to identify teaching material is encouraging considering the large amount of existing online critical data literacy resources examined in chapter 5.1. Apart from this, twelve participants indicated that they create their own resources. Reasons for this included that participants were unhappy with existing materials, have "not found ready-made in exactly what I am teaching" (196), or found that "materials from corporate e-learning providers tend to be inaccurate, and free resources are usually just marketing vehicles for commercial products" (289). In addition, some gave details on how they create this material, for example that they include "current events and debates" (196) or build on ideas that "emerged in situations of (further) training, through experiences and questions of the participants, which led to discussions" (102). Finally, educators indicated that they also find material through institutions or organisations (4 participants), lectures or talks (4), news media (3), colleagues (3) or documentaries (1).

Resources Recommended by Educators

Additionally, many educators provided specific examples of educational resources they have used in the past. This led to novel findings as it gave a first idea of whether the resources examined in chapter 5.1 – and similar ones – are found and used by educators. The first finding here was that existing collections of online resources were mentioned: two educators indicated using the database by the Critical Big Data and Algorithmic Literacy Network and one mentioned the guidebook published by Jess Brand and myself as a source for material. Both of these also acted as sources for the sampling in chapter 5.1. Moreover, two resources from the content analysis itself were mentioned: the video series "Screening Surveillance" by The Surveillance Studies Centre, Canada (R63), and the Advocacy Assembly website with courses on various topics, including privacy (R5).

Apart from that, several resources in a similar style and structure to those analysed in chapter 5.1 were recommended by the educators, for example websites with learning and teaching material specifically for kids (Österreichisches Institut für angewandte Telekommunikation [no date]; Seitenstark e.V. [no date]); a comic-essay on "dimensions and implications of the groundbreaking technology, discussing important opportunities and limitations" (Schneider and Ziyal 2019); and a website on a research project that aims to "support educators in improving their critical data literacies" and includes modules on different topics around data, justice and politics and collects interactive tools (Kuhn et al. [no date]). These recommendations suggest that the online resources analysed in my study seem to be on the right track. Apart from that, novel formats were identified, such as LinkedIn Learning resources, a symposium, exhibitions, theatre plays and movies and institutional websites (for example from state institutes for teacher training or associations of educators). Moreover, several more practice-oriented resources were mentioned (e.g., Bhargava [no date]; Lupi and Posavec [no date]; Utrecht Data School [no date]). These recommendations highlighted the variety of formats and resources that can be used to educate about digital and data technologies.

Usefulness of Specific Formats for Educators

Another goal of the survey was to understand which *formats* of educational resources are most useful for educators who teach about digital and data technologies. Overall, images or infographics and short videos clearly emerged as the most useful formats, with a very high average usefulness of 3.98 each (between 1 – not at all useful, and 5 – extremely useful), and with 80% (images / infographics) and 76% (short videos) of educators indicating that they find these formats very or extremely useful. These results were complemented by the analysis of the open text fields, in which participants highlighted visual approaches such as illustrated texts, infographics, movies, videos of talks, and short videos as useful. This correlates with findings from the previous chapters, in which visualisations and multimedia resources emerged as particularly suitable approaches to make complex issues around datafication tangible and understandable. However, these findings were also contradictory: one educator questioned if videos as a format work well "because we need that larger amount of time to explain context and experience; but people just don't have the time, IMHO [abbreviation for: in my humble opinion] (though I have no analytics on the use of long-form video)" (321).

Figure 20: Average usefulness of resources' formats in the educator survey in descending order.

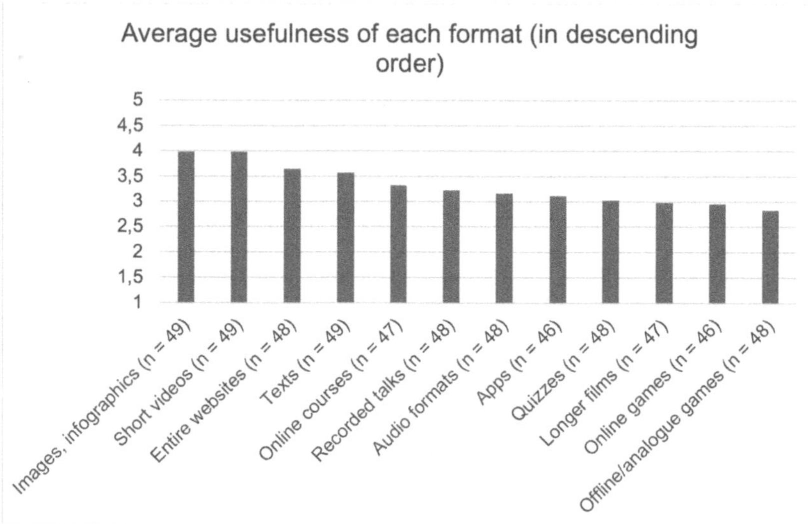

Moreover, "entire websites" emerged as the third most useful format (average 3.65). Before conducting the survey, I was uncertain whether entire websites were actually useful for educators, or if they might see them as overwhelming or not suitable for the classroom. Considering the high number of websites in the content analysis sample, learning that this format is helpful for the surveyed educators was encouraging. Furthermore, texts were also very popular (average 3.57), with 63% of educators indicating they find texts very or extremely useful. The fifth most useful format were online courses (average 3.32), which more than half (51%) of the educators found very or extremely useful. This is another valuable finding as also with this format, I was uncertain about how easily it could be implemented into existing classroom settings.

Formats that the educators identified as somewhat useful included recorded talks (average 3.23), audio formats (3.17), apps (3.11), quizzes (3.02) and longer films

(2.98). Finally, the two game formats the survey asked about raised some questions. Based on the average usefulness, it seems that neither online games (2.96) nor offline or analogue games (2.83) were particularly useful for the surveyed educators (see fig. 20). However, a closer look at the number gives a clearer picture. In both cases, more than a third of the educators indicated they found games very or extremely useful: 37% for online games, 33% for offline games. However, nearly half of the participants saw games as not at all or only slightly useful: 41% for online games, 48% for offline games. This shows the educators' divergent opinions – some seemed to be very convinced of using games for teaching about data, whereas others seemed to entirely disagree. This is a significant finding, particularly considering the emphasis that the interviewed creators laid on playful and interactive approaches in online critical data literacy resources. Moreover, my sample in chapter 5.1 included several games that were developed specifically for educators and classroom settings. Thus, future resources should consider these divergent opinions and ideally offer different formats in each resource to cater to different needs.

The open text analysis further revealed that the surveyed educators generally found resources useful that do not need a long preparation time, are well-structured, provide links to other resources or include a teaching guide. These approaches are in line with many of the resources analysed in chapter 5.1. However, also some novel findings were identified. For example, two educators highlighted that education about digital and data technologies can also take place using analogue material. This argument has been identified in some academic approaches to critical data literacy as well (e.g., Pötzsch 2019), but it did not come up in the expert interviews nor was it strongly emphasised by the resources that were examined in chapter 5.1. Moreover, educators indicated that curricula of colleagues as well as academic texts or blog entries constituted useful resources for them.

Finally, several educators further outlined that for them, the format of a resource is not actually of much importance. They argued that it "all depends on the content, not the format" (345) and that, for example, visual resources only work well "if they are integrated in a good lesson and human communication" (201). This perspective corresponds with the fact that the question about formats showed many "not applicable" answers. Two educators who used the "not applicable" option explained their stance in the next open text field:

> I find this question difficult to answer because in my opinion, it is mainly the teaching format that matters, not the format of the resource. For me, good tasks are important as well as accessible methods, which allow learners to deal with the topics in a proactive manner. The mentioned resources are mainly useful to complement this. (96)

> What applies for every format: depending on the pedagogical design, suitability for the target group and usage context, any format can be useful or not. In my opinion it is particularly important that resources are connected to people's daily lives and that they allow for a behind-the-scenes glimpse with an 'aha effect'. (174)

These arguments emphasise a crucial point: Even having perfect educational resources about digital and data technologies is not a fool-proof 'recipe for success' when it comes to fostering critical data literacy. Instead, the role and importance of the educators themselves cannot be underestimated. For this reason, it is even more relevant to examine which methods and approaches the educators apply in their teaching about data, which will be the focus of the next section.

Educators' Methods and Approaches for Teaching about Data

Two themes concerning the educators' methods and approaches have already been discussed: many educators highlighted that specific formats are useful, whereas others argued that good content and teaching are more important than a resource or its format. As the next paragraphs will highlight, the remaining themes identified in this category showed remarkable parallels to the interview findings presented in chapter 5.2. To highlight these parallels, even subthemes with very small numbers were included in the thematic framework, and colour shades were used to visualise the frequency of each theme.

The strongest main theme in this category was that educators *used interactive, practical and playful approaches* (15 participants). This represents a contrast to the above findings that many of the surveyed educators found playful formats such as quizzes, apps and particularly games less useful. One explanation for this might be that some educators find interactive resources less useful because they already apply interactive, practical or playful approaches in their teaching, for example in the form of individual tasks, group work or discussions. In this case, they might prefer 'passive' resources such as images or videos as teaching material. This would also explain educators' strong agreement with a statement about interactive approaches as a way to engage learners (see next section). However, another possible explanation is that the surveyed educators' perspectives are diverse and that they have divergent opinions about playful approaches, as speculated above.

Twelve educators indicated that they *included practical approaches, such as interactive or exploratory approaches*, in their teaching, making this the strongest subtheme in this category. The arguments here resemble the creator interviewees' calls for engaging formats, including interactive, experiential, or conversational approaches. The educators highlighted the importance of combining theory and practice, and of using active and exploratory tasks, for example asking students to research issues for themselves and to then apply their knowledge practically. In line with this, some educators highlighted that it is *good to give concrete tasks* (2 participants) and that *story-*

telling and play is important (2). These subthemes were not mentioned often, but they show strong parallels to the creator interviewees who argued that it is important to make resources fun and that a story-based approach can help in reaching people. One educator further elaborated: "I use storyb[...]uilding games for children in university work – getting people to play is very important. [...] I wish resources would be more p[...]layful and challenging" (141).

Figure 21: Main themes and subthemes in the category "methods and approaches" in the educator survey.

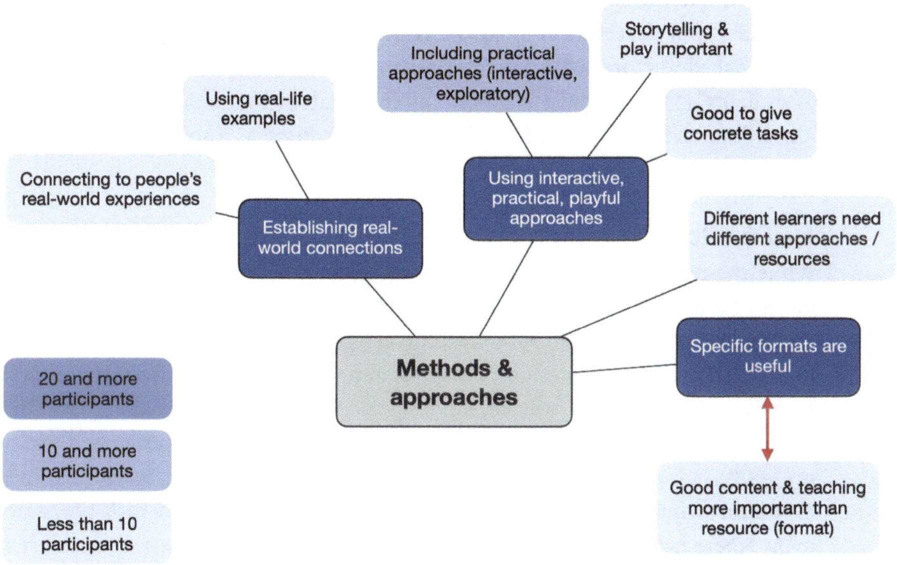

The second main theme regarding educators' methods and approaches is that they wanted to *establish real-world connections* (7 participants). This theme shows strong parallels to the creators' goal to create personal involvement. Six educators indicated aiming to *connect to people's real-world experiences*. As a "proven method" they suggested a "reflection of one's own media biography and current usage patterns (in partner interviews, with recording own usage behaviour, ...)" (102), or recommended to "problematise" (96) topics around digital technologies and to "discuss ambivalences" (122). Moreover, two educators highlighted *using real-life examples*. Despite the small number, this is a significant finding as this approach emerged in every stage of my study, which indicates this as a key approach for fostering critical data literacy. One educator explained that concrete examples can help with people's "'fear' of not being able to understand technology", which should be taken seriously and "the demystification of technology has to be a central goal when working with people who do not normally deal with these topics" (172). These are valuable insights for critical education about datafication, particularly when addressing non-technical and lay audiences, which may otherwise feel resigned in light of the new information (see chapter 2.1).

Finally, five educators highlighted that *different learners need different approaches or resources*. This argument further received most agreement by educators when they were directly asked about it (see next section). One concern that was raised in this context was "the intercultural issue", arguing that it is not enough to provide resources in different languages but that "there is a problem of cultural adaptation and contextualization" as it is questionable that resources can be "applied to several contexts [...] in all sectors of lifelong learning" (209). For these reasons, one participant wished for "sites with activities organized according to the Level and/or age of students" (256) – essentially describing the database by the Critical Big Data and Algorithmic Literacy Network (CBDALN) that was used as a source for my study's content analysis.

Are Educators' Experiences in Line with Key Research Findings?

While the previous sections already provided some insight to parallels between the educators' experiences and scholarly research findings, the survey also directly asked educators about their agreement to ten specific research findings. As detailed in the methodology annotations, the ten statements that were tested were selected with care, intending to cover key findings along with controversial aspects. This approach confirmed some expectations from the literature and prior findings of my study, but also led to several novel findings. Overall, one statement emerged as a clear 'winner': 94% of surveyed educators (strongly) agreed with the statement "There is no one-size-fits-all approach and different learners need different approaches" (average of 4.56, see also fig. 22). This corresponded with the strong emphasis on this perspective in the previous findings chapters – yet, agreement within the survey sample was remarkably high and not a single educator strongly disagreed. The second highest ranked statement equally reiterates prior findings: "Including real-life stories can help learners understand complex issues" (4.32). With 86% of educators (strongly) agreeing and no disagreement at all, this approach seems to constitute a second virtually undisputed best practice for educating about data, which was confirmed in every methodological approach in my study.

Figure 22: Average agreement to research statements in the educator survey in descending order.

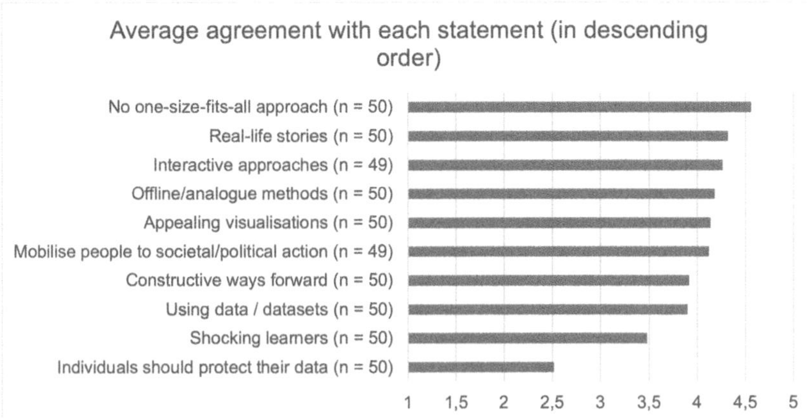

The statement that, on average, received the third highest agreement by the educators was: "Interactive approaches are a great way to engage learners" (4.27). As already discussed above, the comparatively unpopular formats of games, apps and quizzes seemed to have given a wrong impression of educators' perspective to interactive approaches, with 84% (strongly) agreeing and no participant strongly disagreeing to this statement. Thus, it seems that the surveyed educators were almost entirely united in their enthusiasm for interactive approaches for teaching about data, yet they have divergent opinions on certain interactive formats, such as games, when it comes to educational resources. Moreover, the fourth statement "Appealing visualisations of data systems can help learners to engage emotionally" (4.14), with 84% agreement and no strong disagreement clearly confirmed the study's previous findings. Thus, it seems that these four approaches constitute clear best practice approaches for fostering critical data literacy according to my study's samples.

Further statements that received high agreement from the surveyed educators were that "Education about digital technologies can also take place through offline/analogue methods" (average of 4.18; 83% agreement), and that "It is important to not just raise awareness, but also to mobilise people to take societal/political action" (4.12; 86% agreement). Both approaches were already identified in the open text analysis, albeit with very low numbers (two and six participants). This demonstrates the value of combining open and closed questions in this survey, as the statements revealed that two very rare themes in the open text analysis in fact found widespread agreement in the sample when directly asked about. Moreover, the high agreement with societal and political action constituted another parallel to the creator interviews. Furthermore, 68% of surveyed educators agreed that "When educating about critical developments in society, educators should always present constructive ways forward" (3.92). Based on the high agreement with the previous statement on mobilising people and my study's prior empirical and theoretical findings, however, I would have expected even stronger agreement with the importance of constructive advice.

Another novel finding was the educators' strong *disagreement* with the statement: with "It is up to the individuals to protect their data online", which only reached an average agreement of 2.52, and 56% of educators (strongly) *dis*agreed with this approach. Considering that individual data protection emerged as clearly the most common form of constructive advice in the content analysis and that scholars have warned of a shift of responsibility to individuals (e.g., Pangrazio and Selwyn 2019, p. 425), stronger agreement with individual responsibility could have been expected. In total, only 24% (strongly) agreed to individuals' responsibility and 20% neither agreed nor disagreed. These numbers – together with the focus on political or societal action – are very encouraging. It seems that many of the surveyed educators were aware of citizens' limited agency and the systemic nature of challenges of datafication, which cannot be solved by individuals alone.

Finally, two further statements received comparatively low agreement by the educators. The first addressed the ongoing open question of whether critical data literacy approaches should foster people's data skills. Educators' opinions on this seemed to be mixed – yet with overall clearly more agreement (68%) than disagreement (10%). This correlates with scholars' perspectives on this, which are equally divergent (see chapter 2.2). Mixed opinions were further indicated for "Shocking learners in order to make them realise that they are affected by a certain societal issue can be a beneficial approach" (3.48): 56% of the surveyed educators (strongly) agreed, 28% neither agreed nor disagreed and only 16% (strongly) disagreed to the statement. While also the expert interviews revealed some divergent opinions, the overall stance of the creators was that the risks of this approach outweigh its benefits (see chapter 5.2). In light of the strong agreement of the educators, the question of shocking learners thus remains ambiguous and controversial.

5.3.4 What Challenges Emerge? What Do Educators Need and Wish for?

General Challenges When Teaching about Digital Technologies and Data

Ultimately, the analysis identified several challenges that educators encounter and needs and wishes they have for better education about digital technologies and data. Twenty-four survey participants reported challenges in relation to their teaching about these topics (see fig. 23). The most common subtheme was that the educators found it *difficult to engage learners*. This is very much in line with the interview findings, in which creators spoke about how difficult it is to overcome people's "issue fatigue" and to enter their "circle of worry". In the survey, educators argued that learners are often "rooted in their everyday life experiences and knowledge" (226) about digital technologies, and "big data and related dangers are seen as hardly relevant to their own life" (195). This is particularly difficult with younger learners and teenagers, who are often difficult to reach in general and whose "entire attention is captured by their smartphone" (184). For these learners, critical reflection of digital technologies can lead to "cognitive dissonances", which are "understandably uncomfortable" and can evoke resistance rather than a more in-depth examination of the topic (102). Moreover, people's convenience (249) and a "dystopian pull" (174) were highlighted – challenges that are also outlined in the academic literature (e.g., Turow et al. 2015; Draper and Turow 2019; Müller-Peters 2020, p. 125).

Figure 23: Main themes and subthemes in the category "challenges, needs and wishes" in the educator survey.

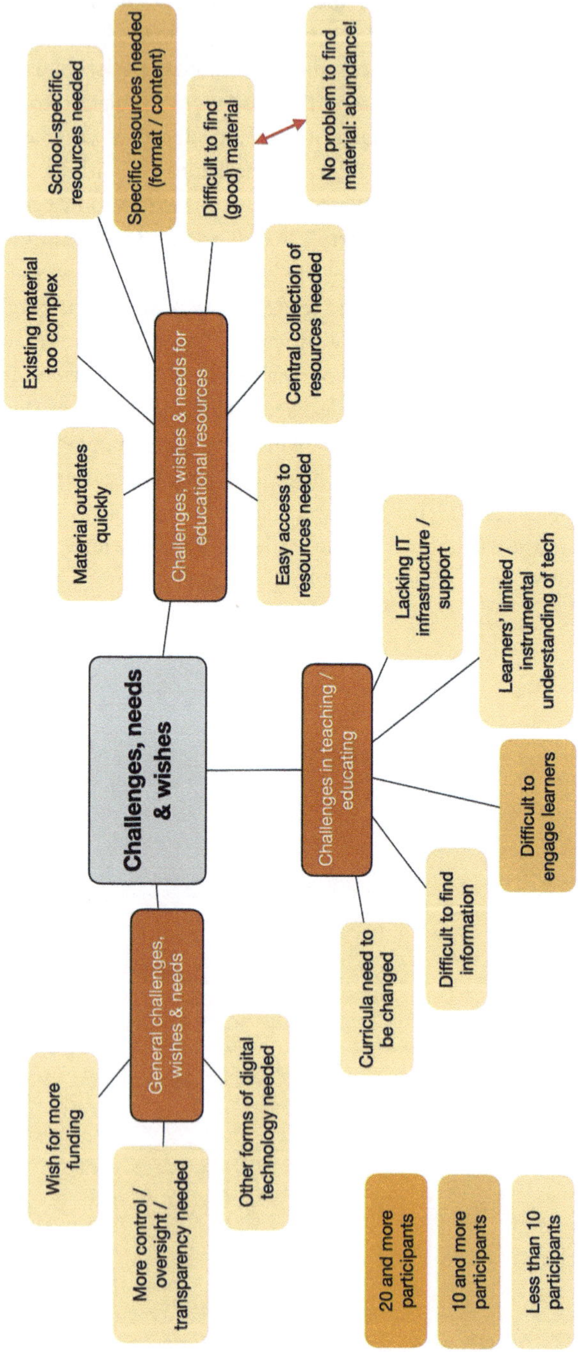

Related to this, several educators identified *learners' limited or instrumental understanding of technology* as a challenge. The educators reported that many learners underestimate the complexity of digital technologies and have little technical knowledge and limited understanding of relations between different technologies, for example of social networks and big data. Particularly learners' instrumental understanding of digital technologies was seen as challenging:

> Historically, I would say the main challenge has been overcoming (on the one hand) instrumental/functional views of technology and (on the other) uncritical enthusiasm about the 'empowering' potential of digital media. (345)

According to this educator, such instrumental views have overall decreased, but are still dominant in schools, where "narrow concerns about internet safety" prevail (345). Another educator made a similar argument about university students, who "have a very instrumental understanding of digital technologies", which is why problematisation is crucial (96).

As further challenges, some survey participants highlighted *lacking IT infrastructure and support*. Some mentioned lacking internet access or access to specific software in their educational institution. Others argued that their school's "digital support unit is less interested in data security" and that they would like to better control the data of their pupils and themselves but would "need competent support by IT Management Systems" for this (201). Similarly, some complained that there is "little willingness to discuss big data among staff and authorities in the field of standard school education" (230), and little interest and understanding particularly by their "younger colleagues" (201). This comment further calls the narrative of "digital natives", who are better skilled at using digital technologies, into question (see e.g., Kirschner and De Bruyckere 2017).

Moreover, some educators called for *curricula to be changed*. They argued that a strong positioning of topics around digital technologies in curricula is missing and that the fact that these topics affect all school subjects leads to a situation in which "no one feels responsible" (218). One educator even called for a "decluttering of all curricula in all school types and education levels", replacing traditional subjects with new ones such as "media usage", "basic social science education" or "the future of work" (218). Similar to some expert interviewees, another educator further highlighted the challenge that teachers need a basic knowledge of digital technologies as well as pedagogical expertise if they want to educate about digital technologies and data (95). Related to this, several educators outlined that they had *difficulties finding information* on data systems due to their "breadth, complexity and opacity" (122) and "the black box problem" (282).

Educators' Challenges, Needs and Wishes for Educational Resources

This leads to another problematic area that 25 educators highlighted: the difficulties they encounter when trying to find and use educational resources as well as their needs and wishes for such resources. In line with the interview findings, one common issue was that *existing material outdates quickly*. Educators criticised that specialist literature is "often already outdated upon publication" (206) and outlined that "the biggest problem" is to view and select the wide range of material and keep up it to date (249). Furthermore, some argued that *existing material is too complex* – with resources being too "difficult for students to access due to complexity of langu[a]ge" (173) and overall being "too technical, too complicated, too detailed and/or ignor[ing] lack of capacity" (316). Several educators outlined that material for beginners and younger kids, for example in primary schools, is missing. Related to this, some educators *called for school-specific resources*. They highlighted a need for textbooks, planned lessons, material that matches the curriculum and resources that are "not several hours long max time we have is 60 mins a lesson" (181). These findings are extremely useful for creators who develop resources for formal educational settings.

Additionally, 13 participants took the opportunity to detail *specific formats and content they need in educational resources* about digital technologies and data. In terms of resource formats, they highlighted a lack of good texts and good videos and called for more offline formats and open-source material. Some further wished for more hands-on interactive resources, playful resources, podcasts and quizzes. Regarding the resources' content, the educators criticised that existing resources often ignore the learners' individual or organisational context – which reinforces the argument that different audiences require different approaches. Moreover, a variety of different needs was outlined, including the need for more practical material, such as resources for practical demonstration, e-learning platforms and material on effective uses of technology; guides to data privacy for parents and teachers; resources that combine different fields; and material that includes ethical thought experiments or covers datafication in more depth. These wishes highlight the variety of educators' needs and that many kinds of resources are required, but they also demonstrate that many of the resources analysed in my study are already on the right track.

Educators' Satisfaction with Existing Educational Resources: "Basically There Is Nothing" versus "The Problem […] Is the Abundance"

The survey further led to divergent findings on educators' overall satisfaction with the existing resources. Seven educators used the open text fields to highlight that they struggled to find good material, arguing that there is "very little teaching material out there if any. […] But basically there is nothing!" (181), and that "almost all the digital resources are needed. None is available here" (148). Others criticised the quality of existing resources, outlining that some resources exist, but they are "way too superficial and factually wrong" (112), that "ther[e] is a lot of nonsense" (201), and

"MS and Co. [Microsoft and others] have a lot of influence" and alternative material is needed (201). Four educators further emphasised that *easier access to resources is needed*, particularly for those not fortunate enough to have access to university library licences, and four called for a *central collection of resources*, such as "a digital library for teaching material that is selected, tagged and commented by experts" (249), a "central pool of material" (218) or for "some form of compendium" (141). These calls are particularly relevant because some such collections already exist – for example the CBDALN database that was used as a source for my study's content analysis. Yet, apart from highlighting the significance of curated collections, these calls also demonstrate the difficulty of reaching the intended audience, as, it seems, these educators were not aware that several such collections already exist.

However, contrary to the arguments made above, four educators also used the open text fields to highlight that is it *no problem for them to find material*. They outline that they have not encountered any problems specific to topics around digital technologies, and that their only challenge is to make a choice on which resource to use out of the large range that exists. One explained that "5 years ago the materials were rather academic. But in the last two years there has been an explosion of very good materials" (209). This educator goes on to name several resource formats and specific resources that were helpful to them and concludes: "The problem, as usual, is the abundance" (209). Unfortunately, the reasons behind these very different perspectives of the educators on the existing material cannot be determined with certainty. One possible solution is that some educators are more informed about the many resources that already exist. Another explanation could be that different educators have different expectations and requirements for resources or – considering the wide range of topics that fall under "education about digital technologies" – that they look for resources on different topics.

These divergent perspectives are not just a singular impression based on the open text field analysis, but they were confirmed by a closed question on participants' satisfaction with their access to information and teaching material about digital technologies and data. Figure 24 demonstrates that the average satisfaction of educators with their access to material was mixed. A little over one third of educators indicated being not at all or slightly satisfied (37%), a little less than one third was moderately satisfied (30%), and exactly one third was very or extremely satisfied (33%).

This picture of mixed opinions remained unchanged when considering the individual topics that were asked about: digital technologies in general, data security, (big) data systems and algorithms, and the way digital media and (big) data affect society. As figure 25 shows, the differences between the topics were marginal, with educators being on average most satisfied with their access to material about digital technologies generally (average of 3.2), followed by data security (2.92), the effects of digital technologies (2.84), and finally (big) data systems and algorithms (2.63).

Across all four topics, divergent opinions could be identified. However, higher satisfaction was indicated towards material on digital technologies in general (41% very or extremely satisfied) in contrast to, for example, (big) data systems and algorithms (26% very or extremely satisfied).

Figure 24: The surveyed educators' average satisfaction (across all four given topics) with access to information and teaching resources in percent (n per topic, see figure 25).

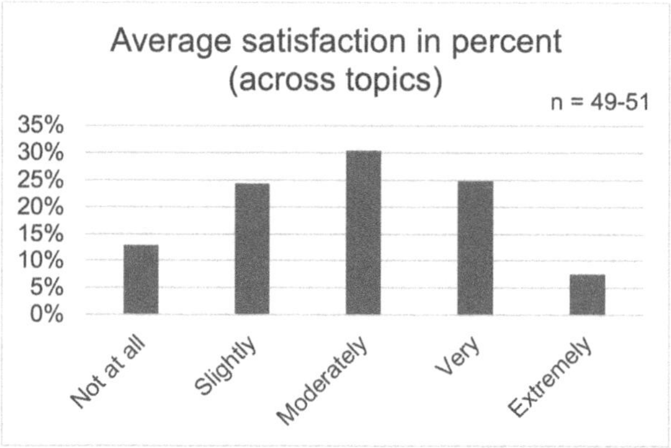

Figure 25: Total numbers of surveyed educators indicating how satisfied they are with their access to information and teaching material on the four given topics.

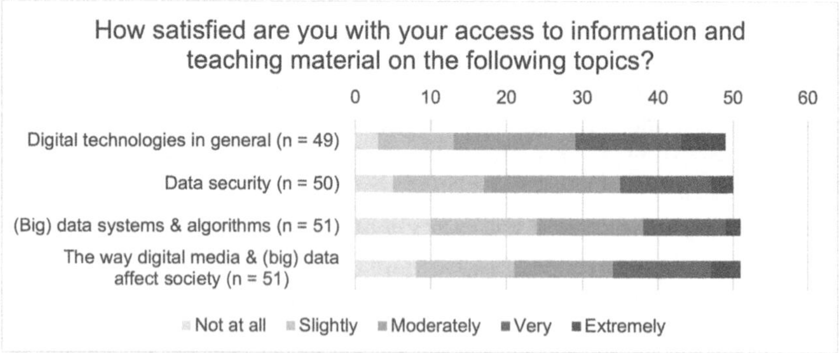

Thus, overall, it can be said that educators' satisfaction with their access to educational resources about digital technologies and data as well as with the resources themselves very much depended on the individual. While the surveyed educators were slightly more content with their access to material on some topics than others, the key finding is one of mixed opinions. Moreover, the numbers for educators' satisfaction with their access to material (averages between 2.63 – 3.2) were consistently significantly lower than the numbers on how well-equipped the educators felt to teach about these topics (averages between 3.41 – 4). This suggests that while the surveyed educators have *some* material to teach about these topics, many do not seem to be very happy with this material.

Educator's Perspectives on Societal Challenges

Finally, some educators took the opportunity to outline societal challenges in relation to digital technologies and data that they saw as most pressing. This gives an idea of their overall attitude to digital technologies and consequently on their motivation for teaching about digital and data technologies. Three key challenges were outlined. First, a small number of educators passionately called for *more control, oversight and transparency of digital technologies*, arguing that technologies need to be turned "back into tools in service to the people rather than degrading people into data suppliers in a data economy" (249), and that more control of companies, less exploitation, and easier data protection for people is needed (321). Related to this, others called for *other forms of digital technologies*, demanding more open data (218); a communal, non-commercial system (201); or "data-minimising and decentral systems, disclosing all source codes, making algorithms transparent and public and giving people data sovereignty" (249). Finally, the *need for more funding for resources and alternative educational formats* was outlined. In this context, educators called for more public support for education about data (184) and more "crowd science" and "collective approaches to generate educational tools" (209). Overall, these final comments of educators highlight the passion and motivation of some educators in addressing challenges around datafication, which suggests that excellent education about data is already being practised.

5.3.5 Conclusion and Discussion

The first key finding of the survey was that a diverse sample of educators could be reached, with educators from 18 different countries and a range of educational settings. Although a dominance of educators in formal education and those living in Germany was determined, the sample's variety nevertheless demonstrated that diverse educators and educational fields are already fostering education about digital technologies and data. Moreover, the participants' information on their subject contexts revealed a remarkable diversity, from journalism to screen writing, IT and data analysis training, or civic or political education, demonstrating for how many different educational contexts these topics are of relevance.

Educators Cover a Variety of Topics in Their Teaching – Often Aiming for Similar Goals as the Resource Creators

This diversity was confirmed in the educators' goals and topics. While educators in the sample overall felt fairly experienced and well-equipped to teach about digital technologies and data, differences between topics were identified. The surveyed educators felt considerably more experienced and well-equipped to teach about digital technologies and their societal implications than about more technical or complex topics such as data security or data and algorithmic systems. In particular, the educators' experience in teaching about societal implications of digital technologies constituted a significant finding in this context. While "implications" is a broad term that can be interpreted in many ways, it was nevertheless encouraging that the surveyed educators go beyond instrumental skills in their teaching, and also include more reflective perspectives on technologies' impacts.

Overall, the educators often provided detailed descriptions of the topics and goals of their education about data, thus giving a good idea of the kind of literacy they aim to foster. Many similarities to the goals of the creators interviewed earlier in my study were identified. A large majority of educators highlighted understanding and critical reflection as key goals. In particular, many educators indicated to educate about how digital technologies and data systems work – including their shortcomings – and how they affect individuals and society. Although the survey did not specifically address educators with a critical stance towards technologies, these goals correspond with the creator interview findings and with my preliminary critical datafication framework. Yet, they represent a contrast to other studies that have found that instrumental and technical approaches to data literacy prevail in the education sector (Raffaghelli and Stewart 2020, p. 446ff). Moreover, novel approaches and goals were identified, such as applying critical thinking and "tech intuition" to new and emerging technologies. Furthermore, the vast majority of participants agreed that mobilising people to take societal or political action was important to them, which represents another parallel to the creator interview findings.

Further novel findings included the educators' objective of teaching about digital and data ethics and laws, and a strong focus on practical skills, such as using office technologies, creating media content, or using and analysing data. This focus on practical skills represents a contrast to many educators' emphasis on critical reflection; yet this perspective was sometimes indicated by the same educators who distinctly called for critical approaches. This significant finding again opens up the question of whether critical education about data should foster people's practical skills – a question that seems unresolved among critical data literacy scholars (see chapter 2.2). For many of the surveyed educators, it seemed that fostering critical reflection alongside practical media usage skills constituted no contradiction – even in relation to skills such as social media marketing, which supports the same business models that many educators wanted learners to critically reflect upon. Overall, a wide range of different topics and goals was determined. This reemphasises the difficulty of defining what education about digital and data technologies entails and which topics should be addressed, but it also highlights the wide range of skills and understandings citizens require to navigate datafied societies.

Parallels to Previous Findings

The analysis further demonstrated that, overall, the approaches that creators of online critical data literacy resources have been taking seem to be in line with educators' needs and requirements. Many of the surveyed educators stated that they search for information and teaching material online, and they found images, short videos, entire websites, texts and online courses very useful. Divergent opinions were identified on whether games – both online and offline – are useful for educators. However, some educators also highlighted that the format of a resource or even the resource itself is not as important as the teaching and pedagogical decisions in which it is embedded. This is a valuable reminder that the role of the educators themselves should not be underestimated when it comes to fostering critical data literacy. Furthermore, several educators recommended specific resources that they found useful, including resources examined in chapter 5.1 and some similar to those. All of these findings are encouraging as they suggest that online resources are useful for educators and that many of the critical data literacy resources examined in my study might be appreciated by educators. Thus, these findings also support the knowledge mobilisation taking place in this study, which, among others, aims to make these resources more easily accessible to educators. Moreover, several educators indicated that they like to create their own resources, which was a novel finding that inspired a section on "creating educational resources" in the knowledge mobilisation project resource (see appendix IX).

Almost all educators used the survey's open text fields to elaborate on the methods and approaches they use when teaching about digital technologies and data. The analysis of this data identified many parallels to the creator interviews, such as wanting to establish real-world connections by relating to people's everyday experiences and using real-life examples, or using interactive, practical and playful approaches including stories. Another strong theme that emerged was that different learners need different approaches. Further research statements the educators agreed on were that interactive approaches work well to engage learners – as found, for example, in my prior research (2020c); that education about digital technologies can also take place through analogue methods – as emphasised, among others, by Pötzsch (2019); and that appealing visualisations can help learners to engage emotionally – as, for example, highlighted by Kennedy and Hill (2018).

A key finding in this context was that the majority of educators did not agree that it is up to individuals to protect their data online. This represents a contrast to the strong emphasis on self-data protection in most resources examined (see chapter 5.1) and in many academic concepts for critical data literacy (see chapter 2.2). A second significant finding was that more than half of the participants agreed that it can be beneficial to shock learners to make them realise that they are affected by a societal issue. The strong agreement with this among many surveyed educators represents a contrast to the divergent opinions on this that were identified in the expert interviews (see chapter 5.2) and in my prior research (2020c, p. 13).

Challenges in Teaching and Finding the Right Material

Several parallels between the challenges highlighted by the educators and the creator interview findings emerged, for example that it is difficult to engage learners and make them realise that they are affected by issues around data systems. Some educators further highlighted structural challenges, such as the need for these topics to be better integrated in curricula and a lack of support for teachers who want to educate about digital technologies. In relation to educational resources, the difficulties of quickly outdating material and insufficient resources for younger children and beginners were outlined. In addition, the educators provided valuable feedback on existing resources, such as that many are too complex, that more school-specific resources are needed, and they called for a central collection of resources. This last point informed this study's knowledge mobilisation project (see appendix IX), but it also demonstrated that existing tools – including an already existing database of resources – often do not reach the intended audience, a challenge that was also raised by the interviewed creators.

Moreover, the analysis identified educators' divergent perspectives on the availability of existing resources. While some indicated being very satisfied with their access to information and material and spoke of an "abundance" of resources, others were not satisfied at all and stated that there was "basically nothing". As discussed above, there could be different reasons for these divergent opinions, for example that the educators were searching for material on different topics, had different expectations towards the material or had different access, with some seeming to be more informed about existing resources than others. For both problems – an abundance of material as well as not knowing of any good resources – a central collection of resources was suggested as a solution. Finally, some educators even highlighted a number of societal challenges in regard to digital and data technologies, demonstrating their passion and motivation for addressing concerns around datafication.

Overall, the survey led to valuable findings regarding educators' goals for teaching about digital and data technologies, the methods and approaches they apply in reaching these goals, and their challenges, needs and wishes when it comes to educational resources and teaching about these topics in general. Particularly the survey's combination of open and closed questions proved valuable in identifying novel findings, while also allowing for generalising statements about the sample's perspectives. With all of these findings, however, it is important to keep in mind that they only represent a small sample of international educators and that no representative statements about all educators can be inferred. Nevertheless, the goal of the qualitative survey – understanding rather than representativeness – was reached and much could be learnt from educators' experiences and perspectives. In addition to many parallels to the creator interview findings, novel approaches and goals were identified, many of which could be highly useful for the future development of critical data literacy resources. Thus, these findings ideally complement the prior two methods that examined existing online resources and their creators' perspectives.

6. Discussion

After the last three chapters presented the findings of each of the study's three empirical perspectives, this chapter aims to interweave and discuss these findings. A key novel finding throughout my study was that many parallels could be identified between the examined resources, the interviewed creators and the surveyed educators. Yet, while many similar themes emerged in all three stages of the empirical research, this did not necessarily entail a unanimous stance of all participants. Rather, many key themes revealed divergent opinions between the participants, which often resembled ongoing debates in the academic literature, for example on the kind of constructive actions that critical education about datafication should encourage, or the appropriate balance between empowering citizens and shifting responsibility to them. Another significant finding was that the study's findings often showed remarkable parallels to those critical-reflective academic data literacy conceptualisations that were identified as most relevant in chapter 2.2 as well as to the selected educational approaches (media literacy, (politische) Bildung, and critical pedagogy) that were analysed in chapter three. Furthermore, a number of new insights were identified, such as ambitious and political goals of some resource creators or thoughtful perspectives on datafication by educators. Overall, the study led to novel findings on the as yet under-researched field of online educational resources about datafication, the intentions and approaches of their creators, and educators' experiences, needs and wishes. All of these provided new insights and strongly informed the further conceptualisation of critical datafication literacy.

6.1 Goals for Understanding Data and Taking Action

6.1.1 Critical Understanding of Datafication

Awareness and Understanding

One key objective of the study was to better understand the goals for critical education about datafication. Here, the analyses of the online resources, the interviews with the creators, and the educator survey showed remarkable parallels. The first key goal that was identified across all empirical stages was that teaching about datafication should aim for increased *awareness* of the use and impact of data technologies as well as *understanding* of how these systems function and how they affect our lives and society. My study's participants aimed to raise awareness of digital technologies' influences and risks and emphasised that they wanted learners to understand how technology functions, including its shortcomings. Many participants wanted to foster critical and reflective understanding rather than mere passing of knowledge, a goal that corresponds with the principles of *Bildung* (e.g., Sander 2018). Equally in line with the concept of Bildung, several study participants highlighted that they view literacy as a never-ending process which continues throughout one's life and argued that a fully literate person does not exist (see e.g., Bauer 2003; Watson 2010). This further resembles critical pedagogy and its understanding of learning as an unfinished process of "becoming" (Freire 2017, p. 57). While these arguments show similarities to key insights from the traditional educational approaches examined in chapter three, they are not common in existing critical data literacy conceptualisations.

A key finding throughout several stages of the research was that many participants shared a goal of *broad, systemic, (infra)structural understanding* of datafication, which goes beyond aspects such as digital media content, data security or personal privacy, and instead aims for understanding of technologies' underlying structures and the wider transformation of society through technology. Many participants highlighted the social, political and economic dimensions of data technologies and thus the political nature of critical data literacy – with one outlining that "this type of engagement is political" (participant 209) – and suggested a need to connect to learners' existing social and political frameworks. As argued in chapter 2.2, such systemic and political approaches to data literacy are rare in the literature, and data literacy concepts have been criticised for "not explicitely engag[ing] with questions of power" and racial and social justice (Jansen 2021, p. 8f). However, this view correlates with critical pedagogy, which defines education or literacy as an inherently political practice (Freire and Macedo 1987; Vossoughi and Gutiérrez 2016). Moreover, a small number of educational approaches about data aim for systemic understanding and for unpacking the politics of data, power, interests and ideologies through data literacy (Pangrazio and Selwyn 2019; Pötzsch 2019; Fotopoulou 2020).

The educators further indicated that fostering such deep structural understanding with learners is *challenging* due to their often *limited and instrumental understanding* of technology, their narrow concerns around internet safety only, and, for some, the fact that they enjoy using data technologies. Other empirical studies have reached similar findings, reporting that people lack the literacy or technology understanding to fully understand critical art pieces about data technologies (Stark and Crawford 2019), or that students found it difficult to think outside the box and beyond cybersecurity, and that the "thrill" of using social media restricted learners' critical reflection (Pangrazio and Selwyn 2020, p. 11). Equally in line with the literature, some participants aimed to foster learners' *technical* understanding while at the same time promoting critical thinking (see e.g., Koltay 2015). Finally, a novel finding was that some educators aimed to teach about the ethics and laws regarding digital and data technologies.

Critical Thinking and Forming One's Own Opinion

A second key goal identified throughout the entire study was *critical reflection* or *critical thinking*. Many study participants placed a particular emphasis on critical *thinking*. This reiterates education scholarship, which outlines the development and promotion of critical thinking as a core goal for education in general (Barrow 2014, p. 257f) as well as for specific approaches such as politische Bildung (Autorengruppe Fachdidaktik 2016, p. 8) and critical pedagogy (Giroux 2010, p. 716). The latter understands critical thinking as a way of fostering a "critical consciousness", an awareness and critical reflection of one's own situation in the world (Freire 2017, p. 42f). However, also some academic critical data literacy concepts have called for critical thinking (e.g., Koltay 2015; Pötzsch 2019; Carmi et al. 2020), or have applied Freire's critical consciousness to education about digital and data technologies (e.g., Hammer 2011; Tygel and Kirsch 2016; Milan 2017; Meng and DiSalvo 2018; Markham 2019).

The study's participants further detailed how they fostered critical thinking in practice. In line with the literature, key identified approaches included educating about the risks and dangers related to data technologies, and demonstrating how *technology affects individuals and society*. Moreover, many participants emphasised to not tell learners what to think, but rather support them in *forming their own opinion*. Instead of convincing learners of a specific perspective through "persuasion and propaganda" (Gaylor interview, 2020), as one creator put it, encouraging them to reach their own conclusions through critical thinking can open learners up to new perspectives and empower them. This corresponds with (politische) Bildung and its goal of Mündigkeit (see below), and with critical pedagogy, which aims for a pedagogy *with* the learner, using dialogue and critical thinking (Freire 2017). Similarly, a small number of data literacy concepts emphasise that educators should not indicate that certain data systems are good or bad, but rather let learners experience and see for themselves how they are tracked (Fontichiaro et al. 2017, p.v; Markham 2019, p. 758), and prompt them with good questions (Markham 2020, p. 231) – approaches that the interviewed educators also suggested. Moreover, Kennedy et al.'s research found that people have (emotional) views on data practices even when they have little understanding (2021a, p. 1759), indicating that these views should be taken seriously instead of convincing learners of other perspectives.

Furthermore, the findings suggested that the ability to think critically and form one's own opinion can help with the *challenges of a fast-changing technology landscape*.

This fast pace comes with many challenges, including keeping online educational resources technically accessible and keeping the content of educational material up to date. One educator suggested that fostering learners' ability to think critically could enable them to apply "ethical thinking on unforeseeable yet emerging technologies" (participant 282). This approach is not yet common in critical data literacy discourses. However, one early data literacy publication made a similar suggestion, aiming to foster "adaptive capacities and resilience rather than teaching platforms and technical languages that are bound to become out-dated" (Data Pop Alliance and Internews 2015, p.iv). This approach is further reminiscent of politische Bildung, which fosters citizens' ability to evaluate and criticise social phenomena, even when these are changing (Autorengruppe Fachdidaktik 2016). Therefore, politische Bildung does *not define any learning objectives*, but argues that whatever challenges individuals' Mündigkeit and democratic self-determination at the time becomes a learning objective (ibid.). While this approach of adapting the topics of teaching to current social challenges is highly relevant for educating about the fast-changing world of data systems, it is difficult to implement in practice as it requires continuous updating of teaching and learning material. More research is needed about how education about datafication could learn from the decade-long experience of politische Bildung regarding these challenges.

Related to critical thinking, two further goals of study participants were to work towards people's *agency* in datafied societies and to *empower* them. While agency is not a particularly common theme in the data literacy discourse (see chapter 2.2), some critical data literacy concepts similarly aim to foster the skills "required to have agency in a datafied world" (Pangrazio and Sefton-Green 2020, p. 214; see also: Pangrazio and Selwyn 2019; Carmi et al. 2020). Empowering individuals, on the other hand, is a pronounced goal of many academic critical data literacy concepts (e.g., D'Ignazio and Bhargava 2015; Pybus et al. 2015; Pötzsch 2019). This goal is further very prominent in critical pedagogy approaches, which aim for "self-determination and civic engagement" (Giroux 2010, p. 716), and want to empower individuals to transform their societal reality (Mihailidis 2018, p. 10). Tygel and Kirsch, who developed a Freirean-inspired critical data literacy, similarly emphasise the emancipatory character of their literacy concept (2016, p. 113f).

6.1.2 Diverse Skills and Paths of Action

Empowering Learners to Become Active

These goals of empowering citizens and providing them with the ability to transform their reality leads to another key goal identified in my study: to *enable learners to take action*. Literacy is sometimes criticised as aiming 'only' for awareness and understanding, without offering constructive next steps. This was not the case for the resources, creators and educators examined in my study, who predominantly placed a strong emphasis on encouraging learners to become active. Similarly, some academic critical data literacy scholars have emphasised the importance of including practical steps toward empowerment (Yates et al. 2021; Bilstrup et al. 2022), and have outlined that agency can also be enacted through "tactical and small forms of engagement" (Gangneux 2020, p. 461). However, as will be further discussed below, citizens' ability to protect their data is limited and if no "adequate pathways forward" are offered, such approach can also lead to frustration and resignation (Jansen 2021, p. 7; Yates et al. 2021). This risk of resignation (see e.g., Hargittai and Marwick 2016; Dencik and Cable 2017; Draper and Turow 2019) was also recognised by some of the surveyed educators, who spoke of a "dystopian pull" (participant 174) in some of their learners.

Many participants further aimed for an *informed participation in datafied societies*. They wanted to enable individuals to make "enlightened choices" (Schekter interview, 2021), and gain a "tech intuition" (participant 316) in order to make informed decisions on technology use without knowing all the details. While also some academic approaches aim to empower citizens to navigate their digital ecosystems and societies in an informed manner (Data Pop Alliance and Internews 2015, p.iv), and work towards "enlightened user[s]" (Milioni and Papa 2019), the notion of a "tech intuition" constitutes a novel and highly relevant approach to educating about fast-changing technology landscapes. Bildung similarly aims for understanding of the world and the ability to make judgements (Sander 2019), and politische Bildung promotes citizens' orientation in the world, political participation and civic involvement (Autorengruppe Fachdidaktik 2016). These objectives correlate with many of the participants' goals, which suggests that many might have called for *Mündigkeit* in regard to datafication if they had been prompted to use this term. Mündigkeit describes the ability of individuals to sustain themselves in and grapple with society, politics and economics in an informed and self-determined manner (Autorengruppe Fachdidaktik 2016). It can be seen as a prerequisite for participating in society successfully, which, one could argue, must include a certain *literacy* regarding digital and data systems in our datafied societies.

While the importance of empowering learners to take action was largely unequivocal, some of the findings identified were less clear. For example, some expert interviewees thought it unrealistic to change people's behaviour and were happy with 'only' aiming for awareness and understanding. Apart from that, the type of constructive actions that should be recommended was not always clear, with some conflicting findings and dilemmas emerging.

Conflicting Findings on the Need for Data Usage Skills

In the academic discourse as well as in debates among critical data literacy practitioners, one question often remains unresolved: Should critical data literacy *also foster people's practical skills of using data*? Some scholars argue that both critical reflection and practical data usage skills are needed (e.g., D'Ignazio and Bhargava 2015), or even that education about data should take place *through* using data (e.g., Pybus et al. 2015; Crusoe 2016; Gray et al. 2018). In contrast, other scholars argue that critical data literacy needs to go *beyond* skills (e.g., Markham 2019; Pangrazio and Selwyn 2019); that fostering digital skills, without also promoting critical reflection, can actually be *harmful* for kids (Livingstone et al. 2021a); and that the (unreflecting) use of digital methods in teaching can come with a "hidden curriculum" – subconsciously suggesting data as direct and accurate measurements (rather than biased, incomplete representations) and building excessive trust, thereby leading to illiteracy (Mertala 2020, p. 14). Similar debates are being held in other fields of literacy research, such as the media literacy field (see chapter 3.1).

In line with these academic debates, the participants of my study showed *diverging opinions* on the question of data usage skills. While the goal of data usage skills was less common in the resource analysis and the expert interviews, the educator survey led to a more mixed outcome, with the majority of educators indicating that in order to understand data systems, learners should use data and datasets themselves. This might be explained by the different samples, as the sampling for the survey did not specifically address educators that aimed to promote critical reflection of data technologies. However, similar to several academic critical data literacy approaches analysed in chapter two (see section 2.2.2), many educators aimed to promote critical reflection *through the use of data* and wanted to foster people's data sovereignty, the use of data for good, and the development of better technologies. Apart from that, educators mentioned practical skills that are more common in information and digital literacy than in data literacy concepts, such as basic usage skills for digital media, digital media content creation, researching skills, and the use of digital technologies for teaching.

The Dilemma of Data Protection Skills and Individual Responsibility

Moreover, the question of whether or not, which, and in what way *data protection skills* should be taught often led to *conflicting findings*. On the one hand, data protection skills were the most common type of advice identified in all three empirical stages. Many study participants argued that such skills can empower individuals, foster their confidence and make them feel safe. They further highlighted that knowing how to (better) protect one's data online can help to avoid a feeling of powerlessness or resignation when learning about data collection and data systems (as also suggested by participants in my prior study, Sander 2020c). Critical data literacy scholars make similar calls, highlighting the empowering nature of such tactics (Young and Pridmore Forthcoming); calling for "resisting" or even "emancipated" users, who resist or abandon the corporate web (Milioni and Papa 2019), or aiming – but finding it difficult – to motivate students to use alternative technologies (Pangrazio and Selwyn 2020).

On the other hand, many study participants emphasised that data protection advice is problematic – some even said pointless – as *systemic solutions are needed*. Several participants outlined that technology is so sophisticated that it cannot and should not be up to the individuals to solve issues around data, and that individual solutions "won't amount to anything" (Gaylor interview, 2021). They drew parallels to the issue of climate activism, arguing that legislation needs to step in and that more control, oversight and transparency is needed. Similar arguments are made in the literature, with scholars outlining that many difficulties in privacy protection are rooted in the "responsibilisation" of individuals (Kazansky 2015, p. 189). The fact that critical education about data can offer learners few alternatives other than opting out from digital services can easily evoke paranoia (Pangrazio and Selwyn 2020; Pangrazio and Sefton-Green 2022), when learners realise that individual data protection is only a "small bandage approach" and that collective and systemic solutions are needed (Young and Pridmore Forthcoming). Moreover, some studies show that young people are annoyed by obfuscation practices and instead see platform providers as responsible for privacy protection (Selwyn and Pangrazio 2018, p. 10) – similar to scholars who argue that responsibility is currently outsourced to the education sector and individuals, whereas it is platforms and regulators who need to act (Livingstone et al. 2021b, p. 233; Yates et al. 2021, p.xii; Livingstone et al. 2022, p. 196).

These arguments are connected to another key finding of the study: that *responsibility to address challenges of datafication should not be shifted to individuals*. Several interviewees highlighted that putting this "burden" on the individual is the "wrong approach" (Gaylor interview, 2021), and also the majority of the surveyed educators indicated that it should not be up to the individuals to protect their data. While self-data protection was a common goal of digital and data literacy concepts in the past, recent critical publications have similarly begun to criticise this shift of responsibility to individuals (e.g., Mihailidis 2018; Pangrazio and Selwyn 2019; Carmi et al. 2020; Pangrazio and Sefton-Green 2020), and called for collective approaches rather than individualised ones (Gangneux 2020, p. 462). Similar arguments can be found in media literacy discourses, with scholars arguing that media pedagogy should support self-determination, but that this self-determination should not be individualised but is dependent on a civic framework for action (Aßmann et al. 2016), and that media literacy should not be restricted to a subjective-individualistic level, but should rather be implemented at a supra-individual, societal level and should foster public discourse (Baacke 1997).

However, finding this *balance between empowerment versus a shift of responsibility* is difficult. The majority of resources analysed in the content analysis only provided individual data protection advice, thereby indirectly shifting responsibility to the individuals, and some even directly urged individuals to take responsibility of their data. Moreover, nearly a quarter of the surveyed educators took this perspective.

These conflicting findings resemble the academic discourse on (critical) data literacy, which, despite the concerns of individual scholars outlined above, overall, still places a strong emphasis on fostering individual skills. Studies have further shown that citizens are so used to individualised approaches to manage the risks of digital data and to remain 'safe' that they view privacy as their own individual responsibility (Shade and Shepherd 2013), and are rarely able to "reimagine data use in more collective, more open and/ or more subversive terms" (Pangrazio and Selwyn 2020, p. 11). This highlights the importance of including alternative and collective forms of action when educating about data, such as those discussed in the next section.

Going Beyond Skills: Alternative and Collective Paths of Action

A novel finding of the study was to identify a number of alternative and collective paths of action as goals for educating about datafication. By far the most common approach in this context was the goal of enabling learners to *take political or societal action*. This approach occurred in small numbers in the analysis of the resources but received strong agreement in the educator survey. Moreover, many of the creator interviewees wanted to support such paths of action, for example by encouraging learners to contact political parties, take part in public debates, or even contribute to a critical data movement. In this context, this study further found that several study participants aimed to provide learners with a *data language*, a shared vocabulary about data that enables them to better articulate their concerns and be heard and seem legitimate in public debates.

These highly motivated and political goals are not common in existing critical data literacy conceptualisations, but resemble "re-active data activism", that aims to educate about data technologies as well as fight against the datafication and its problematic implications (e.g., Milan and Gutiérrez 2015; Milan and van der Velden 2016), albeit possibly with a more disruptive focus than my study participants' goal of citizens enacting their democratic rights. Some participants further aimed to support learners in *actively shaping the digital society*, and argued that to be a citizen in datafied societies means to engage in participatory processes about the control of data extraction, monetisation and usage (209). This perspective is reminiscent of academic definitions of "data citizenship" (Carmi et al. 2020, p. 3) or being a "digital citizen in a datafied society" (Hintz et al. 2019, p. 19) and of Shade and Chan's "digital privacy policy literacy", which promotes citizens' participation in privacy policy-making (2020, p. 336). Similarly, media pedagogy as defined by Aßman et al. aims to help citizens comprehend digital structures and shape them democratically (2016). These goals are closely connected to a hope of *achieving change through education*. This hope was expressed by several participants who aimed to mobilise learners to take political or societal action, to participate in society in an informed manner and to shape this society. Such perspectives reiterate the Freirean understanding of literacy, which sees education as an emancipatory process that can help individuals transform their limiting reality and change social conditions (e.g., Freire and Macedo 1987; Wringe 2012; Freire 2017).

Further alternative actions fostered by study participants included encouraging people to *imagine different data futures*. Their objective to foster an imagination of alternatives in order to motivate learners and steer them away from a resigned attitude resembles Jasanoff and Kim's notion of "sociotechnical imaginaries" that highlight "the capacity to imagine futures" as a crucial element in social and political life, and for formulating and reaching goals (2009, p. 122). The study participants implemented this approach into practice for example by offering learners different data future scenarios – including dystopian and utopian options – or encouraging them with the slogan "To change the future, click here" (Do Not Track, R9). Some – few – academic concepts take similar approaches, aiming to open up people's "infrastructural imagination" of how datasets are created, used and organised through "data infrastructure literacy" (Gray et al. 2018, p. 3), or fostering people's "critical imagination" in data activism projects (Milan 2017, no page number). However, fostering such imagination in practice can prove difficult as learners, such as in my previous study, find it difficult to imagine negative consequences of data disclosure beyond personal safety or cybersecurity (2020a; similar findings by Pangrazio and Selwyn 2020).

Finally, the study participants and the examined resources aimed to foster people's *networks of literacy*. Scholars have emphasised the importance of people's social networks for fostering literacies (Yates et al. 2021), and have highlighted that once people start asking critical questions, this critical awareness starts a "chain reaction" that spreads to their friends and families (Markham 2019). Several such attempts were identified in my study, for example by providing awareness-raising exercises people can do with their friends, public speaking material, or workshop and teaching material that can be used to educate others. Moreover, many educators indicated learning about new topics and resources from their colleagues, and the interviewed creators highlighted empowering people to educate others as one of their goals. Many creators further reported interest from educators in their resources, and one called an educational use of their resource a "dream use case" (Younge interview, 2021). However, they also emphasised that small projects like the ones examined in this study, which often originate from civil society, are not enough and that a *systematic education strategy* for critical data literacy is needed. Similar calls were made by the educators, who nevertheless expressed gratitude about the existing resources (see section 6.2).

6.1.3 Key Insights on Goals for Critical Data Education

Overall, many significant parallels were identified between the study's empirical findings on goals for teaching about data and key theoretical findings from the second and third chapter. These novel insights strongly informed the critical datafication framework developed throughout this study, and they demonstrated how much can be learnt from analysing the practical data education that is already taking place in different contexts. A crucial finding was the strong dominance of *critical and reflexive goals*, aiming for critical and systemic understanding of datafication. In particular, the goal of systemic understanding of the (infra)structural changes in society through datafication provides a novel perspective that does not get much attention in academic data literacy discourses thus far (see chapter 2.2). The content analysis similarly demonstrated that many existing resources did not meet the qualifying criterion asking for a critical perspective. From anecdotal experience, it is likely that a similarly strong focus on instrumental, practical data literacy approaches as identified in chapter 2.2 might be found in a wider scale analysis of educational resources and practical education. A systematic review of literature on higher education data literacy approaches already confirmed this (Raffaghelli and Stewart 2020, p. 446ff).

Moreover, the findings showed a *significant focus on alternative and collective paths of action* for learners. This demonstrates that online educational resources can also go beyond fostering data protection tactics, which has been identified as the dominant approach in this study's content analysis as well as in other studies (Young and Pridmore Forthcoming). Thus, these findings advance previous research in the field and are particularly encouraging as suggestions for collective action allow for a balance between providing constructive advice to avoid learners' resignation while not making learners feel as if it was their responsibility to address the systemic issues around datafication.

6.2 Findings on Resources and Contexts of Teaching

Educational Settings and Challenges for Teaching about Data

The empirical research in my study further led to novel findings on existing online educational resources about datafication and the contexts in which critical data literacy is already being fostered. A wide range of diverse online critical data literacy resources was identified, and the survey demonstrated that topics around digital and data technologies are already addressed in formal and informal education settings, such as schools, universities, teacher training and civil society workshops, and in diverse subject settings from IT through communication and journalism to political literacy. This corresponds with scholarly calls for interdisciplinary approaches to critical data literacy and an implementation of such literacy education in formal as well as informal settings (e.g., Aßmann et al. 2016; Gray et al. 2018; Pangrazio and Selwyn 2019).

Nevertheless, many research participants agreed with scholars that more needs to be done to improve the teaching of critical data literacy. They highlighted a lack of support and IT infrastructure in their institutions, a challenge also identified by Pangrazio and Selwyn (2020). Several surveyed educators further called for a change in curricula in order to include critical perspectives to data technologies. Similarly, already in 2016, Aßman et al. urged that media pedagogy – which, as they argue, should include critical education about big data and data analytics – needs a permanent and sustainable place in curricula (2016). More recently, scholars have argued that school curricula about digital technologies should be more critical (Polizzi 2020a).

Findings on (the Use of) Educational Resources

In light of these challenges and gaps in curricula, many surveyed educators found their own, creative solutions in order to teach about data, such as searching for material online, exchanging ideas and resources with colleagues, or even creating their own resources. Divergent findings were identified on the educators' satisfaction with their access to information and teaching material, with some participants finding it difficult to find good material, highlighting that school-specific, easy-access and up-to-date resources are needed, whereas others were satisfied with their access to material and even spoke of an "abundance" of resources. Several participants wished for a central collection of resources that would make it easier for them to find the right resource for their learners, and many indicated online resources such as the ones that were examined in my study as useful to them.

These novel findings, together with the fact that the content analysis identified a large number of educational resources that foster critical education about datafication without requiring any prior knowledge, suggests that there are already many resources that are useful for educators who are interested in fostering critical data education. Moreover, the analysis demonstrated the diversity of these as yet under-researched resources in terms of their creator background, country of origin and format. Particularly the latter revealed new information on unusual formats and design approaches. Moreover, a large amount of material designed specifically for teaching was identified. This reemphasises the need to better connect these existing resources with educators interested in teaching about data. Yet, one gap remains: as the study only examined resources that are available online (with only few intended for print-out or in-person use), no claims could be made about the formats, content or goals of analogue resources, or about the daily practices and exercises used by educators teaching about data. This is a limitation of my study. An analysis of analogue resources and further approaches educators take in their practical teaching about datafication would be highly interesting for future studies.

However, one significant finding in relation to analogue resources did emerge in the study: the vast majority of educators and also some creators stated that analogue formats are useful for teaching about digital and data technologies as well. This approach tends to be overlooked by most academic critical data literacy concepts, which often instead suggest educating about data systems through the active use of data (e.g., Pybus et al. 2015; Crusoe 2016; Gray et al. 2018). However, it is in line with other scholars, who emphasise that education about digital and data technologies does not have to take place digitally, and that also creative and unusual approaches, for example theatre plays, should be promoted (e.g., Pötzsch 2019; Windeyer 2019; Carmi et al. 2020). Furthermore, studies have shown that embodied, tangible, sensory experiences of data are easier to understand for students than digital approaches (Bilstrup et al. 2022, p. 234), and that gamified online tools might even, especially for young kids, be too thrilling to evoke critical reflection (Pangrazio and Selwyn 2020). Moreover, scholars have highlighted that the (unreflecting) use of digital methods can come with a "hidden curriculum", leading to illiteracy (Mertala 2020). These risks might constitute a limitation of my study's findings, as most resources take digital and playful approaches, and analogue and in-person approaches were not examined. However, this perspective is controversial, as study participants and scholars also highlight the importance of fun and interactive approaches to learning about data (see below).

Challenges and Difficulties of Online Critical Data Literacy Resources

Throughout the different stages of the research, the study identified three key challenges regarding the creation and use of online critical data literacy resources. First, the *funding* of online critical data literacy resources was identified as problematic. Interviewees reported difficulties in finding funding and several of the surveyed educators called for more funding for resources and alternative educational formats. An essential problem was the project-character: funding is usually provided for short-term projects. This leads to time pressures and often means that maintaining or updating the resources is not included in the funding.

Closely related to this, the second challenge was the *sustainability* of online educational resources. With the fast-changing technology landscape, both the content and the technical structure of the resources outdate quickly and need to be maintained and updated regularly. However, in most cases, no permanent funding is available, so maintenance is either unpaid and undertaken in the creators' free time or does not take place at all. Suggested strategies included keeping the resources' content more generic or viewing them as "unupdateable" and focussing on archiving them and creating new resources instead. However, who should be responsible for such archiving work and for providing more permanent funding requires further thought, both from sides of the creators, but also from academia and public and educational institutions.

Finally, the third challenge identified was the dilemma of *evaluating a critical data literacy resource's success and reach* while at the same time protecting the user data. One issue is that it is difficult to evaluate a resource's 'success' in terms of learning outcome as most resources are used independently by learners and their use is not monitored. Moreover, many creators deliberately did not want to collect their users' data in order to keep their integrity and 'practice what they preach' in regard to data privacy. However, for this reason, they were often unable to see how many people used their resource, for how long, or who these users were. Similar conflicts were discussed in Stark and Crawford's analysis of artists working with artificial intelligence (2019). Given these difficulties and knowledge gaps, the usage practices and the 'success' of online critical data literacy resources urgently requires further research.

6.3 New Insights on Strategies for Teaching about Datafication

All three stages of the empirical research in my study further led to novel insights on strategies and methods for fostering critical education about datafication. Besides some conflicting findings, many parallels emerged in the three empirical stages, highlighting best practice strategies recommended by different types of critical data literacy practitioners, which often reiterated approaches from traditional education scholarship.

A Literacy Resource for Everyone is a Literacy Resource for No One

A key insight identified in the literature on critical data literacy as well as in this study's interview and survey findings was that there is *no one-size-fits-all approach* to literacy. The surveyed educators strongly agreed with this and highlighted the importance of considering the different contexts of teaching and cultural backgrounds of different learners. Many of the interviewed creators similarly strongly emphasised the importance of target-group specific resources and detailed how they adapted their resource to their audience. This highlighted new approaches on how to develop target-group specific resources, such as *adapting a resource to the narratives* its target audience already holds about digital technologies and data and *finding their "hook"* – the aspect of data technologies that interests them. This could, for example, be people's sense of justice that encourages them to fight against discrimination, their concern for their kids' safety online, their aversion against economic monopoles, or simply their wish for privacy.

However, while some clearly argued that a "product for everyone is a product for no one" (Jansen, additional material interviews, 2020), others nevertheless addressed broad audiences in their resource (e.g., all Germans). The importance of adapting educational approaches about data to different audiences, considering people's different capacities, being sensitive to diversity and thus developing specifically tailored literacy programmes is also repeatedly emphasised in education literature (e.g., Brüggen 2015; Aßmann et al. 2016; Pangrazio and Selwyn 2019; Carmi et al. 2020). Scholars have further pushed for thinking about literacy as a social practice that is dependent on context and individual, and to thus consider the multiplicity of literacies (e.g., Fotopoulou 2020; Pinney 2020).

The practical implementation of these considerations, however, seems to be less straightforward. Several interviewed creators reported that it can be difficult to reach the intended audience of a resource, and the majority of the resources analysed in this study addressed broad, general groups, such as the general public or all adults and young people. While some addressed specific audiences such as journalists, activists, policymakers or educators, this nevertheless suggests that more online critical data literacy resources should be developed that take the needs, wishes and existing narratives of specific groups and communities into consideration.

Choosing Interactive, Easily Accessible and Involving Formats for Literacy Resources

A key finding that emerged throughout my study was that *interactive formats* are popular and work well for fostering critical data literacy. About half of the examined resources included interactive elements and both the interviewed creators and the surveyed educators praised active and exploratory approaches and saw them as a great way to engage learners. Such "applied and participatory approaches to learning" about data are already suggested by Illiadis and Russo's introduction to Critical Data Studies (2016, p. 5). Some interviewees further argued that a critical data literacy resource should be an "experience" or a conversation with the learner, which should lead to an "essence" or a new insight. This is not a common theme in critical data literacy discourses, but a recent data literacy publication similarly found that connecting "experiential activities" with reflection worked well in supporting students' engagement with data privacy (Agesilaou and Kyza 2021, p. 464). Apart from this, the participants emphasised that resources should be easily accessible, both in terms of technological accessibility and content. They recommended to always consider people's convenience, to not use too much text, to modularise the provided information into chunks, and to take a step-by-step approach – starting from easy-to-understand basics and slowly working towards more complex information. However, they also highlighted that it is often difficult to find a balance between an easily accessible and a technically accurate resource.

In order to capture people's interest and entice them to want to learn more – even about the more complex aspects of datafication – many creators and educators in my study suggested to *foster people's personal involvement*. Both groups reported difficulties in engaging learners and moving data issues into their "circle of worry" (Gaylor interview, 2020), because people suffer from "issue fatigue" (Yusuf interview, 2020). As a solution, they aimed to make people realise that they are personally affected by issues around datafication, and to connect to their own real-world experiences with data technologies. Similar approaches are suggested by critical pedagogy, which confronts learners with real-world problems (Freire 2017, pp. 54; 69), and by some critical data literacy concepts, which suggest using data or examples from the learners' experienced world to let them see the implications of data systems on their lives for themselves (D'Ignazio and Bhargava 2015; Tygel and Kirsch 2016; Markham 2019; Agesilaou and Kyza 2021; Bilstrup et al. 2022). A popular strategy by both the creators and the educators to achieve this was to use real-life examples and stories. Not a single educator disagreed that real-life stories can help learners understand complex issues, and also many creator interviewees strongly emphasised the importance of stories to foster a narrative, communicate complex issues, and to help learners to critically reflect and form their own opinion.

Some creators further recommended *using personas* that lead through the resource, including *real-life dilemmas* and developing resources with a *real-life impact*, and one educator highlighted the use of *story building games*. Moreover, real-life examples were included in two-thirds of the examined resources, suggesting that this strategy is already practiced by many resource creators beyond the interview sample. Thus, these findings reemphasise the value of real-life examples and stories, which was already identified in previous studies (Fontichiaro et al. 2017; Markham 2019; Sander 2020c). In addition, several participants highlighted the importance of *considering representation* when using personas and stories, as the learners should be able to identify with the people represented in the resource.

Should Learning about Datafication Be Fun Instead of Scary?

A final key consideration of the study concerned whether fostering critical data literacy should take a positive, fun and entertaining approach, or rather shock learners with the dangers of technology in order to gain attention and reach personal involvement. Overall, the majority of the findings seemed to recommend *colourful and fun resources*, which are *approachable, playful and entertaining*. The creator interviewees highlighted that people should *enjoy* the experience of using a critical data literacy resource – including the interactive tasks the resource asks users to take – and that particularly for adults, learning must always be fun. This is confirmed for example by literature on the use of serious games in education, which outlines the "motivating and engaging experiences" learners have in serious games (Anastasiadis et al. 2018, p. 139) as well as by data literacy scholarship, which recommends using gamified approaches and creative play scenarios to foster engagement (Agesilaou and Kyza 2021, p. 464; Ahlborn et al. 2021, p. 34). Yet, as outlined above, other studies have also found that gamified approaches can be "too fun" to evoke critical reflection (Pangrazio and Selwyn 2020, p. 11).

Apart from playful approaches, appealing visualisations were recommended by the study's participants. This reiterates literature highlighting the importance of materialising data and of using images and multimedia content (Pangrazio and Selwyn 2020; Alegre 2021). The surveyed educators strongly agreed that appealing visualisations can help learners to engage emotionally, confirming the findings of Kennedy and Hill (2018). The creator interviewees further highlighted that visuals offer another way of understanding for learners, and they warned against stereotypical illustrations, such as locks or zeros and ones. Instead, they recommended tangible and relatable visualisations of data systems, such as the data octopus or "data monster" that were identified in the resource analysis (see chapter 5.1).

Overall, many of the participants seemed to be convinced by visual, entertaining, positive and encouraging resources. Several participants further warned against overly pessimistic approaches, arguing that people will not want to think about issues that are too negative, and that even if their attention is caught, people stop learning when they are scared. This perspective seems supportive of literature on resignation, which has highlighted that some people feel resigned and powerless about the collection and use of their data (e.g., Hargittai and Marwick 2016; Dencik and Cable 2017; Draper and Turow 2019). However, other studies on critical data literacy have recommended that educational interventions should evoke negative emotions to let learners experience their own powerlessness and "how data can be used in ways that are also undesirable for them and their peers" (Bilstrup et al. 2022, p. 233). In my study, some creators similarly argued that *fear can also be helpful* as it gets people's attention and people could get to a "story of hope through a story of fear". Others stated that it depends on the individual whether a pessimistic, shocking approach or a positive, fun approach is more helpful. This corresponds with findings from my own small prior study with university students, which found that some participants saw using fear to learn about data as "not the right approach" and one even began to feel resigned through learning about the wide-reaching implications of data systems, whereas others wanted to be "scare[d] into it" (Sander 2020c, p. 13). The surveyed educators in this study showed equally divergent opinions on this approach, with the majority agreeing that shocking learners can be a beneficial approach to make them realise that they are affected by a certain societal issue, but some (strongly) disagreeing.

How negative and positive emotions affect learning about datafication thus requires further research and the question of whether critical data literacy efforts should evoke negative emotions or rather focus on fun and positive approaches cannot be settled based on the findings of my study. However, in my study, warnings against pessimistic approaches and praises of positive, encouraging and fun approaches overall prevailed. This finding – in combination with other scholars' findings on people's resignation towards the use of their data – suggests that until more research has been conducted, critical data literacy practitioners would be well-advised to refrain from overly pessimistic and scary approaches.

6.4 Insights for an Extended Framework for Critical Datafication Literacy

Overall, the empirical research in my study provided many novel insights on the goals and strategies of those that already practice critical education about data – be it through developing online resources or through their educational work in formal and informal education settings. Key findings included the diversity of educational contexts in which critical data literacy is already fostered, and the variety of online educational resources about these topics. Moreover, significant parallels between the analysed resources, the creators' and educators' perspectives, and the academic literature were identified. This included existing academic research on critical data literacy, but also more established educational approaches, such as media literacy, politische Bildung and critical pedagogy.

The controversies and divergent opinions between the study participants further resembled unresolved academic debates on how best to approach critical education about data technologies. Yet, in some cases it seemed as if the practitioners were several steps ahead of the academic research on critical data literacy, already implementing many insights from traditional educational approaches such as media literacy, Bildung and critical pedagogy, which are only rarely taken into consideration by current critical data literacy concepts. This was demonstrated, for example, through a strong focus on systemic approaches to critical data literacy, on dialogical and experiential methods, and on encouraging citizens to take collective action. These findings advance existing research on the goals and practical implementation of critical data education and confirmed the original intention behind my study: that much can be learnt for the conceptualisation of critical datafication literacy from more established educational fields, but also from practitioners of critical data education. The following paragraphs detail key insights of the study and how they influenced the development of this study's novel critical datafication literacy framework.

A first key insight that emerged was that there is *no single critical education about data*. Already the theoretical chapters of my study identified a variety of different literacies about digital and data technologies with many different approaches and goals. This diversity was confirmed in the empirical research. The content analysis of resources identified many resources that educated about aspects of digital and data technologies but did not foster critical education about datafication in the sense of my study. Similarly, the educator survey identified a variety of approaches and goals for teaching about digital and data technologies. This reemphasises the need for a clear terminology and more thorough critical data literacy conceptualisation, as "education about data" can include various topics and approaches which serve heterogeneous goals.

Diverging perspectives were identified in particular in relation to which practical skills such literacy should foster. The question remains about whether practical usage skills of digital and data technologies are necessary for critical education about data. Apart from this, data protection, or: "digital self-defence", advice emerged as a dilemma: while improving people's skills to better protect their data was the number one constructive action that was recommended throughout all three stages of the research, many participants further voiced the need to go *beyond* individual data protection skills and highlighted the limitations and risks of digital self-defence. This is in line with scholars who criticise this "small bandage approach" and argue that cybersafety approaches can actually be seen as contrary to those of critical data education (Pangrazio and Selwyn 2020; Young and Pridmore Forthcoming).

Based on these insights, an extended framework for critical datafication literacy should thus recognise the *value of data protection skills* in empowering people and instilling confidence in them, while at the same time recognising its *pitfalls* – in that it might suggest that digital self-defence steps are able to solve the systemic issues around datafication and can make individuals feel responsible to solve these issues on their own. Rather than placing a focus on the skills to better – more safely or responsibly – use digital and data technologies, critical datafication literacy should focus on fostering people's *awareness* and *understanding* of the datafication of our societies and support collective forms of action (see below).

In addition, it became clear throughout my study that a key goal of critical datafication literacy should be to foster people's *critical thinking* about data technologies. Instead of aiming for the passing of specific knowledge about data technologies, critical datafication literacy should aim to enable citizens to develop systemic understanding of the datafication of our societies, to think critically about datafication, and to form their own opinion about how and where they want data technologies in their lives and societies. As this study's findings highlighted, this is the only way through which they can – learning from the field of politische Bildung – become *mündige citizens in datafied societies*. In times of fast-changing technologies with wide-reaching implications that may change in unforeseeable ways, the best way to reach an *informed citizenry* is to empower people to develop a "tech intuition" (participant 316), as one educator put it. While details about specific data practices can serve as examples in critical data education, such knowledge will outdate quickly, whereas understanding of the general workings of data systems and their implications and risks; the ability to think critically; and to form one's own opinion can be applied to new and emerging platforms and systems. In this context, critical datafication literacy can learn much from the field of politische Bildung, which does not define any learning objectives, but argues that whatever challenges citizens' democratic self-determination becomes a learning objective (Autorengruppe Fachdidaktik 2016).

Besides empowerment and Mündigkeit in continuously changing datafied societies, another key goal of critical datafication literacy based on this study's findings should be to *enable people to take different forms of action*. The emphasis here lies on "enable" and on "different forms". Regarding the latter, a key theme in the findings was that critical data education should not merely foster people's data protection skills, but also encourage them to take *societal, political and other collective forms of action*. Literacy's *potential for change* was repeatedly emphasised, along with the goal of encouraging learners to *imagine different data futures* and to *actively shape their (datafied) societies*. However, it should be noted that despite these novel approaches, fostering learners' skills to protect their data nevertheless constituted the most common approach in this context.

The other key term, "enable", emphasises that – in line with the goal of citizens forming their own opinion – it should be up to the individual to decide whether or not they want to change their behaviour or take other forms of action. Thus, it could be said that the goal of critical datafication literacy as developed in my study is to create *enlightened users*, who have the opportunity to become *resisting* or even *emancipatory users* according to the user types of data activism projects identified by Milioni and Papa (2019). While an enlightened user is conscious of the way digital systems shape their experiences and create power imbalances, a resisting user goes one step further and tries to actively fight back and rebel, for example through obfuscation (ibid., p. 6). The emancipated user, finally, abandons the corporate web altogether and only uses alternative tools (ibid., p. 7). While it is questionable to what extent the latter position is truly possible considering the wide-spread use of commercial data systems in many areas of life, these user types nevertheless constitute a useful typology for differentiating goals of critical data literacy approaches. Based on my study's findings, however, it seems imperative that the step towards resistance or emancipation should not be something individuals should be persuaded of, but rather a decision that is taken based on people's own deliberations.

Finally, the question of the practical implementation of critical datafication literacy remains. As my study's findings have repeatedly emphasised, *networks of literacy* matter, but there can be *no one-size-fits-all approach to literacy*. When taking this perspective seriously, no specific advice for how best to practically implement critical datafication literacy can be included in a literacy framework, as the practical implementation should differ based on the different learners one is dealing with. However, such translation of abstract objectives of a literacy concept into "a practical model that can be operationalised by educators" is, as argued by Pangrazio and Sefton-Green, challenging (2020, p. 215). While not universally applicable, the findings of my study can help with this challenge as they highlighted the variety of approaches that are possible in critically educating about datafication and identified key best practice strategies recommended by critical data literacy practitioners. This knowledge is further mobilised for educators in the online resource "Teaching about Data" that was developed together with Privacy International in the knowledge mobilisation project as part of this study (Privacy International et al. 2022; see also appendix IX).

A conclusion of key findings of my study, a summary of the key pillars of the framework for critical datafication literacy that was developed throughout the study, a reflection on the study's limitations, and final concluding remarks can be found in the next chapter.

7. Conclusion

7.1 A Theoretically and Empirically Grounded Framework for Critical Datafication Literacy

The overarching goal of my study was to develop a *holistic framework for critical datafication literacy*, grounded in existing academic critical data literacy concepts, an in-depth theoretical analysis of relevant traditional educational approaches, and empirical findings on online educational resources about data – including the perspectives of their creators and of educators who use such resources. All of these insights have informed and shaped this study's framework for critical datafication literacy and were mobilised for educators in a collaborative knowledge mobilisation project with the NGO Privacy International. Thus, the study contributed to gaps in critical data literacy scholarship and to a need for more practical models on how to implement such literacy into practice. The following paragraphs outline this newly developed literacy framework. Critical datafication literacy, as defined in my study, promotes education about datafication by pursuing three key goals: 1) fostering systemic understanding of datafication; 2) encouraging critical thinking; and 3) enabling learners to take different forms of action.

To achieve the first key goal – *systemic understanding of datafication* – learners should be supported in becoming aware of the datafication processes around them, understanding the basic workings – including shortcomings – of data systems, and realising how these systems already affect their lives and our societies, and that these processes come with new opportunities but also manifold risks. Importantly, I argue that such understanding does not necessarily require technical knowledge of data or algorithms but rather aims for societal understanding, or "tech intuition". In contrast to many existing literacy concepts, critical datafication literacy, as presented here, goes beyond mere awareness of data collection practices or a focus on media content or a specific medium. Instead of such specific thematic foci, the objects of learning for critical datafication literacy should be determined by current developments around datafied systems and the risks and challenges, for example to citizen's democratic self-determination, that these systems entail.

As a second key goal, critical datafication literacy aims to *encourage critical thinking*. Rather than placing an emphasis on the passing of specific knowledge about data technologies, which will likely outdate within a short time period, critical datafication literacy aims to provide learners with frameworks to *think differently* about technology, striving to evoke scrutiny and critical reflection of datafication processes. Encouraging people to think critically further empowers them to form their own opinion on an issue, which in turn allows for a more informed societal participation. Thus, one could say that critical datafication literacy ultimately aims for *Mündigkeit* in datafied societies: the ability to grapple with modern society, politics and economy that are increasingly affected and transformed by data technologies in an informed and self-determined manner. In addition, critical thinking equips citizens to deal with fast-changing technology landscapes that are developing in unforeseeable ways, as the ability to scrutinise and critically reflect can be applied to new platforms and systems in the future. Ideally, empowering *some* citizens to critically reflect on data practices might even lead to a "*chain reaction*" of critical thought, in which learners pass on their new perspective on data technologies as they speak to friends, family members and colleagues (for example suggested by Markham 2019).

As a third key goal, critical datafication literacy as conceptualised in this framework aims to *enable learners to take different forms of action*. The first emphasis here lies on "enable". In line with the goal of empowering learners to form their own opinion, the question of whether or not learners even *want* to take any actions should be entirely up to the individual. Critical datafication literacy thus strives for "*enlightened*" *users*, who have the option and the means to become "resisting" or even "emancipatory" users *if they so desire* (see Milioni and Papa's typology, 2019). The second emphasis in this goal for critical datafication literacy is placed on "different forms of action". Advice on actions to take can include steps to better protect one's data, as this can give learners confidence and can help avoid a feeling of resignation. However, the pitfalls of this type of advice should be recognised and addressed: it should be made clear that the challenges around datafication are *systemic issues*, which cannot be solved by individual actions, and individuals should not be made to feel as if this is their responsibility. For this reason, critical datafication literacy places a particular emphasis on going *beyond* individual data protection advice. Thus, constructive advice included in critical datafication literacy approaches should encourage societal and other forms of *collective action* as well, for example by enabling citizens to make their voices heard. Overall, critical datafication literacy aims to prompt learners to *imagine different data futures* and to empower them to work towards such better data futures – attempting to realise literacy's *potential for change*.

Finally, the question of how to implement critical datafication literacy remains. A key insight of my study was that there is *no one-size-fits-all approach* to literacy (as already suggested by other scholars, e.g., Carmi et al. 2020), but that literacy approaches should differ depending on the individual group of learners and contexts of learning. Therefore, I made a conscious decision to differentiate the abstract framework of critical datafication literacy and the practical implementation of this literacy. Instead of providing generic implementation advice and thereby assuming a homogeneous understanding of learners, the educational objectives of critical datafication literacy should rather be adapted to different educational contexts and groups of learners. However, two general recommendations can be made. First, the importance of initially identifying and knowing one's learners and, based on this, *adapting one's approach to these specific learners* cannot be underestimated. Second, it should be stressed that while digital formats constitute suitable, well-established and popular approaches to educating about data, critical datafication literacy *does not need to take place digitally* but can also be fostered by traditional, analogue methods.

7.2 Key Theoretical and Empirical Insights

7.2.1 Insights from the Theoretical Analyses

This new framework for critical datafication literacy was developed out of a close interconnection of theoretical and empirical research in my study. The initial literature review demonstrated the profound transformation of our societies through datafication, the wide-reaching implications of this transformation, and the risks this entails in regard to citizens' privacy, increased surveillance, lacking transparency and public involvement, and bias and discrimination through data technologies. Moreover, studies have identified a "major understanding gap" of citizens regarding how the digital technologies around them work, how they collect and use their data and how they affect their lives (Doteveryone 2018, p. 5; see also Grzymek and Puntschuh 2019; Miller et al. 2020; Yates et al. 2021; Akman 2022). Furthermore, many citizens feel uneasy, concerned or even resigned about the data practices they experience (Bucher 2017; Miller et al. 2018; Worledge and Bamford 2019; Akman 2022). In light of this, many scholars have called for more and better education about datafication (Zuboff 2015; O'Neil 2016; Miller et al. 2018; Müller-Peters 2020), arguing that greater public awareness could open up discussions of new policy solutions for better regulation of data practices (Marwick and Hargittai 2018, p. 14).

Manifold new digital and data literacy concepts have been suggested in recent years. Chapter 2.2 offered a tentative categorisation of these concepts into the overlapping categories of practical-instrumental approaches, those that foster critical reflection through using data, and literacies that promote critical education about datafication. While practical and instrumental data literacy concepts that aim to promote the skills to use and work with data still constitute by far the most common approach in the literature, critical approaches are increasing. Besides more common concepts that aim for critical reflection *when using* data and those that foster critical perspectives on the *content* of digital media, also academic literacy concepts that aim for broader understanding and critical reflection of the way datafication transforms our society are slowly increasing. These approaches strongly informed the development of the framework for critical datafication literacy in my study, for example by calling to go beyond data usage skills (although the extent to which these practical skills should nevertheless be included in critical education about datafication is not always clear); by highlighting the importance of critical thinking; by arguing that inequalities within the society need to be considered and different audiences need different approaches; and by urging not to shift responsibility to the individuals.

Despite several conceptual suggestions, scholars have argued that a more complete theorisation of critical data literacy is urgently required (Pangrazio and Sefton-Green 2020, p. 208). My study aimed to contribute to this research gap by developing a critical datafication literacy framework that is grounded not only in existing critical data literacy concepts, but also in more traditional education scholarship, and in empirical research findings on one of the earliest approaches to critical data education: online educational resources about datafication. To learn from traditional education scholarship, three educational approaches were selected as most relevant, and were analysed in detail. The first educational field, *education about (digital) media*, was perhaps the most obvious educational field to learn from as it has produced a myriad of literacy concepts that aim for better understanding of media technologies. The term "media literacy" is further subject to similar debates as data literacy, with practice-oriented, instrumental conceptualisations, some that focus mostly on media content, but also other, well-established literacy conceptualisations with a strong focus on critical reflection. A highly relevant insight was that literacy should not only be implemented at the individual, but also at the supra-individual and societal level, and should aim to foster a public discourse. Moreover, strong arguments were made for being sensitive towards diversity and for taking vulnerable groups into consideration.

As a second relevant educational approach, key texts from the field of *(politische) Bildung* were analysed. This popular education concept in the German-speaking world proved to be highly relevant for critical education about datafication. The core goal of this approach – Mündigkeit – was identified as a very suitable goal for critical datafication literacy, as it can be seen as a prerequisite to successfully participating in society and is thus exactly what citizens need in order to participate in datafied societies in an empowered manner. Due to these similarities, there are increasing calls to include education about digital and data technologies and their societal implications and power asymmetries into approaches of politische Bildung. Another relevant insight from this theoretical field was the differentiation between education in the sense of Bildung, aiming for understanding one's position in the world, reflection and self-determination, in contrast to education in the sense of a 'mere' acquisition of knowledge – a differentiation that, as outlined above, strongly influenced the final conceptualisation of critical datafication literacy. Related to this, politische Bildung's approach of not defining set learning objectives but addressing whatever currently challenges citizens' Mündigkeit and self-determination emerged as another highly relevant approach for critical datafication literacy.

The third educational approach that was analysed provided many valuable insights for the conceptualisation of critical datafication literacy as well. The *Freirean critical pedagogy* is a transformative educational approach that strives to evoke a critical consciousness in its learners, and that has often been applied to data education in the past (e.g., Tygel and Kirsch 2016; Markham 2019; Špiranec et al. 2019; Dasgupta and Hill 2021). Key tenets of critical pedagogy, such as a focus on dialogue and a pedagogy *with* the learner rather than *for* them as well as the use of real-world problems in teaching constitute valuable approaches for educating about a complex topic like datafication. Moreover, in reaching its core goal of a "critical consciousness", critical pedagogy places particular emphasis on critical thinking as a tool for self-determination and civic engagement, striving to encourage learners to transform their limiting realities. This distinctly transformative and emancipatory character through the use of critical thinking and dialogue strongly informed the conceptualisation of critical datafication literacy as an educational approach that aims to empower learners to actively shape their societies rather than feeling hopeless and resigned about the ubiquity and power of big technology firms.

7.2.2 Novel Findings on Online Resources as One Way to Educate Citizens about Datafication

My study aimed to learn from practitioners of critical data education to better understand the long-standing yet under-researched field of online educational resources about datafication. Novel findings on these resources, the goals of practitioners, and practical strategies for fostering critical data education were identified. Particularly the findings on practitioners' goals strongly informed the development of the critical datafication literacy framework, showing many parallels to key insights from traditional education scholarship and demonstrating similar controversies as highlighted in the literature.

Goals of Critical Data Literacy Practitioners

A first key goal that was identified was that the creators and educators aimed to *raise awareness and understanding* of how digital technologies function, including their shortcomings. Similar to the goals of (politische) Bildung, many aimed for critical and reflective, or even "systemic", understanding of how datafication transforms our societies on a structural level, rather than passing specific knowledge. However, this perspective can be difficult to foster in reality due to learners' limited and instrumental understandings of digital technologies. Related to this, another key goal of the study participants was to promote *critical thinking* about data technologies and to support learners in *forming their own opinion*, for example by demonstrating how data systems already affect people in their everyday lives. Practitioners argued that this can increase learners' agency and empower them and might even help in dealing with fast-changing technology landscapes.

A strong emphasis was further placed on *encouraging learners to become active*. The majority of interviewed creators and surveyed educators wanted to enable people to take action, and similar prompts were found in two-thirds of the examined online resources. These are encouraging findings, as constructive next steps are thought to help avoid learners' resignation when learning about datafication and its risks. Moreover, informed participation in today's datafied societies and citizens' ability to make enlightened choices were repeatedly highlighted as crucial goals – thus seemingly calling for Mündigkeit as defined above, although without using this terminology. Yet, some participants viewed a changed behaviour as an unrealistic goal. Conflicting findings were further found on the question of whether critical education about data should foster people's *data usage skills* as well. Particularly the surveyed educators indicated similarly divergent perspectives on this as identified in academic critical data literacy discourses (see chapter 2.2): some aimed for critical education *through* using data while others saw practical data use as a hindrance or even a risk for critical reflection.

Another key finding was that *data protection advice constituted somewhat of a dilemma*. On the one hand, data protection skills were by far the most common form of practical advice across all stages of the research. The participants highlighted that "digital self-defence" can empower learners, foster their confidence and protect from resignation. On the other hand, many also stated that systemic solutions are needed and that individual approaches are unable to solve the issues around datafication, thus reiterating academic criticisms of a "small bandage approach" (Young and Pridmore Forthcoming). Moreover, many participants agreed that responsibility for data protection should not be shifted to individuals. Yet, the majority of analysed resources provided only individual data protection advice, and some educators indicated that the protection of one's data is up to the individual. Thus, finding a balance between empowering learners through digital self-defence while not making them feel responsible to solve systematic issues around datafication remains difficult.

Besides the popular data protection advice, several participants called to go *beyond skills* and to encourage learners to take *alternative and collective paths of action*. In particular, promoting political and societal action with learners was a common alternative approach. Moreover, some participants wanted to provide learners with a data language to enable them to better take part in public debates and to make their voices heard or wanted to encourage people to imagine different data futures. The objectives of reaching people's "networks of literacy" (Carmi et al. 2020) and starting a "chain reaction" of critical thought (Markham 2019) were further identified in the empirical findings. Overall, the goal of supporting learners in actively shaping the digital society was identified repeatedly and in various forms, suggesting that many participants saw a *potential for change* in literacy education.

Online Critical Data Literacy Resources and Other Contexts of Teaching about Data

The study further led to novel insights on the under-researched field of online critical data literacy resources and the contexts in which critical data education is already fostered. Although topics around data are rarely included in curricula yet, the findings demonstrated that critical data education is *already taking place in various formal and informal education contexts*. Nevertheless, a clear need for a systematic education strategy for critical data literacy and updated curricula was identified. The study further highlighted that a *wide range of diverse online educational resources* about datafication already exist. Key findings on these resources were their various national backgrounds, their diverse creation contexts, and the many different design formats they applied. Moreover, some resources offered different sections for specific target groups or were provided in many languages. Another novel finding was that a large number of resources offered teaching and training material for educators. This suggests that critical research and increasing mainstream interest in topics around datafication is slowly 'trickling down', leading to a greater supply of teaching material on such topics. A comparison of findings on the resources with the surveyed educators' needs and wishes further showed that many of the examined resources already correspond with what the educators called for and saw as useful.

The study further identified different *challenges* when it comes to creating and using online educational resources about data. Divergent findings were identified on educators' satisfaction with their access to educational resources: some were overwhelmed by too many options, whereas others felt unable to find the resources they need. In terms of creating educational resources, *funding* was identified as a particularly difficult hurdle. Many interviewed creators had received project-based funding, which supported only short-term projects and did not allow for longer-term maintenance or updates of the resource. Partly for this reason, the *sustainability* of online resources emerged as another obstacle. With fast-changing technology landscapes, both the resources' content and their technical structure tend to outdate quickly. The findings identified different approaches to this challenge but did not reveal an ideal solution for this problem. The participants clearly called for more permanent funding, and one participant suggested that these resources should be seen as "unupdateable" and be systematically archived instead. Finally, the *evalu-*

ation of online critical data literacy resources was identified as another challenge. The creators highlighted that it is difficult to measure a resource's reach and usage while at the same time ensuring the users' privacy. Moreover, they outlined that evaluating success is a methodological challenge, as it is unclear how "learning success" of critical data literacy resources could even be measured.

Strategies for Practically Implementing Critical Data Literacy

A final set of findings provided new insights on practical strategies for teaching about datafication. A first key finding across all stages of the research was that there is *no one-size-fits-all-approach* to critical data literacy, but that target-group specific resources and teaching are crucial. Resources should, for example, be adapted to the narrative that their target audience holds about data, or try and find their "hook" – what societal or personal issues do these learners care about? However, this was not generally implemented by the examined resources, as most addressed broad groups, such as the general public. Only a third of the examined resources clearly addressed more specific target groups.

Another key finding was that most participants called for *easily accessible, interactive and involving formats* for critical data literacy resources. Interactive formats were overwhelmingly regarded as popular and well-working to engage learners, and they were identified in half of the examined resources in my study. Resources should further be easily accessible both in their content – for example by addressing complex topics in small steps – and in their format, aiming for maximum technological accessibility. Moreover, it was suggested that involving learners personally could help in addressing people's "issue fatigue", for example through connecting to people's personal experiences with data; including real-life stories and examples; or addressing real-life dilemmas around data systems. In all of these cases, the importance of considering representation and making sure the intended audience can identify with the material was emphasised.

Finally, the findings highlighted a controversy around the question of *how fun and light or shocking and scary* a learning resource about data should be. The majority of participants recommended colourful and fun resources, which are approachable, playful and entertaining, and they emphasised that learners should enjoy the experience. Furthermore, appealing visualisations were recommended for engaging people emotionally and fostering understanding of complex issues. Moreover, creative and tangible visualisations, such as the "data octopus" or "data monster" that were identified in the resource analysis, were recommended over stereotypical illustrations of data, such as zeros and ones. Many participants were convinced of such fun, light and entertaining approaches, and warned that overly pessimistic approaches may lead to resignation with the learners. Yet, this perspective was not unanimous, and some participants argued that fear can be helpful as it gets people's attention; that the right approach depends on the individual; or that shocking learners can be beneficial since, as one participant put it, people can get to a story of hope through a story of fear. Thus, the question of how fun and light versus shocking and scary critical data literacy resources should be could not be settled entirely in my study, and the connections between positive or negative emotions and learning about data require more research in the future.

7.3 Contributions of the Study, Limitations and Future Research

Goals and Approach of the Study

Overall, the empirical and the theoretical research in my study provided many novel insights for the development of the critical datafication literacy framework, on the diverse contexts in which critical data education already takes place, and on online critical data literacy resources: what they can look like and aim for; who created them and with what goals and strategies in mind; and how they are being received and what can be learnt from educators. Thus, the three goals set out at the beginning of the study were reached: 1) an *in-depth theoretical framework for critical datafication literacy* was developed; 2) *critical data literacy practices* in the form of online educational resources about data were investigated; and 3) the new knowledge produced in the study was *mobilised for practitioners* together with the NGO Privacy International. A detailed report of how the latter goal was reached can be found in appendix IX.

In working towards each of these goals, the study took a *holistic approach*, continuously *interconnecting theory and practice*. The development of the critical datafication literacy framework was grounded in academic critical data literacy concepts, traditional education scholarship, and in the study's empirical findings on online educational resources and on the practices of creating and using these resources. The study's theoretical and empirical findings further continuously informed each other, with the theory guiding the selection of examined resources and the questions asked in the research, and the empirical findings shaping the further development of the preliminary literacy framework presented in chapter 3.4. Moreover, significant parallels between educational practice and academic literature were identified. In some cases, it seemed like the practitioners of critical data literacy were several steps ahead of the academic research, already implementing many insights from media literacy, Bildung and critical pedagogy, which are not usually taken into consideration by current academic critical data literacy concepts. This reemphasises the original idea behind my study: that much can be learnt from more established educational fields, but also from practitioners of critical data education.

The final stage of the study, the knowledge mobilisation project with Privacy International, took the interconnection of theoretical and practical knowledge particularly seriously. Knowledge exchange took place in several stages throughout the research, with the NGO acting as an advisor and providing useful feedback on different methodological decisions. However, in the final knowledge mobilisation project, the NGO's decade-long practical experience in raising awareness and educating the public about risks surrounding digital technologies proved particularly beneficial. In close collaboration, we examined parallels and divergences between the NGO's experiences and my study's empirical findings on practitioners' year-long experiences in fostering critical understanding of data technologies. This led to many novel insights on best practices for fostering critical data education. To mobilise these findings and support educators, we developed the "Teaching about Data" resource (Privacy International et al. 2022). This website aims to provide educators with information and access to resources for fostering critical datafication literacy in practice (see appendix IX for more details) – thus addressing the need for more practical models on how to practically implement critical education about datafication (see below).

Contributions to Gaps in Academic Knowledge

All three stages of the study contributed valuable new insights to gaps in knowledge and in academic research. As outlined before, a more complete theorisation of critical data literacy is urgently required (Pangrazio and Sefton-Green 2020, p. 208). Only few studies have as yet thoroughly reviewed and analysed existing conceptual suggestions to (critical) data literacy (e.g., Gray et al. 2018; Pangrazio and Selwyn 2019; Pötzsch 2019), and even fewer have connected critical data literacy approaches to more established educational concepts such as Bildung or critical pedagogy that the new and emerging critical data literacy field could learn from (e.g., Tygel and Kirsch 2016; Gapski et al. 2017b; Markham 2019). By developing the theoretical and empirically grounded critical datafication literacy framework, my study addresses these gaps in research and strengthens critical and reflexive approaches to data literacy. These perspectives still constitute an 'underdog' position in academic literacy conceptualisations and in educational practice, research projects, policy interventions and curricula. Yet, critical and systemic understanding of the way datafication affects citizens and society overall is indispensable for an informed citizenry in increasingly datafied societies.

The practices of critical data education constitute another under-researched area. Online educational resources about data are one of the longest-standing and most established approaches to critical data education and provide innovative, creative, diverse and often entertaining approaches to raising critical understanding of data. Nevertheless, these resources have only been examined in very few studies so far (e.g., Milioni and Papa 2019; Sander 2020c; Alegre 2021), and little is known about the many resources that already exist and the ways in which they educate about data. My study addressed this gap in knowledge by providing an extensive – albeit not representative – overview of existing resources and an analysis of their key characteristics; by examining their creators' goals and strategies; and by investigating how such resources are being received and used by educators and what can be learnt from educators' practices of teaching about data.

Another knowledge gap surrounding critical data literacy that has been highlighted by previous studies is the "absence of practical models" on how to implement critical data literacy into practice (Pangrazio and Sefton-Green 2020, p. 215). This is needed because the translation of abstract objectives of an academic literacy concept into "a practical model that can be operationalised by educators is challenging" (ibid., p. 211). My study aimed to address this knowledge gap by examining practices of critical data literacy practitioners – specifically in relation to online educational resources – and mobilising these findings in the form of a learning resource that provides educators with practical suggestions on why and how to educate about datafication, and how to find, use and create online educational resources for this (see appendix IX).

Limitations of the Study

Despite addressing these gaps in knowledge and research and producing many new insights, my study nevertheless came with limitations. A key limitation was that the study's findings are *not representative*. Although every stage of the empirical research aimed for a sample that is as wide and diverse as possible, the findings still – as is usually the case for qualitative research – cannot be generalised beyond the specific samples of resources, creators and educators examined in the study. Moreover, the study only examined resources that are *available online* (with only few intended for print-out or in-person use), although the surveyed educators emphasised that analogue resources are also useful in educating about digital and data technologies. Thus, it is unknown whether the study's findings on goals and strategies for critically educating about data would be similar if examining analogue educational resources or the practices and exercises used by educators in the classroom. More research on these areas of critical data education is urgently needed.

Related to this, the study has a *specific question focus*, aiming to learn about the goals and strategies of the resources, creators and educators in order to develop the framework for critical datafication literacy, and to be able to provide practical suggestions for the implementation of this framework for educators. By taking this perspective, other lines of questions that may have led to interesting insights had to be omitted. For example, it would have also been fascinating to learn more about how critical data literacy resource creators decide on the topics, examples and stories they use to illustrate the wide and complex topic area of datafication, or about the experiences educators may have with resignation and a feeling of powerlessness in their learners.

Finally, my study did not examine the actual learning outcome of any resources or education about data, but only the *intentions* of creators and educators. Thus, nothing can be said about how well the strategies that were identified work, and if the goals for learners are being reached. This is a significant limitation of my study, as it allows no conclusions on the 'success' and the learning outcome of the educational approaches identified. For example, while the participants of my study overwhelmingly recommended interactive and fun resources, other scholars have warned that, particularly for young kids, gamified online tools with similarities to social media might be too thrilling and fun to evoke critical reflection (Pangrazio and Selwyn 2020). Ambiguities such as this should be further investigated in future research.

Ideas and Needs for Future Critical Data Literacy Research

Based on these limitations and the study's findings, several ideas, inspirations and needs for future research have emerged. Related to the previous paragraph, one major area that crucially needs more research is the question of the learning outcome of critical data literacy resources: do these approaches in fact achieve their goals in terms of understanding, critical reflection, and ability for action? Which strategies that the creators and educators outlined affect the learning outcome most positively? And how can this literacy and the learning outcome of critical data literacy efforts be measured? These questions were touched upon by my small prior study that examined how online critical data literacy resources affected university students' privacy attitudes and behaviour (Sander 2020a), but they urgently need to be researched more systematically and on a much larger scale.

Another area that desperately needs more research are critical data literacy practices beyond online resources. For example, traditional material such as books or worksheets could be analysed in terms of what type of data education is supported and how critical datafication literacy could better be promoted through these formats. Equally, learning more about educators' practices in the classroom when educating about data would be highly interesting. Furthermore, less formal educational approaches such as museum exhibitions, theatre plays, board games, role plays or even data activism projects constitute inspiring formats that are already used to educate about data as well, but that are not yet thoroughly researched.

Moreover, both the creators and the educators that participated in my study called for a more systematic approach to critical data education and for changes in curricula to include these topics. In order to achieve such a more systemic education strategy, however, we first need more research on what works well in fostering critical understanding of datafication. This study's findings provide valuable first insights on goals and practical strategies for critical data literacy along with detailed findings on online educational resources about data, but they focus on only *one way* of educating about datafication and are not representative. Thus, more, and more systematic research on different approaches to promoting critical datafication literacy in various educational settings is needed as a basis for policy interventions and updated curricula. As other scholars have highlighted, simply tasking educators with the responsibility to address the systemic challenges around datafication is misdirected as also legislators and regulatory authorities need to act (Livingstone et al. 2022, p. 197).

Overall, it can be said that critical data literacy constitutes a young research field, which still has more questions than it has answers, but which will only gain in importance and relevance over the coming years. This study hopes to open up a more in-depth academic as well as practice-oriented discourse about what kind of critical data education we need, and how we can critically educate about the ways in which datafication processes are affecting our societies, economy, politics, and our personal lives and social relations. It provides a theoretical conceptualisation for such critical datafication literacy together with empirical findings that it is hoped are useful for future academic research, and for practitioners who are already taking on the difficult task of promoting critical understanding of datafication in their educational work.

References

Ada Lovelace Institute. 2020. *Rethinking Data. Changing narratives, practices & regulations*. London: Ada Lovelace Institute. Available at: https://www.adalovelaceinstitute.org/wp-content/uploads/2020/01/Rethinking-Data-Prospectus-Print-Ada-Lovelace-Institute-2019.pdf [Accessed: 30 August 2022].

Ada Lovelace Institute. 2022. *Who cares what the public think?* London: Ada Lovelace Institute. Available at: https://www.adalovelaceinstitute.org/evidence-review/public-attitudes-data-regulation/ [Accessed: 30 August 2022].

Agesilaou, A. and Kyza, E.A. 2021. Empowering Students to be Data Literate: The Design and Implementation of a Learning Environment to Foster Critical Data Literacy. In: de Vries, E., Hod, Y., and Ahn, J. eds. *Proceedings of the 15th International Conference of the Learning Sciences – ICLS 2021*. Bochum, 1–7 June, 2021. Bochum: International Society of the Learning Sciences, pp. 458–465.

Ahlborn, J., Verständig, D. and Stricker, J. 2021. Embracing Unfinishedness: Kreative Zugänge zu Data Literacy. *Medienimpulse* 59(3), pp. 1–42. https://doi.org/10.21243/MI-03-21-18

Akman, P. 2022. A Web Of Paradoxes: Empirical Evidence On Online Platform Users And Implications For Competition And Regulation In Digital Markets. *Virginia Law & Business Review* 16(2), pp. 217–292. https://doi.org/10.2139/ssrn.3835280

Alegre, N.L.S. 2021. *Evaluating a Web Documentary Through the Cognitive Theory of Multimedia Learning*. Quezon, Philippines: Department of Curriculum, Pedagogy, and Assessment, Gokongwei Brothers School of Education and Learning Design. Ateneo de Manila University. pp. 1–12.

Algorithm Watch. 2019. *Automating Society. Taking Stock of Automated Decision-Making in the EU*. Berlin, Germany: AlgorithmWatch & Bertelsmann Stiftung. Available at: https://algorithmwatch.org/en/wp-content/uploads/2019/02/Automating_Society_Report_2019.pdf [Accessed: 11 November 2019].

Aliakbari, M. and Faraji, E. 2011. Basic Principles of Critical Pedagogy. In: *Proceedings of the 2nd International Conference on Humanities, Historical and Social Sciences – IPEDR vol.17*. Cairo, 21 October, 2011. Singapore: IACSIT Press, pp. 77–85.

Anastasiadis, T., Lampropoulos, G. and Siakas, K. 2018. Digital Game-based Learning and Serious Games in Education. *International Journal of Advances in Scientific*

Research and Engineering 4(12), pp. 139–144. https://doi.org/10.31695/IJASRE.2018.33016

Andrejevic, M. 2014. The Big Data Divide. *International Journal of Communication* 8, pp. 1673–1689.

Aronowitz, S. 2009. Foreword. In: Macrine, S. L. ed. Critical Pedagogy in Uncertain Times: Hope and Possibilities. New York: Palgrave Macmillan, pp.ix–xi.

Aßmann, S., Brüggen, N., Dander, V., Gapski, H., Sieben, G., Tillmann, A. and Zorn, I. 2016. Digitale Datenerhebung und -verwertung als Herausforderung für Medienbildung und Gesellschaft. Ein medienpädagogisches Diskussionspapier zu Big Data und Data Analytics. In: Brüggemann, M., Knaus, T., and Meister, D. M. eds. *Kommunikationskulturen in digitalen Welten*. München: kopaed Verlag, pp. 131–142.

van Audenhove, L. and Donders, K. 2019. Talking to People III: Expert Interviews and Elite Interviews. In: Van den Bulck, H., Puppis, M., Donders, K., and Van Audenhove, L. eds. *The Palgrave Handbook of Methods for Media Policy Research*. Cham: Springer International Publishing, pp. 179–197.

Autorengruppe Fachdidaktik. 2016. *Was ist gute politische Bildung? Leitfaden für den sozialwissenschaftlichen Unterricht*. 2nd ed. Schwalbach/Ts: Wochenschau Verlag.

Baack, S. 2015. Datafication and empowerment: How the open data movement re-articulates notions of democracy, participation, and journalism. *Big Data & Society* 2(2), pp. 1–11. https://doi.org/10.1177/2053951715594634

Baack, S. 2018. Civic Tech at mySociety: How the Imagined Affordances of Data Shape Data Activism. *Krisis JOURNAL for contemporary philosophy – Special Issue: Data Activism* (1), pp. 44–56.

Baacke, D. 1997. *Medienpädagogik*. Tübingen: Niemeyer.

Baacke, D. 2001. *Was ist Medienkompetenz?* Available at: https://dieter-baacke-preis.de/ueber-den-preis/was-ist-medienkompetenz/ [Accessed: 29 October 2020].

Bailenson, J.N. 2021. Nonverbal Overload: A Theoretical Argument for the Causes of Zoom Fatigue. *Technology, Mind, and Behavior* 2(1). https://doi.org/10.1037/tmb0000030

Barbas, Á. 2019. Educommunication for social change. In: Stephansen, H. C. and Treré, E. eds. *Citizen Media and Practice*. Critical perspectives on citizen media. 1st ed. London: Routledge, pp. 73–87.

Barrow, R. 2014. Education, Concept of. Phillips, D. C. ed. *Encyclopedia of educational theory and philosophy*. Los Angeles: SAGE Publications, pp. 256–259.

Bartlett, S. and Burton, D. 2016. *Introduction to education studies*. Los Angeles: SAGE Publications.

Bassett, C. 2015. Plenty as a response to austerity? Big Data expertise, cultures and communities. *European Journal of Cultural Studies* 18(4-5), pp. 548–563. https://doi.org/10.1177/1367549415577394

Bauer, M.W. 2000. Classical Content Analysis: A Review. In: Bauer, M. W. and Gaskell, G. eds. *Qualitative Researching with Text, Image and Sound. A Practical Handbook.* London; Thousand Oaks; New Delhi; Singapore: SAGE Publications, pp. 131–151.

Bauer, W. 2003. Introduction. *Educational Philosophy and Theory* 35(2), pp. 133–137. https://doi.org/10.1111/1469-5812.00014

Behr, D. 2018. Translating questionnaires for cross-national surveys: A description of a genre and its particularities based on the ISO 17100 categorization of translator competences. *The International Journal of Translation and Interpreting Research* 10(2), pp. 5–20. https://doi.org/10.12807/ti.110202.2018.a02

Beraldo, D. and Milan, S. 2019. From data politics to the contentious politics of data. *Big Data & Society* 6(2). https://doi.org/10.1177/2053951719885967

Berelson, B. 1952. *Content Analysis in Communication Research*. Glencoe: Free Press.

Bhargava, R. [no date]. *Data Therapy*. Available at: https://datatherapy.org/ [Accessed: 2 June 2022].

Biesta, G. 2012. Philosophy of Education for the Public Good: Five challenges and an agenda. *Educational Philosophy and Theory* 44(6), pp. 581–593. https://doi.org/10.1111/j.1469-5812.2011.00783.x

Bilstrup, K.-E.K. et al. 2022. Supporting Critical Data Literacy in K-9 Education: Three Principles for Enriching Pupils' Relationship to Data. In: *Proceedings of the 2022 Interaction Design and Children Conference*. Braga, Portugal, June 27–30, 2022. New York: ACM, pp. 225–236. Available at: https://dl.acm.org/doi/10.1145/3501712.3530783 [Accessed: 21 November 2022].

Bogner, A., Littig, B. and Menz, W. 2009. Introduction: Expert Interviews – An Introduction to a New Methodological Debate. In: Bogner, A., Littig, B., and Menz, W. eds. *Interviewing experts*. Research methods series. Basingstoke; New York: Palgrave Macmillan, pp. 1–13.

Bowker, G.C. 2014. The infrastructural imagination. In: Mongili, A. and Pellegrino, G. eds. *Information Infrastructure(s): Boundaries, Ecologies, Multiplicity.* Cambridge, UK: Cambridge Scholars Publishing, pp. xii–xiii.

boyd, d. and Crawford, K. 2012. Critical Questions For Big Data: Provocations for a cultural, technological, and scholarly phenomenon. *Information, Communication & Society* 15(5), pp. 662–679. https://doi.org/10.1080/1369118X.2012.678878

Boyte, H.C. 2014. Deliberative Democracy, Public Work, and Civic Agency. *Journal of Deliberative Democracy* 10(1). Available at: https://delibdemjournal.org/article/id/461/ [Accessed: 19 December 2022].

Brand, J. and Sander, I. 2020. *Critical data literacy tools for advancing data justice: A guidebook*. Cardiff: Data Justice Lab. Available at: https://datajustice.files.wordpress.com/2020/06/djl-data-literacy-guidebook.pdf [Accessed: 10 July 2020].

Braun, V. and Clarke, V. 2006. Using thematic analysis in psychology. *Qualitative Research in Psychology* 3(2), pp. 77–101.

Braun, V., Clarke, V., Boulton, E., Davey, L. and McEvoy, C. 2021. The online survey as a qualitative research tool. *International Journal of Social Research Methodology* 24(6), pp. 1–14. https://doi.org/10.1080/13645579.2020.1805550

Brinda, T. et al. 2019. Das „Frankfurt-Dreieck“. Ein interdisziplinäres Modell zu Bildung und Digitalisierung. *Medienimpulse* 57(2), pp. 1–19. https://doi.org/10.21243/MI-02-19-05

Brodsky, J.E., Zomberg, D., Powers, K.L. and Brooks, P.J. 2020. Assessing and fostering college students' algorithm awareness across online contexts. *Journal of Media Literacy Education* 12(3), pp. 43–57. https://doi.org/10.23860/JMLE-2020-12-3-5.

Brown Epstein, H.-A. 2020. Virtual Meeting Fatigue. *Journal of Hospital Librarianship* 20(4), pp. 356–360. https://doi.org/10.1080/15323269.2020.1819758

Brüggen, N. 2015. Gedanken zur Neuausrichtung der Medienkompetenzförderung angesichts Big Data. In: Gapski, H. ed. *Big Data und Medienbildung: Zwischen Kontrollverlust, Selbstverteidigung und Souveränität in der digitalen Welt*. Schriftenreihe zur digitalen Gesellschaft NRW. Düsseldorf, München: kopaed, pp. 51–62.

Bryman, A. 2016. *Social research methods*. Fifth Edition. Oxford: Oxford University Press.

Bucher, T. 2017. The algorithmic imaginary: exploring the ordinary affects of Facebook algorithms. *Information, Communication & Society* 20(1), pp. 30–44. https://doi.org/10.1080/1369118X.2016.1154086

Büchi, M., Festic, N. and Latzer, M. 2022. The Chilling Effects of Digital Dataveillance: A Theoretical Model and an Empirical Research Agenda. *Big Data & Society* 9(1), pp. 1–14. https://doi.org/10.1177/20539517211065368

Buckingham, D. 2018. Going Critical: Zu den Problemen und der Notwendigkeit von Medienkritik. In: Niesyto, H. and Moser, H. eds. *Medienkritik im digitalen Zeitalter*. München: kopaed, pp. 45–58.

Cadwalladr, C. and Graham-Harrison, E. 2018. Revealed: 50 million Facebook profiles harvested for Cambridge Analytica in major data breach. *The Guardian*. 17 March. Available at: https://www.theguardian.com/news/2018/mar/17/cambridge-analytica-facebook-influence-us-election [Accessed: 1 November 2022].

Calzada, P.J. and Marzal, M.A. 2013. Incorporating data literacy into information literacy programs: Core competencies and contents. *Libri* 63(2), pp. 123–134.

Carlson, J.R., Fosmire, M., Miller, C. and Nelson, M.R.S. 2011. Determining data information literacy needs: A study of students and research faculty. *Portal: Libraries and the Academy* 11(2), pp. 629–657.

Carmi, E., Yates, S.J., Lockley, E. and Pawluczuk, A. 2020. Data citizenship: rethinking data literacy in the age of disinformation, misinformation, and malinformation. *Internet Policy Review* 9(2). https://doi.org/10.14763/2020.2.1481

Claes, A. and Philippette, T. 2020. Defining a critical data literacy for recommender systems: A media-grounded approach. *Journal of Media Literacy Education* 12(3), pp. 17–29. https://doi.org/10.23860/JMLE-2020-12-3-3

Clark, T., Foster, L., Sloan, L. and Bryman, A. 2021. *Bryman's social research methods*. 6th ed. New York: Oxford University Press.

Couper, M.P. 2004. Internet Surveys. Lewis-Beck, M., Bryman, A., and Futing Liao, T. eds. *The SAGE Encyclopedia of Social Science Research Methods*. Thousand Oaks: Sage Publications. pp. 505–506.

Critical Big Data and Algorithmic Literacy Network. 2022. Information Sheet New Members.

Critical Big Data and Algorithmic Literacy Network. [no date]. *Database – Critical Big Data and Algorithmic Literacy Network (CBDALN)*. Available at: https://www.bigdataliteracy.net/database/ [Accessed: 21 April 2021].

Crusoe, D. 2016. Data Literacy defined pro populo: To read this article, please provide a little information. *The Journal of Community Informatics* 12(3), pp. 27–46. https://doi.org/10.15353/joci.v12i3.3276

Dalton, C. and Thatcher, J. 2014. What does a critical data studies look like, and why do we care? *Society & Space*. Available at: https://www.societyandspace.org/articles/what-does-a-critical-data-studies-look-like-and-why-do-we-care [Accessed: 12 May 2020].

Dander, V. 2014. Von der ‚Macht der Daten' zur ‚Gemachtheit von Daten'. Praktische Datenkritik als Gegenstand der Medienpädagogik. *Mediale Kontrolle unter Beobachtung. Datenkritik* 3(1), pp. 1–21. https://doi.org/10.25969/MEDIAREP/13783

Dander, V. 2021. Datenpolitiken ‚von unten' zwischen Aktivismus und Politischer Medienbildung. *Medienimpulse* 59(3), pp. 1–37. https://doi.org/10.21243/MI-03-21-07

Dander, V. and Aßmann, S. 2015. Medienpädagogik und (Big) Data: Konsequenzen für die erziehungswissenschaftliche Medienforschung und -praxis. In: Gapski, H. ed. *Big Data und Medienbildung: Zwischen Kontrollverlust, Selbstverteidigung und Souveränität in der digitalen Welt*. Schriftenreihe zur digitalen Gesellschaft NRW. Düsseldorf, München: kopaed, pp. 33–50.

Dasgupta, S. and Hill, B.M. 2021. Designing for Critical Algorithmic Literacies. *Algorithmic Rights and Protections for Children*. https://doi.org/10.1162/ba67f642.646d0673

Data Literacy, LLC. [no date]. *Data Literacy. Learn the Language of Data*. Available at: https://dataliteracy.com/ [Accessed: 6 September 2022].

Data Revolution Group. 2014. *A World That Counts: Mobilising the Data Revolution for Sustainable Development*. New York: United Nations Secretary-General's Independent Expert Advisory Group. Available at: https://www.undatarevolution.org/wp-content/uploads/2014/12/A-World-That-Counts2.pdf [Accessed: 19 June 2020].

Data-Pop Alliance and Internews. 2015. *Beyond Data Literacy: Reinventing Community Engagement and Empowerment in the Age of Data*. Harvard Humanitarian Initiative, MIT Media Lab, Overseas Development Institute and Internews. Available at: https://datapopalliance.org/wp-content/uploads/2015/11/Beyond-Data-Literacy-2015.pdf [Accessed: 20 June 2020].

Davies, H.C. 2022. Rescuing Data Literacy from Dataism. In: Currie, M., Knox, J., and McGregor, C. eds. *Data Justice and the Right to the City*. Studies in Global Justice and Human Rights. Edinburgh: Edinburgh University Press, pp. 146–164.

Davies, M.M. and Mosdell, N. 2009. *Practical research methods for media and cultural studies: Making people count*. Edinburgh: Edinburgh Univ. Press.

Deacon, D., Pickering, M., Golding, P. and Murdock, G. 2007. *Researching Communications: A Practical Guide to Methods in Media and Cultural Analysis*. 2nd ed. London; New York: Hodder Arnold; Distributed in the U.S.A. by Oxford University Press.

Degeling, M., Utz, C., Lentzsch, C., Hosseini, H., Schaub, F. and Holz, T. 2019. We Value Your Privacy ... Now Take Some Cookies: Measuring the GDPR's Impact on Web Privacy. In: *Proceedings 2019 Network and Distributed System Security Symposium*. San Diego, 24–27 February, 2019. Available at: http://arxiv.org/abs/1808.05096 [Accessed: 12 May 2020].

Demertzis, N., Mandenaki, K. and Tsekeris, C. 2021. Privacy attitudes and behaviors in the age of post-privacy: An empirical approach. *Journal of Digital Social Research* 3(1), pp. 119–152. https://doi.org/10.33621/jdsr.v3i1.75

Dencik, L. 2018. Surveillance Realism and the Politics of Imagination: Is There No Alternative? *Krisis JOURNAL for contemporary philosophy* (1), pp. 31–43.

Dencik, L. and Cable, J. 2017. The Advent of Surveillance Realism: Public Opinion and Activist Responses to the Snowden Leaks. *International Journal of Communication* 11, pp. 763–781.

Dencik, L., Hintz, A. and Cable, J. 2016. Towards data justice? The ambiguity of anti-surveillance resistance in political activism. *Big Data & Society* 3(2), pp. 1–12. https://doi.org/10.1177/2053951716679678

Dencik, L., Hintz, A., Redden, J. and Treré, E. 2022. *Data Justice*. London; Thousand Oaks; New Delhi; Singapore: SAGE Publications.

Derntl, M. [no date]. *Data Literacy Certificate*. Available at: https://uni-tuebingen.de/en/study/finding-a-course/transdisciplinary-competencies/certificates/data-literacy-certificate/ [Accessed: 6 September 2022].

Detjen, J. 2013. *Politische Bildung: Geschichte und Gegenwart in Deutschland*. 2nd ed. München: Oldenbourg.

Deutscher Bundestag. 1949. *Basic Law for the Federal Republic of Germany*. Available at: https://www.btg-bestellservice.de/pdf/80201000.pdf [Accessed: 1 November 2022].

Diakopoulos, N. 2015. Algorithmic Accountability: Journalistic investigation of computational power structures. *Digital Journalism* 3(3), pp. 398–415. https://doi.org/10.1080/21670811.2014.976411

D'Ignazio, C. 2017. Creative data literacy: Bridging the gap between the data-haves and data-have nots. *Information Design Journal* 23(1), pp. 6–18. https://doi.org/10.1075/idj.23.1.03dig

D'Ignazio, C. and Bhargava, R. 2015. Approaches to Building Big Data Literacy. In: *Proceedings of the Bloomberg Data for Good Exchange Conference*. New York, September 28, 2015. Available at: http://www.kanarinka.com/wp-content/uploads/2021/01/DIgnazio-and-Bhargava-Approaches-to-Building-Big-Data-Literacy.pdf [Accessed: 18 February 2020].

D'Ignazio, C. and Bhargava, R. 2018. Cultivating a Data Mindset in the Arts and Humanities. *Public. A Journal of Imagining America* 4(2). Available at: https://public.imaginingamerica.org/blog/article/cultivating-a-data-mindset-in-the-arts-and-humanities/ [Accessed: 28 February 2020].

Directorate-General for Communications Networks, Content and Technology. 2018. *algo:aware. Raising awareness on algorithms*. Brussels: European Commission.

Doteveryone. 2018. *People, Power and Technology: The 2018 Digital Attitudes Report*. London: Doteveryone. Available at: https://attitudes.doteveryone.org.uk [Accessed: 10 July 2019].

Draper, N.A. and Turow, J. 2019. The corporate cultivation of digital resignation. *New Media & Society* 21(8), pp. 1824–1839. https://doi.org/10.1177/1461444819833331

Edwards, R. and Holland, J. 2013. *What is Qualitative Interviewing?* London: Bloomsbury Academic.

Eslami, M. et al. 2015. 'I always assumed that I wasn't really that close to [her]': Reasoning about Invisible Algorithms in News Feeds. In: *Proceedings of the 33rd Annual ACM Conference on Human Factors in Computing Systems – CHI '15*. Seoul, Republic of Korea, 18–23 April, 2015. New York: ACM Press, pp. 153–162. Available at: http://dl.acm.org/citation.cfm?doid=2702123.2702556 [Accessed: 12 May 2020].

EU Science Hub – European Commission. [no date]. *DigComp. Digital Competence Framework for citizens*. Available at: https://ec.europa.eu/jrc/en/digcomp [Accessed: 28 October 2021].

Eubanks, V. 2018. *Automating Inequality: How High-Tech Tools Profile, Police, and Punish the Poor*. New York, NY: St. Martin's Press.

European Commission, Directorate-General for Justice and Consumers, and TNS Opinion & Social. 2015. *Data protection: Report*. Brussels: European Commission. Available at: http://dx.publications.europa.eu/10.2838/552336 [Accessed: 12 May 2020].

Felizi, N. and Varon, J. [no date]. *What is the Datasucker and where has he been?* Available at: https://chupadados.codingrights.org/en/intro/ [Accessed: 15 December 2021].

Flores, M.A. 2018. Linking teaching and research in initial teacher education: knowledge mobilisation and research-informed practice. *Journal of Education for Teaching* 44(5), pp. 621–636. https://doi.org/10.1080/02607476.2018.1516351

Fontichiaro, K., Lennex, A., Hoff, T., Hovinga, K. and Oehrli, J.A. eds. 2017. *Data Literacy in the Real World: Conversations & Case Studies*. Michigan, US: Michigan Publishing, University of Michigan Library. Available at: http://hdl.handle.net/2027/spo.mpub9970368 [Accessed: 3 April 2020].

Forbrukerrådet. 2018. *Deceived by design. How tech companies use dark patterns to discourage us from exercising our rights to privacy*. Oslo, Norway: Forbrukerrådet. pp. 1–43.

Fotopoulou, A. 2020. Conceptualising critical data literacies for civil society organisations: agency, care, and social responsibility. *Information, Communication & Society*, pp. 1–18. https://doi.org/10.1080/1369118X.2020.1716041

François, K. and Monteiro, C. 2018. Big Data Literacy. In: Sorto, M. A., White, A., and Guyot, L. eds. *Looking back, looking forward. Proceedings of the Tenth International Conference on Teaching Statistics*. Kyoto, Japan, 8–13 July, 2018. Voorburg, The Netherlands: International Statistical Institute, pp. 1–6.

Frank, M., Walker, J., Attard, J. and Tygel, A. 2016. Data Literacy – What is it and how can we make it happen? *The Journal of Community Informatics* 12(3), pp. 4–8.

Freedman, D.A. 2004. Sampling. Lewis-Beck, M., Bryman, A., and Futing Liao, T. eds. *The SAGE Encyclopedia of Social Science Research Methods*. Thousand Oaks: Sage Publications. pp. 987–990.

Freire, P. 2017. *Pedagogy of the Oppressed [1970]*. London: Penguin Books.

Freire, P. and Macedo, D.P. 1987. *Literacy: Reading the Word and the World*. London: Routledge and Kegan Paul.

Gangneux, J. 2020. Tactical agency? Young people's (dis)engagement with WhatsApp and Facebook Messenger. *Journal of Research into New Media Technologies* 27(2), pp. 458–471. https://doi.org/10.1177/1354856520918987

Gapski, H. 2015. Medienbildung in der Medienkatastrophe – Big Data als Herausforderung. In: Gapski, H. ed. *Big Data und Medienbildung: Zwischen Kontrollverlust, Selbstverteidigung und Souveränität in der digitalen Welt*. Schriftenreihe zur digitalen Gesellschaft NRW. Düsseldorf, München: kopaed, pp. 63–79.

Gapski, H. 2019. Mehr als Digitalkompetenz. Bildung und Big Data. *Aus Politik und Zeitgeschichte* 27–28 (Bildung und Digitalisierung), pp. 24–29.

Gapski, H., Oberle, M. and Staufer, W. 2017a. Einleitung. In: Gapski, H., Oberle, M., and Staufer, W. eds. *Medienkompetenz: Herausforderung für Politik, politische Bildung und Medienbildung*. Bonn: Bundeszentrale für politische Bildung, pp. 17–30.

Gapski, H., Oberle, M. and Staufer, W. eds. 2017b. *Medienkompetenz: Herausforderung für Politik, politische Bildung und Medienbildung*. Bonn: Bundeszentrale für politische Bildung.

Gapski, H., Tekster, T. and Elias, M. 2018. *Bildung für und über Big Data. Gutachten im Rahmen von ABIDA – Assessing Big Data*. Marl: Grimme-Institut.

Garcia, A., Mirra, N., Morrell, E., Martinez, A. and Scorza, D. 2015. The Council of Youth Research: Critical Literacy and Civic Agency in the Digital Age. *Reading &*

Writing Quarterly 31(2), pp. 151–167. https://doi.org/10.1080/10573569.2014.962203

Gaylor, B., Upian, National Film Board of Canada, ARTE, and Bayrischer Rundfunk (BR). 2015. *Do Not Track*. Available at: https://donottrack-doc.com/en/ [Accessed: 29 October 2019].

Gaylor, B., Upian, National Film Board of Canada, ARTE, and Bayrischer Rundfunk (BR). 2015. *Do Not Track – S01E07 – To Change The Future, Click Here*. Available at: https://episode7.donottrack-doc.com/en/ [Accessed: 15 December 2021].

Gee, J.P. 2005. The New Literacy Studies: From 'socially situated' to the work of the social. In: Barton, D., Hamilton, M., and Ivanic, R. eds. *Situated Literacies: Theorising Reading and Writing in Context.* London and New York: Routledge, pp. 177–193.

Gesellschaft für Politikdidaktik und politische Jugend- und Erwachsenenbildung (GPJE) ed. 2004. *Nationale Bildungsstandards für den Fachunterricht in der Politischen Bildung an Schulen: ein Entwurf.* 2nd ed. Schwalbach/Ts: Wochenschau-Verlag.

Giroux, H.A. 2010. Rethinking Education as the Practice of Freedom: Paulo Freire and the Promise of Critical Pedagogy. *Policy Futures in Education* 8(6), pp. 715–721. https://doi.org/10.2304/pfie.2010.8.6.715

Golden, N.A. 2017. Critical digital literacies across scales and beneath the screen. *Educational Media International* 54(4), pp. 373–387. https://doi.org/10.1080/09523987.2017.1391523

Goll, T. 2018. Mediatisierung und Medienkompetenz. Aufgabenfelder für die politische Bildung. In: Kalina, A., Krotz, F., Rath, M., and Roth-Ebner, C. eds. *Mediatisierte Gesellschaften. Medienkommunikation und Sozialwelten im Wandel*. Baden-Baden: Nomos, pp. 207–224.

Gontcharov, I., Kobayashi, K. and Grenier, A. 2021. Knowledge Mobilization for an Engaged Researcher. In: Sixsmith, A., Sixsmith, J., Mihailidis, A., and Fang, M. L. eds. *Knowledge, Innovation, and Impact.* International Perspectives on Social Policy, Administration, and Practice. Cham: Springer, pp. 33–42.

Gould, R. 2017. Data literacy is statistical literacy. *Statistics Education Research Journal* 16(1), pp. 22–25. https://doi.org/10.52041/serj.v16i1.209

Graham, M., Kitchin, R., Mattern, S. and Shaw, J. eds. 2019. *How to Run a City Like Amazon, and Other Fables*. London, UK: Meatspace Press.

Gran, A.-B., Booth, P. and Bucher, T. 2021. To be or not to be algorithm aware: a question of a new digital divide? *Information, Communication & Society* 24(12), pp. 1779–1796. https://doi.org/10.1080/1369118X.2020.1736124

Gran, L. 2019. Digital Bildung from a teacher's perspective. *Nordic Journal of Studies in Educational Policy* 5(2), pp. 104–113. https://doi.org/10.1080/20020317.2019.1615368

Gran, L., Petterson, D. and Mølstad, C.E. 2019. Digital Bildung: Norwegian Students' Understanding of Teaching and Learning with ICT. *Nordic Journal of Digital*

Literacy 14(1-2), pp. 23–36. https://doi.org/10.18261/issn.1891-943x-2019-01-02-03

Gray, J., Gerlitz, C. and Bounegru, L. 2018. Data infrastructure literacy. *Big Data & Society* 5(2), pp. 1–13. https://doi.org/10.1177/2053951718786316

Grimm, P. and Kimmel, B. 2015. Big Data und der Schutz der Privatsphäre – Medienethik in der medienpädagogischen Praxis. In: Gapski, H. ed. *Big Data und Medienbildung: Zwischen Kontrollverlust, Selbstverteidigung und Souveränität in der digitalen Welt*. Schriftenreihe zur digitalen Gesellschaft NRW. Düsseldorf, München: kopaed, pp. 111–129.

Grzymek, V. and Puntschuh, M. 2019. *Was Europa über Algorithmen weiß und denkt. Ergebnisse einer repräsentativen Bevölkerungsumfrage*. Gütersloh: Bertelsmann Stiftung. Available at: https://doi.org/10.11586/2019006 [Accessed: 10 July 2019].

Guest, G., MacQueen, K.M. and Namey, E.E. 2012. *Applied thematic analysis*. Thousand Oaks: SAGE Publications.

Gummer, E.S. and Mandinach, E.B. 2015. Building a Conceptual Framework for Data Literacy. *Teachers College Record* 117(4), pp. 1–22.

Hammer, R. 2011. Critical Media Literacy as Engaged Pedagogy. *E-Learning and Digital Media* 8(4), pp. 357–363. https://doi.org/10.2304/elea.2011.8.4.357

Hanna, P. and Mwale, S. 2017. 'I'm Not with You, Yet I Am ...'. Virtual Face-to-Face Interviews. In: Braun, V., Clarke, V., and Gray, D. eds. *Collecting Qualitative Data*. 1st ed. Cambridge: Cambridge University Press, pp. 256–274. https://doi.org/10.1017/9781107295094.013

Hansen, A. 1998. Content Analysis. In: Hansen, A., Cottle, S., Negrine, R., and Newbold, C. eds. *Mass Communication Research Methods*. London: Palgrave, pp. 91–129.

Hargittai, E. and Marwick, A. 2016. "What Can I Really Do?" Explaining the Privacy Paradox with Online Apathy. *International Journal of Communication* 10, pp. 3737–3757.

Harkness, J., Pennell, B.-E. and Schoua-Glusberg, A. 2004. Survey Questionnaire Translation and Assessment. In: Presser, S., Rothgeb, J. M., Couper, M. P., Lessler, J. T., Martin, E., Martin, J., and Singer, E. eds. *Methods for Testing and Evaluating Survey Questionnaires*. Wiley Series in Survey Methodology. Hoboken: John Wiley & Sons, Inc., pp. 453–473.

Harkness, J.A., Villar, A. and Edwards, B. 2010. Translation, adaptation, and design. In: Harkness, J. A., Braun, M., Edwards, B., Johnson, T. P., Lyberg, L., Mohler, P. P., and Smith, T. W. eds. *Survey methods in multinational, multiregional, and multicultural contexts*. Hoboken: John Wiley & Sons Inc, pp. 115–140.

Hartong, S. and Förschler, A. 2019. Opening the black box of data-based school monitoring: Data infrastructures, flows and practices in state education agencies. *Big Data & Society* 6(1), pp. 1–12. https://doi.org/10.1177/2053951719853311

Hautea, S., Dasgupta, S. and Hill, B.M. 2017. Youth Perspectives on Critical Data Literacies. In: *Proceedings of the 2017 CHI Conference on Human Factors in Computing*

Systems. Denver, 6–11 May, 2017. New York, ACM Press, pp. 919–930. Available at: http://dl.acm.org/citation.cfm?doid=3025453.3025823 [Accessed: 17 March 2020].

Helbig, C. 2016. Partizipation und Kulturelle Medienbildung in einer digitalen Medienwelt. *KULTURELLE BILDUNG ONLINE*. Available at: https://www.kubi-online.de/artikel/partizipation-kulturelle-medienbildung-einer-digitalen-me dienwelt [Accessed: 29 October 2020].

Hepp, A., Jarke, J. and Kramp, L. 2022. New Perspectives in Critical Data Studies: The Ambivalences of Data Power – An Introduction. In: Hepp, A., Jarke, J., and Kramp, L. eds. *New Perspectives in Critical Data Studies: The Ambivalences of Data Power*. Transforming Communications – Studies in Cross-Media Research. Cham: Palgrave MacMillan, pp. 1–23.

Herder, J.G. 1774. *Auch eine Philosophie der Geschichte zur Bildung der Menschheit: Beytrag zu vielen Beyträgen des Jahrhunderts*. Riga: Hartknoch.

Herzig, B. and Martin, A. 2017. Erfassung und Messbarkeit von Medienkompetenz als wichtige Voraussetzung für politische Bildung. In: Gapski, H., Oberle, M., and Staufer, W. eds. *Medienkompetenz: Herausforderung für Politik, politische Bildung und Medienbildung*. Bonn: Bundeszentrale für politische Bildung, pp. 126–135.

Hesse-Biber, S. 2010. Qualitative Approaches to Mixed Methods Practice. *Qualitative Inquiry* 16(6), pp. 455–468. https://doi.org/10.1177/1077800410364611

Hinrichsen, J. and Coombs, A. 2013. The five resources of critical digital literacy: A framework for curriculum integration. *Research in Learning Technology* 21, pp. 1–16. https://doi.org/10.3402/rlt.v21.21334

Hintz, A. 2022. Data and Citizenship. In: Dencik, L., Hintz, A., Redden, J., and Treré, E. eds. *Data Justice*. London; Thousand Oaks; New Delhi; Singapore: SAGE Publications, pp. 73–87.

Hintz, A., Dencik, L., Redden, J., Treré, E., Brand, J. and Warne, H. 2022. *Civic Participation in the Datafied Society: Towards Democratic Auditing?* Cardiff: Data Justice Lab, Cardiff University.

Hintz, A., Dencik, L. and Wahl-Jorgensen, K. 2019. *Digital citizenship in a datafied society*. Medford, MA: Polity Press.

Hintz, A. and Milan, S. 2018. "Through a Glass, Darkly": Everyday Acts of Authoritarianism in the Liberal West. *International Journal of Communication* 12, pp. 3939–3959.

Hitlin, P. and Rainie, L. 2019. *Facebook Algorithms and Personal Data*. Washington, D.C., USA: Pew Research Center. Available at: http://www.pewinternet.org/2019/01/16/facebook-algorithms-and-personal-data/ [Accessed: 24 January 2019].

Hoffmann, C.P., Lutz, C. and Ranzini, G. 2016. Privacy cynicism: A new approach to the privacy paradox. *Cyberpsychology: Journal of Psychosocial Research on Cyberspace* 10(4). https://doi.org/10.5817/CP2016-4-7

Hsieh, H.-F. and Shannon, S.E. 2005. Three Approaches to Qualitative Content Analysis. *Qualitative Health Research* 15(9), pp. 1277–1288. https://doi.org/10.1177/1049732305276687

Hug, T. 2019. From Literacy to an Ecology of Literacies? Reflections on Some Conceptual Issues. In: Stadler-Altmann, U. and Gross, B. eds. *Beyond erziehungswissenschaftlicher Grenzen. Diskurse zu Entgrenzungen der Disziplin*. Opladen, Berlin, Toronto: Barbara Budrich, pp. 144–160.

von Humboldt, W. 1986. Theorie der Bildung des Menschen. Bruchstück [1793]. In: Tenorth, H.-E. ed. *Allgemeine Bildung: Analysen zu ihrer Wirklichkeit, Versuche über ihre Zukunft*. Weinheim; München: Juventa-Verlag, pp. 32–39.

von Humboldt, W. 2000. Theory of Bildung. In: Westbury, I., Hopmann, S., and Riquarts, K. eds. *Teaching as a Reflective Practice: The German Didaktik Tradition*. Mahwah, NJ: Lawrence Erlbaum Associates, pp. 57–61.

Iliadis, A. and Russo, F. 2016. Critical data studies: An introduction. *Big Data & Society* 3(2), pp. 1–7. https://doi.org/10.1177/2053951716674238

Jansen, F. 2021. Critical is not political: The need to (re)politicize data literacy. *Seminar.net* 17(2). https://doi.org/10.7577/seminar.4280

Jasanoff, S. and Kim, S.-H. 2009. Containing the Atom: Sociotechnical Imaginaries and Nuclear Power in the United States and South Korea. *Minerva* 47(2), pp. 119–146. https://doi.org/10.1007/s11024-009-9124-4

jfc Medienzentrum. [no date]. *BIG DATA | Aktiv werden*. Available at: http://bigdata.jfc.info/aktiv-werden.html [Accessed: 15 December 2021].

Johnson, M., Steeves, V., Shade, L.R. and Foran, G. 2017. *To Share or Not to Share: How Teens Make Privacy Decisions about Photos on Social Media*. Ottawa: MediaSmarts. Available at: https://mediasmarts.ca/sites/default/files/publication-report/full/to-share-or-not-share.pdf [Accessed: 9 June 2021].

Kant, I. 1964. Beantwortung der Frage: Was ist Aufklärung? (1783). In: Weischedel, W. ed. *Kants Werke in sechs Bänden. Bd. 6. Schriften zur Anthropologie, Geschichtsphilosophie und Pädagogik*. Darmstadt: WBG.

Kazansky, B. 2015. FCJ-195 Privacy, Responsibility, and Human Rights Activism. *The Fibreculture Journal* (26), pp. 189–207. https://doi.org/10.15307/fcj.26.195.2015

Kennedy, H. and Hill, R.L. 2018. The Feeling of Numbers: Emotions in Everyday Engagements with Data and Their Visualisation. *Sociology* 52(4), pp. 830–848. https://doi.org/10.1177/0038038516674675

Kennedy, H. and Moss, G. 2015. Known or knowing publics? Social media data mining and the question of public agency. *Big Data & Society* 2(2), pp. 1–11. https://doi.org/10.1177/2053951715611145

Kennedy, H., Oman, S., Taylor, M., Bates, J. and Steedman, R. 2020. *Public understanding and perceptions of data practices: a review of existing research*. Sheffield: The University Of Sheffield. Available at: http://livingwithdata.org/current-research/publications/ [Accessed: 24 October 2022].

Kennedy, H., Steedman, R. and Jones, R. 2021a. Approaching public perceptions of datafication through the lens of inequality: a case study in public service media. *Information, Communication & Society* 24(12), pp. 1745–1761. https://doi.org/10.1080/1369118X.2020.1736122

Kennedy, H., Taylor, M., Oman, S., Bates, J., Medina-Perea, I., Ditchfield, H. and Pinney, L. 2021b. *Context and prior awareness matter in public concerns about data uses. Findings from the 2020 Living With Data Survey*. Sheffield: The University of Sheffield.

Kirschner, P.A. and De Bruyckere, P. 2017. The myths of the digital native and the multitasker. *Teaching and Teacher Education* 67, pp. 135–142. https://doi.org/10.1016/j.tate.2017.06.001

Kitchin, R. 2014. *The data revolution: big data, open data, data infrastructures & their consequences*. Los Angeles: SAGE Publications.

Kitchin, R. 2017. Thinking critically about and researching algorithms. *Information, Communication & Society* 20(1), pp. 14–29. https://doi.org/10.1080/1369118X.2016.1154087

Kitchin, R. 2021. *Data lives. How data are made and shape our world*. Bristol: Bristol University Press.

Kitchin, R. and Lauriault, T.P. 2014. *Towards critical data studies: Charting and unpacking data assemblages and their work. The Programmable City Working Paper 2*. Maynooth: National University of Ireland Maynooth.

Klafki, W. 1991. Grundzüge eines neuen Allgemeinbildungskonzepts. Im Zentrum: Epochaltypische Schlüsselprobleme. In: Klafki, W. ed. *Neue Studien zur Bildungstheorie und Didaktik. Zeitgemäße Allgemeinbildung und kritisch-konstruktive Didaktik*. 2nd ed. Weinheim; Basel: Beltz Verlag, pp. 43–81.

Knaus, T. 2020. Technology criticism and data literacy: The case for an augmented understanding of media literacy. *Journal of Media Literacy Education* 12(3), pp. 6–16. https://doi.org/10.23860/JMLE-2020-12-3-2

Koltay, T. 2015. Data literacy: in search of a name and identity. *Journal of Documentation* 71(2), pp. 401–415. https://doi.org/10.1108/JD-02-2014-0026

Koska, C. 2015. Zur Idee einer digitalen Bildungsidentität. In: Gapski, H. ed. *Big Data und Medienbildung: Zwischen Kontrollverlust, Selbstverteidigung und Souveränität in der digitalen Welt*. Schriftenreihe zur digitalen Gesellschaft NRW. Düsseldorf, München: kopaed, pp. 81–93.

Kuhn, C., Atenas, J., Havemann, L., Timmerman, C. and Raffaghelli, J. [no date]. *Understanding Data: Praxis and Politics*. Available at: https://datapraxis.net/ [Accessed: 18 May 2022].

Laney, D. 2001. *3D-Data Management – Controlling Data Volume Velocity and Variety*. Stamford: Application Delivery Strategies – META Group Inc. Available at: https://blogs.gartner.com/doug-laney/files/2012/01/ad949-3D-Data-M

anagement-Controlling-Data-Volume-Velocity-and-Variety.pdf [Accessed: 20 November 2019].

Lange, D. 2008. Citizenship Education in Germany. In: Georgi, V. B. ed. *The Making of Citizens in Europe: New Perspectives on Citizenship Education*. Schriftenreihe. Bonn: Bundeszentrale für politische Bildung, pp. 89–95.

Lankshear, C. and Knobel, M. 2011. *New Literacies. Everyday Practices and Social learning*. Maidenhead: Open University Press.

Larsson, S., Jensen-Urstad, A. and Heintz, F. 2021. Notified But Unaware: Third-Party Tracking Online. *Critical Analysis of Law* 8(1), pp. 101–120.

Lauwerys, J.A. et al. 2019. Education. *Encyclopædia Britannica*. Chicago: Encyclopaedia Britannica, Inc. Available at: https://www.britannica.com/topic/education [Accessed: 23 January 2020].

Leaning, M. 2017. *Media and Information Literacy. An Integrated Approach for the 21st Century*. Cambridge, Kidlington: Chandos Publications, Elsevier. https://doi.org/10.1016/B978-0-08-100170-7.00007-X

Leineweber, C. 2021. Digitale Aufklärung? Datenkritik und Urteilsfähigkeit. In: Leineweber, C. and de Witt, C. eds. *Algorithmisierung und Autonomie im Diskurs – Perspektiven und Reflexionen auf die Logiken automatisierter Maschinen*. Medien im Diskurs. Online: FernUniversität in Hagen, pp. 125–154. Available at: http://www.medien-im-diskurs.de [Accessed: 18 November 2022].

Littig, B. and Pöchhacker, F. 2014. Socio-Translational Collaboration in Qualitative Inquiry: The Case of Expert Interviews. *Qualitative Inquiry* 20(9), pp. 1085–1095. https://doi.org/10.1177/1077800414543696

Livingstone, S. et al. 2022. Children's privacy and digital literacy across cultures. Implications for education and regulation. In: Pangrazio, L. and Sefton-Green, J. eds. *Learning to Live with Datafication. Educational Case Studies and Initiatives from Across the World*. London and New York: Routledge, pp. 184–200.

Livingstone, S., Mascheroni, G. and Stoilova, M. 2021a. The outcomes of gaining digital skills for young people's lives and wellbeing: A systematic evidence review. *new media & society*, pp. 1–27. https://doi.org/10.1177/14614448211043189

Livingstone, S., Stoilova, M. and Nandagiri, R. 2021b. Data and privacy literacy: the role of the school in educating children in a datafied society. In: Stapf, I., Ammicht Quinn, R., Friedewald, M., Heesen, J., and Krämer, N. eds. *Aufwachsen in überwachten Umgebungen*. Baden-Baden: Nomos Verlagsgesellschaft mbH & Co. KG, pp. 219–236.

Louie, J. 2022. Critical data literacy: Creating a more just world with data. In: *Proceedings of the National Academy of Sciences' Workshop on Foundations of Data Science for Students in Grades K-12*. Washington / online, 13–14 September, 2022. Washington: National Academy of Sciences, pp. 1–16.

Louie, J. [no date]. *Strengthening Data Literacy across the Curriculum*. Available at: https://www.edc.org/strengthening-data-literacy-across-curriculum [Accessed: 6 September 2022].

Lovlie, L. and Standish, P. 2002. Introduction: Bildung and the idea of a liberal education. *Journal of the Philosophy of Education* 36(3), pp. 317–340. https://doi.org/10.1111/1467-9752.00279

Lüders, J. 2007. Soziale Arbeit und „Bildung“. Ein foucaultscher Blick auf ein umstrittenes Konzept. In: Anhorn, R., Bettinger, F., and Stehr, J. eds. *Foucaults Machtanalytik und Soziale Arbeit*. Wiesbaden: VS Verlag für Sozialwissenschaften, pp. 185–199.

Lupi, G. and Posavec, S. [no date]. *Dear Data*. Available at: http://www.dear-data.com [Accessed: 2 June 2022].

Lyon, D. 2017. Surveillance Culture: Engagement, Exposure, and Ethics in Digital Modernity. *International Journal of Communication* 11, pp. 824–842.

Lyon, D. 2018. *The Culture of Surveillance: Watching as a Way of Life*. Cambridge; Medford: Polity Press.

Macedo, D.P. 2014. Introduction to the Anniversary Edition by Donaldo Macedo. In: Freire, P. ed. *Pedagogy of the oppressed*. New York; London: Bloomsbury Academic, pp. 11–27.

Malterud, K., Siersma, V.D. and Guassora, A.D. 2016. Sample Size in Qualitative Interview Studies: Guided by Information Power. *Qualitative Health Research* 26(13), pp. 1753–1760. https://doi.org/10.1177/1049732315617444

Manolev, J., Sullivan, A. and Slee, R. 2019. The datafication of discipline: ClassDojo, surveillance and a performative classroom culture. *Learning, Media and Technology* 44(1), pp. 1–16. https://doi.org/10.1080/17439884.2018.1558237

Manzel, S. 2017. Medienkompetenz als eine Schlüsselkompetenz für politische Urteils- und Handlungsfähigkeit. In: Gapski, H., Oberle, M., and Staufer, W. eds. *Medienkompetenz: Herausforderung für Politik, politische Bildung und Medienbildung*. Bonn: Bundeszentrale für politische Bildung, pp. 207–217.

Markham, A.N. 2019. Critical Pedagogy as a Response to Datafication. *Qualitative Inquiry* 25(8), pp. 754–760. https://doi.org/10.1177/1077800418809470

Markham, A.N. 2020. Taking Data Literacy to the Streets: Critical Pedagogy in the Public Sphere. *Qualitative Inquiry* 26(2), pp. 227–237. https://doi.org/10.1177/1077800419859024

Marreiros, H., Tonin, M., Vlassopoulos, M. and Schraefel, M.C. 2017. “Now that you mention it”: A survey experiment on information, inattention and online privacy. *Journal of Economic Behavior & Organization* 140, pp. 1–17. https://doi.org/10.1016/j.jebo.2017.03.024

Marwick, A. and Hargittai, E. 2018. Nothing to hide, nothing to lose? Incentives and disincentives to sharing information with institutions online. *Information, Communication & Society*, pp. 1–17. https://doi.org/10.1080/1369118X.2018.1450432

Mason, J. 2004. Semistructured Interview. Lewis-Beck, M., Bryman, A., and Futing Liao, T. eds. *The SAGE Encyclopedia of Social Science Research Methods*. Thousand Oaks: Sage Publications. pp. 1020–1021.

Masschelein, J. and Ricken, N. 2003. Do We (Still) Need the Concept of Bildung? *Educational Philosophy and Theory* 35(2), pp. 139–154. https://doi.org/10.1111/1469-5812.00015

Maugain, O. 2022. *The Data Literacy Course: Learn How to Work With Data*. Available at: https://www.udemy.com/course/the-data-literacy-course-learn-how-to-work-with-data/ [Accessed: 6 September 2022].

Maybee, C. and Zilinski, L. 2015. Data informed learning: A next phase data literacy framework for higher education. *Proceedings of the Association for Information Science and Technology* 52(1), pp. 1–4. https://doi.org/10.1002/pra2.2015.1450520100108

Mayer-Schönberger, V. and Cukier, K. 2013. *Big data: A revolution that will transform how we live, work and think*. London: Murray.

McDonald, A.M. and Cranor, L.F. 2008. The Cost of Reading Privacy Policies. *I/S: A Journal of Law and Policy for the Information Society* 4(3), pp. 543–568.

Meier, Y., Schäwel, J. and Krämer, N.C. 2020. The Shorter the Better? Effects of Privacy Policy Length on Online Privacy Decision-Making. *Media and Communication* 8(2), pp. 291–301. https://doi.org/10.17645/mac.v8i2.2846

Meng, A. and DiSalvo, C. 2018. Grassroots resource mobilization through counter-data action. *Big Data & Society* 5(2), pp. 1–12. https://doi.org/10.1177/2053951718796862

Mertala, P. 2020. Data (il)literacy education as a hidden curriculum of the datafication of education. *Journal of Media Literacy Education* 12(3), pp. 30–42. https://doi.org/10.23860/JMLE-202012-3-4

Meuser, M. and Nagel, U. 2009. The Expert Interview and Changes in Knowledge Production. In: Bogner, A., Littig, B., and Menz, W. eds. *Interviewing experts*. Research methods series. Basingstoke; New York: Palgrave Macmillan, pp. 17–42.

Michael, M. and Lupton, D. 2016. Toward a manifesto for the 'public understanding of big data'. *Public Understanding of Science* 25(1), pp. 104–116. https://doi.org/10.1177/0963662515609005

Mihailidis, P. 2018. Civic media literacies: Re-Imagining engagement for civic intentionality. *Learning, Media and Technology* 43(2), pp. 1–13. https://doi.org/10.1080/17439884.2018.1428623

Milan, S. 2017. Data-logies: The conditions of possibility for democratic agency in the datafied society (Keynote Address). In: *Recording of Data Power Conference*. Carleton University, Ontario, Canada, 23 June, 2017. Available at: https://www.youtube.com/watch?v=zy3evUmv9Kg&t=4s [Accessed: 3 April 2020].

Milan, S. and Gutiérrez, M. 2015. Citizens' media meets big data: the emergence of data activism. *MEDIACIONES* 11(14), pp. 120–133. https://doi.org/10.26620/uniminuto.mediaciones.11.14.2015.120-133

Milan, S. and Treré, E. 2019. Big Data from the South(s): Beyond Data Universalism. *Television & New Media* 20(4), pp. 319–335. https://doi.org/10.1177/1527476419837739

Milan, S. and van der Velden, L. 2016. The Alternative Epistemologies of Data Activism. *Digital Culture & Society* 2(2), pp. 57–74. https://doi.org/10.14361/dcs-2016-0205

Milioni, D.L. and Papa, V. 2019. The hidden, meta- and anti-affordances of data activism: a discursive-material analysis of how data activists contest the power of social media. In: *Proceedings of the Data Power Conference*. Bremen, Germany, 12–13 September, 2019.

Miller, C., Coldicutt, R. and Kitcher, H. 2018. *People, Power and Technology: The 2018 Digital Understanding Report*. London: Doteveryone. Available at: http://understanding.doteveryone.org.uk/ [Accessed: 10 November 2019].

Miller, C., Kitcher, H., Perera, K. and Abiola, A. 2020. *People, Power and Technology: The 2020 Digital Attitudes Report*. London: Doteveryone. Available at: https://doteveryone.org.uk/report/peoplepowertech2020 [Accessed: 14 April 2022].

Moats, D. and Seaver, N. 2019. "'You Social Scientists Love Mind Games'": Experimenting in the "'divide'" between data science and critical algorithm studies. *Big Data & Society* 6(1), pp. 1–11. https://doi.org/10.1177/2053951719833404

Moser, H. 2018. Medienkritik im Rahmen von Digital Citizenship. In: Niesyto, H. and Moser, H. eds. *Medienkritik im digitalen Zeitalter*. München: kopaed, pp. 77–90.

Müller-Peters, H. 2020. Big Data: Chancen und Risiken aus Sicht der Bürger. In: Knorre, S., Müller-Peters, H., and Wagner, F. eds. *Daten-Souveränität in digitalen Lebenswelten*. Berlin: Springer, pp. 124–153.

Naidorf, J.C. 2014. Knowledge Utility: From Social Relevance to Knowledge Mobilization. *Education Policy Analysis Archives* 22(89), pp. 1–31. https://doi.org/10.14507/epaa.v22n89.2014

Neff, G., Tanweer, A., Fiore-Gartland, B. and Osburn, L. 2017. Critique and Contribute: A Practice-Based Framework for Improving Critical Data Studies and Data Science. *Big Data* 5(2), pp. 85–97. https://doi.org/10.1089/big.2016.0050

Nguyen, D. 2021. Mediatisation and datafication in the global COVID-19 pandemic: on the urgency of data literacy. *Media International Australia* 178(1), pp. 210–214. https://doi.org/10.1177/1329878X20947563

Niesyto, H. 2018. Medienkritik – Entwicklungslinien und aktuelle Herausforderungen. In: Niesyto, H. and Moser, H. eds. *Medienkritik im digitalen Zeitalter*. München: kopaed, pp. 59–75.

Noble, S.U. 2018. *Algorithms of oppression. How search engines reinforce racism*. New York: New York University Press.

Nordenbo, S.E. 2002. Bildung and the Thinking of Bildung. *Journal of the Philosophy of Education* 36(3), pp. 341–352. https://doi.org/10.1111/1467-9752.00280

Oberle, M. 2017. Medienkompetenz als Herausforderung für die politische Bildung. In: Gapski, H., Oberle, M., and Staufer, W. eds. *Medienkompetenz: Herausforderung für Politik, politische Bildung und Medienbildung*. Bonn: Bundeszentrale für politische Bildung, pp. 187–196.

Ofcom. 2019. *Online Nation. 2019 Report*. London: Ofcom.

Ofcom. 2022. *Online Nation. 2022 Report*. London: Ofcom.

O'Neil, C. 2016. *Weapons of math destruction: How big data increases inequality and threatens democracy*. London: Allen Lane, Penguin Books.

Österreichisches Institut für angewandte Telekommunikation. [no date]. *Saferinternet.at*. Available at: https://www.saferinternet.at/ [Accessed: 2 June 2022].

Overdiek, M. and Petersen, T. 2022. *Was Deutschland über Algorithmen und Künstliche Intelligenz weiß und denkt. Ergebnisse einer repräsentativen Bevölkerungsumfrage: Update 2022*. Gütersloh: Bertelsmann Stiftung. Available at: https://www.bertelsmann-stiftung.de/de/publikationen/publikation/did/was-deutschland-ueber-algorithmen-und-kuenstliche-intelligenz-weiss-und-denkt-all [Accessed: 20 October 2022].

Pangrazio, L. 2016. Reconceptualising critical digital literacy. *Discourse: Studies in the Cultural Politics of Education* 37(2), pp. 163–174. https://doi.org/10.1080/01596306.2014.942836

Pangrazio, L., Godhe, A.-L. and Ledesma, A.G.L. 2020. What is digital literacy? A comparative review of publications across three language contexts. *E-Learning and Digital Media* 17(6), pp. 442–459. https://doi.org/10.1177/2042753020946291

Pangrazio, L. and Sefton-Green, J. 2020. The social utility of 'data literacy'. *Learning, Media and Technology* 45(2), pp. 208–220. https://doi.org/10.1080/17439884.2020.1707223

Pangrazio, L. and Sefton-Green, J. 2022. Learning to live well with data. Concepts and challenges. In: Pangrazio, L. and Sefton-Green, J. eds. *Learning to Live with Datafication. Educational Case Studies and Initiatives from Across the World*. London and New York: Routledge, pp. 1–16.

Pangrazio, L. and Selwyn, N. 2018. "It's Not Like It's Life or Death or Whatever": Young People's Understandings of Social Media Data. *Social Media + Society*, pp. 1–9. https://doi.org/10.1177/2056305118787808

Pangrazio, L. and Selwyn, N. 2019. 'Personal data literacies': A critical literacies approach to enhancing understandings of personal digital data. *New Media & Society* 21(2), pp. 419–437. https://doi.org/10.1177/1461444818799523

Pangrazio, L. and Selwyn, N. 2020. Towards a school-based 'critical data education'. *Pedagogy, Culture & Society*, pp. 1–18. https://doi.org/10.1080/14681366.2020.1747527

Peel, E.A. 2017. Pedagogy. *Encyclopædia Britannica*. Chicago: Encyclopaedia Britannica, Inc. Available at: https://www.britannica.com/science/pedagogy [Accessed: 23 January 2020].

Peters, R.S. 1966. *Ethics and Education*. London: Allen & Unwin.

Philip, T.M., Schuler-Brown, S. and Way, W. 2013. A Framework for Learning About Big Data with Mobile Technologies for Democratic Participation: Possibilities, Limitations, and Unanticipated Obstacles. *Technology, Knowledge and Learning* 18(3), pp. 103–120. https://doi.org/10.1007/s10758-013-9202-4

Pinney, L. 2020. Is literacy what we need in an unequal data society? In: Engebretsen, M. and Kennedy, H. eds. *Data Visualization in Society*. Amsterdam: Amsterdam University Press, pp. 223–238.

Pleines, J.-E. 1989. Die Pädagogische Bedeutung des Begriffs "Bildung" (Original: 1971). In: *Studien zur Bildungstheorie*. Darmstadt: Wissenschaftliche Buchgesellschaft, pp. 7–62.

Pohl, K. ed. 2016. *Positionen der politischen Bildung 2. Interviews zur Politikdidaktik*. Schwalbach/Ts: Wochenschau Verlag.

Polizzi, G. 2020a. Digital literacy and the national curriculum for England: Learning from how the experts engage with and evaluate online content. *Computers & Education* 152, pp. 1–13. https://doi.org/10.1016/j.compedu.2020.103859

Polizzi, G. 2020b. Information Literacy in the Digital Age: Why Critical Digital Literacy Matters for Democracy. In: Goldstein, S. ed. *Informed societies: why information literacy matters for citizenship, participation and democracy*. 1st ed. London, UK: Facet Publishing, pp. 1–23.

Pötzsch, H. 2019. Critical Digital Literacy: Technology in Education Beyond Issues of User Competence and Labour-Market Qualifications. *tripleC: Communication, Capitalism & Critique. Open Access Journal for a Global Sustainable Information Society* 17(2), pp. 221–240. https://doi.org/10.31269/triplec.v17i2.1093

Prietl, B. 2019. Big Data: Inequality by Design? In: *Proceedings of the Weizenbaum Conference 2019 'Challenges of Digital Inequality – Digital Education, Digital Work, Digital Life'*. Berlin, 16–17 May, 2022. Berlin: WI – Weizenbaum Institute for the Networked Society, pp. 1–10. Available at: https://www.ssoar.info/ssoar/handle/document/62586 [Accessed: 27 October 2022].

Privacy International, Hosein, G. and Sander, I. 2022. *Teaching about Data*. Available at: https://media.privacyinternational.org/videos/embed/e139ba03-4464-4fbe-bb02-6cea3466263a [Accessed: 7 November 2022].

Pybus, J., Coté, M. and Blanke, T. 2015. Hacking the social life of Big Data. *Big Data & Society* 2(2), pp. 1–10. https://doi.org/10.1177/2053951715616649

QlikTech International AB. 2018. *Lead with Data™. How to Drive Data Literacy in the Enterprise*. QlikTech International AB. Available at: https://www.qlik.com/us/bi/-/media/08F37D711A58406E83BA8418EB1D58C9.ashx?ga-link=datlitreport_resource-library [Accessed: 6 September 2022].

QlikTech International AB. [no date]. *The Data Literacy Project*. Available at: https://thedataliteracyproject.org [Accessed: 6 September 2022].

Raffaghelli, J.E. 2020. Is Data Literacy a Catalyst of Social Justice? A Response from Nine Data Literacy Initiatives in Higher Education. *Education Sciences* 10(9), pp. 1–20. https://doi.org/10.3390/educsci10090233

Raffaghelli, J.E. 2022. Educators' data literacy. Understanding the bigger picture. In: Pangrazio, L. and Sefton-Green, J. eds. *Learning to Live with Datafication. Educational Case Studies and Initiatives from Across the World*. London and New York: Routledge, pp. 80–99.

Raffaghelli, J.E. and Stewart, B. 2020. Centering complexity in 'educators' data literacy' to support future practices in faculty development: a systematic review of the literature. *Teaching in Higher Education* 25(4), pp. 435–455. https://doi.org/10.1080/13562517.2019.1696301

Redden, J. 2018a. Democratic governance in an age of datafication: Lessons from mapping government discourses and practices. *Big Data & Society* 5(2), pp. 1–13. https://doi.org/10.1177/2053951718809145

Redden, J. 2018b. The Harm That Data Do. *Scientific American*. 1 November. Available at: https://www.scientificamerican.com/article/the-harm-that-data-do/ [Accessed: 12 May 2020].

Redden, J. 2022. Data harms. In: Dencik, L., Hintz, A., Redden, J., and Treré, E. eds. *Data Justice*. London; Thousand Oaks; New Delhi; Singapore: SAGE Publications, pp. 59–72.

Redden, J., Brand, J., Sander, I. and Warne, H. 2022. *Automating Public Services: Learning from Cancelled Systems*. Cardiff, UK: Data Justice Lab, Cardiff University. Available at: https://www.carnegieuktrust.org.uk/publications/automating-public-services-learning-from-cancelled-systems/ [Accessed: 31 October 2022].

Regmi, P.R., Waithaka, E., Paudyal, A., Simkhada, P. and Van Teijlingen, E. 2017. Guide to the design and application of online questionnaire surveys. *Nepal Journal of Epidemiology* 6(4), pp. 640–644. https://doi.org/10.3126/nje.v6i4.17258

Reichenbach, R. 2014. Bildung. Phillips, D. C. ed. *Encyclopedia of educational theory and philosophy.* Los Angeles: SAGE Publications. pp. 86–89.

Reja, U., Manfreda, K.L., Hlebec, V. and Vehovar, V. 2003. Open-ended vs. Close-ended Questions in Web Questionnaires. *Developments in Applied Statistics* (19), pp. 159–177.

Richterich, A. 2018. *The Big Data Agenda: Data Ethics and Critical Data Studies*. London: University of Westminster Press.

Rochester Institute of Technology. [no date]. *Data Literacy Foundations*. Available at: https://www.edx.org/course/data-literacy-foundations [Accessed: 6 September 2022].

Ruppert, E. et al. 2015. A Social Framework for Big Data. *CRESC, The University of Manchester and The Open University: Goldsmiths Research Online*. Available at: https://research.gold.ac.uk/id/eprint/13483/1/SFBD.pdf [Accessed: 13 November 2019].

Ruppert, E., Isin, E. and Bigo, D. 2017. Data politics. *Big Data & Society* 4(2), pp. 1–7. https://doi.org/10.1177/2053951717717749

Sander, I. 2020a. Critical Big Data Literacy Tools – Engaging Citizens and Promoting Empowered Internet Usage. *Data & Policy* 2(5). https://doi.org/10.1017/dap.2020.5

Sander, I. 2020b. *Warum unsere Daten wertvoll sind*. Available at: https://www.politische-bildung.nrw.de/digitale-medien/digitale-demokratiekompetenz/big-data/ [Accessed: 10 July 2020].

Sander, I. 2020c. What is critical big data literacy and how can it be implemented? *Internet Policy Review* 9(2). https://doi.org/10.14763/2020.2.1479

Sander, W. 2017. Von der Medienkompetenz zur Medienkritik? Plädoyer für eine Neuorientierung im Umgang mit digitalen Medien in der politischen Bildung. In: Gloe, M. and Oeftering, T. eds. *Perspektiven auf Politikunterricht heute. Vom sozialwissenschaftlichen Sachunterricht bis zur Politiklehrerausbildung*. Baden-Baden: Nomos, pp. 129–148.

Sander, W. 2018. *Bildung: ein kulturelles Erbe für die Weltgesellschaft*. Frankfurt/M: Wochenschau Verlag.

Sander, W. 2019. The Concept of Education (Bildung) as a Cultural Heritage: Transcultural Traditions and Perspectives. *Global Education Review* 6(4), pp. 19–30.

Sander, W. and Pohl, K. eds. 2022. *Handbuch politische Bildung*. 5th ed. Frankfurt/M: Wochenschau Verlag.

Schneider, J. and Ziyal, L.K. 2019. *We Need to Talk, AI*. Available at: https://weneedtotalk.ai/ [Accessed: 18 May 2022].

Schüller, K., Busch, P. and Hindinger, C. 2019. Future Skills: Ein Framework für Data Literacy. *Hochschulforum Digitalisierung* (47), pp. 1–114.

Schüller, K., Koch, H. and Rampelt, F. 2021. *Data Literacy Charter*. Berlin: Stifterverband.

Seitenstark e.V. [no date]. *Seitenstark*. Available at: https://seitenstark.de/ [Accessed: 2 June 2022].

Selwyn, N. and Pangrazio, L. 2018. Doing data differently? Developing personal data tactics and strategies amongst young mobile media users. *Big Data & Society* 5(1), pp. 1–12. https://doi.org/10.1177/2053951718765021

Seymoens, T., Van Audenhove, L., Van den Broeck, W. and Mariën, I. 2020. Data literacy on the road: Setting up a large-scale data literacy initiative in the DataBuzz project. *Journal of Media Literacy Education* 12(3), pp. 102–119. https://doi.org/10.23860/JMLE-2020-12-3-9

Shade, L.R. and Chan, S. 2020. Digital Privacy Policy Literacy: A Framework for Canadian Youth. In: Frau-Meigs, D., Kotilainen, S., Pathak-Shelat, M., Hoechsmann, M., and Poyntz, S. R. eds. *The Handbook of Media Education Research*. 1st ed. Hoboken: John Wiley & Sons, pp. 327–338.

Shade, L.R. and Shepherd, T. 2013. Viewing youth and mobile privacy through a digital policy literacy framework. *First Monday* 18(12). Available at: https://firstmonday.org/ojs/index.php/fm/article/view/4807 [Accessed: 25 September 2020].

Shaull, R. 2014. Foreword. In: Freire, P. ed. *Pedagogy of the oppressed*. New York; London: Bloomsbury Academic, pp. 29–34.

Sieben, G. 2015. Big Data – ein Thema für die Jugendmedienarbeit. In: Gapski, H. ed. *Big Data und Medienbildung: Zwischen Kontrollverlust, Selbstverteidigung und Souveränität in der digitalen Welt*. Schriftenreihe zur digitalen Gesellschaft NRW. Düsseldorf, München: kopaed, pp. 131–140.

Siljander, P. 2014. The Comeback of the Concept of Bildung. *Erwägen, Wissen, Ethik* 25(2), pp. 327–329.

Simanowski, R. 2018. *Stumme Medien: Vom Verschwinden der Computer in Bildung und Gesellschaft*. Berlin: MSB Matthes & Seitz.

SoSci Survey GmbH. [no date]. *SoSci Survey. Professionelle Onlinebefragung made in Germany*. Available at: https://www.soscisurvey.de/ [Accessed: 21 June 2022].

Špiranec, S., Kos, D. and George, M. 2019. Searching for critical dimensions in data literacy. *Information Research* 24(4). Available at: http://informationr.net/ir/24-4/colis/colis1922.html [Accessed: 15 November 2022].

Stark, L. and Crawford, K. 2019. The Work of Art in the Age of Artificial Intelligence: What Artists Can Teach Us About the Ethics of Data Practice. *Surveillance & Society* 17(3/4), pp. 442–455. https://doi.org/10.24908/ss.v17i3/4.10821

Stifterverband. [no date]. *Data Literacy Education*. Available at: https://www.stifterverband.org/data-literacy-education [Accessed: 6 September 2022].

Street, B. 1997. The Implications of the 'New Literacy Studies' for Literacy Education. *English in Education* 31(3), pp. 45–59. https://doi.org/10.1111/j.1754-8845.1997.tb00133.x

Tableau Software LLC. [no date]. *Data Literacy for All*. Available at: https://www.tableau.com/learn/data-literacy [Accessed: 6 September 2022].

Tactical Technology Collective. 2018. *Training Methodologies*. Berlin: Tactical Technology Collective.

Taibi, D. [no date]. *DATALIT*. Available at: https://datalit.pa.itd.cnr.it/en/ [Accessed: 6 September 2022].

Trindade, R.F. 2020. *Data Privacy as a strategic competitive advantage*. Master Thesis, São Paulo: Escola De Administração De Empresas De São Paulo.

Turow, J., Hennessy, M. and Draper, N. 2018. Persistent Misperceptions: Americans' Misplaced Confidence in Privacy Policies, 2003–2015. *Journal of Broadcasting & Electronic Media* 62(3), pp. 461–478. https://doi.org/10.1080/08838151.2018.1451867

Turow, J., Hennessy, M. and Draper, N.A. 2015. *The tradeoff fallacy: How marketers are misrepresenting American consumers and opening them up to exploitation.* Philadelphia: University of Pennsylvania. Available at: https://dx.doi.org/10.2139/ssrn.2820060 [Accessed: 1 December 2019].

Tygel, A.F. and Kirsch, R. 2016. Contributions of Paulo Freire to a Critical Data Literacy: a Popular Education Approach. *The Journal of Community Informatics* 12(3), pp. 108–121.

Urbšienė, L., Varanavičiūtė, J. and Nelson Mauro, A. [no date]. *Data Literate. Digital Data Literacy for Education*. Available at: https://www.dataliterateproject.eu/ [Accessed: 6 September 2022].

Utrecht Data School. [no date]. *Data Ethics Decision Aid (DEDA)*. Available at: https://dataschool.nl/en/deda/ [Accessed: 2 June 2022].

Valhalla Foundation. [no date]. *Data Literacy*. Available at: https://valhalla.org/data-literacy/ [Accessed: 6 September 2022].

Van Audenhove, L., Van den Broeck, W. and Mariën, I. 2020. Data literacy and education: Introduction and the challenges for our field. *Journal of Media Literacy Education* 12(3), pp. 1–5. https://doi.org/10.23860/JMLE-2020-12-3-1

Van Dijck, J. 2014. Datafication, dataism and dataveillance: Big Data between scientific paradigm and ideology. *Surveillance & Society* 12(2), pp. 197–208. https://doi.org/10.24908/ss.v12i2.4776

Verständig, D. 2021. Critical Data Studies and Data Science in Higher Education: An interdisciplinary and explorative approach towards a critical data literacy. *Seminar.net* 17(2). https://doi.org/10.7577/seminar.4397

Vogel, P. 2008. Bildung, Lernen, Erziehung, Sozialisation. In: Coelen, T. and Otto, H.-U. eds. *Grundbegriffe Ganztagsbildung*. Wiesbaden: VS Verlag für Sozialwissenschaften, pp. 118–127.

Vossoughi, S. and Gutiérrez, K.D. 2016. Critical Pedagogy and Sociocultural Theory. In: Esmonde, I. and Booker, A. eds. *Power and Privilege in the Learning Sciences*. London: Routledge, pp. 139–161.

Waldis, M. 2020. „Civic media literacy", „digital citizenship" und Politische Kompetenz – Annäherungen an ein theoretisches Rahmenmodell für die digitale Politische Bildung. In: Binder, U. and Drerup, J. eds. *Demokratieerziehung und die Bildung digitaler Öffentlichkeit*. Wiesbaden: Springer Fachmedien Wiesbaden, pp. 55–70.

Warren, C.A.B. 2004. Interviewing in Qualitative Research. Lewis-Beck, M., Bryman, A., and Futing Liao, T. eds. *The SAGE Encyclopedia of Social Science Research Methods.* Thousand Oaks: Sage Publications. pp. 521–524.

Wasson, B. [no date]. *DaLi. Data Literacy for Citizenship*. Available at: https://dalicitizens.eu/ [Accessed: 6 September 2022].

Watson, P. 2010. *The German genius. Europe's third renaissance, the second scientific revolution and the twentieth century*. London: Simon & Schuster.

Williamson, B. 2017. *Big data in education: the digital future of learning, policy and practice*. 1st edition. Thousand Oaks: SAGE Publications.

Windeyer, R.C. 2019. Faces between numbers: re-imagining theatre and performance as instruments of critical data studies within a liberal arts education. *Research in Drama Education: The Journal of Applied Theatre and Performance* 24(3), pp. 316–332. https://doi.org/10.1080/13569783.2019.1615873

Wolff, A., Gooch, D., Cavero Montaner, J.J., Rashid, U. and Kortuem, G. 2016. Creating an Understanding of Data Literacy for a Data-driven Society. *The Journal of Community Informatics* 12(3), pp. 9–26. https://doi.org/10.15353/joci.v12i3.3275

Wolff, A. and Kortuem, G. 2015. Visualising energy: teaching data literacy in schools. In: *Proceedings of Sencity 2 workshop*. Osaka, 8 September, 2015.

Worledge, M. and Bamford, M. 2019. *Adtech Market Research Report*. London; Cheshire: Ofcom; International Commissioner's Office.

Wringe, C. 2012. Education and Society. In: *Democracy, Schooling and Political Education*. Routledge Library Editions: Education. New York: Routledge, pp. 1–6.

Xie, W. and Karan, K. 2019. Consumers' Privacy Concern and Privacy Protection on Social Network Sites in the Era of Big Data: Empirical Evidence from College Students. *Journal of Interactive Advertising*, pp. 1–15. https://doi.org/10.1080/15252019.2019.1651681

Yates, P.S.J., Carmi, D.E., Lockley, D.E., Wessels, P.B. and Pawluczuk, D.A. 2021. *Me and My Big Data: Understanding Citizens Data Literacies. Research Report*. Liverpool: Nuffield Foundation.

Yates, S., Carmi, E., Pawluczuk, A., Lockley, E., Wessels, B. and Gangneux, J. 2020. *Understanding citizens' data literacies: thinking, doing & participating with our data*. Liverpool: University of Liverpool.

Yeung, K. 2017. 'Hypernudge': Big Data as a mode of regulation by design. *Information, Communication & Society* 20(1), pp. 118–136. https://doi.org/10.1080/1369118X.2016.1186713

Yeung, K. 2018. Algorithmic regulation: A critical interrogation. *Regulation & Governance* 12, pp. 505–523. https://doi.org/10.1111/rego.12158

Young, S. and Pridmore, J. Forthcoming. Finding Agency in Resistance through Tactical Communication: Privacy and Data Surveillance. In: Sarat-St. Peter, H. A. and Kimball, M. A. eds. *Tactical Approaches to Technical Communication: Re-Shaping Institutions, Changing Society*. New York: State University of New York Press.

Yousef, A.M.F., Walker, J. and Leon-Urrutia, M. 2021. Defining Data Literacy Communities by Their Objectives: A Text Mining Analysis. In: *Proceedings of the WebSci '21 – 13th ACM Web Science Conference 2021*. Online, 21 June, 2021. New York:

ACM Press, pp. 26–33. Available at: https://dl.acm.org/doi/10.1145/3462741.3466663 [Accessed: 10 November 2022].

Zorn, I. 2015. Warum sich Medienpädagogik mit Big Data Analytics befassen sollte. In: Gapski, H. ed. *Big Data und Medienbildung: Zwischen Kontrollverlust, Selbstverteidigung und Souveränität in der digitalen Welt*. Schriftenreihe zur digitalen Gesellschaft NRW. Düsseldorf, München: kopaed, pp. 19–32.

Zuboff, S. 2015. Big other: surveillance capitalism and the prospects of an information civilization. *Journal of Information Technology* 30(1), pp. 75–89. https://doi.org/10.1057/jit.2015.5

Zuboff, S. 2019. *The age of surveillance capitalism: the fight for a human future at the new frontier of power*. First edition. London: Profile Books.

Appendix

Appendix I: Methodology Annotations

I.I Annotations for Section 4.2: Identifying, Analysing, and Selecting Online Critical Data Literacy Resources

I.I.I Section 4.2.2: Conducting the Content Analysis - Sources and Sampling

Detailed description of how the sampling for the content analysis was conducted:
As outlined in the methods chapter, the content analysis aimed for a sample that is as-broad, diverse and comprehensive as possible. As no list of online critical data literacy resources exists, no sampling frame was available and a representative sampling not possible. Instead, a broad and diverse sample was reached by identifying resources through a number of different sources. As a first step to find resources for my sample, all online resources identified in my prior work were examined. This included my 2018 snowball sampling (2020c), which led to 31 resources; an informal mapping and analysis of German-language data literacy resources I undertook in 2020 (see Sander 2020b), which included 41 resources, and a guidebook on critical data literacy tools I co-developed with Jess Brand (2020) with 15 resources. As a next step, I examined all recommendations by the project partners, the *Data Justice Lab* and the NGO *Privacy International*. Eight resource recommendations emerged during the *Data Justice Conference 2021*, and *PI* recommended 24 resources as particularly relevant for my content analysis.

After this, I examined resources that were included in the online database by the Critical Big Data and Algorithmic Literacy Network (CBDALN) as of 07.05.2021 ([no date]). CBDALN is an international network of critical data literacy scholars and practitioners I co-founded in 2020 and that at the time of writing has 22 members. The database collects online resources that critically educate about datafication and that were recommended by network members. The database's criteria for inclusion are similar to my study's selection criteria for critical data literacy resources. The resources should:

- Raise awareness about the collection, analysis and use of our data.
- Emphasise the long-term social implications of such data systems and of this "datafication" on our societies and on individual citizens.
- Critically examine the technological basis of data systems and highlight influences on human interactions and social systems.
- Foster critical thinking, support the ability to form one's own opinion and critically reflect the collection and analysis of personal data.
- Be available (at least) in English or German (Critical Big Data and Algorithmic Literacy Network 2022).

The database can be filtered by language, format, target audience, and license of the resources. I examined all resources that are available in English or German and that were categorised as "introduction", indicating that there is no prior knowledge required. At the time of sampling, this included 90 resources. While I co-developed the database and have added some resources myself, I do not have any influence on the resources that are recommended by other network members. The database thus constitutes a valuable collection of resources that experienced critical data literacy scholars and practitioners view as 'good' literacy tools, therefore making it an ideal source for my sample. In light of the similar inclusion criteria, it is not surprising that the database emerged as the most 'successful' source, leading to the identification of 39 resources that fit my study's criteria for critical data literacy resources.

Finally, these sources were complemented by a list of potential critical data literacy resources I had maintained for two years prior to starting the content analysis. It includes all online resources that I came across or that others had recommended and that, on first glance, seemed to be educating about datafication. All 66 resources on this list were examined, but not all qualified for the sample. Moreover, nine additional resources were identified via other, already included, resources and were examined because they seemed particular relevant for my study. In total, these eight sources led to the identification of 250 resources. Several of those were recommended by two, three or even four of the different sources. For reasons of transparency, I recorded the source and which selection criteria were met for each resource that was examined.

I.I.II Section 4.2.2: Conducting the Content Analysis - Codebook and Coding Sheet

Detailed description of the coding sheet and methodological considerations behind its design: As detailed in the methods chapter, the coding sheet consisted of four sections with a total of 19 variables. Of the 19 variables in total, ten identified the unit of analysis and provided information on the first two research questions outlined before. Nine further variables aimed at answering the third and fourth research question on the resource's similarity to the preliminary theoretical framework for critical datafication literacy. The following paragraphs present the variables and methodological considerations behind the design of the coding sheet and codebook in more detail.

The first three variables (1. Title; 2. URL; 3. Origin of resource) make up section A of the codebook (see appendix III), and record which resource is being coded and from which source it originated. This aimed to ensure transparency and traceability. The next three variables constitute the qualifying criteria for this sample (section B): 4. Education about datafication, 5. Critical reflection, 6. No prior knowledge. If a resource met all three criteria, it was included in the sample and the next categories were coded. If a resource did not meet *all three* of these basic criteria, it was excluded from further analysis.

For every resource that met the qualifying criteria, the next seven variables (section C) were coded, aiming at describing the resource and its creator: 7. Creator name; 8. Creator background; 9. Country of origin; 10. Format; 11. Language(s); 12. Publication date; and 13. Target group. These variables were either open fields (e.g., creator name) or included several answer options that were selected based on my prior research (e.g., creator background). Moreover, these variables always included an "other" option if no predefined option was suitable. In this case, the full answer was entered in the field. All answer options for all variables as well as detailed descriptions of each variable can be found in the codebook (see appendix III). Section C further checked for the age of the resource. If no publication date could be identified – as often the case with online resources – this field was omitted. However, if a resource that was older than 2015 was identified, it was excluded from further coding. Due to the fast pace of technology development and the profound changes related to the datafication of our societies in the last years, resources older than 2015 will likely not include current issues of datafication. Also the field '13. Target group' could be omitted if the target audience of a resource was not obvious from using the resource.

The last section D (variables 14–19) examined to what extent a resource was in line with the preliminary framework for critical datafication literacy and thus tested for research questions three and four, including the variables: 14. Interactive design; 15. Different audiences; 16. Practical advice; 17. Individual responsibility; 18. Real-life examples; and 19. Special category. As some of these variables require a certain amount of interpretation or judgement from the coder, I followed Hansen's recommendation of laying down "very clear interpretation guidelines" for these variables (1998, p. 115). The codebook included not only extensive definitions for these variables, but also provided examples of how each variable has been implemented in critical data literacy resources that were identified in my prior study (see appendix III). The variables 14–19 describe the resource's content as well as format. All categories (except for variable 16: practical advice, and 19: special category) were represented as Yes/No fields that were ticked if the resource fit the category. During piloting, these fields were further differentiated (see section I.I.III). The more criteria a resource met, the better it fit my literacy framework. However, none of these criteria were compulsory, but they were only intended to guide the selection of expert interviewees and provide more information about the analysed resources.

Finally, the last variable, "19. Special category" requires some further explanation. This variable was intended to highlight resources that take an unusual approach (content or format), fit the project focus extremely well or were especially recommended by established practitioners. This variable was included for a number of reasons. First of all, content analysis focuses on frequencies and can sometimes neglect "the rare and the absent" (Bauer 2000, p. 148). As online critical data literacy resources are still very under-researched, this open variable helped to avoid the risk of asking the 'wrong' questions in the content analysis and thus overlooking relevant but unexpected aspects. Related to this, a "special category" variable further helped to avoid a 'self-fulfilling prophecy' in which resources are analysed in respect to a certain framework, and then, indeed, fit this framework. As the intention was to learn from the content analysis for further developing the preliminary theoretical framework, it was important to record and highlight unusual or unexpected approaches. Finally, variable 19 helped to stay open-minded in the final selection of interviewees because it allowed to highlight unusual resources but also those that came highly recommended from project partners and established practitioners. This enabled an open-minded final selection of resource creators for the expert interviews, not only rigidly following predefined criteria, but opening up the possibility to think and research outside the box. Moreover, a "comments" category was included, in which first impressions of each resource or further explanations in relation to the coding of the resource could be noted in a logbook-style.

Coding itself took place using an Excel table that included all variables. To save time and due to the large number of resources, I decided against creating individual coding sheets for each resource. Using an Excel table further allowed me to quickly enter responses to Yes/No variables and also record open text for other variables. To simplify coding and prevent errors, the columns in the Excel table were colour-coded according to the sections A-D, and initials for different answer options were used rather than numbering them (e.g., N for "NGO/Civil Society" in variable 8). As recommended in the literature, I also kept a logbook during coding to make notes and in case I "encounter certain examples that do not fit neatly within [my] pre-designed categories" (Deacon et al. 2007, p. 130). In this case, once I decided on a coding solution, I noted it and could be consistent in my coding in similar cases in the future. In these situations and generally throughout the content analysis, being the only coder helped minimise reliability challenges such as inter and intra-coder reliability (see Bauer 2000, p. 143f.).

I.I.III Section 4.2.2: Conducting the Content Analysis - Piloting

Detailed description of changes made during and after the content analysis pilot:
A number of changes were made to the coding sheet based on the pilot study. The first finding of the piloting was that coding directly into the excel table was a very time-efficient method and worked well. Furthermore, some changes to the order of variables were made, moving the qualifying criteria to the front so that I would not have to collect a lot of information on a resource that then ended up being excluded from the sample. Moreover, in an effort for more transparency and traceability, I decided to add the variable "3. Origin of Resource" as it may be useful to know how a resource ended up in my sample and also which resources were identified through more than one source. Piloting further confirmed using initials instead of numbers to signify different answer options as time-efficient and error-reducing. Moreover, I decided to highlight in bold font if a resource fit a category extremely well and by "(X)" if a resource only somewhat fit a variable. For example, it might be useful to differentiate between resources that include one interactive element, like a short quiz, in contrast to those that take a fundamentally interactive approach, such as "Do Not Track" that stops playing without input from the user.

I further came across a number of problematic issues in my pilot study. First, a number of resources recommended further resources about datafication, and I was uncertain whether I should follow these recommendations, leading to a snowballing effect. Given the large number of resources already included in my sample's sources, I decided against examining these recommendations immediately. Instead, I decided to highlight these cases as "C – collection of resources" (variable 10. Format). In case my existing sources would not have led to a sufficient sample, I could have used these to find further resources. Only one exception was made: I identified several highly suitable and very unusual resources via a website created by Tijmen Schep for the Project Sherpa. These nine resources were analysed and four fit my criteria and were fully coded.

I further realised that a number of resources were too extensive and time-consuming to analyse in whole, such as an online course containing five one-hour lessons or a podcast with possibly hundreds of episodes. In these cases, I could not always be entirely certain if the resource, for example, included real-life examples hidden in the many hours of content. To record this uncertainty, these cases were coded as "??". Moreover, the coding revealed the volatility of online resources that are prone to change and develop over time, making it difficult to determine which version of a website I coded in my content analysis. To prevent this at least to a certain extent, I decided to save a local copy of each resource's home page on my computer. While this does not allow for further browsing in the resource, it at least records a first impression of each resource in the sample.

After receiving feedback on the variables and pilot study findings from the project supervisors and the project partner Gus Hosein from Privacy International, it was further decided to differentiate several answer options for variable 16. "practical advice" in order to collect more in-depth data and to allow for cross-comparisons.

I.II Annotations for section 4.3: Learning from the Experts

I.II.I Section 4.3.2: The Sampling Process and the Final Sample - Sample Selection Process

Detailed description of the sample selection process

In order to narrow down my initial sample of 75 resources that were analysed in the content analysis to a final sample of 10 resources for the expert interviews, several selection steps needed to be taken. As the next paragraphs will outline, some selection steps aimed at identifying the 'best' resources based on criteria informed by theoretical and empirical research, while others aimed at a high *diversity* in the final sample. As argued in chapter 2.2, research on critical data literacy suggests that there is no "one-size-fits-all" approach when it comes to literacy, and different audiences with different capacities as well as different learner types require different approaches to learning about datafication (e.g., Aßmann et al. 2016; Carmi et al. 2020; Pinney 2020). Thus, the final sample should include resources with different formats, thematical foci, that originated in different countries, and that were developed in different creation backgrounds. It was further important to me to keep an open mind during this selection process and to put special emphasis on unusual approaches and resources, hoping to broaden my horizon and gain new perspectives for my theoretical framework.

The *first and second selection step* were informed by existing research on critical data literacy as well as my prior experience in this field. *First,* I decided to exclude all resources that did not include any practical advice for citizens.[1] The importance of constructive advice on how to protect one's data, use alternative tools, make one's voice heard or other constructive 'next steps' has been highlighted in my prior research as well as in other studies (Pangrazio and Sefton-Green 2020, p. 218; Sander 2020c, p. 13; Bilstrup et al. 2022, p. 234). The rationale behind this is that constructive next steps can encourage learners to take action, thus giving them an (albeit limited)

1 For some resources, this could not be determined with certainty, mainly due to their extensiveness (see also I.I.III). Given the importance of constructive advice, these were also excluded in this step.

sense of agency, as well as helping to prevent resignation in light of new knowledge about the risks of datafication.

As a *second step*, all resources that placed particular emphasis on the responsibility of individuals to protect their data were excluded. During coding the resources as part of the content analysis, I noticed that some resources convey the impression that it should be up to the individuals to protect their data in order to avoid negative consequences of datafication. As highlighted in the theoretical framework chapters, this notion is highly problematic. A shift of responsibility to individuals can overwhelm users and potentially lead to discouragement and resignation. Moreover, citizens' agency to protect their data is limited and data collection often takes place in contexts in which citizens do not have a choice to opt out (Aßmann et al. 2016; Mihailidis 2018; Pangrazio and Selwyn 2019; Carmi et al. 2020).

These first two selection steps narrowed down my sample to 55 highly suitable resources. In order to select ten final resources from these 55, I took four different approaches:

a) Examining which resources fit *all* content analysis criteria (7 resources);
b) Identifying which resources were highlighted as *unusual, particularly interesting or very suitable* through the "special category" and / or the comments section of my content analysis (11 resources);
c) Identifying *outliers* (17 resources);[2] and
d) Taking *practical considerations* into account (5 resources).[3]

Through these parallel approaches, a total of 27 resources were identified, including several that were selected in more than one of the four approaches. In order to narrow down to a final sample of ten resources, I examined which resources were *selected in several of these four approaches*. Moreover, I reassessed the resources in light

2 As I aimed for diversity in my final sample and was interested in learning from different and diverse resources, I decided to place particular focus on unusual resource characteristics that stood out from the content analysis findings. Such outliers included, for example, an unusual creator background (e.g., museum); country (e.g., Brazil); format (e.g., email, app or yoga instructions); or target group (e.g., activists, parents, or technologists and policymakers). Moreover, resources that were offered in more than four languages or that applied more than four different formats were considered outliers.

3 As outlined in chapter four, several preliminary expert interviews informed the preparation and conduct of the final interviews. When these preliminary interviews took place, the final sample of my study was not yet determined. However, four resource creators that were interviewed in these preliminary interviews and who had agreed to a follow-up interview at a later point in time emerged in the sample at this point in the selection process. Selecting these came with the advantage that they had already agreed to be interviewed, thus reducing the risk of being rejected and having to find an alternative interviewee.

of my *project focus* and compared key characteristics such as format, country of origin, and creator background, aiming for an equal distribution of *diverse perspectives* in my final sample. This led to a *preselection of 'finalists'*, which were then discussed with the project collaborator Privacy International (represented by Gus Hosein) in detail, and a sample of ten resources was decided.

Unfortunately, out of the ten resource creators selected in this process, only six agreed to be interviewed. Some others expressed their interest or even agreed, but then could not be reached anymore. Therefore, four other resources had to be selected. Here, the same criteria as described above were considered and I tried to replace each of the four resources with a similar one in order to maintain the diversity of different characteristics in the sample.

I.II.II Section 4.3.4: Preparing and Conducting the Interviews

Privacy and methodological considerations around the use of virtual face-to-face interviews: As outlined in the methods chapter, all interviewees chose to be interviewed via video call. Using virtual face-to-face interviews came with several specific benefits, such as lifting geographical restrictions, but also "*ease and flexibility of scheduling*", including saving money and time spent travelling; "*virtual and visual interaction*", allowing for synchronous visual interaction; "*ease of data capture*" by using audio recording software; "'*public' places and 'private' spaces*", as video calls from home offer privacy from the public and also from the researcher; and "*greater control for participants*" when they are invited to choose their preferred interview format – and, in my case, platform (Hanna and Mwale 2017, p. 259ff, emphasis in original). While giving participants the choice of platform provided more convenience for them, it required flexibility and a certain privacy pragmatism from my side. Considering my research topic, I would have preferred to use privacy-sensitive tools such as Jitsi and Big Blue Button. Unfortunately, these often do not work as smoothly as other platforms, and many people are not as familiar with them. Thus, adapting to my interviewees' wishes and aiming for a smooth conversation without technical disruptions meant using less privacy-sensitive tools.

However, I did not use the built-in recording options of the video calling platforms because the data flows of the recorded data and the companies' access to this data was not transparent and safe enough in order for me to ensure the protection of my participants' data. Instead, the interviews were recorded through software on my local device, with participants giving consent in written form as well as verbally. Audio-recording qualitative interviews helps to gather accurate data while also allowing the researcher to "focus on the flow of the interview, to think about follow up questions, [...] and build up rapport with the interviewee" (van Audenhove and Donders 2019, p. 192).

The normalisation of video calling for work and for staying in touch with loved ones during the COVID-19 pandemic likely helped to foster a natural conversation flow in my interviews. However, video interviewing is not without limitations. In 2021, many people – especially those working from home – experienced a certain frustration, or "Zoom fatigue", in light of too many video calls (cf. Brown Epstein 2020; Bailenson 2021). Moreover, technical problems and poor internet connection can have an impact on the quality of conversation and on "rapport and ultimately on the quality of data collected" (Hanna and Mwale 2017, p. 267). Apart from this, participants need appropriate equipment for video calls (ibid., p. 261). Yet, in my study with creators of online resources, this latter aspect was less problematic. Overall, conducting virtual face-to-face interviews was thus not only a workaround, but in fact a suitable method for my study's goals and sample. Furthermore, already having conducted several expert interviews in person, via telephone and through video calling in research projects in the past helped me navigate the process and its challenges.

I.II.III Section 4.3.5: Analysing the Interviews

Detailed description of how the different steps of the thematic analysis combined deductive and inductive elements:

The first step after transcribing the interviews was to create a list of deductive nodes and categories based on the theoretical framework for critical datafication literacy and the research questions for the interviews. Three categories and nine nodes were developed. However, as will be outlined below, the analysis later showed that only some of the deductive nodes fit the codes derived from the data and an inductive, 'bottom-up' approach worked better to capture key themes and patterns in the data. Thus, the majority of themes in the final thematic framework were identified inductively. The three deductive categories "understanding of literacy", "strategies and principles on how to foster this literacy" and "challenges and practical considerations", however, proved helpful in sorting and gaining an overview of the large number of initial codes (see below).

The next steps in the analysis followed the recommendations for conducting a thematic analysis of Meuser and Nagel (2009) in combination with Braun and Clarke (2006). In the first phase of the analysis, I familiarised myself with the data by reading it several times (Braun and Clarke 2006, p. 16f), and I paraphrased the entire interview transcripts.[4] The paraphrase followed the "unfolding of the conversation" and aimed to "give account of the interviewee's opinions" (Meuser and Nagel 2009,

4 Key information on the resource creator's background and on the resource itself, such as position or training background of the creator or year of publication of the resource were not paraphrased or coded but saved in a separate document.

p. 35). Additionally, I collected particularly catchy quotes that might be used in the findings chapter in a separate document so that they are not lost in the large number of codes later on. In the second phase, the initial codes were created in NVivo. This process condenses the material and "order[s] the paraphrased passages thematically", while keeping close to the text and, if possible, adopting the language of the interviewee (Meuser and Nagel 2009, p. 36). In line with Braun and Clarke's recommendations, the goal was to create as many codes as possible in order to capture all data extracts and all potentially interesting aspects of the data (2006, p. 19). Thus, the initial list of codes consisted of 332 codes, which were used 1–13 times in the interviews.

In the next analytical phase, this long list of codes was revised, and the initial themes were identified. A first attempt to sort the initial codes into the deductive nodes quickly showed that several of these nodes did not fit the codes and others were too broad, not leading to any meaningful themes. Thus, I switched to a bottom-up, inductive approach of identifying themes, which was more productive and 'natural' – sticking close to the data. However, the three deductive categories outlined above proved helpful in providing a first overview of the large number of initial codes. Thus, in a first step, all 332 initial codes were sorted into one of the three categories, with only few codes remaining in an "other" category. After this, I checked and revised all codes in each of the categories, combining similar codes, differentiating too broad codes and in some cases deleting codes that were irrelevant for the research questions (see Meuser and Nagel 2009, p. 36). At the same time, I searched for patterns in the codes, considering how "different codes may combine to form an overarching theme" (Braun and Clarke 2006, p. 19). Also here, a bottom-up approach proved most valuable – first identifying *subthemes* and later examining which broader patterns can be found among these subthemes, leading to the *main themes* of the analysis. Throughout this process, codes and themes were continuously revised, merged with others and sometimes moved between the categories.

This led to an initial framework of 14 main themes and 61 subthemes. As outlined in chapter four, this was visualised in the form of a mind map. In the next, fourth phase of the analysis, all themes (including their total of 680 extracts as well as notes made during initial paraphrasing and coding) were reviewed and edited in several rounds of revision. The goal was to ensure that each theme formed a coherent pattern; was distinct; that the themes overall "'accurately' portrayed the meanings evident in the data set as a whole" (Braun and Clarke 2006, p. 19); and that they were relevant for the research questions.

Through this extensive revision, a final thematic framework with 12 main themes and 45 subthemes was developed. The next analytical phase then consisted of finalising the names of the themes and categories. Based on Braun and Clarke's recommendations, the names should capture the "essence" of each theme and ideally be "concise, punchy, and immediately give the reader a sense of what the theme is about" (2006, pp. 22; 23). After this, the mind map visualising the thematic framework was updated to represent the final themes and theme names. Moreover, the key quotes collected at the beginning of the analysis were complemented and sorted corresponding to the final thematic framework. Finally, as outlined in chapter four, the themes were analysed according to the "story" they and the data overall tell (ibid., p. 22), and connections to academic literature, prior findings and my study's theoretical framework for critical datafication literacy were drawn (Meuser and Nagel 2009, p. 35f).

I.III Annotations for section 4.4: Learning from the Educators

I.III.I Section 4.4.2 – The Survey Sample – Finding the Sample

Detailed description and reflection on the process of reaching a diverse survey sample:
As outlined in the methods chapter, the population of interest for my study's qualitative online survey consisted of educators from Germany, the United Kingdom and other places in Europe, who are interested in teaching about digital technologies and datafication. As most relevant groups, I identified teachers, student teachers, teacher trainers, higher education lecturers, adult educators, media education centres, and trainers in civil society.

To reach this population, the most appropriate communication channel(s) for each educational profession in each of the three (supra)national contexts had to be identified. This selection was not only informed by my prior experience in the field of critical data literacy research, but also by several experts I contacted. These included, among others, researchers directly working with educators from different backgrounds, and current and former civil society activists in the field of critical data literacy. In discussion with these experts, the project partner Privacy International, and the project supervisors, a list of communication channels was assembled through which the survey would aim to reach a broad and diverse sample of educators from different fields (see appendix VII). Attention was paid to aiming at as much diversity as possible, yet ensuring consistency throughout the different contexts. In line with Clark et al. (2021, p. 186), the list included mailing lists, social media channels, and individual contacts who would be able to distribute the questionnaire even further, aiming to reach as many members of my target population – educators from different backgrounds interested in educating about datafication – as possible. Moreover, every contact was invited to share the survey information and link with other educators they know who might be interested in the survey's topic.

Clark et al. further highlight the typically low response rates for online surveys (2021, p. 186). This proved to be a limitation of my study as well, although I took considerable efforts to reach a big sample. As represented in appendix VII, a large number of educational organisations, groups, mailing lists and interested individuals were contacted. However, a limitation of this sampling technique is that it is unknown how many and which people the survey invitation reached, as it is not always possible to determine whether an organisation or individual shared the information about the study within their organisation or mailing list. Yet, in some cases, I received confirmation. Therefore, it can be said with certainty that the survey link was circulated:

- In the members newsletter of the German society for media pedagogy scholars (GMK);
- In the mailing list by the British Media, Communication and Cultural Studies Association (MeCCSA);
- In the Weekly Digest mailing list by the European Communication Research and Education Association (ECREA);
- In a German newsletter for educators interested in learning more about digital educational technologies (UNBLACK THE BOX);
- By the social media channels of several educational organisations, such as The Media Education Association and the Association for Citizenship Teaching;
- Among several relevant German and European educational research projects;
- In a German teacher training centre;
- By several teachers in Germany and the UK;
- And by several higher education colleagues in different European countries, who shared the survey in their personal networks.

Already through these channels – particularly through the large mailing lists by different associations – it is likely that the survey information reached several thousand people. Additionally, the promotion via Twitter was successful, with many individuals as well as organisations retweeting the survey invitation, including the Association for Teacher Education in Europe, the British Media Education Association, an Irish educational research journal, a European association for media and learning, a German media pedagogy association, a popular German guide to teaching material (bildungsserver.de), a research institute and several researchers and media pedagogues. In total, the main English-language tweet reached 6,907 impressions and generated 49 link clicks, and the main German tweet reached 1,683 impressions with 26 link clicks.

Moreover, I sent several rounds of invitations in order to reach a sample that is as diverse and equally balanced as possible. In a first round of invitations, I contacted 46 groups and individuals via email, website contact forms and sometimes Twitter in the end of November 2021. A first examination of the collected data by the beginning of January 2022 showed that 38 people had completed the full questionnaire, but there was a predominance of German participants and those from formal education fields. I tried to address this imbalance, in a second round of invitations.

This included sending several reminders to those groups and individuals from a UK and EU background who had not responded yet, and sending invitations to 29 new contacts from British or European background, including many from the non-formal education sector. This helped to balance the sample and was complemented by a third round of invitations in the end of January 2022, with several reminders as well as invitations to four new groups and individuals, again aiming for a diverse and balanced sample. Through these steps, a diverse and fairly balanced sample was achieved (see also chapter 5.3.1).

I.III.II Section 4.4.3 - Developing the Questionnaire - Pilot Study

Detailed description of changes made to the questionnaire after the pilot study:
As outlined in the methods chapter, the survey pilot testers provided detailed and extensive feedback and constructive suggestions. Most comments related to small changes in wording, which were all implemented. There were several issues related to translation, mainly regarding the different German terms that can be used for "educator" and "teaching". In the German language, there are no common broad terms that summarise all kinds of teaching and being an educator. Instead, the German language tends to differentiate for example between teaching in schools ("unterrichten") and being a school teacher ("Lehrer/in") in contrast to teaching in university ("lehren") and being a lecturer ("Dozent/in" or "Lehrende"). It was thus difficult to find a wording that included all areas of education and I decided to use more than one term in some instances (e.g., by writing "unterrichten/lehren").

The pilot testers further recommended separating several of the open questions because they were asking about too many aspects in one question. In several places, the pilot testers suggested adding examples in order to clarify the question or the answer options, or they suggested smaller changes in question or answer option wording. These suggestions were implemented in all instances. For example, several answer options in question five were renamed: such as "non-formal education (e.g., media education centre)" instead of "media education". In question 17, the first statement "Interactive approaches work well and are popular with learners" was changed to "Interactive approaches are a great way to engage learners" (see appendix VIII). This captures my intended meaning similarly well without – as criticised by pilot testers – asking about two different things in one question. Moreover, more details on my research project were added to the landing page.

I.III.III Section 4.4.3 – Developing the Questionnaire – Final Questionnaire

Detailed information on the methodological considerations behind the questionnaire design: Apart from recommendations from the methodological literature, the development of the questionnaire was strongly influenced by my study's previous theoretical and empirical findings. The survey aimed to investigate if these findings corresponded with educators' daily lived experience and thus aimed to examine the following questions:

a) To what extent are topics related to datafication already being covered and critical data education already fostered by educators?
b) Does the predominance of practical digital and data skills over critical reflection of the societal implications of datafication that I found in the theoretical literature as well as in many resources I analysed correspond with the topics that educators predominantly covered in their teaching?
c) How well-equipped do educators feel to teach about these different dimensions of critical data literacy?
d) Do educators know about the resources I analysed in my content analysis and if yes, what do they think of them?
e) Does the popularity of certain formats I found in my prior study (Sander 2020c) correspond with the formats educators prefer?
f) Do educators – based on their practical experience – agree with key findings on 'best-practice' approaches to educate about datafication that have emerged from my own and other scholars' research on critical data literacy?
g) And finally: What do educators need in order to better educate about datafication and what are their wishes for future critical data literacy resources?

After I created a first draft questionnaire, it was revised and condensed several times based on feedback from the project collaborator Privacy International as well as based on recommendations from methodological literature (see e.g., Reja et al. 2003; Braun et al. 2021; Clark et al. 2021). The final questionnaire used in my survey consisted of a landing page that provided information about the study; a short demographics section (1); a section on educators' experience with topics around digital technologies, (big) data and datafication (2); a section on educational resources about datafication, including a final open question asking for additional comments (3); and a last page that thanked for the participation in my study and asked participants if they were interested in testing and providing feedback for the resource developed with PI (for whole final questionnaire, see appendix VIII).

The landing page contained information on my research project and its goals, details on the survey and data handling as well as contact information for participants who had questions or wanted to express their interest in the study's findings. As outlined in the methods chapter, this also included information necessary for *informed consent* (see e.g., Regmi et al. 2017, p. 642; Braun et al. 2021, p. 8f). Moreover, the landing page specified the study's target population and stated the estimated completion time for the questionnaire, giving a realistic estimation, as recommended in the literature (Clark et al. 2021, p. 187).

The first section on demographics then asked for a small number of basic personal details (age in groups; gender, providing sufficient options and including the option to self-describe; country of residence; and nationality) that would help to situate findings within these contexts. Moreover, one question asked about the area of education that participants worked in (multi-select question, providing nine options and an "other" field) and another invited them to describe their individual position or role in an open text field. These questions aimed at understanding in which educational contexts aspects of datafication might already be covered, but also discovering if the survey was successful in reaching diverse educators from different fields and countries, as had been intended.

The second section asked about the educators' experiences with teaching about topics such as digital technologies, (big) data systems and their implications on society. This section included five questions. The first two used a rating scale to examine how *well-equipped* and how *experienced* educators felt in teaching about different aspects of digital technologies and (big) data. Here, and in all other rating questions, a 5-point rating scale was used. This gave participants the opportunity to indicate if they felt neutrally about a certain option. A "N.A." option further allowed to indicate if a question was not applicable to participants. Adding a visual scale above the numbers and using the same 5-point scale for all rating questions further aimed at a user-friendly design.

For both questions (7 and 8), the broad thematical field of digital and data technologies was separated into four key topics: Digital technologies in general; data security; (big) data systems and algorithms; and the way digital media and (big) data affect society. These four topics were informed by findings that highlight the prevalence of concerns around digital technologies in general and data security questions in contrast to less known issues around algorithmic systems and the way these systems affect society (see literature review as well as Sander 2020). I was curious to see if the same prevalence could be found in educators' knowledge and experiences. In order to clarify each topic, pilot testers suggested to add example questions for each topic, which were displayed in smaller font below each topic. Both rating questions were placed on the same page for ease of use. Moreover, an explanatory sentence was added for each question based on pilot tester feedback, emphasising what was meant by "well-equipped" and "experienced".

Subsequently, three open questions (9–11) asked about more details on the educators' experience with teaching about digital and data technologies, such as the exact topics covered, the key skills and understanding aimed for, and inviting participants to add further information on the context, methods, successes and challenges they encountered in teaching about these topics.

The third section focussed on educational resources about datafication. This section included four open and three rating questions and investigated how educators inform themselves on topics around digital technologies and data (12), how they find teaching material on these topics (and if there are any challenges) (13), and how satisfied they are with their access to information and teaching material about digital technologies and (big) data (14). In addition, educators were asked to rate the usefulness of 12 different design formats of educational resources from "not at all useful" to "extremely useful" (15). The selection of formats was made based on findings from my prior research and this study's analysis of online critical data literacy resources (see chapter 5.1). Examples were provided for formats that might be unclear. The rating question was followed-up by an open question (16) inviting participants to name examples of useful resources they have used and to provide more details on what makes a resource useful for them.

The next and penultimate question of the survey (17) was likely the most complex question to design. It asked participants to indicate to what extent they agree with ten statements about how best to educate about digital technologies and data systems. In order to develop these ten statements, I reviewed my prior empirical findings (Sander 2020c), findings from this study's literature review and theoretical framework, further theoretical literature on how best to implement critical data literacy as well as first findings from this study's content analysis of online critical data literacy resources. In a second step, I tried to condense all these findings into simple statements that reflected academic findings on critical data literacy as well as ongoing academic debates, for example on whether or not practical data skills are necessary for critical data literacy. I deliberately included controversial issues, such as the question of "individual responsibility" or "shocking learners", in these statements. The statements were revised, condensed and simplified several times to make them as concise and clear as possible. Key terms for each questions were underlined for further clarification and ease of reading. Feedback from pilot testers about this question was consistently very positive, indicating that efforts for simplification and clarification were successful.

Finally, as recommended in the literature, the questionnaire ended with a final open question, inviting participants to share final remarks and additional comments that may have not been covered by the questionnaire thus far. As Braun et al highlight, this can often generate "unanticipated and useful data" (2021, p. 8). In addition to this open invitation, several suggestions were made on what participants could comment on: for example, on what they would need to be better able to educate about digital technologies and data systems, whether there are any particular kinds of resources they need but can't find, or on their overall wishes for educational resources. Through these suggestions, I hoped to inspire and nudge participants to elaborate more freely on their needs and wishes when it comes to critical data literacy resources.

After participants submitted their answers, the survey ended with a final thank-you-page, which also invited the participants to contact me via email if they were interested in testing and providing feedback on a new educational resource that was being developed with Privacy International as part of this project. In order to ensure anonymity in the collected data, I asked the educators to email me rather than collecting their email addresses through the survey. This likely led to fewer (8) responses from potential testers, but anonymity was ensured.

Appendix II: Content Analysis Sample

Nr.	**Title**	**URL** (all: analysed in April/May 2021, last accessed: March 2024)
R1	Your data matters	https://ico.org.uk/your-data-matters/
R2	My data and privacy online. A toolkit for young people	http://www.lse.ac.uk/my-privacy-uk
R3	Breaking the Black Box	https://www.propublica.org/article/breaking-the-black-box-what-facebook-knows-about-you
R4	The Privacy Paradox. Note to Self	Main: https://project.wnyc.org/privacy-paradox/ Also (newer): https://www.wnycstudios.org/podcasts/notetoself
R5	Advocacy Assembly – Courses about Privacy	https://advocacyassembly.org/en/courses/ – Topic: Privacy
R6	Chupadados the Datasucker. The hidden faces of our beloved technologies	https://chupadados.codingrights.org/en/
R7	Youngdata	https://www.youngdata.de/
R8	Digital Shred. Privacy Literacy Toolkit	https://sites.psu.edu/digitalshred/
R9	Do Not Track	https://donottrack-doc.com/en/
R10	Me and My Shadow	https://myshadow.org/
R11	Privacy International	https://privacyinternational.org/
R12	Surveillance Self-Defense, EFF	https://ssd.eff.org/
R13	A data-day	https://tacticaltech.org/news/a-data-day/
R14	The Power of Privacy — Documentary	https://www.youtube.com/watch?v=BvQ6I9xrEuo
R15	Free your data	https://freeyourdata.org/de/

R16	Daten, Daten, Daten	https://www.politische-bildung.nrw.de/themen/big-data-story
R17	Anna. Das vernetzte Leben	https://www.annasleben.de/
R18	Lernparcours Big Data	http://bigdata.jfc.info/lernparcours.html
R19	Deine Daten Deine Rechte / Your Data Your Rights	https://deinedatendeinerechte.de/
R20	DATASELFIE	https://dataselfie.jnw-sdm.ch/
R21	How to Selbstauskunft. Kampf um meine Daten	https://www.br.de/puls/themen/netz/selbstauskunft-kampf-um-meine-daten-100.html
R22	Selbstdatenschutz und digitale Selbstverteidigung	https://www.selbstdatenschutz.info/ [Not available anymore. Analysed version: https://web.archive.org/web/20210417193332/https://www.selbstdatenschutz.info/]
R23	Privacy-Handbuch	https://www.awxcnx.de/
R24	Selbstdatenschutz! Tipps, Tricks und Klicks	https://www.blm.de/files/pdf1/blm-selbstschutz.pdf
R25	Dein Algorithmus – meine Meinung! Algorithmen und ihre Bedeutung für Meinungsbildung und Demokratie	https://www.mabb.de/files/content/document/UEBER%20DIE%20MABB/Download-Center/Publikationen/Broschueren/Algo-Broschur_20170403_mabb_neu.pdf
R26	Big Data und politische Bildung	https://www.bpb.de/lernen/digitale-bildung/medienpaedagogik/bigdata/ [Not available anymore. Analysed version: https://web.archive.org/web/20210507040640/https://www.bpb.de/lernen/digitale-bildung/medienpaedagogik/bigdata/]
R27	Dein Netz	https://dein-netz.org/hi/ [Not available anymore. Analysed version: https://web.archive.org/web/20210517035140/https://dein-netz.org/hi/]
R28	Klicksafe	http://www.klicksafe.de/
R29	Dein Tag in Daten	http://www.watchyourweb.de/assets/watchyourweb/mdb/2/Infografik_Datentag.png
R30	Watch your web: Big Data	http://www.watchyourweb.de/p2304197173_564.html#fd8ee25326f243a432e5cefe8ae8ac55
R31	Digital Defense Playbook. Community Power Tools for Reclaiming Data	https://www.odbproject.org/wp-content/uploads/2019/03/ODB_DDP_HighRes_Single.pdf

R32	Unbias Fairness Toolkit and Youth Jury resource pack	https://unbias.wp.horizon.ac.uk/fairness-toolkit/ And: https://uyj.wp.horizon.ac.uk/overview/
R33	Automating NYC and (en)coding inequality?	https://automating.nyc/
R34	#Nachgeschaut – Big Data Erklärvideo	https://www.mediasmart.de/2019/03/nachgeschaut-big-data-erklaervideo/
R35	Behind the Buzzwords – Big Data	https://www.bbc.co.uk/sounds/play/m000lghg
R36	Von der flächendeckenden Überwachung zur flächendeckenden Lenkung der Bürger. Big Data als Lenkungswerkzeug	https://media.ccc.de/v/pw17-93-von_der_flachendeckenden_uberwachung_zur_flachendeckenden_lenkung_der_burger#t=3
R37	Big Data verstehen. Lehrer*innen-Leitfaden: Big Data	https://www.erlebe-it.de/Unterrichtsmaterialien/Big-Data-verstehen
R38	Big Data-Forscher Dirk Helbing über den „perfekten Sturm" der Digitalisierung	https://www.youtube.com/watch?v=83cEm-kPEeg
R39	Lehrmittel Big Data – Museum für Kommunikation	https://www.mfk.ch/bigdata/
R40	Big Up 4 Big Data	https://medienfachberatung.de/wp-content/uploads/2017/03/Spielanleitung-Big-Up-4-Big-Data_MFB-Schwaben.pdf
R41	Datak – Spiel um deine Daten	https://www.datak.ch/#/start
R42	Daten, Algorithmen, Kontrolle der Zukunft	https://www.surveillance-studies.org/daten-algorithmen-kontrolle-der-zukunft/
R43	Digital Literacy Best Practices	https://www.netliteracy.org/digital-literacy/
R44	Unterrichtsprojekt Digitalisierung – Leben in einer digitalen Welt	https://www.bpb.de/lernen/grafstat/304602/digitalisierung
R45	Zukunftswerkstatt: Digitopia	https://www.bpb.de/lernen/digitale-bildung/medienpaedagogik/bigdata/253169/zukunftswerkstatt
R46	Future Influencer – Die smarte Schule!?	https://future-influencer-prototype.jimdofree.com/

R47	Online-Konferenz Weiterbilden: Ich habe doch nichts zu verbergen! – für den verantwortungsvollen Umgang mit Daten sensibilisieren	https://www.gutes-aufwachsen-mit-medien.de/informieren/themen/news-detail/detail/online-konferenz-weiterbilden-ich-habe-doch-nichts-zu-verbergen-fuer-den-verantwortungsvollen-umgang-mit-daten-sensibilisieren
R48	Big Data – inform@21	https://inform21.ch/de/big-data/
R49	Big Data | Medienportal der Siemens Stiftung	https://medienportal.siemens-stiftung.org/de/big-data-111955
R50	nano-Magazin Wissen: Big Data	https://www.3sat.de/wissen/nano/big-data-104.html [Not available anymore. Analysed version: https://web.archive.org/web/20210127145203/https://www.3sat.de/wissen/nano/big-data-104.html]
R51	nano-Magazin Wissen: Datenspuren	https://www.3sat.de/wissen/nano/datenspuren-100.html [Not available anymore. Analysed version: https://web.archive.org/web/20210120035638/https://www.3sat.de/wissen/nano/datenspuren-100.html]
R52	Panel Discussion "Big Data"	https://digitallearninglab.de/unterrichtsbausteine/panel-discussion-big-data
R53	Podcasts zu Digitalisierung und Privatheit	https://www.leopoldina.org/themen/digitalisierung-und-demokratie/big-data-podcasts-1/
R54	Stadt | Land | DatenFluss	https://ki-campus.org/datenfluss
R55	Überwacht und verkauft	https://projekte.sueddeutsche.de/artikel/digital/digitale-privatsphaere-ueberwacht-und-verkauft-e784992/
R56	Understanding predictive privacy harms	https://www.journalismfestival.com/programme/2016/understanding-predictive-privacy-harms
R57	Unterrichtsmaterial: Rund um Daten	https://appcamps.de/unterrichtsmaterial/unterrichtsmaterial-zu-datenschutz/
R58	Watching You	https://www.studioimnetz.de/projekte/watchingyou/
R59	Data Literacy in the Real World: Conversations & Case Studies	http://datalit.sites.uofmhosting.net/wp-content/uploads/2017/08/data_literacy_in_the_real_world.pdf
R60	The Internet of Everything	https://www.arte.tv/de/videos/RC-019504/internet-of-everything/ [Not available anymore. Analysed version: https://web.archive.org/web/20210620001719/https://www.arte.tv/de/videos/RC-019504/internet-of-everything/]
R61	Mijente #TakeBackTech Curriculum Materials	https://drive.google.com/drive/folders/147CCSTLyN8OsfwFpUtw7mU-VCnJN58SX Background: https://notechforice.com/

R62	Center for Humane Technology	https://www.humanetech.com/
R63	Screening Surveillance | The Surveillance Studies Centre	https://www.sscqueens.org/projects/screening-surveillance
R64	Erklärfilm: Der Weg der Daten	https://www.bpb.de/mediathek/318379/erklaerfilm-der-weg-der-daten
R65	The emotion business: How companies are learning to read your mind	https://ig.ft.com/emotion-recognition/
R66	How normal am I?	https://www.hownormalami.eu/
R67	Project Sherpa – Videos	https://www.project-sherpa.eu/category/videos/
R68	What is mathwashing?	https://www.mathwashing.com/
R69	Social Cooling – big data's unintended side effect	https://www.socialcooling.com/
R70	STEALING UR FEELINGS	https://www.stealingurfeelin.gs/
R71	Datensammlung – Big Data (Modul)	https://de.digitale-lernwerkstatt.com/lehrer/sammlung/5f0c222cef587a00113e1748
R72	Schule macht Daten	https://ki-campus.org/courses/datenschule-jt2021
R73	Daten- und Algorithmenethik	https://ki-campus.org/courses/daethik
R74	Coveillance: Watching the watchers	https://coveillance.org/
R75	Clear Your Tracks	https://www.clearyourtracks.org [Not available anymore. Analysed version: https://web.archive.org/web/20210511094939/http://clearyourtracks.org/]

Appendices III - IX

The remaining appendices can be found online:

https://tvl.ink/9783839473788

These include:

Appendix III: Content Analysis Codebook
Appendix IV: Participant Information Sheet
Appendix V: Participant Consent Form
Appendix VI: Expert Interview Guide
Appendix VII: Educator Survey Sampling
Appendix VIII: Educator Survey Questionnaire
Appendix IX: Report on Collaboration with Privacy International